Access 2003 Power Programming
with VBA

Access 2003
Power Programming
with VBA

Allen G. Taylor and Virginia Andersen

WILEY

Wiley Publishing, Inc.

Access 2003 Power Programming with VBA

Published by:
Wiley Publishing, Inc.
111 River Street
Hoboken, NJ 07030-5779
www.wiley.com

Library of Congress Control Number: 2003101931.

ISBN: 0-7645-2588-3

Printed in the United States of America

10 9 8 7 6 5 4 3 2 1

1Q/RU/RQ/QT/IN

Distributed in the United States by Wiley Publishing, Inc.

For general information on our other products and services or to obtain technical support, please contact our Customer Care Department within the U.S. at (800) 762-2974, outside the U.S. at (317) 572-3993 or fax (317) 572-4002.

Wiley also publishes its books in a variety of electronic formats. Some content that appears in print may not be available in electronic books.

Credits

ACQUISITIONS EDITOR
Terri Varveris

PROJECT EDITOR
Pat O'Brien

TECHNICAL EDITOR
Greg Guntle

COPY EDITOR
John Edwards

PROJECT COORDINATOR
Courney MacIntyre

GRAPHICS AND PRODUCTION SPECIALISTS
Beth Brooks
Carrie Foster
Kristin McMullan
Heather Pope

QUALITY CONTROL TECHNICIANS
John Greenough
Andy Hollandbeck
Carl William Pierce
Charles Spencer

PROOFREADING AND INDEXING
TECHBOOKS Production Services

About the Authors

Allen G. Taylor is a 30-year veteran of the computer industry and the author of 22 books, including *Crystal Reports 9 For Dummies, Database Development For Dummies, SQL For Dummies,* and *SQL Weekend Crash Course.* He lectures internationally on databases, networks, innovation, and entrepreneurship. He also teaches database development through a leading online education provider, and he teaches digital electronics at Portland State University. Allen teaches computer hardware via distance learning at the International Institute for Information, Science & Technology in Shanghai, China. For the latest news on Allen's activities, check out www.allengtaylor.com. You can contact Allen at allen.taylor@ieee.org.

Virginia Andersen is also an "old timer" in the computer industry. She saw her first computer in 1951 after Grace Hopper told her there was a future for women in high-speed digital computers. During her career as a systems analyst/programmer, Virginia used computers on many diverse projects, such as mapping the moon for the first Apollo moon landing, serving as the reliability engineer for the parachute recovery system, and even conducting undersea surveillance. She also taught computer science, mathematics, and systems analysis at the graduate and undergraduate level for 12 years at the University of Southern California and other western colleges. Since she retired from the "power suit and nylons" industry, she has written over 35 books about personal-computer–based applications, including *Access 2002 The Complete Reference, Peter Norton's Guide to Microsoft Access 2000 Programming, Troubleshooting Access Databases,* and finally her memoirs, *Digital Recall.*

*This book is dedicated to all the seekers who are trying to find their way
in the world. May you find what you seek.*

Acknowledgments

First and foremost, I appreciate the great work of my coauthor, Virginia Andersen. We make a great team. I would also like to thank my project editor, Pat O'Brien, and my acquisitions editor, Terri Varveris, for their key contributions to the production of this book. As always, thanks to my agent, Matt Wagner, of Waterside Productions for his support of my career.

Allen

I certainly want to thank Allen for inviting me to join him in this important work. I have enjoyed working with him. I also owe thanks to Pat O'Brien and Terri Varveris for their fine support. My agent, Matt Wagner, of Waterside Productions has always provided much-appreciated guidance and help in finding new and challenging projects.

Virginia

Contents at a Glance

Contents

Part IV   **Advanced Access Programming Techniques
with VBA**

Introduction

Welcome to a new edition of the popular Power Programming series, *Access 2003 Power Programming with VBA*. You will find many helpful ways to create Access databases that even novices can use successfully. If you are only interested in perfecting your programming skills for your own use, you can't go wrong with this book.

Why we wrote this book

Due to its inclusion in Microsoft Office, Microsoft Access is the most widely used database management system in the world. Many books are available that describe how to use the standard features of Access. Other books, aimed at highly experienced professional programmers, explain in highly technical terms how to develop major applications using Access and VBA. This book is a bridge between those two extremes – in that middle ground where people want to go beyond what the stock Access offers without having to become a career VBA programmer. With this book and a general comprehension of programming principles, you can greatly expand the power and professional appearance of the applications that you build with Access.

What you need to know

If you are new to Access or any other relational database system, you need to start with a more instructional book for beginners, such as *Microsoft Access 2003 For Dummies.*

To make the most use of this book, you need to have some fairly high-level experience with Access – not necessarily with Access 2003 but with version 2000 or 2002. You need to be comfortable with Access and all its objects: tables, queries, forms, reports, macros, and modules. You should be able to perform the following tasks:

- Create tables, enter data, and save the design and the data
- Create queries to extract the data that you need, including summaries
- Create forms for data entry with user-friendly controls
- Design and print reports that group and summarize data
- Work in the Windows environment

If you are experienced with previous versions of Access, you should get a lot out of this book. You will learn how to automate your applications with VBA. Chapter 1 gives you an idea of what Access and VBA can do together for you while you are developing an application.

What you need to have

To begin with, you need a copy of Access. This book was written to focus on version 2003, but much of the information presented also applies to Access 2000 and 2002.

This book was written considering Access running in a Windows environment, although much of the information in the book may also apply to Macintosh operating systems.

You will be more satisfied with running large programs such as Access if you have a relatively fast computer (a Pentium III PC is marginal, and a Pentium 4 is preferred). The Office suite of programs takes up a lot of space, which can seriously bog down a slower machine with a limited amount of memory.

Conventions used in this book

We have included several typographic conventions that can aid you in interpreting the meaning of the text.

KEYBOARD CONVENTIONS

Data is usually entered via the keyboard. We have used different fonts and font styles to highlight the data entry, menu and toolbar selections, VBA code, and function names.

USER INPUT   When an example includes data that you are to enter via the keyboard, the characters appear in boldface — for example, enter **<#7/31/2003#** in the Criteria row. If the expression is longer, it may appear in monofont, as follows:

```
=Format([DARDate],"ddd")
```

VBA CODE   You will find a bounty of VBA code throughout this book. Some examples are merely small blocks of a statement, and others are complete procedures or functions that are ready to use. The listings appear in monofont, and each line of code usually takes up a single line, as follows:

```
DoCmd.OpenReport rs![Argument], acPreview
```

The exception is when the line of code exceeds the width of the book page. Then we add a continuation mark (an underline character) and place the rest of the code on the next line. The continuation lines are usually indented. Although indentation is not required, it makes the code easier to read.

```
Me.Filter = "[ItemNumber] = 0 AND [Switchboard]= " & _
      rs![Argument]
```

FUNCTIONS, FILENAMES, AND NAMED OBJECTS   Function syntax appears in the text in boldface but, when used in code, the function appears in monofont. Keywords and statements within text appear in boldface.

MOUSE CONVENTIONS

We have used the standard terminology for working with the mouse: click, double-click, right-click, and drag. You are probably already so used to the mouse it has become a member of the family.

What the icons mean

One of the most helpful features of the Power Programming series is the use of margin icons to point out important items. You find the following icons in this book:

- ◆ **New Feature:** This icon highlights material that is new to Access 2003. If you are working with earlier versions of Access, you can skip these new features.

- ◆ **Note:** This icon indicates that the accompanying paragraph contains important information. The information may apply to the task at hand or may be a clue to material that comes later.

- ◆ **Tip:** This icon is just that – it points out other ways to accomplish a task or introduces work-arounds.

- ◆ **Caution:** You should pay special attention to text that accompanies this icon. This icon points out problems that can occur with the current operation unless you pay particular attention to the instructions that we provide.

- ◆ **Cross Reference:** This icon refers you to other chapters that contain additional information about the subject you are working on.

How this book is organized

We have grouped the chapters in this book into parts. We also include appendices, which contain detailed reference information.

PART I: ACCESS APPLICATION DEVELOPMENT

The first four chapters of this book introduce you to Microsoft Access as an application development environment. Chapter 1 places Access in its historical context and describes how Access has evolved over time to become the versatile tool that it is today. Chapter 2 lays down the fundamental principles of application development. You should be firmly committed to following these principles before embarking on any development project.

Chapter 3 describes the tools that Access provides for application development without programming. You can build a variety of useful applications without writing one line of VBA code. The chapter introduces you to that mode of development. Chapter 4 goes into detail about how to create your own custom menus and toolbars, again without VBA.

PART II: UNDERSTANDING VISUAL BASIC FOR APPLICATIONS

This extensive part of the book contains seven chapters that are devoted to describing VBA from A to Z. In Chapter 5, we discuss the concept of VBA and introduce the elements that make up the programming structure. Chapter 6 describes in more detail all the language elements and gives examples of various program structures. Chapter 7 presents the Visual Basic Editor environment and shows how to make the best use of all the options that it offers. Chapter 8 takes a closer look at the VBA elements and includes many examples of code that is used with Access forms, reports, tables, and queries.

Chapter 9 focuses on designing and writing sub procedures. Chapter 10 is devoted to detecting and correcting errors that can occur with VBA code. The final chapter in this part, Chapter 11, describes how to use built-in functions and how to create custom functions as well as how to run and debug a new function.

PART III: PROGRAMMING USER INTERACTIONS WITH VBA

The three chapters that make up Part III focus on the interface between the Access application and the end user. Chapter 12 discusses user input and the methods for requesting and processing it. Chapter 13 presents examples of modifying the command bars that the user has access to during operation, including setting command bar properties, creating new menus and toolbars, and limiting user access to certain command bar controls. Chapter 14 contains information about setting startup options and default database options with VBA code. It also discusses the process of running conditional compilation during debugging or for developing an application for different computer systems or languages.

PART IV: ADVANCED ACCESS PROGRAMMING TECHNIQUES WITH VBA

Part IV, which consists of Chapters 15 through 19, is the most code-heavy part of the book. Chapter 15 details how to create database objects such as databases, tables, queries, and recordsets. It also covers how to manipulate database data. Chapter 16 introduces event-driven programming, explaining the major event types that Access responds to. Chapter 17 breaks you out of the isolation of a single application by explaining how your application can interact with other programs and resources. Chapter 18 discusses Access's ability to import, export, and store data in XML format, making your data accessible to any other XML-compatible system, from PDA to supercomputer. Chapter 19, which focuses on add-ins, describes how you can build custom wizards to extend the capabilities of Access.

PART V: DEVELOPING APPLICATIONS WITH VBA

Chapter 20 gives pointers on how to develop applications that are easy for their intended audience to understand and use. Chapter 21 discusses the additional issues that must be considered in a multiuser installation. Security and reliability considerations become much more important.

APPENDICES

The following five appendices contain reference information for programming with VBA:

- ◆ Appendix A contains important information about Access online resources.

- ◆ Appendix B is a reference guide for all the VBA statements and functions.

- ◆ Appendix C is a reference guide for all the VBA enumerated constants.

- ◆ Appendix D is a reference guide for all the trappable errors.

- ◆ Appendix E is a reference guide for the ANSI codes.

How to use this book

This is an intermediate- to advanced-level book. You may read it cover to cover as a way to raise yourself from the ranks of Access power users into the heady atmosphere of VBA programmers. However, we suspect that most people will use the book as a reference, reaching for it when presented with a thorny application development problem. Because each chapter is essentially complete within itself, it is perfectly acceptable to flip to any chapter that you need at the moment and start reading.

Feedback

The publisher and we want to hear from you. After you have had an opportunity to use the book, visit the Wiley Web site (`www.wiley.com`), register your book, and give us your comments. If we can improve anything in future editions, we want your input on how we can do so. You can also contact Allen directly at `allen.taylor@ieee.org`.

Part I

Access Application Development

Chapter 1

Access Application Development

IN THIS CHAPTER

- ◆ The various versions of Access and how they differ
- ◆ Developing database applications with Access
- ◆ The future of Access

MICROSOFT ACCESS WAS INTRODUCED as a desktop database management system (DBMS) in 1992, and in the years that followed, became a leader in its category. As a part of the popular Microsoft Office suite of applications, Access is used daily by millions of people. Since its inception, Access has grown progressively more capable and easier to use. The most recent versions, while retaining their position as the most popular desktop DBMS in the world, enable developers to build applications that access information from large networked client/server databases based on Microsoft's enterprise scale SQL Server client/server DBMS.

Although many people use Access to perform relatively simple data management tasks that don't require any kind of programming, the Visual Basic for Applications (VBA) language gives Access the power to host systems that are customized to meet the exact needs of a wide variety of organizations, regardless of their size or the kinds of tasks that they need to perform.

The purpose of this book, after laying a little groundwork, is to take you from a non-programming Access power user to a developer who is comfortable using the full power of VBA to build sophisticated applications that execute complex tasks while making things easy for the user.

Access Versions

Access 1.0 appeared in 1992, shortly after the appearance of Microsoft Windows. Access 1.1 came along in 1993, and in 1994, Access 2.0 arrived on the scene. Each new version was an incremental improvement that built on the strengths of the prior versions. Access 95 followed in 1995, Access 97 in 1997, Access 2000 in 1999, and Access 2002 in 2001. With each new version, Access has grown easier to use and has expanded its data-handling capability.

Access 1.0, 1.1, and 2.0

When Access 1.0 first saw the light of day, it introduced features that were new to personal database products, or for that matter, any kind of database products:

- ◆ *OLE technology* in Table Designer enabled users to create databases that contained graphical images and audio and video files, in addition to text and numbers. OLE stands for *object linking and embedding,* which is rather descriptive of what OLE does. Users were even able to incorporate Word documents and Excel spreadsheets into an Access database.

- ◆ The *Forms Package* enabled users to create custom forms by dragging form elements onto a blank page. This was a major step forward in ease of use.

- ◆ The Report Wizard made report creation equally easy.

- ◆ The *drag-and-drop Query Designer* used *query by example* (QBE) technology to enable users to create queries without writing program code.

- ◆ The *Graph Wizard* turned chart production into an intuitive step-by-step process.

- ◆ In addition to its native files, Access 1.0 could also operate on dBASE, Paradox, and Btrieve files with native drivers, as well as others, such as Sybase SQL Server, DEC Rdb, and FoxPro) via an ODBC interface.

  ODBC stands for Object DataBase Connectivity, and provides a common application programmer's interface (API) to a large number of different and mutually incompatible databases.

Access 1.1 added the following improvements:

- ◆ Enhanced ODBC and Btrieve support.

- ◆ Improved connectivity to FoxPro.

- ◆ Easy data export to Word for mail-merge applications.

- ◆ Database sizes up to 1GB (about eight times larger than 1.0 could handle).

- ◆ An Access *runtime* became available. Developers could create applications that could operate without Access installed on the system.

Access 2.0 added more capabilities:

- ◆ Wizards that automated tasks that had previously required coding on the part of the application developer.

- ◆ More sophisticated event handling.

- ◆ A debugger in the development tools, plus an automatic documenter and an Add-in Manager.

- ◆ Jet database engine improvements, allowing more complex databases to be built and making queries run over twice as fast.

Access 95

Access 95 was the first version to officially be a part of Microsoft Office. Its controls were brought into conformance with the other members of the Office application suite.

♦ VBA was one of several development tools that Access shared with other Office programs, such as Word and Excel.

♦ The Import Wizard and the PivotTable Wizard were added.

♦ The Form and Report Wizards were improved.

Access 97

Access 97 became more Web-aware:

♦ It stored hyperlinks as a native data type and allowed saving to HTML. Users could publish database objects to the Web, and extract data from an HTML document that contained a table, and then put the data into a database table.

♦ Class modules could contain the definition of a new object.

♦ Procedures in a module could hold the properties and methods of that object.

♦ Conditional compilation enabled developers to create both debug and production compilations of their applications by setting flags in the code.

♦ Developers could remove source code from an application, thus speeding execution and preventing people from viewing and copying it.

♦ New ActiveX controls were introduced, and compatibility with source code control systems was added to the Developer Edition of Office 97.

Access 2000

Many aspects of Access were enhanced for this version, improving performance and expanding capability. This Access version introduced these features:

♦ ActiveX Data Objects (ADO) replaced practically all the data access functions that were previously performed with Data Access Objects (DAO).

♦ Access Project (.adp) files work with SQL Server and Microsoft Data Engine files as smoothly as .mdb files work with the Jet engine.

♦ Data access pages (DAPs) were introduced, enabling you to put things that look like Access forms and reports on the Web.

Access 2002

The previous Access release added these features:

- The Data Access Page Designer was improved with these features:
  - Multi-level undo and redo
  - Better grouping with multi-table data entry
- Enhanced support for the SQL Server Desktop Engine was included, plus cascading updates and deletes.
- The Upsizing Wizard converted applications written to drive the Jet engine so they work with the SQL Server Desktop Engine.
- XML support was added.

Access 2003

New features of Access 2003 include:

- Improved ease of use
- Expanded ability to import, export, and work with XML data files
- Flagging of common errors
- Identification of object dependencies

Access as an Application Development Environment

Access provides a particularly congenial application development environment for several different classes of developers. It is congenial for the following reasons:

- **Low barrier to entry.** You can start developing useful applications with a minimum of study or training.
- **Intuitive.** As you use Access more and increase your proficiency, you can tackle more complex assignments, thus using more of Access's power.
- **Part of the Office suite.** Access can draw on the capabilities of the other members of Microsoft Office, such as Word and Excel.

◆ **Help from wizards.** The many wizards that automate a wide variety of tasks can dramatically reduce development time.

◆ **Tight integration with Microsoft SQL Server.** Because of this, Access is applicable to a broad range of development tasks, from the smallest personal database application to enterprise-wide applications for large multinational firms. Other DBMS products typically aim for one end of the size spectrum or the other.

The difference between databases and database applications

Sometimes people fail to make the distinction between databases and database applications. This is particularly true of people who "learn by doing" with Access rather than of those who take a formal course in database theory. Access lumps *database development* and *database application development* together, with no apparent separation of the two:

◆ A *database* is a self-describing collection of integrated records. It is *self-describing* because the information that describes the structure of the database is included in the database. The records are *integrated* because relationships between data items are explicitly maintained. These two characteristics differentiate a database from a mere collection of data items.

A database is a structured collection of data. By itself, it doesn't solve any problem or serve any purpose. The database application uses the data in the database to solve problems or to accomplish a purpose.

◆ A *database application* is a program that works with a database to maintain and deliver desired information. A database application developer may write the database application or it may be generated semi-automatically by a DBMS, such as Access.

In a relational database, the data is stored in tables, which give the data its structure. A database application may include forms and reports that enable users to interact with the data in the database, with the objective of accomplishing some purpose.

The Database window

When you enter Access and specify the name of the database that you want to work on, the Database window shown in Figure 1-1 is displayed.

The column shown on the left lists the kinds of objects that it deals with: *tables, queries, forms, reports, pages, macros,* and *modules.*

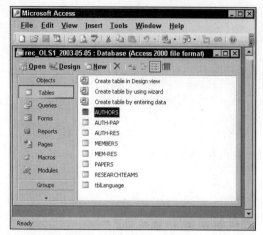

Figure 1-1: Database window.

For example, if Tables is selected, the pane on the right displays the names of all the tables in the current database plus three options for creating tables, either in Design View, with a wizard, or just by entering data. Similarly, selecting Forms displays the names of any forms that have been created, and gives you the option of creating a new form either in Design View or by using a wizard. Access makes it supremely easy to create all the different database objects that you may need for your application.

Creating tables

Because this is an advanced book on programming with Access, we assume that you can already create a table using Design View. Figure 1-2 shows an example of Design View after entering the specification for the first field of a table. You enter the field name, data type, and description of the field, and then specify some of its properties, such as field length and whether the field is indexed. After you have done this for all the fields in a table, name and save the table. That is all that's involved in creating a database table. Of course, we assume that you have already carefully thought about what fields should be included in the table, what their data types should be, what properties the fields should have, and how this table relates to other tables in the database.

After you have created the tables, you have created the database skeleton or structure. All you need to do now to complete the database is to fill it with data. You can do this in several ways, including through a data-entry form, by typing directly into the table, or by filling the table automatically from an existing file.

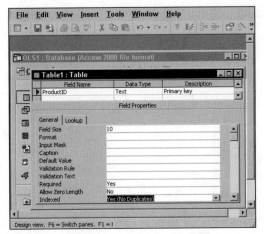

Figure 1-2: Design View of table creation.

The following sections are about creating parts of a database application (forms, reports, data access pages, and so forth), and are not about creating the database itself. Unlike tables, forms, reports, and data access pages are all involved in performing specific tasks or answering specific questions.

Creating forms

For most applications, users see and interact with forms. Access forms are flexible tools. Forms can be different sizes, and they can contain such objects as controls, text, and graphics. For example, you can

- ◆ Create switchboard forms that control navigation around an application from one screen to another.

- ◆ Use a form to
  - ■ Enter data into one or more database tables
  - ■ Modify existing table data
  - ■ Delete data from tables
  - ■ View the data in one or more tables

Figure 1-3 shows a blank form.

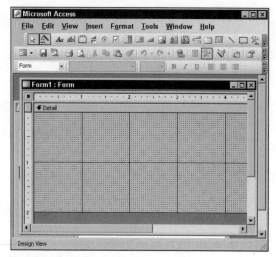

Figure 1-3: Design View of form creation.

Creating reports

The report creation process is similar to the form creation process. The main difference is that reports are more likely to be multi-page documents, and as a result, are more likely to be divided into sections, such as report header and footer, page header and footer, detail section, and group sections. Forms can also have form and page headers and footers, but often do not. Figure 1-4 shows the Design View of a blank report. You can add controls and other objects from the toolbox to appropriate sections of the report to achieve the report that you want.

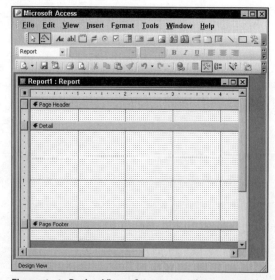

Figure 1-4: Design View of report creation.

Creating data access pages

Data access pages, introduced in Access 2000, provide an easy way to display information on the Web that on a local machine would be contained in forms and reports. Data access pages are HTML files that are bound to data in a data source. With data access pages you can

◆ Browse through the records in a data source

◆ Add, modify, and delete data

◆ Display the data either *sorted* or *grouped*

You can display database data on the Web in other ways, but data access pages, which are specifically designed for the task, provide an easy way to put your data online.

Using macros

Macros are simple constructs for executing a sequence of operations. Before VBA became available to Access developers, macros provided the only way to automate execution. Now, there is little reason to use macros for any serious development. The many advantages of VBA make it the preferred alternative.

◆ VBA has these capabilities that are missing from macros:

  ▪ Case structure

  ▪ Loops

  ▪ Constants

  ▪ Variables

  ▪ Functions

  ▪ Transactions

  ▪ Database objects creation

  ▪ Graceful error handling

  ▪ User-defined functions

  ▪ Access Windows API functions

  ▪ Automated operations with OLE and DDE

◆ Macros may be appropriate for these uses:

  ▪ Quick prototyping of an application

  ▪ A simple application that only runs on single-user systems

◆ Both VBA and macros support an *if-then-else* structure.

Using modules

When you write code in VBA to perform operations on database data, the code is stored in *modules*. VBA is migrating toward becoming an object-oriented language, and is becoming more object-oriented with each release, although it still lacks some essential features of an object-oriented language.

In Chapter 6, we discuss modules in-depth. For now, all you need to know is that modules are the containers that hold the VBA code that you write to make your application perform the tasks that you want it to perform.

Creating classes

In addition to the predefined objects that Access provides, you can create your own objects that apply specifically to the task at hand. You can also create classes of objects. Each class has its own particular attributes. A class can have multiple instances; each is different from another in some way, but all share the common attributes that define the class. A class's attributes are called *properties* and *methods,* which are mentioned in the next section and described in detail in Chapter 5.

Properties and methods

In Access, data and program components are *encapsulated* into objects. In this architecture, class attributes are data items that are called *properties,* and program components are processes that operate on the object and are called *methods.*

All the objects in an object class share the same properties and methods.

The Visual Basic Editor (VBE)

The Visual Basic Editor, known to its friends as VBE, is the primary tool Access provides you for developing VBA applications. Chapter 7 describes VBE and tells you how to use it to code the procedures that comprise your application. As you follow the examples in this book, you will become familiar with VBE and all the things it can do for you.

 VBE is an Access application developer's most important tool.

Toolbars

Access comes with over two dozen *standard* toolbars. You can also create your own *custom* toolbars, which we describe in Chapter 4.

Using the Database toolbar, you can quickly access database functions by clicking on an icon. Figure 1-5 shows the Database toolbar.

Figure 1-5: Database toolbar.

All of the Database toolbar functions deal directly with the database or with the application that you are building, based on that database. The functions on the toolbar are, from left to right:

◆ New

◆ Open

◆ Save

◆ Search

◆ Print

◆ Print Preview

◆ Spelling

◆ Cut

◆ Copy

◆ Paste

◆ Undo

◆ Office Links

◆ Analyze

◆ Code

◆ Microsoft Script Editor

◆ Relationships

◆ New Object Autoform

◆ Microsoft Access Help

The second standard toolbar type is the Task Pane toolbar. Shown in Figure 1-6, the Task Pane, usually anchored to the right edge of the Database window, presents you with the option of opening one of several recently used databases or the option of creating a new database. You may also connect to Microsoft Office Online for information or support.

Figure 1-6: Task Pane.

The functions of the options on the Task Pane are:

◆ Open a file

◆ New

◆ New from existing file

◆ New from template

After you select a database file to work on, you can dismiss the Task Pane. It has done its job and you won't need it any more.

The Web toolbar is the third and final standard toolbar in Access. It gives you access to the most basic Web browser functions, as shown in Figure 1-7.

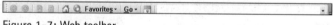

Figure 1-7: Web toolbar.

The functions on the Web toolbar are:

◆ Back

◆ Forward

◆ Stop

◆ Refresh

◆ Start Page

◆ Search the Web

◆ Favorites

◆ Go

◆ Show Only Web Toolbar

◆ Address

   Clicking on any of the icons in the Web toolbar launches your browser and performs the indicated function. These functions are handy when you are building a database application for access over the Web.

Access's Role in Microsoft's Strategy

Microsoft Office is a key part of Microsoft's overall strategy for providing business tools that apply to the vast majority of businesses. By continually enhancing and expanding the capabilities of Office, the folks at Microsoft have shown that they consider Access to be a major element of their future product plans. Access is one of the core components of Office. It is the tool of choice for developing business applications that involve the storage, manipulation, and retrieval of important data.

   More than 600,000 Access developers worldwide are building applications based on the Access DBMS. They are operating in different environments. Some are developing applications of limited scope that are used by a small number of people, or perhaps only one person at a time. Other developers, working in large enterprises, build applications that share data among hundreds or even thousands of users. Recently, demand has grown for database applications that are available to potentially millions of users over the Web.

   As the market for database products has evolved, Microsoft's strategy for Access has evolved with it. The vision Microsoft has for Access is much larger than what it was when Access 1.0 first hit the market in 1992.

Access as a personal database management system

Access was originally designed as a personal database management system to run on personal computers, but in 1992, PCs were not nearly as powerful as they are now. Furthermore, the connection of PCs in an organization using a local area network (LAN) was not common. Access was easy to learn and use and gradually took market share from competing products, such as dBASE, R:BASE, and Paradox.

   True to its heritage, the latest versions of Access are still suited for small personal database applications. However, Access has gained additional capabilities that make it a valuable tool for much larger, more complex problems.

Access in the enterprise

With each version of Access, support for larger, more complex applications has grown. Key to this evolution is the ability of Access to handle data generated by other data sources, first through the ODBC connectivity standard, then by OLE DB, and most recently (in Access 2002), by XML and XSL.

These advances allow Access to seamlessly integrate with enterprise data sources. SQL Server, an enterprise class DBMS from Microsoft, integrates even more tightly with Access because Access can handle native-mode SQL Server data directly through the Access Data Projects feature. Applications written with an Access front end and a SQL Server back end suffer no performance degradation due to format translations.

Access and the Web

The browser-based technology pioneered on the World Wide Web is now widely used on corporate intranets. This has driven the expansion of Access's capabilities to ever-greater support of Web-based database operation:

♦ Access 2000 introduced data access pages, which provide a method for creating HTML pages that are bound to data and that can be displayed either over an intranet or on the Web.

♦ Access 2002 brought enhancements to data access pages that improve reliability and give stronger drill-down capability.

♦ Access 2002 supports Web-based operation in other ways:

■ You can save any Access report as a Web page by using the Save As Data Access Page feature.

■ You can save a report as an XML document. Doing so reduces demand on the database when people later want to view the report.

■ You can use the enhanced PivotTable and PivotChart capability to improve analysis and presentation capabilities. Because you can save PivotTables and PivotCharts as data access pages, the power of these analysis tools can be made available to Web-based users.

♦ Access 2003 does everything that Access 2002 does for Web-based operation, plus it has expanded ability to deal with XML.

Access and .NET

.NET is Microsoft's much ballyhooed software technology for connecting dissimilar, incompatible systems, devices, data sources, and people. It uses XML Web services to connect discrete, building-block application components and complete applications via the Internet. Microsoft Windows .NET Server 2003 builds XML natively into the operating system, giving an unprecedented level of interoperability to far-flung systems.

With its support of XML, Access 2002 enables the development of applications that can fully share data at the enterprise level and beyond. Access 2003's expanded XML support makes that data sharing even easier. It is evident that Access is a key component of Microsoft's vision of the future of enterprise computing.

Summary

Access has been in a constant state of evolution in two directions for more than a decade. First, the continual addition of wizards and other new tools makes databases and database applications easier to create without programming. Second, the continual addition of powerful features has expanded the scope of the problems to which an Access solution can be applied. The folks at Microsoft have shown by their actions and words that they consider Access to be a key part of their overall solution to the problems of businesses, and to the problems of organizations of all kinds. Learning to program and operate with Access is an investment of time and energy that is well spent. The skills gained are relevant and marketable for the fore-seeable future.

Chapter 2

Essentials of Database Application Development

IN THIS CHAPTER

♦ Organizing programming teams

♦ Systems Development Life Cycle

IN THE OLD DAYS (a couple of years ago), many considered Access a "toy" database management system that would never be used by professional developers for serious database application development. Now, application developers frequently use Access to prototype systems that are slated to migrate later to SQL Server, and to build robust applications that execute under the Access Jet engine. In the past, a lone developer may have used Access to build very simple systems that did not involve any programming. These days, however, it's becoming more common for teams of programmers to use Access to build major projects.

Whether you are a lone programmer developing relatively small applications, or a member of a team building larger systems, an organized approach to system conceptualization, design, and development is essential to building a successful project. In this chapter, we describe an approach that, if followed, virtually guarantees success.

The Systems Development Life Cycle

The Systems Development Life Cycle divides a software development effort into several distinct phases that are executed one after another. Each phase must be completed before the next is started. We will recommend the following seven-phase SDLC model:

♦ Definition

♦ Requirements

♦ Evaluation

♦ Design

♦ Implementation

♦ Final Documentation and Testing

♦ Maintenance

25

The importance of a systematic methodology

Overconfidence is the biggest threat to the successful development of Access applications. After your client has told you what he wants, it is tempting to fire up Access, build database tables, create screen forms, fill the tables with data, and then develop reports that retrieve what your client requested. Unfortunately, this straightforward approach almost never works. Problems arise from

- Client's lack of understanding of what is required.
- Lack of consensus of all of the people in the client organization who are affected by the new system.
- A communication gap between the client and the developer.
- Inadequate time allowance.
- Inadequate resource allowance.
- Inadequate documentation to maintain the system.
- Inadequate system testing during development.

All of these problems are addressed and eliminated by following the phased approach of the Systems Development Life Cycle.

You as a Programming Team Member

You may have several reasons for wanting to divide a development effort among several programmers rather than doing the whole job yourself. The primary motivator is usually schedule pressure. Generally, when clients want a new application, they want it as soon as possible. A single programmer must develop each part of the application serially, one after the other, because she can only perform one task at a time. A programming team, however, can develop an application in parallel, with each team member tackling a different module. The speedup on development time is proportional to the degree to which the effort can be subdivided.

As you begin to work on larger projects, you will find yourself as either a member or a leader of a programming team. If you are a team leader, it is critical that you organize the development effort in a systematic way. If you are a team member, it is important that you understand the system and why it is necessary. The Systems Development Life Cycle (SDLC) is a widely used approach to conducting a software development project. By adhering to all its phases, you can ensure that you do not overlook any important aspect of the development process.

The dangers of Access's user-friendly design environment

Paradoxically, systems developed with Microsoft Access are particularly susceptible to serious problems because Access is so easy to use. People who have no formal training in software development think that they can develop Access applications. After all, it is part of Microsoft Office, like Microsoft Word and Microsoft Excel.

Many self-taught Word and Excel users expect to develop database applications with Access without any training. Access's intuitive user interface reinforces this perception. Access makes it easy to create database tables, data entry forms, and reports without any programming of any kind. This situation can lead to the construction of databases and applications that exhibit poor performance, or even worse, databases that are susceptible to data corruption.

Even experienced programmers can produce databases and applications that don't meet the real needs of the client if the programmers don't follow a structured approach that goes through all the needed steps, and if they don't constantly consult the client to make sure that the evolving project continues to meet the client's needs. So, even though it is really easy to create database tables, forms, and reports with Access, it is important to resist the temptation to do so immediately. The first four phases of the SDLC should be completely executed before you create your first table.

The Definition Phase

Like any development project of any kind, the database development project must be sharply defined to reach a satisfactory conclusion for both the client and the developer. All too often, a client may have only a nebulous idea of what he wants the system to look like and what he wants it to do. If the developer takes that vague specification and builds a system based on her interpretation of it, she may find that she has produced a system that does not meet the client's needs.

Define the problem to be solved

In the Definition Phase of the SDLC, the client and developer agree on exactly what the system must do. Typically, the client has a problem that the proposed system must solve. At this early stage, it is imperative to precisely define the problem and agree upon the solution to it. Good client/developer communication at this stage can save the developer from reworking code that is based on incorrect assumptions. Good communication can also help prevent a serious strain on client/developer relations. In this phase, the developer comes to understand exactly what the client wants. The client comes to understand what is possible and what is not possible within the constraints of time and budget. Generally, some compromise is reached in which the client gets substantially what he wants, and the developer gets the time and budget that she needs to make it happen.

Determine project scope

After you know exactly what your application must do in order to satisfy your client's needs, you can determine the project's difficulty. Based on your experience with similar projects, you can estimate what the project will require in expertise, software tools, access to the client's facility, access to key client personnel, travel expenses, and time. Collectively, the combination of all these items is called the *project scope*. It is critically important to accurately determine project scope so that you know what it will cost you to do the job.

Determine feasibility

After you determine the project scope, and you have a good idea of the resources that you can apply to the project, consider whether the project is feasible. Do you have – or can you get – the resources to satisfactorily complete the project within the time and budget available? Is this particular project the highest and best use of the resources that it requires, or are those resources better deployed elsewhere? When I speak of *resources,* I am primarily referring to your time and expertise, as well as the time and expertise of your coworkers who join you on the project. A worthwhile project makes sense economically and professionally.

If you decide that you can't complete the project within the time and budget available, it is best to say so at the outset. Don't plunge in, then risk running out of time, money, or both, before you are able to deliver a completed system. If you state your concerns upfront, you may get the client to relax the requirements or perhaps allocate more time or money to the project. At the very least, you will not be a party to a disaster.

Partition the project into functional blocks

Any application that's more complex than the simplest practical application can probably be divided into semi-independent functional blocks. One block may be the creation of the database. Another may be the overall organization and navigation of the application program that accesses the database. A third block may be the user interface, and a fourth block may be the data access part of the application program. Each of these tasks requires a different developer skill set, so each task is best performed by the person who can offer the best match of skill set to task. If a project is big enough to require the efforts of more than one developer, then properly dividing the tasks between the developers gives you and the client the best result.

Choose your project team

Assuming that the project is big enough to require the efforts of more than one person, select members of the development team based on which people have the knowledge, training, and experience to do the best job on each block. Ideally, you already have people with the requisite skills on your staff, and they are available to take on a new project. If this situation does not match your reality, you must decide whether to train existing staff or hire new staff—either permanently or on a contract basis for this one job. Your decision depends on *time and budget constraints* and *your prospects for follow on work*.

Document problem definition, scope, feasibility, partitioning, and team membership

One common element applies to each phase of the SDLC: You must thoroughly document everything that you discover, decide, and do in that particular phase. In the Definition Phase, document a succinct definition of the problem, the agreed-upon scope of the effort, the rationale behind and the result of the feasibility study, and the membership of your development team and each member's qualifications. This documentation is an important record, but beyond that, it tells both you and your client when the project is complete.

Even if you aren't a team leader, you will be an active participant in the Definition Phase. You will help to define that part of the overall problem that pertains to the block for which you are responsible. You will have input into the estimate of the scope of your part of the project. Indeed, you may decide whether your assigned block is even feasible, given the available time and budget. Ideally, each member of the development team, plus representatives from all the client's constituencies, will contribute to the decisions made in the Definition Phase.

The Requirements Phase

After the project is defined and the definition is properly documented, it's time to get very specific. You must determine *exactly* what the system must do and how well it must perform to satisfy all the people who will use it, as well as the people who will act upon the information that it produces. These people, called *stakeholders*, may have conflicting requirements.

Interview a representative sample of all stakeholders

It's probably impractical for you to interview everyone who will either use or receive information from the proposed system. However, you should listen to people who represent each different class of stakeholder, to see what is most important to them—what they want, and what they don't care about. You are likely to hear a wide range of opinions.

Some people may say that Feature A is absolutely necessary, Feature B would be nice to have but is not important, and Feature C is not needed at all. The fun starts when you interview the representative of another group of stakeholders, who say just the opposite.

Formulate system requirements that all stakeholders can agree upon

After interviewing representatives of all stakeholders, your challenge is to determine which features *really* need to be included in the project, and which can be left out. The surviving feature set forms the basis for the formal Statement of Requirements. Because the requirements that you settle upon probably don't agree 100 percent with the stated requirements of all the stakeholder groups, you must go back to them and solicit agreement with the feature set that you have decided to implement. As always, time and budget constraints, as well as technical feasibility, may limit what you can do. However, your ultimate solution must satisfy the minimum requirements of all stakeholder groups.

Create a users' data model

When a stakeholder tells you what she wants the system to do, she has a model in her mind of the way the various parts of the system fit together. Each such stakeholder, or system user, has a mental model of what the system should be. These mental models may differ from one person to another. It is your job, as the system developer, to consolidate those models into a single users' data model that all the various constituencies will accept. It is vital that all interested parties agree on the logical structure of the system to be built. After you have that agreement, you can formalize the model and specify exactly what the new system will deliver in a written Statement of Requirements.

Create a formal Statement of Requirements

As you may guess, the formal, written Statement of Requirements is the main product of the Requirements Phase. The Statement of Requirements performs these functions

- ◆ States exactly what data the proposed application will store, how that data will be entered into the database, and how it will be retrieved.

- ◆ Describes what the user interface will be like to people either entering data or making queries.

- ◆ States what the reports produced by the system will contain.

- ◆ Specifies a required level of performance and a required level of security. (Optional)

- ◆ Specifies how the system will be documented. (Optional)

Obtain client signoff on the Statement of Requirements

Just to make sure that the Statement of Requirements represents universal agreement on what is to be done, both the responsible party on the development team and the responsible party at the client organization should sign and date the Statement of Requirements. If questions are raised later, you can refer back to the signed and dated Statement of Requirements. As long as it is a clear, unambiguous statement of what the project is to deliver, there should be no controversy at the end of the project as to whether all objectives are satisfied.

The Evaluation Phase

The Statement of Requirements is like a roadmap that tells you exactly where you want to go with the project. Once you know where you want to go, you are in a position to decide how you will get there. Also, now that you know the scale of the project, you can choose the most appropriate development tools for the job.

Choose the best development tools

After you know the size and complexity of the job you are facing, you can choose the development tools that will do the best job. For database applications that support a dozen or so simultaneous users, Microsoft Access is a convenient, affordable tool. Access is probably not appropriate for a major application based on a large client/server database. However, Access may still be the best development choice because it offers a smooth migration path to a Microsoft SQL Server database. SQL Server is capable of handling enterprise-level databases and applications.

Many developers of large applications prototype their database and application with Access, then migrate it to SQL Server for the production version. This method saves time because Access is easier to learn and work with than SQL Server or any of the other popular client/server DBMS (database management systems) products, such as IBM's DB2 or Oracle Corporation's Oracle.

Create job descriptions for team members

A written, formal description of each team member's job reduces confusion about who is responsible for each part of the overall task. This formal description also eliminates wasteful duplication of effort and also helps to ensure that nothing important is left undone.

These job descriptions, like all the other forms of written documentation that are generated during the project, become a part of the final project documentation.

Reassess feasibility

Determine whether the project is really doable in the time available, considering the resources and budget that you can apply. As the overall picture comes into sharper focus, you may decide that the project is *not* feasible as proposed. If that is the case, it is better to admit as much at this point, before a substantial investment is made, than to proceed with a project that is doomed to fail.

You can address the infeasibility problem in several ways. For example, you can take your documentation to the client and discuss the problem. This discussion may lead to the client relaxing some requirements, stretching the schedule, expanding the budget, or a combination of all three. If a solution can't be worked out that is satisfactory for all concerned, your best course may be to decline to proceed with the project. It is better for both you and the client to cut your losses by walking away than to proceed on the project and fail to deliver a satisfactory solution to the client's problem.

Document tool choice, job descriptions, feasibility analysis, scope determination

Everything that you generate in the Evaluation Phase becomes a part of the project documentation.

♦ Document which development tools you have chosen and the reasons why they are the best for the job.

♦ Include the job descriptions of each team member.

♦ Document all the considerations that went into the feasibility analysis and the conclusion that the analysis led to.

♦ Document any modifications in project scope that resulted from the feasibility analysis. Restate the schedule and budget for the project based on the latest, most accurate information.

The Design Phase

After you the developer and the client agree on exactly what the project will produce, the developer can translate the client's requirements into a software product. The design and subsequent development effort has two major components:

♦ **Database:** The repository where all the data of interest is stored. It is structured to facilitate the retrieval of desired information. Building this structure properly is the key to producing an efficient and reliable system.

♦ **Database application:** The program that interacts with the database. Generally, it gives users these abilities:

- Add, change, and delete database data

- Run queries

- Publish reports

In some cases, multiple different applications that are aimed at different user communities will operate on the same database. Data entry people may use one application to maintain the database, while administrators may use another application to generate status reports or other documents, based on the current state of the database.

Designing the database

The users' data model that you constructed, based on conversations with your client, makes sense to both you and the users, but is not in a form that can be directly translated into a database design. You must first convert it to a model that follows one of the formal modeling systems that bridge the gap between human understanding and the needs of a computerized relational database management system. A number of such modeling systems exist, some more appropriate for certain applications than others. A couple of popular examples are the entity-relationship (E-R) model and the semantic object model (SOM). You should become an expert in at least one of the available modeling systems and at least be aware of the major benefits and deficiencies of several more. Chances are, you will be able to employ the modeling system with which you are most familiar. Otherwise, you will at least know where else to look for an appropriate system.

TRANSLATE THE USERS' DATA MODEL INTO A FORMAL ENTITY-RELATIONSHIP MODEL

Probably the most widespread model across a broad spectrum of application categories is the *entity-relationship model*. The E-R model deals with these four main elements:

- **Entity:** An item that the user can identify and that is relevant to the objectives of the project. An *entity class* is a set of entities that share one or more common attributes. An example of an entity class in a business organization's E-R model may be the EMPLOYEE entity class. An example of an entity that is a member of the EMPLOYEE class may be Sam Taylor. Most organizations want to keep track of certain facts about their employees. Those facts are the employee's attributes.

- **Attribute:** An aspect of an entity that users consider to be worth tracking.

  In the case of the EMPLOYEE entity class, you probably want to keep track of each employee's home address. Thus, the home address would be an attribute of EMPLOYEE in the database that you are constructing. On the other hand, the organization is probably not interested in an employee's shoe size, so shoe size would *not* be considered an attribute. Every employee has a shoe size, but that doesn't matter. The organization does not care to track the size of its employees' feet.

◆ **Identifier:** An attribute or a combination of attributes that uniquely identifies a particular instance of an entity class (an entity).

In an EMPLOYEE entity, the employee's identification number usually serves as a unique identifier. For entities that don't include an attribute that is guaranteed to be unique, combinations of attributes work. In the worst case, all of an entity's attributes can be an identifier. This assumes that it isn't possible for two entities in an entity class to have all attributes in common. In that case, you need to add or change attributes so that all entities are guaranteed to be distinguishable from each other.

◆ **Relationships:** Define the way entities in an E-R model relate to each other. For example, an EMPLOYEE may make a SALE to a CUSTOMER. EMPLOYEE is related to SALE and SALE is related to CUSTOMER. A relationship between two entities, such as that between EMPLOYEE and SALE, is termed a *binary relationship*. Although higher order relationships are certainly possible, most common situations can be adequately modeled using binary relationships.

There are three principal kinds of binary relationships:

◆ **One-to-one relationships:** Relate one instance of an entity class to one (and only one) instance of another entity class.

These are the simplest relationships. An example of a one-to-one relationship is the relationship between a SHIP and its CAPTAIN. A SHIP has one and only one CAPTAIN, and a CAPTAIN commands one and only one SHIP. (Officers who command more than one ship are either commodores or admirals.) Figure 2-1 shows an *E-R diagram* representing a one-to-one relationship.

Figure 2-1: One-to-one relationship between a SHIP and its CAPTAIN.

◆ **One-to-many relationships:** Relate one instance of one entity class to multiple instances of a second entity class.

An example of a one-to-many relationship is the relationship between an EMPLOYEE and an INVOICE. An EMPLOYEE may write multiple INVOICEs (and hopefully will, if she wants to remain employed as a salesperson), but each INVOICE is written by one and only one EMPLOYEE. Figure 2-2 shows a one-to-many relationship.

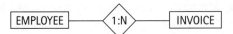

Figure 2-2: One-to-many relationship between
an EMPLOYEE and multiple INVOICEs.

◆ **Many-to-many relationships:** Relate multiple instances of one entity class
to multiple instances of a second entity class. This is the most complex
binary relationship. The relationship between the STUDENT class and the
COURSE class in a college is an example of a many-to-many relationship.
A STUDENT may enroll in multiple COURSEs in a given term, and each
COURSE may enroll multiple students. Figure 2-3 represents a many-to-
many relationship.

Figure 2-3: Many-to-many relationship between
multiple STUDENTs and multiple COURSEs.

The E-R model that you construct is the basis for the relational database that you
will build using Access. Give the E-R model visible existence by drawing an E-R
diagram that shows all the entities and the relationships between them. Seeing the
E-R diagram will often remind you of important things that have been left out, or
relationships that are not quite right. By explaining the E-R diagram to your client,
you can get valuable feedback that confirms your conception of the system agrees
with what the client wants. Figure 2-4 shows the relationships between some of the
entity classes in a college.

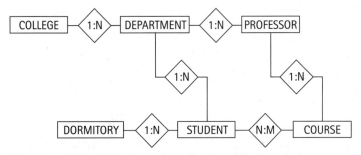

Figure 2-4: E-R model of part of a college's academic operation.

A college can have multiple departments, but each department is a member of one
and only one college, so the relationship between COLLEGE and DEPARTMENT is
one-to-many. A department can have multiple professors and multiple students, so

those relationships are also one-to-many. A dormitory can house multiple students and a professor can teach multiple classes, so those relationships are one-to-many too. A student can take multiple courses and a course can enroll multiple students so the relationship between STUDENT and COURSE is many-to-many.

TRANSFORM THE E-R MODEL INTO A RELATIONAL MODEL

Relational databases, which are the kind of databases that Access is designed to build, must adhere to the relational model, which was conceived by E. F. Codd in 1970 (an employee of IBM at the time). Codd and other computer scientists have refined the relational model over the years in order to produce a system that is both robust and that preserves a high degree of data integrity.

The E-R model is not the same thing as the relational model, but a specific E-R model can be translated into a corresponding relational model in a fairly straight-forward manner. This translation is described in *Database Development For Dummies* by Allen G. Taylor, published by Wiley Publishing, Inc. Part of the translation process is to convert any many-to-many relationships in the E-R model into pairs of one-to-many relationships. Eliminating many-to-many relationships greatly simplifies the model, and reduces the chance that data will become corrupted when additions, deletions, and updates are made. Figure 2-5 shows a relational model that corresponds to the E-R model illustrated in Figure 2-4.

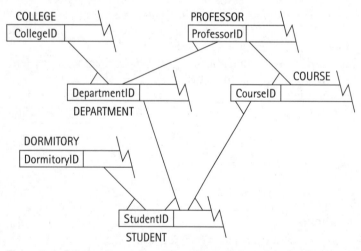

Figure 2-5: Relational model corresponding to E-R model of college academic operation.

When you convert from an E-R model to a relational model, the nomenclature changes. An entity in an E-R model corresponds to a *relation* in the corresponding relational model. Happily, an attribute in an E-R model corresponds to an attribute in the relational model also. An entity instance in an E-R model corresponds to a *tuple* (rhymes with couple) in the relational model, and an identifier in an E-R model translates to a *key* in the relational model. If more than one attribute of an entity uniquely identifies an instance of the entity, choose one of them to be the *primary key* in the relational model. You can retrieve a single tuple by searching for its primary key.

Each rectangle in Figure 2-5 represents a relation. The primary key of each relation is shown, but other attributes are not, since they do not contribute to the relationships. The lines between relations represent the relationships. The many side of a relationship is shown as a "bird's foot." One-to-many relationships have a bird's foot on one end and many-to-many relationships have bird's feet on both ends.

You reduce a many-to-many relationship in an E-R model to a pair of one-to-many relationships in the corresponding relational model by placing an intersection relation between the two relations that correspond to the two original entities that were joined by a many-to-many relationship. Each of the two original relations is on the one side of a one-to-many relationship with the intersection relation, instead of being on the many side of a many-to-many relationship with each other. Figure 2-6 shows a simplified version of the relational model in Figure 2-5, with the many-to-many relationship removed. The intersection relation STU-COURSE, which was created to decompose a many-to-many relationship, has a primary key made up of the primary keys of the two tables it is directly related to, the STUDENT table and the COURSE table.

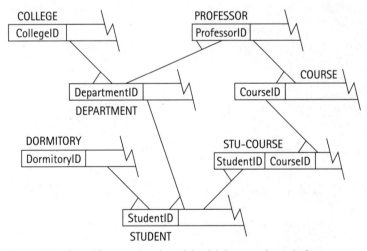

Figure 2-6: Simplified relational model, with intersection relation.

A relational model is directly translatable into a relational database consisting of tables with columns and rows. The model's relations become the database's tables. A relation's attributes become the columns of its corresponding table. The relation's tuples become the rows of the database table. Figure 2-7 shows some example data in a database table.

EMPLOYEE

Employee	Department	Manager
Kris Howcraft	Logistics	Neil Stryker
Luis Mangler	Human Resources	Theodore Ursa
Walter Salvador	Administration	Tim Krieger

Figure 2-7: Example of a relational database table.

NORMALIZE THE RELATIONAL MODEL

Relational databases are subject to problems called *modification anomalies.* Modification anomalies can occur whenever you modify a database, either by adding a new row to a table, changing the data in an existing row, or deleting a row altogether. Figure 2-7 shows an example. It shows a few rows of the EMPLOYEE table. Suppose that employee Kris Howcraft wins the Powerball lottery and decides to resign to pursue a new career as a karaoke singer. If you delete his row from the table, you not only remove him from the table, but you also lose the information that shows that Neil Stryker is the manager of the Logistics Department.

The problem occurs because the EMPLOYEE table is being used to track two distinct kinds of data: the department an employee is in, and the names of the managers of all the departments. *Normalizing* the EMPLOYEE table entails breaking it into two tables (Figure 2-8): one table tracks employee department membership and another table records department managers.

EMPLOYEE

Employee	Department
Kris Howcraft	Logistics
Luis Mangler	Human Resources
Walter Salvador	Administration

EMPLOYEE

Department	Manager
Logistics	Neil Stryker
Human Resources	Theodore Ursa
Administration	Tim Krieger

Figure 2-8: EMPLOYEE table is normalized by splitting it into two tables, each with a single purpose.

Now, if Howcraft leaves to pursue a singing career, the information about who manages the Logistics department is not lost. Refer to books on database development for more on normalizing a database.

DOCUMENT YOUR DATABASE DESIGN DECISIONS

When you have arrived at your final database design, thoroughly document every step in the process. Print out and file your E-R model diagram, your relational model diagram, and the formal descriptions of each table – including columns, rows, keys, item name, data type, and description. Figure 2-9 shows the way that Access represents relationships in a database and Figure 2-10 shows an example of an Access table definition.

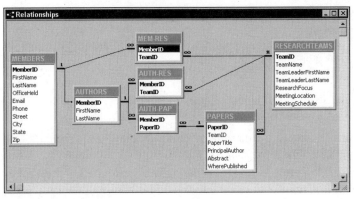

Figure 2-9: Relationships in an Access database.

The diagram shows four primary tables named MEMBERS, AUTHORS, PAPERS, and RESEARCHTEAMS, and three intersection tables named MEM-RES, AUTH-RES, and AUTH-PAP. The one-to-many relationships between primary tables and intersection tables are identified by a numeral "1" on the one side of the relationship and an infinity symbol on the many side. The intersection tables were added to the relational model to simplify many-to-many relationships that existed between members and research teams, authors and research teams, as well as between authors and papers. This particular database is for a scientific organization whose members can belong to multiple research teams. Each research team, of course, can have multiple members (otherwise it wouldn't be a team). Similarly, scientific paper authors can be members of multiple teams; authors can write multiple scientific papers; and a scientific paper can have multiple co-authors.

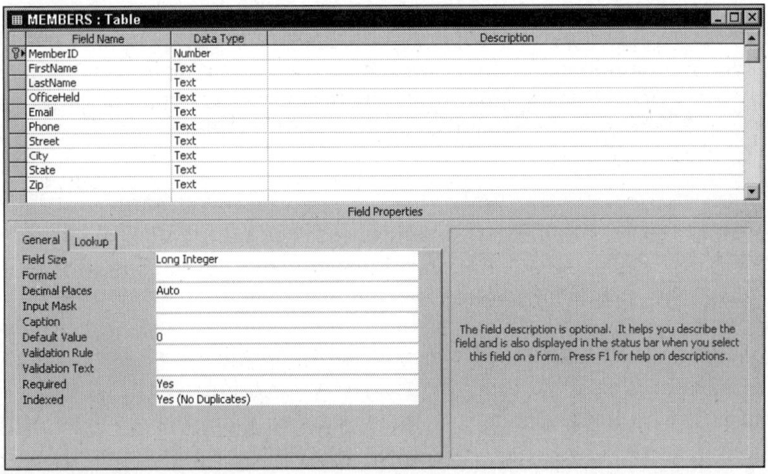

Figure 2-10: Example Access table definition.

The structure of the MEMBERS table is completely described by the `Field Name`, `Data Type`, and `Description` columns. The key symbol in the left column indicates that the `MemberID` field is the table's primary key. The Field Properties box at the bottom of the window gives details about the properties of the currently selected field (`MemberID`).

Designing the database application

Database applications let users put data into the database, manipulate the data after it is in the database, and retrieve useful information out of the database. Access provides tools that enable you to build an application without doing any programming. Such programs have a generic appearance and perform common functions.

To give your applications an extraordinary appearance and perform uncommon functions, you can create database applications by using the VBA programming language. Whether you are using VBA to create a simple, non-programmed application or an elaborate application, several considerations are common to both types of development.

DESIGN THE APPLICATION'S USER INTERFACE

The process of retrieving information must be intuitively easy and natural to the target audience of your application. Different audiences have different needs and your application should be tuned to the specific needs of its users. This consideration affects the appearance and the functionality of the user interface's screens. When you design that interface, you must accommodate how users work and what they need. You probably need to mock up a prototype of the proposed user interface to show to the various user communities. Feedback at this point can save you from a lot of rework later.

DESIGN THE APPLICATION'S FLOW OF CONTROL

Moving from one function to another should be a logical process and make sense to the user. A structure that makes a lot of sense to you may not be nearly so intuitive to a user. Find out what they are comfortable with and design your program so their experience will be pleasant. Avoid ways of doing things that the users will find frustrating or obscure.

DESIGN ERROR TRAPPING

Despite your best efforts, we can almost guarantee problems in your application. Perhaps your code will have bugs. Maybe users don't adequately communicate to you what they need. Users will do things with the application that you didn't anticipate. To minimize the damage that can be caused by any of these occurrences, anticipate possible errors ahead of time. If the flow of execution ever deviates from what you expect for a program that is operating normally, include code in your application to handle the error. This error-trapping code may be simple, such as displaying a warning message to the user, or it may be more complex, perhaps deducing the source of the error and correcting it on the fly, without the user even being aware that a problem occurred. Try to anticipate potential problem areas, and build error-trapping routines at those spots. If intermediate results are not as anticipated, the error-trapping code is executed instead of continuing with the main program.

DESIGN SECURITY FEATURES

Hacker attacks are pretty common these days, so database security is more important than ever before. Design your database application so it gives users only the level of access that they are authorized to have.

Database applications should display warnings to the user before obeying commands that may have a major effect on the database, such as DELETE TABLE. Mistakes by authorized users can be as devastating as malicious tampering by outsiders.

DOCUMENT THE DESIGN

Detailed documentation is important in the Design Phase. This is when you precisely structure your system — then you create that structure on paper (or electronic paper, as the case may be). Document why you have chosen to design the system one way and not any of the other possible ways. Note the pros and cons of all design possibilities and show that, in consideration of all the relevant facts, the design you have chosen is the best possible.

OBTAIN CLIENT SIGNOFF OF THE DESIGN DOCUMENT

After your design is complete and fully documented, present it to your client. When the client reads the design document and understands it, have him or her sign and date it; this shows that the client agrees with what you are proposing to provide. Your signature shows that you are committed to providing what the design document describes.

Obtaining the client's signature on the design document can stop "feature creep." Feature creep occurs when the client comes to you in mid-development and asks about a feature that you didn't agree to deliver. Generally the client wants this new feature included in the project at no added cost and without lengthening the schedule. At this point, you can refer to the signed design document; it shows what was agreed upon. If the new feature is not described in the design document, you are not obligated to provide it. You may decide to provide it, but as a separate project with its own budget and schedule.

The Implementation Phase

The Implementation Phase is where you actually build the system. Fingers touch keyboards and code gets written. This phase consists of several parts, each part corresponding with a part of the Design Phase. Building the database is one major piece, followed by building the database application that connects the database with the users. Of course, documenting what you produce here is just as — and probably more — important as it is in all the other phases. After the database is complete, someone can fill it with data while someone else writes the application program.

Build the database

The documentation you created in the Design Phase should provide a detailed roadmap of what to do in the Implementation Phase. You can use Access's tools to build database tables and establish the relationships between them. No programming is required for this task. We assume that you know how to use the Access tools to build a database.

 Building the database should occur only after you have performed all the jobs specified for the preceding phases of the system development cycle.

Document the database

Access does a great job of creating documentation about the structure of the database that you create, so you don't need to do much extra work at this point:

◆ Make hard copies of the definitions of all the tables that you create and of the relationships between the tables.

◆ Keep records of why you detoured from your original design concept, and what precise steps you took along the way to arrive at your final implementation.

◆ Your design will probably evolve as you get into it and you will go through several iterations for at least some of the tables. This information is a valuable reference to help you justify any alterations you had to make in the design specified in the design document. It may also help you on future projects.

Write the database application program

At last! This is where you actually get to do some programming. To a dedicated coder, the temptation is great to skip the preceding steps and start coding right away. If you do that, expect problems. If you have not done justice to the Definition, Requirements, and Evaluation Phases, it is likely (because of less than full communication with the users), that you will build a system that does not fully meet their needs. If you have not spent enough time and effort on the Design Phase, you may have structural problems that lead to data corruption. However, if you have given the preceding phases the attention that they deserve, you can now embrace the challenge of writing the code that makes your paper design into a reality that meets the client's needs. Aside from your financial compensation, perhaps a happy client is your greatest reward.

You can build much of your application without doing any programming. Access has graphical tools for building user interface screens, menus, and reports. You don't need to program for any of those tasks. This saves considerable time and also eliminates a major source of errors. Take advantage of Access' Design View to create the forms, queries, and reports that will form the bulk of your application's interactions with the users. Any programming that you do will most likely operate under the surface, controlling the flow of execution, making calculations, or performing data retrievals.

Document the program code

Regardless of how fluent you are with VBA and SQL, program logic can get convoluted. Six months after you complete the project, it is difficult for you to follow what your logic was when you wrote the code. If you are called upon to make updates or modifications to the program, it helps immensely if you liberally intersperse comments with the code. Document the purpose and main algorithm of each functional block. Give extra attention to any actions that may be obscure. You may work on this code again. Even more likely, a maintenance programmer who is totally unfamiliar with the code may need to modify it. As a professional, you want to give that person all the help you can. Her job already is hard enough.

Fill the database with data

After you have created the application, data entry operators can start entering data into the database by using the screens you have created for that purpose. Alternatively, you can transfer the data directly from where it currently resides, if it is in electronic form, by using a *data transfer utility*. You may be able to find one that already exists, or you may write one yourself. The details of that utility depend on the format of the data, and how you want it to appear in your Access database. After a representative amount of data is entered into the database, you can move on to the next phase, the Testing and Final Documentation Phase.

The Testing and Final Documentation Phase

After you have built your application and it is functioning the way you want it to function, it is okay to congratulate yourself, but it is not yet time for a big celebration. You have much work yet to do. First, your application must be thoroughly tested to make sure it does everything it should, does it as well as it should, and does it in all environments where it should. Furthermore, the application must not behave badly, regardless of what the users do to it. The only way to guarantee that the system will act as desired is to try every function under all possible operating conditions and to misuse the system in all the ways that users could possibly misuse it.

Employ a professional tester

The people who build the database and application, and the folks who write the code that perform the application's functions, are not the best people to conduct the Testing Phase. If they have blind spots in their thinking about the application that caused them to miss something while they were building it, those same blind spots are likely to cause them to miss the problems that arise. Ideally, testers should be people who are highly skilled in the art of testing software, but who had nothing to do with the development effort. Unlike the developers, whose goal is to create a flawless system, the primary goal of the tester is to make the system fail. It is much better to expose a flaw at this stage than to have the client discover it later when live data is in the database and your reputation is on the line.

Employ regression testing

Any system of sufficient size and complexity is apt to contain problems when it exits the Implementation Phase. These problems may be outright bugs or they may be usability problems, such as a confusing user interface. If, in the process of running a series of tests, your testing function detects a problem and brings it to your attention, fixing it is your job.

One unfortunate aspect of software development is that whenever you modify an existing system, the modification that you make may have unexpected consequences. It may alter the behavior of the application in an area that seems to be totally unrelated to the function that you fixed. Because of this, when you return the application to the testers to resume testing, they can't pick up where they left off when they discovered the original problem. They must run all their tests again from the beginning to see whether the modification you made introduced new problems in the functionality that they had already tested. This practice of rerunning tests from the beginning after the correction of a problem is called *regression testing*. Regression testing, even though it takes additional time and effort, is a vital part of any development effort if you want to deliver a reliable system.

Test the system for functionality, performance, and compatibility

In the Testing Phase, the first order of business is to determine whether the system does everything it should. You can accomplish this by referring to the Statement of Requirements. Exercise the system with the test data that you have entered to see that you can perform all the functions specified in the Statement of Requirements and that results of all operations are as expected.

In the process of testing for functionality, you can note whether performance is satisfactory. For example, do database retrievals take too long? This is something you can only discover if the test database that you are working against is about as big as the production database that the system will operate on. Performance problems typically don't surface when you test against a database whose tables have only a small number of records. Make sure that your test data is representative of production data.

Compatibility may or may not be an issue. If the production system will only be run on computers that are configured identically to the one on which the system was developed, you should not encounter any compatibility problems. However, you should check the system being developed under all possible combinations of operating conditions if it will be run on computer systems with different *memory configurations, disk subsystems, printers, processors,* or *operating systems.* This becomes an almost impossible task, unless standards are in place that limit the number of possible configurations. This is one reason why many organizations standardize on one configuration for all computers in the organization.

Test the system's response to unexpected user behavior

You never know what a user is going to do. You may make it perfectly clear how to use the system, both in printed documentation and on-screen instructions. Users will still find ways to misunderstand, misinterpret, or merely forget what they are supposed to do. They do what makes sense to them at the time, and in so doing, send your application in a direction that you never anticipated. When this happens, you want your system to respond gracefully and direct the user to the proper way to operate. You don't want the system to suddenly lock up or, even worse, give the user erroneous information.

The Testing Phase should specifically include a full suite of tests in which the tester *does not* follow directions. These tests should explore everything that a user might conceivably do. If they expose a system response that is less than helpful, you should modify the system so that it behaves in a benign manner, even when abused.

Produce online help

One of the most useful forms of documentation that you can provide with a system is a comprehensive and well-organized system of online help. Explanations of how to perform all system functions, with definitions of all relevant terms, should be included in the online help files. Often, printed documentation and instruction sheets are not close at hand, but online help is always available and easy to access. Online help that tells the users what they are likely to want to know is an important component of the total system package.

Produce final printed documentation

As the developer, you should retain this documentation and give a copy to the client as a package:

- The documentation maintained throughout all the phases of the system's development.

- Complete records of the testing, including results of each test, any fixes applied, and results of subsequent retests

- A printed copy of the online help

- Operating instructions for the users

Obtain client acceptance and signoff

When you deliver the completed system and the final documentation package to the client, demonstrate how everything works and show that all the items specified in the Statement of Requirements are satisfied. After the client understands that everything that was agreed upon was delivered, obtain a signature that signifies acceptance. At this point, it is appropriate to ask for final payment for your work. Now you can celebrate!

Celebrate successful completion

Celebration is good for the soul and it is good for your development team. Do something special to show that you appreciate the work that has been done, and that something important has been achieved. The celebration provides an end point to the development effort, but it does not mean that you are completely finished with this particular application. Once a system is in service, it may need to be modified, upgraded, or repaired from time to time. These are jobs for the Maintenance Phase of system development.

The Maintenance Phase

When most people worked on farms, folks had a saying that went something like this, "A man works from sun to sun, but a woman's work is never done." In many ways, the application developer's lot in life is similar to that of the farmer's wife. Even after you deliver the product and are paid, you are not "done." Old projects keep coming back – for a number of reasons.

Fixing latent bugs

One reason is the possibility that bugs in the code may cause the application to malfunction. How can there be bugs in the code? All the bugs were discovered and corrected in the testing phase, weren't they? The reality is, probably not. Even a very thorough test program doesn't typically find 100 percent of the bugs in an application. Obscure bugs that require an unusual combination of conditions, or are present in sections of code that is infrequently exercised, may not manifest themselves for weeks, months, or even years. The Y2K bug, for instance, was almost 50 years in the making before it was recognized as a problem. Once acknowledged, that problem inspired a panicked effort and cost millions of dollars before it was fixed.

Because no one is more familiar with an application than the team that developed it, you are likely to be called upon to fix it when problems arise. At this point, you will be glad that you have extensive documentation. If a couple of weeks have passed since you finished the project, it will already have started to fade from your memory. If the problem that you are being called in to fix is from an error on your part, you may be obligated to fix it for free. If the problem is from another cause, providing ongoing maintenance can be a good steady source of income for you.

Providing enhancements and updates

Because you are the person most familiar with the application and thus the one most likely to understand how to modify it, you may need to make enhancements. As organizational needs change, the applications that support the organization must change, too. Perhaps new functions must be added. Maybe existing functions have become obsolete and should be deleted. The legal or regulatory environment may have changed, thus requiring changes to the software. There are many reasons why software you have written must be updated on an ongoing basis, and that's not a bad thing. This need can be the basis for a good, stable source of income for you. Every successful installation that you do becomes a possible source of residual income in the months and years after you complete the project.

Client Communication

A vital factor in the success of any development project is close communication between the developer and the client. The developer must have a clear idea of what the client wants, and the client must have a clear idea of what to expect from the developer.

Controlling client expectations

Many people who aren't computer-savvy find computers almost magical. They believe that you can do practically anything with a computer. This mistaken idea often translates into unrealistic expectations of what your application can do for them. After the client tells you what he wants, it is up to you to communicate what can reasonably be done with the available time and budget. Because unforeseen problems almost always occur, it is wise to be conservative in your estimate. It is much better to underpromise and overdeliver than it is to overpromise and underdeliver.

At the end of any project, you want clients to feel that they received more than they expected, not the reverse.

Resisting schedule pressure

Clients always seem to want new applications to be delivered faster than is humanly possible. They pressure the developer to speed up the process and deliver early. Generally, the only way for a developer to deliver early is to cut corners, and usually that means skimping on testing and documentation. The client probably doesn't realize it, but pressuring the developer to accelerate the schedule at the expense of testing or documentation is almost always a bad idea. The long-term consequences of inadequate testing and documentation usually far outweigh the short-term benefit of putting the system into service a little sooner.

In the best interests of the client, and to reduce your stress level, you must convince the client that it is better to do the job right than it is to do it fast. Take the time to do it right, so that later you won't have to do it again.

The client may suggest adding developers to accelerate the project. This rarely helps; often, additional personnel slow down a project instead of speeding it up. The time that you would have to take to bring the new people to the point where they are productive is better spent just doing the work. The larger a development group is, the more time that must be spent in meetings. Coordination of activity takes up time that a smaller group could have applied to the work at hand. Sometimes adding staff to a project is the right thing to do, but often it is not. Evaluate each situation carefully before deciding to add to a team that is already working well.

Summary

To build a robust system that does an important job efficiently and reliably by using data stored in an Access database, follow a structured approach to system development. This approach should include close communication with the client for whom you are building the system and a step-by-step approach to the specification, design, implementation, testing, and documentation of the system. You should also consider maintaining the system after it has gone into operation. Every phase of the system's development life cycle is important. Make sure that each phase gets the attention that it deserves.

Chapter 3

Access Application Development without VBA

IN THIS CHAPTER

- ◆ Access and database architecture
- ◆ What Access applications are good for
- ◆ What Access applications are made of
- ◆ Developing simple applications without programming
- ◆ Event-driven operation
- ◆ Using templates to shortcut the development process
- ◆ Deciding whether an application requires programming

ALTHOUGH THE MAIN PURPOSE of this book is to give you pointers on building Access applications by using the VBA programming language, Access provides a set of tools that enable you to build applications without any programming on your part. Before we get into VBA, then, let's look at an overview of application development and the tools that Access provides to perform that development.

The whole point of developing application programs is to perform some function that is of use to one or more people. Databases form the core of many applications because they contain data, and useful functions generally require data of some sort. The tool used for connecting the application to the data is usually a *database management system* (DBMS), and more specifically, a *relational database management system* (RDBMS). Depending on the size of the installation and the number of users that may need data access at the same time, different configurations are used.

Database Management System Architecture

The three main kinds of database systems are personal, workgroup, and enterprise. A personal database system consists of a database, a DBMS, and a database application. All components of the system reside on a single computer and are used by one person at a time. In a workgroup database system, a single computer, called the *server*, hosts the database and distributes information to multiple client computers that are running application programs. An enterprise database system may have multiple servers distributing information to hundreds or even thousands of client computers. Microsoft Access is typically considered a personal database product, but it can play a role in workgroup and enterprise systems as well.

Different Access Uses

Access is an application development environment built around a relational database management system. Although it was originally conceived as a personal RDBMS, Access works in a multiuser environment

- ◆ With a file server
- ◆ With a replication strategy
- ◆ In a client/server configuration

Using Access with a file server

A *file server* is a computer that is configured to be relatively "dumb." It holds the database in a file or in a collection of related files, and is connected to a network that is also connected to other computers. An application, running on one of those other computers, requests a file from the file server. The file server responds by locating the requested file and sending it over the network to the computer running the application.

The file server network architecture is a rather crude way of distributing computer power. Access stores all the tables, forms, reports, and other database objects in a single .mdb file. An application may need only a single record from a database table, but the file server sends the entire database in response to any request, because it isn't smart enough to do anything more than determine which database contains the requested record and then send the database out over the network to the requesting client computer. The main problem with this approach is poor performance, because so much unneeded data is being sent across the network. When the number of simultaneous users reaches a certain threshold value, performance plummets.

Replicating the database

One solution to the bandwidth saturation problem that plagues a file server system is to do away with the file server, and instead, replicate the database on all the computers that are running the applications. This overcomes the performance problem because the data is on the same machine as the application, thus bypassing the network bottleneck.

Replication has a couple of problems:

◆ Synchronizing multiple copies of the database. If a user on one system makes a change to a record in her copy of the database, that change must be broadcast to all the other copies before a second user on another machine requests that same record. This requires a DBMS that is quite complex, but at the same time robust and error-resistant.

◆ Equipping all the computers running the applications with high capacity, high-speed storage. This is needed because the database is stored redundantly on each of the computers.

Working with SQL Server to create a client/server system

The most efficient approach, and the only one that can scale to enterprise class networks, is the client/server approach. This scheme employs an intelligent server in contrast to the dumb server in a file server system. The intelligent server is smart enough to accept an SQL command, execute it to perform an operation on the database, and then send a result back to the requesting client computer.

Access does not have the power to support client/server architecture. To provide a full spectrum of solutions to an organization's database needs, Microsoft combines Access with its full powered client/server RDBMS – SQL Server. By combining Access's easy-to-generate user interface with the intelligence and power of SQL Server, you can generate applications that are easy to build and use, while at the same time being scalable to enterprise class installations. Access provides the "front end" on the client machines, while SQL Server functions as the "back end" on the intelligent server machine.

What Access Applications Do

You may wonder why a person would use an Access application in the first place. What kinds of things can you do with Access that you couldn't do equally well with a spreadsheet program, such as Microsoft Excel?

Keeping track of things

Databases act primarily as repositories of data. Spreadsheets also hold data, but in a different way. The great value of storing data in a database is that you can use SQL statements to retrieve datasets containing the exact information that you want – excluding everything else. The options available to the application developer are much greater than they are with a spreadsheet. Here are two examples:

◆ The order in which items are stored in database tables doesn't matter because a properly written SQL statement retrieves precisely the information that you specify, regardless of how it is stored in the database.

◆ You can apply constraints to the data in a database that prevent the inadvertent incorporation of invalid data.

Overall, the relational database model is a much more powerful way of representing a set of interrelated facts or items than the spreadsheet model provides.

Recording transactions

Databases are particularly valuable for creating a record of items that change frequently. Retail operations keep track of sales with databases; airlines record and maintain reservations with databases; financial institutions track securities trades with databases. The world economy depends on the function and reliability of databases. Databases provide a record – theoretically, a permanent record – of most of the commercial and financial activity that takes place throughout the modern world.

Performing computations

Database applications can do much more than merely store and retrieve database data. Through the use of programming languages such as VBA, in combination with SQL, you can perform a wide variety of mathematical and logical operations on your data. This capability enables you to maintain, and retrieve on demand, the key information that you need to make the best decisions regarding the real-world enterprises that your databases are modeling.

The Parts of an Application

You can think of a database application as being divided into three main parts:

◆ User communication

◆ Execution of functions that the application is designed to perform

◆ Database communication

Each of the three parts is important, although the skills to perform them differ. Figure 3-1 shows how the three parts of an application fit into a complete system.

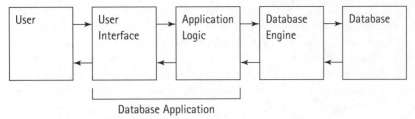

Figure 3-1: Block diagram of an information processing system.

The database application is the heart of the overall system. The database contains the data, but it isn't in a particularly useful form. At the other end of the chain, the user has questions and is seeking answers. The application is the part of the system that translates the user's questions into a form that the database engine can understand. The database engine, in turn, extracts the wanted information from the database and sends it back to the application, which then passes it on to the user.

Creating a user interface

The user interface of an Access application generally consists of screen forms. You, as a developer, create those screen forms, perhaps supplementing them with menu bars and dialog boxes. It pays to put considerable effort into the design of the user interface because if your application is not easy to understand and use, your organization won't get the full benefit from it. Applications with poorly designed user interfaces, or interfaces that are not appropriate for the users, often fall into disuse, thus wasting the investment put into their development.

Having the prospective users of your system review and critique a prototype of your user interface is a critical part of system development. This review should occur in paper form during the Design Phase of the System Development Life Cycle, and then again with a mockup at the beginning of the Implementation Phase. Continue to refine the user interface as development progresses until your contact in the user community is completely happy with the way it looks and the way it functions.

Dealing with data

The data is located at the opposite end of the processing chain from the user. The database engine component of Access, which is either the Jet engine or the SQL Server engine, deals with the data. Your application accesses the data via the database engine. To do so, it communicates with the engine by using either DAO or ADO. DAO is an older technology that is being replaced by ADO. When creating new applications, it is better to use ADO, which Microsoft will support for a long time. In many cases, the ADO commands are generated by Access, based on actions that the user takes. In other, usually more complex cases, you would write ADO commands to perform the exact operations that you want performed. These ADO commands would be part of the program control code that you would write using VBA. Because this chapter is about application development without programming, don't worry about the database engine, ADO, or VBA. You can create applications that tell the database engine what to do without knowing or using SQL or VBA. We discuss VBA in Chapter 5 and ADO in Chapter 15.

Controlling what the user can do

When you write a full-blown application using VBA, you have complete control over what the application does, and how it responds to user actions, such as menu selections and button clicks. When you write a simple application that doesn't involve VBA programming, the control that you have over what can occur is much more limited. You can do the following:

- ◆ Create screen forms that allow the user to make selections, enter or modify database data, or merely read information that the database contains.

- ◆ Create reports that the user can view and print out.

- ◆ Give the user the option of navigating from one screen form to another by way of menu selections or hyperlinks.

This list sums up what you can do for the user without the benefit of programming. To do more, use VBA.

An Application Developed without Programming

To illustrate some of the features of an Access application, consider a simple application that was developed without programming. This application keeps some basic records for a fictional non-profit organization named The Oregon Lunar Society. The Oregon Lunar Society (OLS) is a research and educational organization. Members are scientists who do research in lunar geology and exploration. Members with common interests join research teams that investigate problems, and then publish results in papers presented at conferences. The main items that the OLS database tracks are the following:

- ◆ Society members
- ◆ Research teams

◆ Scholarly papers produced by research teams

◆ Members who serve as authors of papers

This information is stored in database tables named MEMBERS, RESEARCHTEAMS, PAPERS, and AUTHORS. Figures 3-2 through 3-5 show the definitions of these four tables.

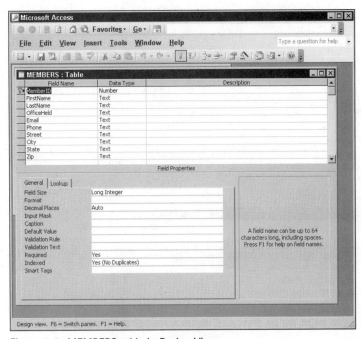

Figure 3-2: MEMBERS table in Design View.

Figure 3-2 shows the names and data types of all the fields in the MEMBERS table. In the lower part of the window, the figure shows the field properties for the `MemberID` field, which is the primary key of the table. Every table must have a primary key, which uniquely identifies each row in the table. The field that the cursor is located within determines which set of field properties is displayed. Because `MemberID` is the primary key, it was given the property that it must contain a value (Required), and that it is Indexed and duplicate values are not allowed. Because the primary key of every record in a table must be unique, neither duplicates nor null values are allowed.

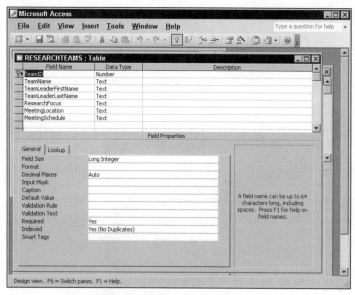

Figure 3-3: RESEARCHTEAMS table in Design View.

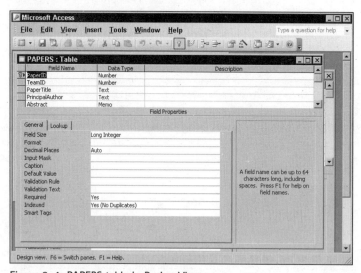

Figure 3-4: PAPERS table in Design View.

Handling relationships

One entity can be related to another entity in a number of different ways. Of most practical interest are the binary relationships, in which one entity relates to one other entity. Tables in a relational database can have the same kinds of binary relationships that we described when discussing the E-R model in Chapter 2.

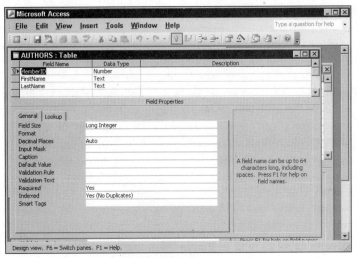

Figure 3-5: AUTHORS table in Design View.

ONE-TO-ONE RELATIONSHIPS

One-to-one relationships are the simplest, in which one instance of one entity corresponds to one and only one instance of the second entity. A relational database example of such a relationship is a corporate database that maintains one table of unrestricted data about employees, such as their employee ID numbers, their names, their departments, and their office telephone extensions. A second table, available only to authorized human resources personnel, contains their employee ID numbers, their hire dates, their job classifications, and their current salaries. One record in the first table corresponds to one and only one record in the second table. Figure 3-6 shows a schematic representation of the relationship. The "1" symbol on each end of the line connecting the tables shows that it is a one-to-one relationship. As shown in Figure 3-6, the two tables in a one-to-one relationship share the same primary key.

Emp ID	Name	Dept	Phone
10	Anne Aray	Dock	2985
20	Bob Reed	Dock	3423
30	Cy Hart	Intake	3425

Emp ID	Start	Job	Salary
10	10/4/1979	Manager	41472
20	10/3/1994	Assist	34848
30	8/2/1997	Manager	67608

Figure 3-6: One-to-one relationship.

ONE-TO-MANY RELATIONSHIPS

One-to-many relationships are common in many application areas. In a one-to-many relationship, one instance of one entity corresponds to multiple instances of a second entity. For example, such a relationship occurs in a retailer's database, in which one customer may correspond to multiple purchases. Figure 3-7 shows a schematic representation of this relationship. The "1" symbol on one side and the "∞" symbol on the other side of the line connecting the two tables shows that it is a one-to-many relationship. As you can see from Figure 3-7, the table on the many side of a one-to-many relationship includes the primary key of the table on the one side.

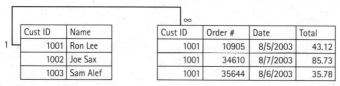

Cust ID	Name		Cust ID	Order #	Date	Total
---------	----------		---------	---------	----------	-------
1001	Ron Lee		1001	10905	8/5/2003	43.12
1002	Joe Sax		1001	34610	8/7/2003	85.73
1003	Sam Alef		1001	35644	8/6/2003	35.78

Figure 3-7: One-to-many relationship.

MANY-TO-MANY RELATIONSHIPS

In a many-to-many relationship, one instance of one entity can correspond to multiple instances of a second entity, and one instance of the second entity can correspond to multiple instances of the first entity. Whereas one-to-one and one-to-many relationships are pretty easy to grasp and to deal with, many-to-many relationships are significantly more complex and somewhat problematic. College classes provide an example of this kind of relationship. One student can enroll in multiple classes in any given term. Similarly, one class can (and should) enroll multiple students in a given term. It is hardly worth offering a class if only one student can take it at a time. Figure 3-8 shows a schematic representation of this relationship. The infinity symbol on both ends of the line connecting the two tables shows that the relationship is many-to-many.

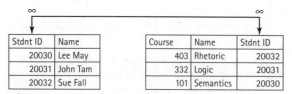

Stdnt ID	Name		Course	Name	Stdnt ID
----------	----------		--------	-----------	----------
20030	Lee May		403	Rhetoric	20032
20031	John Tam		332	Logic	20031
20032	Sue Fall		101	Semantics	20030

Figure 3-8: Many-to-many relationship.

PROBLEMS WITH MANY-TO-MANY RELATIONSHIPS

Many-to-many relationships suffer from some structural problems. Consider the STUDENTS/CLASSES relationship. Because a student may enroll in multiple classes, the primary key of STUDENTS should be part of the primary key of CLASSES.

Because a course may enroll multiple students, the primary key of CLASSES should be part of the primary key of STUDENTS. You can't have a situation where A is a part of but not all of B, and at the same time B is a part of but not all of A. Computer scientists have devised several ways to avoid this dilemma, but the most commonly used solution employs intersection relations.

INTERSECTION RELATIONS

Adding intersection relations to a database model is a way to trade one form of complexity for another. A many-to-many relationship between two tables is difficult to handle. You can overcome this difficulty by placing a new table, called a *junction table,* based on an intersection relation, between the two original tables. This new table sits on the many side of a one-to-many relationship with each of the original tables. You have added to the complexity of the database by adding a table, but you have also reduced the complexity by transforming the many-to-many relationship into two one-to-many relationships. Additional tables are a lot easier to handle than many-to-many relationships, so the transformation yields a net benefit to the database developer. Figure 3-9 represents the STUDENT/CLASSES relationship after it was transformed by introducing the STU-CLASS junction table between the two original tables.

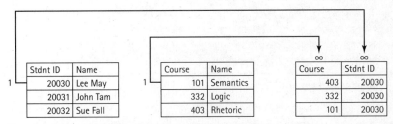

Figure 3-9: Many-to-many relationship transformed by the addition of a new table based on an intersection relation.

Modeling relationships for the OLS database

The Oregon Lunar Society has members, research teams, papers, and authors. Relationships are as follows:

- ◆ A member may join multiple research teams and a research team may have multiple members. (Relationship type: many-to-many)

- ◆ A research team may produce multiple papers, but each paper will be the product of one and only one research team. (Relationship type: one-to-many)

- ◆ A paper may have multiple authors and each author may write multiple papers. (Relationship type: many-to-many)

◆ A member may be an author and an author may be a member. (Relationship type: one-to-one)

◆ An author may join multiple research teams and a research team may have multiple authors. (Relationship type: many-to-many)

With three many-to-many relationships, your first step is to transform them to one-to-many relationships by adding three tables based on intersection relations. Figure 3-10 shows a relational diagram of the transformed database. Three new tables are added and three many-to-many relationships are converted into six one-to-many relationships.

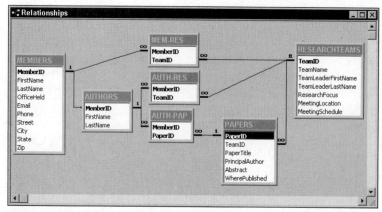

Figure 3-10: Relational diagram of OLS database.

The tables based on the intersection relations – MEM-RES, AUTH-RES, and AUTH-PAP – consist of the primary keys of the two tables that they connect. They don't contain any non-key fields.

Creating the OLS application

After you have the database structure finalized, you can begin building your application. Follow all the phases of the System Development Life Cycle. For the Oregon Lunar Society, you want the application to do a few simple things:

◆ Allow users to

■ Enter into the MEMBERS table pertinent information about new members when they join.

■ Change information about existing members when addresses or phone numbers change.

■ Delete records for members who don't renew their memberships.

◆ Perform the same types of maintenance tasks (as detailed in the previous list) on the tables for research teams, authors, and papers.

◆ Automatically update intersection tables when the data in related primary tables changes.

◆ Generate desired reports, such as a members' e-mail list, a list of papers produced by a particular research team or authored by a particular member, and so forth.

The user interface of an application must respond to the actions of the user. From the application's point of view, every user action is an event.

Events

Microsoft Windows is an event-driven operating system. Actions are taken in response to events. For example, when you click on the Windows Start button, the Start menu appears. Clicking the button is an event and the display of the menu is Windows' response to that event. Microsoft Access is also an event-driven program. As with Windows, it responds to mouse hovers, button clicks, double-clicks, and a number of other events. The applications that you create, either with Access's graphical tools or with VBA, are also event-driven.

Event-driven operation is based on a discipline called *object-oriented programming*. Object-oriented programming deals with objects, which are characterized by properties and methods.

Objects, properties, and methods

All the major elements of a database are objects, including *tables, forms, reports,* and *queries*. Properties are attributes of objects, and an object can have many properties. Methods are actions that objects perform; an object may have multiple methods. For example, a button can have a method that determines what happens when the mouse cursor hovers over the button. Another method can determine what happens when the button is clicked. Yet another method may determine what happens when the button is double-clicked.

Objects respond to user-initiated events, such as button clicks, or to a programmed event caused by the execution of a VBA command. With a VBA command, you can cause an event to "fire" (execute) an object's method.

Event procedures

Event procedures, written in VBA, are short, single-purpose programs that are executed in response to an event. After you become proficient at writing VBA code, you write your own custom event procedures. Whether you know it or not, you are creating event procedures even when you develop Access applications without writing a single line of VBA code. Access writes the VBA code for you.

Retrieving data with a button press event

This is an intermediate to advanced level book on Access, so we are assuming that you can design a screen form and place objects (such as buttons) on it. Consider the form created for the OLS application shown in Figure 3-11.

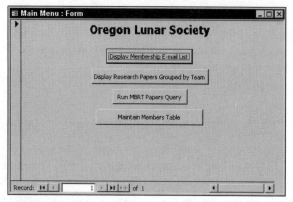

Figure 3-11: Main menu screen form for the OLS application.

The menu consists of several buttons, one of which is titled "Display Membership E-mail List." When the user clicks this button, Access retrieves the desired information from the MEMBERS table and displays it on the user's screen. This action did not require any programming on the developer's part, but code was generated as an event procedure.

You can view the code that was generated to respond to the button's click method by invoking the Visual Basic Editor (VBE). In the Main Menu form, select the "Display Membership E-mail List" button, and then right-click on it. This action displays the pop-up menu shown in Figure 3-12.

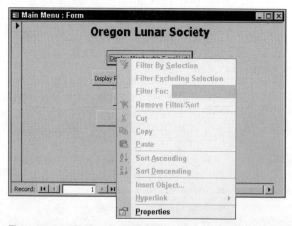

Figure 3-12: Option menu for a button on a form.

From the menu, select Properties. This displays the Property Sheet shown in Figure 3-13, which lists all the events to which the button may respond. Currently only the click event is defined and an event procedure for it is present.

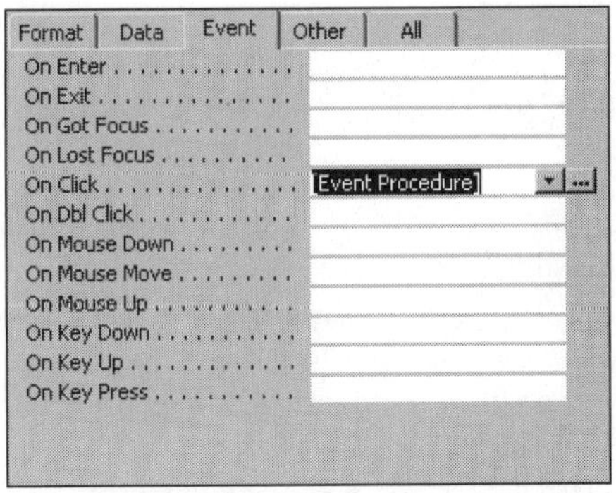

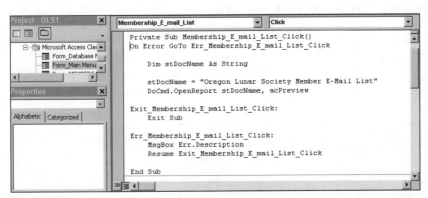

Figure 3-13: Defining information window for the selected command button, with the Event tab selected.

By clicking on the ellipsis at the right edge of the line for the click event, you invoke VBE. It displays the VBA code for the button-click event procedure, as shown in Figure 3-14.

Figure 3-14: Event procedure for the button-click event.

Let's take a quick look at the code in the event procedure.

```
Private Sub Membership_E_mail_List_Click()
On Error GoTo Err_Membership_E_mail_List_Click

    Dim stDocName As String

    stDocName = "Oregon Lunar Society Member E-Mail List"
    DoCmd.OpenReport stDocName, acPreview
```

```
Exit_Membership_E_mail_List_Click:
    Exit Sub

Err_Membership_E_mail_List_Click:
    MsgBox Err.Description
    Resume Exit_Membership_E_mail_List_Click

End Sub
```

The first line identifies this code as a private subroutine named `Membership_E_mail_List_Click()`. The second line redirects execution to an error handling routine if an error condition is detected at this point.

The third line declares a variable named `stDocName` and assigns it a `String` type. The fourth line fills the variable `stDocName` with the name of the report to be generated, "Oregon Lunar Society Member E-Mail List."

The fifth line, starting with `DoCmd`, is the first line to actually do something. It opens the named report and directs its output to the screen. The sixth and subsequent lines just tie up loose ends by exiting the event procedure, exiting the subroutine, and specifying what the error handling routine does.

All the code in the preceding VBA subroutine was created automatically by Access in response to the way the application developer defined the button when he placed it on the form.

Updating an existing record

An event such as a click on a button need not start the execution of an event procedure. It can cause a macro to execute instead. Consider the "Maintain Members Table" button on the OLS application's main menu, as shown in Figure 3-11. Right-clicking on this button displays the shortcut menu shown in Figure 3-15.

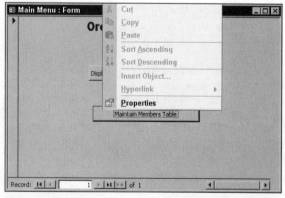

Figure 3-15: Shortcut menu for Maintain Members Table button.

Selecting Properties from the menu displays the command button dialog box shown in Figure 3-16. The On Click event is the only one that is defined and it says MEMBERS form. The developer has specified that clicking on the button opens the MEMBERS form, thus displaying the first record in the table, as shown in Figure 3-17.

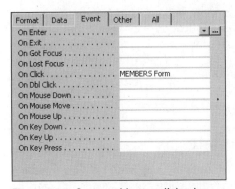

Figure 3-16: Command button dialog box.

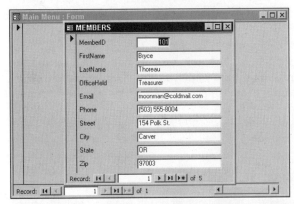

Figure 3-17: Form invoked by the "Maintain Members Table" button.

With the MEMBERS form, you can change the information in an existing record, move back and forth through the records, or add new records. You don't need VBA or programming of any kind, although you can also perform this kind of table maintenance with VBA code, as discussed in Chapter 9.

Speeding Development with Pre-defined Templates

Maybe the application you have in mind for an Access database is completely different from anything that anyone has ever done before. Then again, maybe it is not *completely* different. For example, your application may share some common elements with applications that others have developed or even that you have developed in the past. Particularly in business, some kinds of requirements appear again and again, regardless of the company or even of the industry. People tend to track things in similar ways, even when the things being tracked are not similar at all.

Borrowing a database template

If someone has already developed a database similar to the one that you are about to start creating, why not take advantage of that earlier work instead of starting from scratch? You can use the structure of the earlier database as a template for the one that you are developing. It's a lot easier to modify something that substantially meets your requirements and that already exists than it is to build the whole thing from the ground up.

Several templates for common database tasks come with Access 2003. If one of these tasks is a fairly close match for what you want, you can save a lot of time and effort by starting with the template and modifying it into the database structure that you need. One side benefit of this approach is that the template structure has already been tested and thoroughly debugged. You still need to test everything, but the Testing Phase should go smoothly because much of the system is proven.

Example of a database template

Access 2003 provides ready-made database templates for several common business applications. Figure 3-18 shows what the screen looks like when you start Access.

In the Open pane on the right, one option is Create a new file. Click on that option to show the menu in Figure 3-19.

The New File menu offers several starting points for a new database, including the use of templates, either online or on the local computer. Contact Management and Asset Tracking are also listed, because they were used recently. When you click on Templates on Office Online, the screen in Figure 3-20 appears.

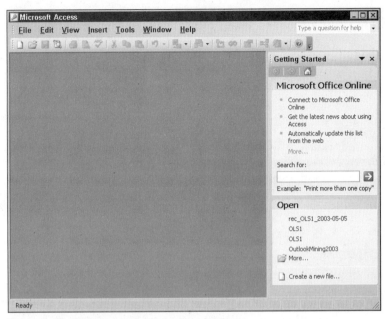

Figure 3-18: Choices for creating a new database.

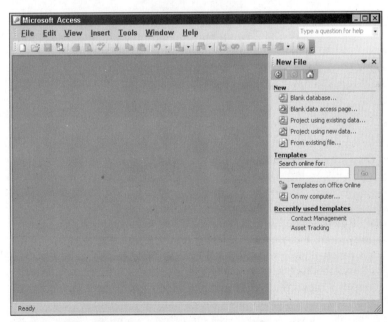

Figure 3-19: New File menu.

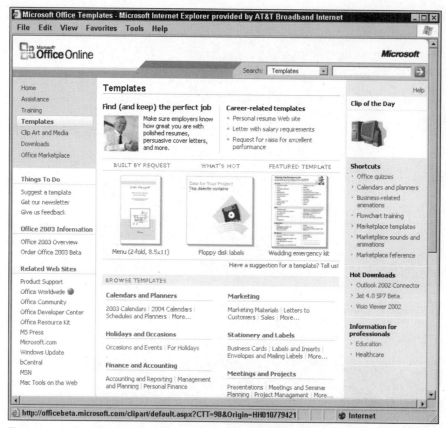

Figure 3-20: Ready-made templates available on Microsoft's Web site.

There are hundreds of templates to choose from. These templates cover many of the most common needs of a wide variety of businesses as well as personal needs. In some cases, they are all that you need – so you won't have to create your database from scratch. You can build on the core provided by one of the templates. In some cases, none of the templates may apply to your situation, so you won't be able to take advantage of work that somebody else has done.

A look at one of these templates will show how you may incorporate one like it into a system that you are building. We selected an asset tracking template, which is a full, although simple database application. In response, Access starts the database application's switchboard form shown in Figure 3-21.

The switchboard is a menu that gives the user access to the data that the database holds. Each option on the menu leads to the data in a database table. Figure 3-22 displays what you see when you select Enter/View Employees.

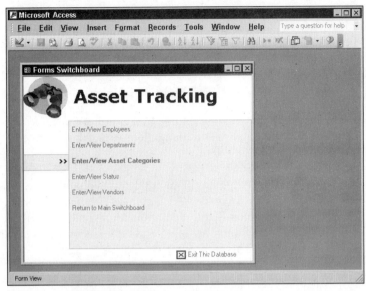

Figure 3-21: Asset Tracking Database Template.

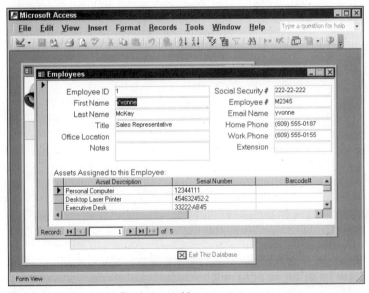

Figure 3-22: Record in Employees table.

Figure 3-22 shows a record for a fictional employee, along with the assets assigned to her. To customize the forms such as the one shown in Figure 3-21, switch to Design mode, where you can change the form to meet your needs that differ from those of the stock template.

Not only can you change the forms, but you can change everything else including the structure of the tables. You could add new tables, delete ones you don't want, or modify the ones you keep. Modifying a template is just like modifying a database that you have built from scratch.

Creating a form template without coding

Creating a form template is similar to creating a form. You just don't take the task all the way to completion. A form template is nothing more than a form that contains common elements.

When you create a form with the Form Wizard, you are first asked for the table on which the form is based, and the fields from that table that will appear on the form. Next, you are asked to specify a layout, which can be *Columnar, Tabular, Datasheet, Justified, PivotTable,* or *PivotChart.* Next, you are asked to specify a style for the background of the form from a list of several different styles. Finally, you are asked to give the form a title. This is the same set of steps that you followed when creating the forms for the Contact Management database.

For a template, if you are basing multiple forms on a specific table, specify that table in the Form Wizard. Also specify all the fields in that table so they are available; later you can delete the fields that you don't want in any particular form. You will probably want all the forms that are derived from your template to have the same layout and style, so you can also specify those two characteristics. Finally, for the report title, just enter some placeholder title that you can change as appropriate for each form that you derive from the template.

Save the finished template with a descriptive name. To create a form from the template, call it up in Design View and make whatever modifications, deletions, or additions that are needed to give the form the exact functionality that you desire, and then save the result under a new name. The work required to make those modifications is typically considerably less than is required to build each form from scratch. You get the additional benefit of a uniform appearance for all the forms that you create with the template, without referring to the forms that you have already created.

Creating a report template without coding

The process of creating a report is pretty similar to that of creating a form. Consequently, the discussion in the previous section of creating a form template applies equally well, with slight adjustments, to creating a report template. The main thing to remember is that creating a report template is just like creating a report, but opting for generality, not specificity. The resulting template should be easy to customize into the desired report by removing unwanted fields and perhaps rearranging the layout to emphasize whatever is the most important material in any specific report.

Switchboard Forms

Switchboard forms are forms that are specifically designed to provide navigation for an application. They may contain graphics, but primarily, they hold buttons that, when clicked, send execution to other switchboard forms or to the forms or reports that comprise the functional part of the application. Creating a switchboard form is just like creating any other form, except that you restrict what the form contains to graphics; perhaps a title; possibly some explanatory text; and the buttons that navigate to other switchboard forms, ordinary forms, or reports. When creating a switchboard form, Access can guide you step-by-step with the Switchboard Manager. Alternatively, you can easily create a switchboard form the same way you create an ordinary form, and you have more flexibility in the design of it, in exchange for only a little bit more complexity.

Enhancing switchboard appearance

You can enhance the appearance of a switchboard form with the well-considered inclusion of graphic images, such as the one on the left and side of the switchboard Another enhancement is the reversed color font and drop shadow of the form title. You can let your creativity loose here to give your switchboard forms an appearance that communicates on a non-verbal as well as a verbal level.

Multi-level menus

Making a selection on the switchboard form that is the main menu can lead to another switchboard form that is a submenu. You can create as many levels of menus as you need, providing navigation back to the main menu from each one, as appropriate. Exiting the application should be one of the choices on the main menu (probably the last option).

Is Programming Needed?

This is a question to ask yourself when you enter the Implementation Phase of any development project. As you have seen in the preceding sections of this chapter, it is quite possible to develop a fairly elaborate application without doing any VBA programming. For some projects, you may be able to create a satisfactory application without doing any programming. For others, the requirements demand the power that only comes from custom programming. You, in combination with your client, must decide whether a non-programming solution can work. If it can, you can save a lot of time and effort and deliver a finished application sooner. If programming is required, make sure that the client understands what that means in terms of development, testing, and documentation time.

Summary

In this chapter, we covered the different kinds of database architectures and what database applications do. We showed you that you can develop a useful Access application without doing any programming. We discussed event-driven operation and the object-oriented structure that Access supports. We talked about how the use of templates can save time, effort, and money. Switchboard forms provide an easy-to-create and easy-to-use method of providing navigation to an application. Using switchboard forms, no programming is required to allow users to move around within an application. Whenever you are presented with a new development task, analyze it to determine whether the required application can be developed without programming. If so, you will probably save time by doing so.

Chapter 4

Customizing Menus and Toolbars

IN THIS CHAPTER

- ◆ Manipulating Built-in Command bars
- ◆ Editing Built-in Command Bars
- ◆ Creating Custom Command Bars
- ◆ Importing Custom Command Bars
- ◆ Converting macros to VBA

IN THE DAYS BEFORE ACCESS 97, you needed at least an advanced degree in cryptology to be able to change the built-in menus and toolbars or – even more complicated – to create your own command bars to fit your application. Recent versions of Access, however, provide many more helpful and understandable tools to modify and create menus, toolbars, and even the handy shortcut menus. In addition to the built-in assistance, you can use VBA code to create and modify existing and custom toolbars and menus. (This chapter focuses on the built-in tools; Chapter 13 shows you how to build your own special purpose command bars.)

All three types of these user interaction objects now fit into the classification of *command bars* and share much of the same appearance and behavior. You can also use most of the same techniques to work with all three.

About Access Command Bars

Menu bars and toolbars are the basic user interaction tools. Menu bars and toolbars are both considered command bars. Figure 4-1 illustrates the parts of the Access command bars.

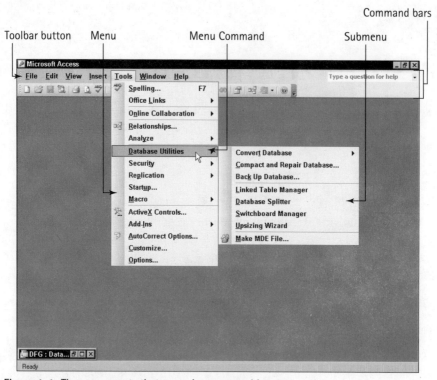

Figure 4-1: The components that comprise command bars.

♦ **Command:** The basic element of a command bar that you choose to carry out an action, such as opening a form or running a query. Either a *menu command* or a *toolbar button* can execute this.

♦ **Command bar:** A set of *menus, toolbar buttons,* or both. The command bar usually appears at the top of your screen but you can usually place it anywhere you want it.

♦ **Toolbar button:** An item in the command bar that carries out a specific action when you click it.

♦ **Menu:** An item on a command bar that, when clicked, displays a list of commands from which you can choose.

♦ **Menu command:** An item in the list displayed by the menu. When you click it, just like a toolbar button, it carries out a specific action.

♦ **Submenu:** A list of menu commands that are accessible when you rest the mouse pointer on one of the items in the menu list. You can tell which menu items lead to a submenu by the right-pointing arrow located next to the text.

TIP A menu item showing ellipses (...) opens a dialog box.

◆ **Shortcut menu:** A special list of commands that appears when you right-click in an area on the screen. The commands in the list differ depending on where you are when you right-click.

Access provides three command bar types:

◆ **Built-in command bars:** Automatically displayed by Access with specific database views. For example, the Form Design command bar appears when you are creating or modifying a form design.

◆ **Global command bars:** Custom tools that you make accessible to any database or application in your system.

◆ **User-defined custom command bars:** Custom tools that you create in a specific database. You can specify a custom command bar that automatically displays with a certain form or other view.

Manipulating Built-in Command Bars

Access provides 25 built-in toolbars but only one built-in menu bar. The menus on the menu bar change when you change views in your database. For example, the Records menu is added to the menu bar when you open a form in Form view. This menu gives you the capability to filter and sort records, save the current record, or add a new record. Two global toolbars, Utility 1 and Utility 2, are also in the list of toolbars in the Customize dialog box. These have no commands at first but you can create global toolbars bearing these names. They can contain any mixture of toolbar buttons, menus, and even some items that you create.

Moving and resizing command bars

By default, the command bars are *docked* — they are fixed along one side of the screen. Usually, they appear at the top of your screen but you don't have to leave them there. You can drag them to another side or drag them away from the edge altogether and let them float in the window. To move the bar, click and drag on the moving handle (the stack of small dash lines at the left end of the bar). You can also click on any empty space or a separator bar in the command bar and drag it away from the edge.

After a command bar is floating, you can change the height and width by dragging the borders. To close a floating toolbar, just click the Close button in the title bar. You can't close a floating menu bar because it doesn't include a Close button; however, you can drag it back to where it belongs. Figure 4-2 shows a floating menu bar with a floating toolbar.

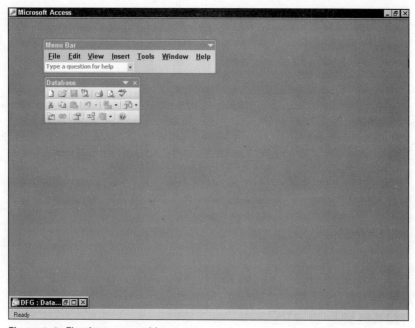

Figure 4-2: Floating command bars.

To dock the command bar at another side of the window, drag it to that side until it spreads out to the full height or width of the window.

To put two toolbars on the same row at the top of your screen, click and drag the lower toolbar by its move handle up to the row above. This should place the lower toolbar to the left of the upper one. You can change the order of the toolbars by dragging the upper one down a notch then dragging it back up to join the other one.

Give it a try; it's not as complicated as it sounds.

Showing and hiding command bars

Specific command bars appear by default in certain views; other command bars are available if you need them. Table 4-1 lists the default and optional command bars that appear with each view. You can choose to display other command bars or remove the default command bars from the screen.

TABLE 4-1 AVAILABLE COMMAND BARS IN ACCESS VIEWS

View	Default or Optional Command Bars
Database Window	Database
Filter By Form or Filter/Sort	Advanced Filter/Sort
Form Design view	Form Design, Formatting (Form/Report), Toolbox
Form view	Form View, Formatting (Form/Report)*
Macro Design view	Macro Design
Page Design view	Data Outline, Field List, Formatting (Page), Page Design, Toolbox
Page view	Page View, Formatting (Page)*
Print Preview	Print Preview
Query Datasheet view	Query Datasheet, Formatting (Datasheet)
Query Design view	Query Design
Relationships window	Relationships
Report Design view	Report Design, Formatting (Form/Report), Toolbox
Table Datasheet view	Table Datasheet, Formatting (Datasheet)
Table Design view	Table Design
Visual Basic Editor view	Standard, Debug, Edit, UserForm

The formatting command bars are available only when the Allow Design Changes property of the form or page is set to All Views.

To remove one of the default toolbars from the screen, do either of these:

◆ Right-click an empty space in the toolbar or menu bar and clear the check mark next to the command bar name in the list.

◆ On the View menu, point to Toolbars and click the toolbar that you want to remove.

TIP To return the toolbar to the screen, repeat the action and check the name again.

Three toolbars on the list are always available but not displayed automatically:

♦ **Toolbox:** The toolbar you use while working in a Form or Report Design window.

♦ **Web:** The standard Web navigation toolbar.

♦ **Task Pane:** Options for working with new or existing files, like when you start Access 2003.

To display one of the toolbars that is not a default for the view you are using or not on the list of available toolbars, open the Customize dialog box with one of the following steps:

♦ Right-click again and this time choose Customize from the drop-down list.

♦ Click the Toolbar Options arrow and point to Add or Remove Buttons, and then click Customize.

♦ On the View menu, point to Toolbars and choose Customize.

♦ On the Tools menu, choose Customize.

In the Customize dialog box shown in Figure 4-3, you can see the list of built-in command bars, including the Menu bar. Because the Form Design and Formatting (Form/Report) toolbars are checked, they are currently displayed with the Menu bar. If you scroll down the list, you also see Shortcut Menus (discussed later in this chapter). Check any of the toolbars that you want to add to the window, and then click Close. Any non-default toolbars that you add to the view remain on-screen after you leave that view.

Three toolbars in this list are not associated with any specific view and appear only when you ask for them:

♦ **Source Code Control toolbar:** Displays buttons to control changes in VBA code while you are working in a multiple-developer environment.

♦ **Utility toolbars:** Two global toolbars that you can design for an application.

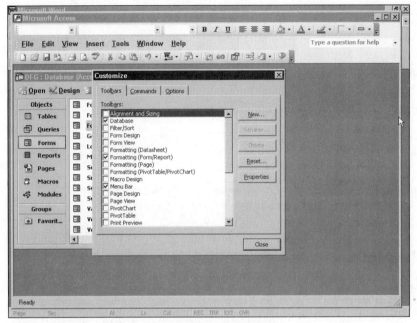

Figure 4-3: Adding toolbars to the screen with Customize.

To clear or display built-in toolbars, do the following:

◆ **Remove a toolbar from the window:** Right-click in a command bar and click the check mark to clear it.

If you remove a default toolbar from the screen in the view where it normally appears, it doesn't appear the next time you open that view but it is still in the list of available toolbars.

◆ **Restore a toolbar:** Right-click in the command bar and check the toolbar in the list of available toolbars.

A non-default toolbar is removed from the drop-down list of available toolbars the next time you look at it.

You can't remove the Menu Bar from the screen this way unless you have changed the menu's Allow Showing/Hiding property. You can find more about changing command bar properties later in this chapter.

Showing and hiding toolbar buttons

You don't have to display all the buttons on the built-in toolbars. You can hide any of them that you don't need. This is handy when you want to place more than one command bar in a single line so you can see all the useful buttons and menus without scrolling to the right. The Toolbar Options button (the one at the right of the toolbar with the question mark and the drop-down arrow) chooses which buttons to display on the default toolbar. Just click the Toolbar Options button and point to Add/Remove Buttons, and then point to the name of the current view.

Figure 4-4 shows the buttons that are available on the Query Design toolbar.

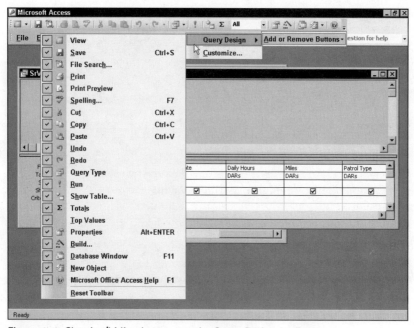

Figure 4-4: Showing/hiding buttons on the Query Design toolbar.

 When the Menu bar or toolbar is floating, the Toolbar Options button is in the title bar next to the Close button.

If you are designing a database for an end-user who doesn't need to access the Help topics, you can hide the Type a question for help control in the title bar.

- ◆ With the Customize dialog box open, do the following:

    1. Right-click the Type a question for help control.

    2. Clear the checkmark next to Show the Ask a Question Box option.

    3. Close the Customize dialog box.

- ◆ To get the control back, do the following:

    1. Open the Customize dialog box.

    2. Right-click the Type a question for help control.

    3. Check the Show the Ask a Question Box option.

    4. Close the Customize dialog box.

Editing Built-In Command Bars

You aren't stuck with the built-in command bars the way that Access delivers them to you. You can change their appearance, properties, and behavior to suit the activities of the intended user. You can move the buttons and menus around on the command bar and actually change the text or image on the button or menu.

You have a lot of options with command bars, such as

- ◆ Allowing the command bar to be moved

- ◆ Controlling the length of menus

- ◆ Showing screen tips and help text

These settings are optional and can easily be changed.

Setting Command bar options

After you open the Customize dialog box, click the Options tab to take a look at the properties you can change (see Figure 4-5).

The upper pane contains options that affect the way that Office personalizes the menus and toolbars, depending on its interpretation of your usage. The intent is to reduce the space occupied by unused menu commands and toolbar buttons. Sometimes this is a nuisance, so Access lets you set your own preferences:

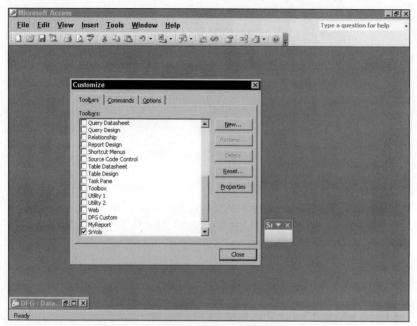

Figure 4-5: Setting options for the menu bars and toolbars.

- ◆ **Show Standard and Formatting toolbars on two rows:** Controls how the two default toolbars appear when you are editing a chart in Access.

- ◆ **Always show full menus:** Displays all the menu commands when you click a menu instead of the ones that Access thinks you will need.

- ◆ **Show full menus after a short delay:** Selected by default, but overridden when you select *Always show full menus.*

  This option can be cleared if you choose to show full menus. If it is cleared and you don't choose to show full menus, you must click the down-arrows at the bottom of the menu list to see the rest of the commands.

- ◆ **Reset my usage data:** Performs three functions:

  - ■ Clears the history of your toolbar button and menu command selections

  - ■ Returns the built-in toolbars to their original button display

  - ■ Returns the menu command lists to their original items

The *lower pane* contains options that affect the appearance and behavior of all *toolbar buttons* and *menu commands:*

◆ **Large icons:** Shows toolbar buttons with much larger images. This doesn't affect menu bars. This changes all Office programs.

◆ **List font names in their font:** Refers to the list of available fonts in the drop-down list in the Formatting toolbars. The font names are displayed in their own font so you can see what you are dealing with.

◆ **Show ScreenTips on toolbars:** Displays the name of the button when you rest the mouse pointer on it. This changes all Office programs.

◆ **Show shortcut keys in ScreenTips:** Displays the shortcut key as an underlined character in the name of the button. This doesn't affect the underlined shortcut keys in menus. This changes all Office programs except Excel.

◆ **Menu animations:** Gives you control of the animation action when menus open and close. Check them out and find the one that works best for you.

Changing toolbar properties

You can change some of the properties of individual command bars separately:

◆ **Set the properties of a specific toolbar:** Select the toolbar name in the Toolbars list on the Toolbars tab of the Customize dialog box, and then click the Properties button.

Figure 4-6 shows the properties for the built-in Form Design toolbar.

■ **Toolbar Name and Type:** Name your custom toolbar and choose the type: *toolbar, menu bar,* or *pop-up* (a shortcut menu).

You can't change the name or type for a built-in toolbar.

■ **Show on Toolbars Menu:** Lists this custom toolbar in the Toolbars submenu in the View menu.

Built-in toolbars are always shown on the Toolbars submenu.

■ **Docking:** Offers *Allow Any* (default), *Can't Change, No Vertical,* or *No Horizontal.*

■ The four **Allow** properties, when checked, let the user *customize, resize, move,* or *show/hide* the toolbar. These are available with all toolbars.

◆ **Change the properties of other toolbars:** Click the down-arrow next to the Selected Toolbar control and choose another toolbar from the list.

You see the same list as in the Toolbars tab of the Customize dialog box. This is just a shortcut. Click Close when you finish these changes.

◆ **Return the toolbar to its original appearance and behavior:** Click Restore Defaults in the Toolbars Properties dialog box.

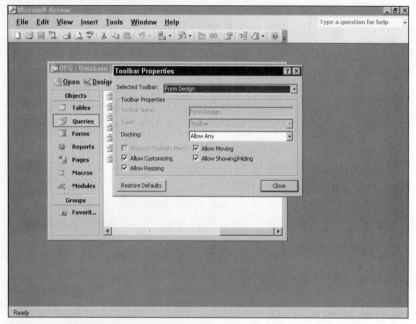

Figure 4-6: Setting toolbar properties.

Changing built-in buttons or commands

After you are satisfied with the look and feel of the command bars themselves, you can change the appearance of any of the buttons or commands on the command bars. To change one of the properties, do the following:

1. Right-click in the toolbar and choose Customize from the shortcut menu.

2. Select the toolbar in the Toolbars list that you want to change to make sure it is visible.

3. Right-click the button or menu that you want to change to display the shortcut menu.

For example, Figure 4-7 shows the editing options that are available for the Print Preview toolbar button. Table 4-2 describes each of the editing options in the menu. The image-editing options are discussed separately.

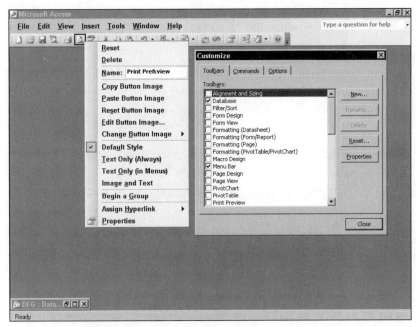

Figure 4-7: Editing the Print Preview toolbar button.

TABLE 4-2 BUTTON AND MENU EDITING OPTIONS

Menu Command	Description
Reset	Restores the default properties for the built-in menu, menu command, or button. Not available for custom items because they have no "default" properties.
Delete	Removes menu, menu command, or button from the toolbar. Built-in items are still available in the Commands box if you need to use them again.
Name	Edit or enter a new name for the built-in or custom menu, menu command, or button. An ampersand (&) in the name indicates that the next character is the access key. Press Alt and the character to carry out the command.
Default Style	Shows only an image on a button, but both text and image (if one exists) on a menu command.

Continued

TABLE 4-2 BUTTON AND MENU EDITING OPTIONS *(Continued)*

Menu Command	Description
Text Only (Always)	Shows only text on buttons and menu commands.
Text Only (in Menus)	Shows text with no image on menu commands and only an image on buttons.
Image and Text	Shows both an image (if there is one) and text on both buttons and menu commands.
Begin a Group	Adds a dividing line to the left or above the button, menu, or menu command.
Assign Hyperlink	Assigns or removes a link to the command.
Properties	Opens the Control Properties dialog box for the active toolbar, menu bar, or shortcut menu.

Not all of the options on the shortcut menu are available for all the buttons and menus. For example, when you right-click the Undo button, only the Delete, Name, Begin a Group, and Properties commands are available.

 If you rename a built-in button, you see the new name in the ScreenTip even if the button shows only an image.

If you think your toolbar is taking up too much room and you have hidden all the buttons you don't need, you can still reduce the width of one of the combo box controls. For example, the Font combo box is wide enough to show most of the font names and maybe you don't need to see all that. To shrink the control, follow these steps:

1. With the Customize dialog box open, click the combo button on the toolbar.

   A black rectangle appears, framing the button.

2. Place the mouse pointer on either the left or right edge; when the pointer changes to a double-pointed arrow, drag the edge of the box to a better width.

For the image options on the shortcut menu, you can

◆ Copy the image from this button to the Clipboard and paste it to another button later

◆ Paste an image from the Clipboard to this button

◆ Reset the original image

To change the image, choose Change Button Image to open a palette of available images (see Figure 4-8). Select the one you want.

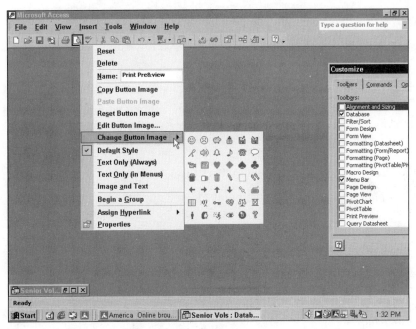

Figure 4-8: Choosing a different button image.

To get creative and customize the image in place, choose Edit Button Image to start the Button Editor, as shown in Figure 4-9.

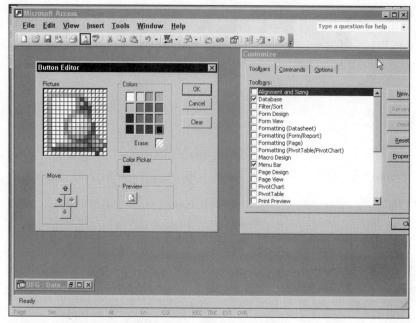

Figure 4-9: Using the Button Editor to modify the image.

If you mess up with the Button Editor, you can reset the image and start over. The original icon is still in the library of commands in the Commands box.

◆ To start over with a blank button, click Clear.

◆ To add to the image, click a color button and draw the image in the grid by clicking in individual cells or by dragging the pointer over several cells.

◆ To erase some cells, click the Erase button and drag the pointer over the cells that you want to clear.

◆ To move the image on the grid, click the Move buttons. One click moves the image one row or column. If it is up against a side of the grid, that Move button is not available. In Figure 4-9, only the down Move button is available.

If the button doesn't show the new image when you finish your artwork, the style may be set to Text Only.

You can change one more set of properties for menu and toolbar controls. Select Properties on the control's shortcut menu to open the Control Properties dialog box. Figure 4-10 shows the property sheet for the Print Preview button on the Database toolbar. Table 4-3 describes these control properties and how to set them.

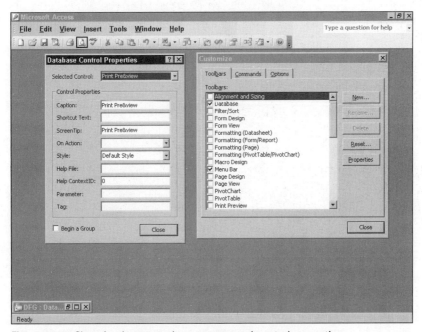

Figure 4-10: Changing button and menu command control properties.

TABLE 4-3 TOOLBAR CONTROL PROPERTIES

Property	Description
Caption*	Enter the name of the control. An ampersand (&) precedes the access key.
Shortcut Text	Enter the text to display that specifies the shortcut key combination for this control. For example, Ctrl+X is the shortcut for the Cut toolbar button.
ScreenTip*	Enter the text to display when the mouse pointer rests on the control.

Continued

TABLE 4-3 TOOLBAR CONTROL PROPERTIES *(Continued)*

Property	Description
On Action*	Enter the name of a macro or VBA function to execute when the control is selected. If you use a function procedure, precede the name with an equal (=) sign.
Style	Choose from the same list of four styles as shown on the shortcut menu.
Help File*	Enter the path and file name of the Help file that contains the text to display when you click the What's This? button.
Help ContextID*	Enter the Context ID number for tip text in the compiled Help file specified in the Help File property.
Parameter	If a parameter is passed to the event procedure named in the On Action property, enter the name.
Tag	An identifier string that can refer to the control in an event procedure.

* Property applies to both menus and buttons.

The changes that you make to a toolbar or menu bars are stored with that command bar and are not propagated to other instances of the button or menu on other command bars.

Changing built-in shortcut menus

Modifying built-in shortcut menus is a little different from working with toolbars and menu bars. Access stores all the shortcut menus in one block. When you select Shortcut Menus in the Toolbars list, a menu appears, showing a list of categories of shortcut menus. When you click one of the menus, you see a list of all the shortcut menus associated with that item. The list shows the areas of a form where right-clicking results in a pop-up shortcut menu. When you click on one of these, you see the actual shortcut menu.

Figure 4-11 shows the shortcut menu that appears when the form is in Datasheet view and you right-click in a column of the datasheet. Changing a command on a shortcut menu is the same as changing one in a regular menu. Right-click the command and make the changes as before, including altering the command's properties.

Figure 4-11: Modifying a shortcut menu command.

Looking Ahead

Toolbars, menu bars, and shortcut menus are all Access objects in VBA with sets of properties that reflect the settings you are working with through the customizing mode.

When you make changes via the Customize dialog box, they are stored with the toolbar or menu and used later — whether you want it or not.

◆ Chapter 13 shows that you can make run-time modifications to menu bars with VBA statements. For example, you can add an item to a menu, change a button style, or specify a procedure to run when the user clicks a button. You can even add a shortcut menu at run time. This comes in handy if you want to make changes temporarily for a special purpose. After the activity is completed, the toolbar or menu reverts to its original appearance and behavior.

◆ Chapter 14 shows you how to use VBA to program startup options for command bars, including specifying which custom command bars to show and restricting the user's ability to make changes.

Restoring built-in command bars

Access provides three levels of restoration for command bars. All these actions require an open Customize dialog box:

◆ Remove all the changes to the built-in toolbar, menu bar, or shortcut menu, including any changes made to the buttons or menus, and restore all the original property settings.

■ To restore the command bar to its original appearance and behavior, select the toolbar or menu bar from the Toolbars list and click Properties, and then click the Restore Defaults button.

 If you haven't made any changes to the selected command bar, the Restore Defaults button is not available.

■ To restore the buttons and menus, select the toolbar name in the Toolbars list and click Reset, and then click OK to complete the reset process.

◆ Restore the changes made to all of the individual buttons and menus on the command bar without changing other command bar properties, such as screen location or size.

◆ Reset individual menu, button, or menu command settings.

■ To reset an individual menu command, click (left-click) first on the menu that contains the command, and then right-click the command itself and choose Reset in the shortcut menu. You will be asked to confirm the action.

■ To reset the appearance and behavior of an individual menu, toolbar button, or shortcut menu command, right-click the item and choose Reset in the shortcut menu.

Figure 4-12 shows the shortcut menu for the Forms menu command in the Database Objects submenu.

 You can't use Reset to get the original image back to the toolbar button if the button opens a list of options. Use Reset Button Image instead.

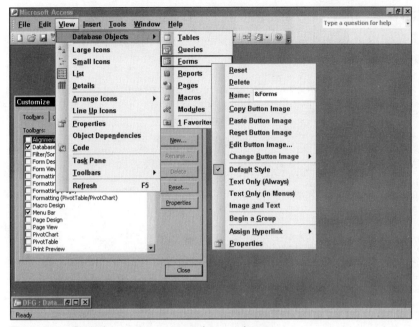

Figure 4-12: Resetting a menu command on a submenu.

Creating Custom Command Bars

Modifying built-in command bars and creating custom ones use most of the same methods and techniques.

However, modified built-in command bars and your own custom toolbars have one basic difference:

◆ Built-in command bars are available to *all databases*.

◆ Your own custom toolbars are available only to the *active database*.

Two *global toolbars,* Utility 1 and Utility 2, are available to all your databases and clients.

Starting a new toolbar

Working with toolbars and menu bars requires an open Customize dialog box. To start a new toolbar, do the following:

1. Right-click in the toolbar and choose Customize on the shortcut menu.

2. Click New on the Toolbars tab.

3. Enter the name for the new toolbar in the New Toolbar dialog box.

4. Click OK.

The new toolbar name appears at the bottom of the Toolbars list and a small empty toolbar appears next to the Customize dialog box as shown in Figure 4-13.

Figure 4-13: Starting a new toolbar.

To set the toolbar properties, click Properties. If you are building a new menu bar or shortcut menu, use the Properties dialog box to change the Type to Menu Bar or Pop-up (for a shortcut menu).

ADDING BUTTONS AND MENUS

You can add buttons and menus to the new toolbar in a couple of ways:

◆ Copy a built-in button or a previously created custom button from another toolbar.

◆ Select a button or menu from the Command list on the Commands tab of the Customize dialog box.

The commands are arranged by category. After you select a category, you can see the list of commands that it includes. (See Figure 4-14.)

When you find the command that you want to add to the toolbar, do the following:

1. Click and drag it to the new toolbar.

2. When you see the dark I-beam, drop the command where you want it to appear.

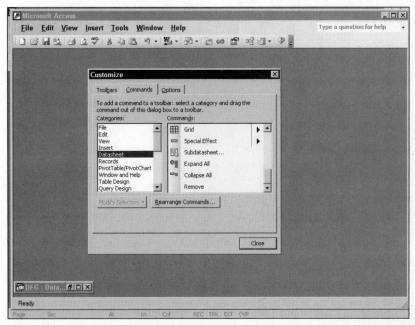

Figure 4-14: Commands arranged by category.

 TIP   You may have to look around in the Categories lists for the command that you want. Some of them are stored in odd places.

If the button is not in the right position after you add a few more commands, you can move them around on the command bar by doing the following:

1. Click the Rearrange Command button on the Commands tab of the Customize dialog box to open the dialog box (see Figure 4-15).

2. Select the menu or toolbar you want to change.

3. Select the menu command or toolbar button you want to move and click the Move Up or Move Down button.

You can also use the Rearrange Commands dialog box to add or delete commands.

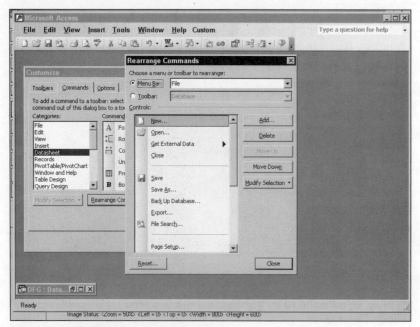

Figure 4-15: Rearranging menu commands.

 If you are using Access 2002, you can still rearrange the commands by dragging them to another position on the menu or toolbar.

The following are some special categories of commands in the list:

◆ **ActiveX Controls:** Lists all the ActiveX controls available to your database, such as the Calendar Control and a ton of Microsoft controls.

The sets of **All Forms, All Queries, All Reports, All Tables,** and All **Web Pages** display the names of the objects you have available to your current database. When you add one of these to the toolbar, the button opens the object in the default view. Forms are opened in Form View, reports in Print Preview, and so on.

◆ **All Macros:** Lists the available macros and the toolbar button that runs the selected macro. Figure 4-16 shows the beginnings of a toolbar with a button that opens the Activity Codes form in Form View. We added the vertical lines between the buttons by right-clicking a button and choosing Begin a Group in the shortcut menu.

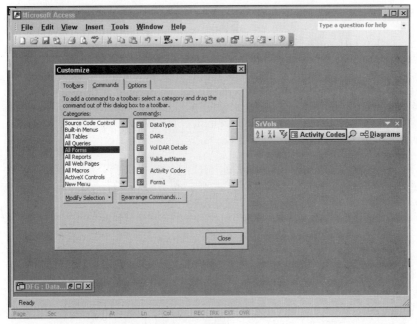

Figure 4-16: Adding buttons to a new toolbar.

You can copy a button from another toolbar. Be sure both toolbars are visible, then do the following:

◆ With the Customize dialog box open, hold down the Ctrl key while you drag the button from one to the other.

◆ If the Customize dialog box is not open, hold down Ctrl+Alt and drag the button.

 The copy is still part of the original button. If you make changes to the copy, they are reflected in the original button as well. If you intend to make changes, you are better off creating a button by dragging a command from the Commands list.

If you want to move the button from one toolbar to another, with both toolbars visible, do the following:

◆ In Customize mode, just drag the button from one to the other.

◆ If you are not in Customize mode, hold down the Alt key while you drag the button.

To remove a button or menu from a visible command bar, open the Customize dialog box and drag the button or menu off the command bar. Without the Customize dialog box open, you can still remove the button or menu by holding down the Alt key while you drag it off the command bar.

You can also choose a built-in menu to add to your new toolbar. Select Built-In Menus in the Categories list to see the menus in the Commands list. Drag the menu that you want to the toolbar and drop it when you see the dark vertical line. The built-in menu on the toolbar has the same menu commands as appear in the built-in menu.

CREATING A NEW MENU OR SUBMENU

You can add a new menu to a toolbar then add menu commands or submenus to it. To create a new menu for the toolbar, do the following:

1. Click New Menu in the Categories box.

2. Drag the new menu from the Commands dialog box to the toolbar (see Figure 4-17).

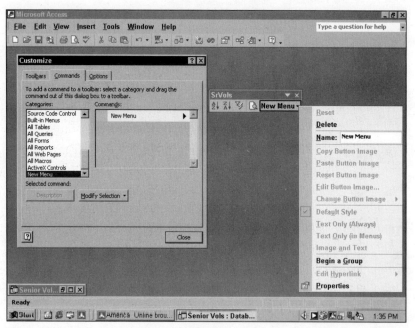

Figure 4-17: Adding a new menu to a toolbar.

3. Right-click the New Menu menu item and enter a name for the new menu in the Name box on the shortcut menu. If you are indicating access keys in the menu names, be sure to use a different character for each menu that you add.

Now you are ready to place commands on the new menu:

◆ Choose the first command from the list and drag it to the empty box below the new menu.

◆ Add other commands by dragging them to the list forming below the menu itself.

◆ If you change your mind about a menu command, just drag it off the toolbar.

◆ To create a new submenu, add a new menu and give it a name, and then add commands to the submenu by dragging them to the box to the right of the submenu itself (see Figure 4-18).

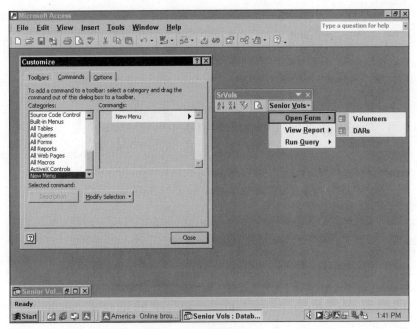

Figure 4-18: Adding commands to a new submenu.

GROUPING BUTTONS AND COMMANDS

Aligning buttons and commands into groups of related activities speeds up user interaction and helps avoid errors. Built-in toolbar and menu group items have something in common. For example, Cut, Copy, and Paste are grouped in the Database toolbar and in the Edit menu.

To arrange buttons and menus in groups, do the following:

- To start a group, right-click the button or menu you want as the first member of the group and choose Begin a Group in the shortcut menu.

- To add the end divider, first right-click the button or menu outside the group and choose Begin a Group again.

- To add another command inside the group, just drag and drop it anywhere between the two group markers.

- To remove the group marker, repeat the process and clear the check mark next to Begin a Group.

ASSIGNING A HYPERLINK

You can include a custom button or menu command that jumps to another location in the current database or on your hard drive, LAN or to a Web page.

1. Right-click the custom button and point to Assign Hyperlink.

2. Click Open.

3. In the resulting Assign Hyperlink – Open dialog box click the source you want to link to in the Link to pane.

4. Select the options you want. You can browse through the list of files in the Current Folder or other locations for the hyperlink address.

ADDING HELP

One quick way to provide help to your users is to add a ScreenTip that displays when you rest the mouse pointer on the control.

If you think a more elaborate explanation is called for, you can add some text to the compiled Help file that Office uses to store responses when you click the What's This? button.

This property comes in two parts:

- The path and file name of the compiled Help file
- The context ID number of the text that applies to this button

For example, the Help File property may be set to C:\MyHelp\Custom.hlp. The text for the button is item 47 in the file so set the HelpContextID property to 47.

More about adding custom help features with VBA in Chapter 20.

ADDING A FUNCTION

When you add a custom command, you can use it to run a function (either a built-in function or one you create with VBA). To add a custom command to a toolbar button, do the following:

1. Open the Customize dialog box.

2. Open the File category on the Commands tab. The Custom command is the first in the list.

3. Drag the Custom command to the new toolbar or menu bar.

4. Right-click the menu and choose Properties in the shortcut menu.

5. Go to the On Action property and enter the function. Be sure to include the equal sign. For example, Figure 4-19 shows a new Custom menu that runs this MsgBox function.

```
=MsgBox (IIf(WeekDay(Date())=6,"Hoorah! It's Friday.","Sit
down. It's not Friday."))
```

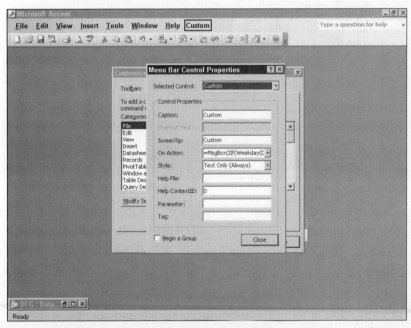

Figure 4-19: Adding a Custom menu that runs a function.

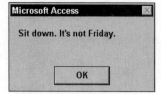

Figure 4-20: The result of clicking the Custom menu.

Starting a New Shortcut Menu

Creating a new shortcut menu is much the same as building a new toolbar. After you enter a name for the new menu, do the following:

1. Click Properties on the Toolbars tab of the Customize dialog box.

2. Change the Type to Popup. You are warned that if you change the toolbar type to Popup, it will seem to disappear (see Figure 4-21). But you can find it in the list of Custom shortcut menus by choosing Shortcut Menus in the Toolbars list.

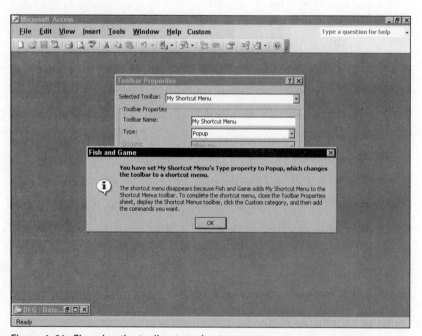

Figure 4-21: Changing the toolbar to a shortcut menu.

Adding menus and buttons to the shortcut menu is the same as adding them to a toolbar or menu. Click the Custom menu in the Shortcut Menus bar and drag the buttons and menus to the right of the new shortcut menu. Figure 4-22 shows My Shortcut Menu under construction.

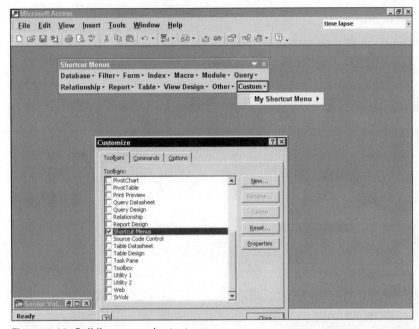

Figure 4-22: Building a new shortcut menu.

Shortcut menus are either global or context-sensitive. To make the menu global, set the Shortcut Menu Bar option in the Startup dialog box to the name of the custom shortcut menu. Context-sensitive shortcut menus contain commands that are related to a specific Access object.

Attaching a Custom Command Bar to an Object

Forms, reports, and controls have properties to attach a custom toolbar, menu bar, or shortcut menu. This determines which command bar is visible when you open or right-click the object. These properties are located on the Other tab of the Properties dialog box (see Figure 4-23):

◆ **Menu Bar property:** Specifies the menu bar to display when the database, form or report has focus. If you leave it blank, the default menu bar appears.

◆ **Toolbar property:** Specifies the toolbar to use when you open a form or report. Again, if blank, the default toolbar appears.

◆ **Shortcut Menu Bar property:** Specifies the shortcut menu to display when you right-click a form, report, or one of the controls on a form (not on a control or report).

If blank, the default shortcut menu appears unless you have set a global shortcut menu in the Startup settings.

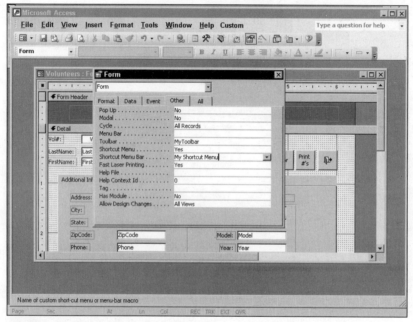

Figure 4–23: Setting command bar properties.

 If you don't want the user to be able to open a shortcut menu while viewing a form, you can set the form's Shortcut Menu property to No in the Property sheet.

Importing Custom Command Bars

If you have spent a lot of time creating custom command bars for another application and would like to have them available for a new application, it is easy to import them. With the receiving database open, choose Get External Data on the File menu then choose Import.

Locate the database containing the custom command bars and open the Import Object dialog box. Click Options and in the Import group in the lower pane (see Figure 4-24), select Menus and Toolbars then click OK.

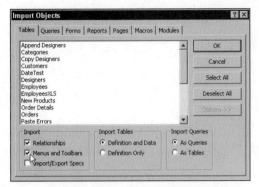

Figure 4-24: Importing menus and toolbars.

 Access doesn't import a command bar that has the same name as one already in the receiving database.

Storing Custom Command Bars

When you delete a custom command bar, it disappears completely, unlike the built-in ones that remain in the Customize dialog box list. If you have spent a lot of time and thought on creating custom command bar items and may have a use for them later, instead of deleting them, place them in a storage toolbar.

Start a new toolbar and give it a name, such as DryStorage. Then move or copy the buttons you want to keep to the new toolbar. When you close the new toolbar, you can see the name in the toolbars list and can access it when you want to retrieve the buttons or commands.

Summary

In this chapter, we have discussed customizing toolbars, menus bars, and shortcut menus using the tools of Access. We have edited built-in command bars and created new ones. In the next chapter, we begin our in-depth coverage of the Visual Basic Language for Applications by introducing the elements of the language and how they are used. We also give you a quick tour of the Visual Basic Editor window and point out some of the features that help create clean and accurate VBA code.

Part II

Understanding Visual Basic for Applications

Chapter 5

Introducing Visual Basic for Applications

IN THIS CHAPTER

◆ Looking at the BASIC Background

◆ Investigating the Basics of VBA

◆ Understanding Objects and Collections

◆ Working with Properties and Methods

◆ Some Things to Know About Objects

◆ A Quick Introduction to the Visual Basic Editor

PROGRAMMING ACCESS WITH VBA is simply the art of writing instructions that Access can handle. You tell Access what to do with which object. This chapter introduces you to the language and identifies the Access objects that you will deal with.

Where VBA Came From

Just in case you thought that we didn't have computer programming back in the Dark Ages, BASIC (Beginner's All-Purpose Symbolic Instruction Code) has been around since the early 1960s. The industry already had FORTRAN and COBOL programming languages, but for the most part, only scientists and engineers used these languages. So the academic community came up with BASIC as a simpler learning tool for the students. Another advantage of BASIC was that it required less memory because the program itself was not stored — only the interpreter.

The original BASIC was an interpretive language; in other words, each instruction executed when the student entered it. The program was not compiled as a whole and then run all at once from beginning to end like FORTRAN and COBOL. When IBM introduced the PC in 1982, a version of BASIC (GW-BASIC) shipped with the DOS operating system. This version was cumbersome and not popular with programmers (the authors included).

Then along came Microsoft Visual Basic in the new Windows form, which became an important bridge for developing applications that involved exchange among different applications. Visual Basic for Applications is a special version of Visual Basic that also provides access to a lot of third-party functions and objects, such as Dynamic Link Libraries and OLE Controls.

The result is that when you develop an application in this versatile language, you are able to extend the solution to other applications.

The Concept of VBA

VBA is an object-oriented language that has become the standard for Windows-based applications. VBA is included with all Office packages from 2000 to 2003, as well as with programs from other suppliers.

Another factor is that VBA is *event-driven,* which means that it doesn't execute any code until some event takes place. For example, an event occurs when you move the mouse pointer, click a button, or open a form. VBA responds to system events as well, such as moving focus from one control to another or formatting a report page prior to printing.

VBA with Access applications

To be able to use VBA in an Access application, you need to know about Access's object model and the objects that Access exposes to VBA. For example, the Access object model exposes tables, queries, forms, reports, and data access pages (DAP), as well as hundreds of built-in functions and expressions. Using these within VBA, you can create procedures to automate almost any activity that you can imagine.

So to start out, let's take a quick look at what comprises VBA and then we'll move on to see how the Access object model fits in. We cover each of these subjects in more detail later in this chapter.

A skeleton of VBA

The VBA framework consists of four major components:

♦ *Modules* that contain the instructions.

♦ *Objects* that identify the focus of the actions.

♦ *Variables* that contain values used during execution.

♦ *Constants* that are fixed values used during execution.

The following paragraphs describe these components in more detail.

English is also object-oriented

Think about the English language; it's also object-oriented in its own way. Nouns are objects and verbs are methods. For example, consider this sentence: "I'm going to buy (method) a shirt (object)." Adjectives are like properties; for example, "I'm going to buy a white (property) shirt." VBA is not quite a simple as that, but that's a start.

MODULES

When you write VBA code, it is stored in *modules*. Access uses two types of modules:

- ◆ **Form and report modules:** Attached to and stored with the host object.

- ◆ **Standard modules (also called module objects):** Standalone objects that are listed on the Modules page in the Database window.

Modules are made up of *procedures*. A procedure is a set of statements that carries out a specific action. There are two types of procedures:

- ◆ A *sub procedure* performs one or more operations but does not return a value. This is the most common type of procedure. For example, the following procedure displays the current system date:

```
Sub GetToday()
     MsgBox "Today is "& Date()
End Sub
```

- ◆ A *function* procedure returns a value. A function procedure can be either assigned as the source of a control value in a form or report or called from another procedure.

  For example, the following function returns the discounted Sale value:

```
Function GetDiscount(Sale As Single) As Single
     GetDiscount = Sale*.85
End Function
```

OBJECTS

VBA works with Access objects. The Access object model includes 80 classes of objects, such as tables, forms, and reports. It also includes screens, printers, command bars, and database diagrams.

The object model is hierarchical. For example, the Application object is at the top of the chain and may contain one or more forms, reports, modules, references, data access pages, and a number of other objects. The CurrentProject object hosts currently active forms, reports, and so forth, while the CurrentData object organizes the tables, queries, views, stored procedures, functions, and database diagrams.

Some objects, such as CurrentProject, are limited to a single instance, but you may have many instances of other types. Like objects form a collection. For example, the Reports collection in the CurrentProject object contains all the active reports in the current database. To refer to a specific report in the Reports collection, you need to call the report out by name:

```
Application.CurrentProject.Reports("SrVols")
```

To refer to a specific control in a report, all you need to do is add the control name to the statement, like this:

```
Application.CurrentProject.Reports!SrVols.Controls!Vol#
```

You have several ways to refer to objects and properties. If the reference is to an Access-named object or property, use the "dot" operator (.); for example, Application.CurrentProject. If you refer to something that you named, you have a couple of ways of doing so: Use the "bang" operator (!) or enclose the name in quotation marks.

All Access objects have the following properties and methods:

♦ **Properties:** Actions that you can set or just examine. For example, the SrVol report has two related properties called Filter and FilterOn that you can use to include only specific records in the report. For example, to include only the names of the volunteers who have e-mail addresses, use the following:

```
Reports!SrVols.Filter = "[email] Is Not Null"
Reports!SrVols.FilterOn = True
```

♦ **Methods:** Actions that can be executed with the object. Each type of object has its own set of methods. For example, if you are working with an Access form, you can use the GoToRecord method to move to a specific record. The following example displays the tenth record in the Volunteers form:

```
DoCmd.GoToRecord acDataForm, "Volunteers", acGoTo, 10
```

Introducing the Senior Volunteer Database

We are using an existing application, called the Senior Volunteer Database, in many of the examples in this book. Hopefully, this will make the material seem more real and less like a trip to outer space. The Volunteers application tracks senior volunteers who work with a law enforcement agency. They are not asked to carry a weapon or to be confrontational, but they do perform an important service to the agency. Seniors provide public safety information, deliver citations to courthouses, inspect facilities for code violations, and so forth.

The database is intended to track the daily activities of each volunteer and summarize the hours spent on the different activities. This sounds simple — and it is, which is why we are using it as an example. Visualizing how VBA works with Access is much easier if the examples are not too complicated.

The principal mode of data entry is the DAR (Daily Activity Report) form shown in the following figure.

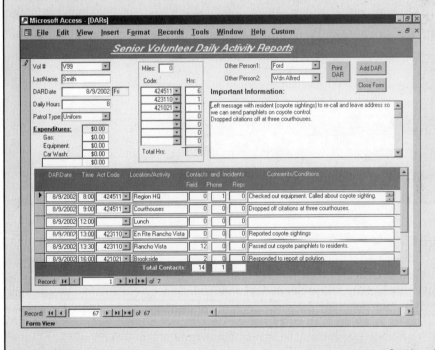

Continued

Introducing the Senior Volunteer Database *(Continued)*

The overall summary of work accomplished by the volunteers is presented in the report shown in the following figure.

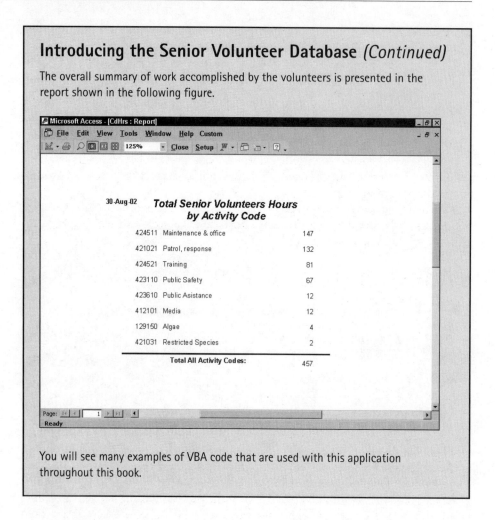

You will see many examples of VBA code that are used with this application throughout this book.

VARIABLES

VBA uses *variables* to name the values that you are using in a procedure. A variable is actually a named storage location that contains data and can be changed during program execution. When you declare a variable, you give it a name; you can also specify a data type. Here are some examples of declaring variables:

```
Dim strTitle As String
Dim dteStartDate As Date
Dim intAge As Integer
```

If you don't specify a data type, the variable assumes the default Variant data type, which can contain any type of data.

CONSTANTS

You can declare symbolic *constants* in a VBA procedure. A constant is a named item that retains its assigned value throughout the program execution. Here are a couple of examples of declaring symbolic constants:

```
Const conVoteAge As Integer = 18
Const conState As String = "CA"
```

Other types of constants include system-defined or intrinsic constants that are provided by Access or by a referenced library, and constants that are used during program compilation.

Now that we have covered the bare skeleton of VBA, let's get into how it works with Access by examining the structure of the Access objects and collections.

Understanding Objects and Collections

An *object model* is nothing more than a hierarchy of all the items in Access that you use to create an application:

◆ Tables and their fields

◆ Forms and their controls

◆ Controls and their properties

If you look at the Help topics about object models, you can see all the members and how they relate.

When you tackle Access databases with VBA, you can pick from more than one object library: the Access object library, the Data Access Object (DAO) library, and the VBA object library. Many more libraries are available through the Visual Basic Editor, but let's start with these basic libraries.

About the Access object model

If you look at the Microsoft Access Object Help topic, you will see quite a complicated hierarchical structure. A simplified application can include forms, reports, modules, and data access pages. In a more complete (and more complex) structure, you will see additional objects and collections, such as printers, modules and references.

The Access object model includes some additional items that you can work with in VBA. For example, the CommandBars collection represents all the command bars in the application. Each command bar object contains buttons, combo boxes, and pop-up controls that you can work with in VBA.

The application object also hosts the DoCmd object that comes in very handy when writing VBA code.

If you look at the CurrentProject and CurrentData branches of the tree, you can find objects related more to the database and the data that it contains. For example, forms, reports, and macros are on the CurrentProject branch, while tables, queries, stored procedures, and functions are included in the CurrentData branch.

A group of like objects forms a collection of that object. The following example adds a new command bar, SrVols1, to the collection and displays it as a floating toolbar.

```
Set cBar1 = CommandBars.Add(Name: = "SrVols1"), Position: = _
msoBarFloating
cBar1.Visible = True
```

If a line of code exceeds the width of the screen (as it does in the preceding line of code), you can continue the statement on the next line by adding a space followed by an underline character. VBA treats the two lines as a single statement.

The application is referred to as the *parent* of the forms. A form is the parent of the controls in the form design, and so on. To refer to an object in VBA code, you use the parental structure. For example, refer to a specific table in the application with either of these designations:

```
CurrentData.AllTables("Volunteers")

CurrentData.AllTables!Volunteers
```

If the table name includes a space, you must enclose it in square brackets when you use the bang (!) operator. For example, CurrentData. AllTables![Activity Codes]

About the Data Access Object model

The DAO model represents the structure of your database as well as the data that it contains. With VBA, you can use DAOs to create and modify tables and queries, secure the database against unauthorized users, interface with external sources, and a lot of other tasks.

The tree contains familiar names. For example, a database contains these objects:

◆ The TableDef object (Table Definition; one for each table in the database), contains a group of fields and usually one or more indexes.

◆ The QueryDef object (Query Definition) contains a group of fields and possibly a parameter, too.

◆ The Recordset object represents the data contained in the records in either the base table or the results of running a query.

◆ The Container object contains documents with information about all the saved databases, tables, queries, and relationships.

◆ The Relation object represents a relationship between fields in tables and queries.

About VBA Objects

VBA objects are a little different from Access objects. The VBA object library contains hundreds of built-in functions and statements, as well as many predefined constants that you can make use of when writing VBA code.

One of the most useful built-in function objects is the `MsgBox` function that you can use as a quick solution to an ordinary dialog box. You can use it to display a value or to prompt for and then return a user's answer to a question.

The first example displays a simple message box showing the current weekday, as shown in Figure 5-1:

```
MsgBox "Hello. Today is " & WeekDayName(WeekDay(Date()))
```

Figure 5-1: A simple message box.

Three additional VBA functions that are nested in this `MsgBox` statement:

◆ The `Date()` function returns the current system date.

◆ The `WeekDay()` function then extracts the weekday number from the current date.

◆ The `WeekDayName()` function converts the weekday number to the full weekday name.

The second example is a little more elaborate; it seeks a user response by asking a question, as shown in Figure 5-2:

```
MsgBox "Do you really want to delete this record?",307,
    "Delete Record"
```

Figure 5-2: Requesting user response.

After formulating the question in the message, the second argument (the number 307) tells Access which buttons and icons to display in the box. It also assigns one of the buttons as the default. Each of these features has a numeric value and 307 represents the unique sum of the three settings. The last argument is the text that you want to display in the title bar. If you don't specify a title, "Microsoft Access" appears in the title bar.

This is just a peek at one of VBA's functions. You'll get to investigate more of them in Chapter 6 and see additional examples throughout this book.

Understanding Properties and Methods

Properties are attributes or characteristics of an object. Properties are not unique to any single object – many objects share the same properties. A property can specify

♦ *Attributes,* such as the color, size, or location of an object

♦ The *state* of an object, such as whether it is visible or enabled

A *method* is either an *action* that an object can perform or a procedure that *acts on* the object. Each object has a set of methods that apply to it. Between VBA and Access objects, nearly 160 methods are at your disposal.

About Properties

All objects have a set of properties that you can view or set with VBA. Here are a few examples:

◆ Forms have an OrderBy property that specifies the sort order of the records in Form view. Reports share this and many other properties with forms.

◆ The BorderStyle property is shared by all controls except toggle buttons, command buttons, tabs, and pages.

◆ The TabStop property setting determines whether you can use the Tab key to move to a control in Form view.

You can use the MsgBox() function to check the property settings of an object. The following procedure returns True if the TabStop property of the LastName text box control is set to Yes.

```
Sub IsTab()
    MsgBox Form_DARs.LastName.TabStop
End Sub
```

You can also use VBA to set property values on the fly. The following example changes the BorderStyle property of a rectangle control from the previous setting to dots. The list of valid settings is indexed beginning with 0. The setting for the BorderStyle that shows dots has the index value 4.

```
Sub DotBorder()
    Forms!DARs.[Important Info].BorderStyle = 4
End Sub
```

Access provides most properties with a default setting to save you the trouble. For example, a form's DataEntry property is set to No by default. If it were set to True, then the form would open with a blank form for adding new records with no existing records displayed. Access assumes that you prefer to see the records, so the default is set to No.

Some special properties are the event properties. You attach a macro or VBA procedure to these properties in order to carry out an action. For example, the OnClick event property applies to many objects and controls and is set to the procedure that you want to execute when you click the object.

The following example is attached to the OnClick event property of a command button and moves to a new blank record in the form:

```
Private Sub AddDAR_Click()
    DoCmd.GoToRecord , , acNewRec
End Sub
```

Another event property that comes in handy is the one that you can use to respond to a user trying to enter a value in a combo box that is not on the lookup list that you provided. The event occurs when focus moves to the next control in

the form and tries to update the combo box control that you just left. Set the
`OnNotInList` property, for example, to a `MsgBox` that asks if the user really wants
to enter an unlisted value.

About Methods

Each method applies to one or more objects and uses a precise syntax that further
specifies the action to take and the object involved. The following are examples of
methods:

- ◆ Filtering records for a report

- ◆ Displaying a message when an error occurs

- ◆ Maximizing a form when it opens in Form view

- ◆ Adding a new item to a combo box or list box

Here are some quick examples of using VBA methods. The first example uses the
`SetFocus` method to move focus to the `LastName` field in the Volunteers form.

```
Forms!Volunteers!LastName.SetFocus
```

The next example uses the `DoMenuItem` method to carry out the Find command
on the Edit menu in Form view.

```
DoCmd.DoMenuItem acFormBar, acEditMenu, 8, acMenuVer70
```

The following example comes in handy if you are creating an application for a
user who gets spooked by warnings about deleting or appending records. You can
use the `SetWarnings` method to turn off the warnings temporarily and then turn
them back on.

```
DoCmd.SetWarnings False
      ......Statement1
      ......Statement2
      ...........
DoCmd.SetWarnings True
```

Over 50 of the VBA methods are used with the DoCmd object to carry out the
equivalent of macro actions.

Figure 5-3 shows a partial list of `DoCmd` methods.

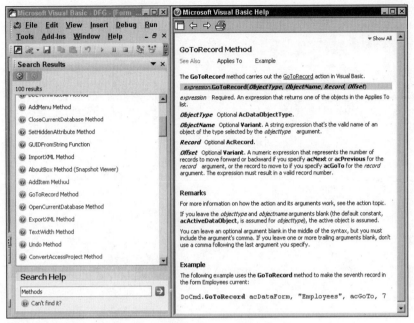

Figure 5-3: VBA methods used with the `DoCmd` object.

About Arguments

You can't just say, "go." You need to say where to go and who to go with. These specifics are the *arguments* that you provide so the method can complete its mission. Some arguments are required while others are optional.

The `OpenForm` method shown in the previous paragraphs requires the name of the form but the other six arguments are optional (including the `View`, `FilterName`, and `WhereCondition`). In this example, the optional `WhereCondition` property is set to limit the records to a specific value in the `LastName` field.

```
DoCmd.OpenForm "DARs", , , "LastName = 'Andersen'"
```

The commas in the preceding example are placeholders that indicate the positions of optional arguments that were not included (in this example, the optional arguments are `View` and `FilterName`). Arguments are listed in a specific order in a method statement. You can find more about this picky feature and how to deal with it in Chapter 8.

Practice with Form and Control Objects

A *form object* is a member of the Forms collection, which is the group of currently open forms. If you are working with only one form at a time, the collection has only that one member. The form is the parent of all the controls in its design. You have two ways to refer to a control on an active form – *implicitly* or *explicitly*.

To refer to the LastName text box on the Volunteers form:

```
Forms!Volunteers!LastName               'Implicit reference
Forms!Volunteers.Controls!LastName      'Explicit reference
```

Form objects in VBA enjoy over 190 properties that you can set or examine with code; see Figure 5-4 for some examples. Each type of control has a set of properties that you can also set or examine with code. Both forms and controls also have applicable methods that you can use to create a complete and user-friendly application.

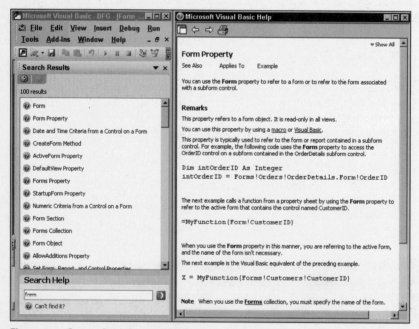

Figure 5-4: Some of the form properties.

Form Object Properties

To set a form property with code, use either the implicit or the explicit reference to the form and add the name of the property. If you are working with code in the form's class module, you can use the Me keyword instead of the full reference.

The following are a few examples of setting form properties. The first example centers the form on the screen when it opens:

```
Forms.Form!Volunteers.AutoCenter = True
```

Another example assigns a custom menu bar to the form to replace the default menu bar:

```
Forms.Form!Volunteers.MenuBar = "VolunteersMenu"
```

If you want to return to the default menu later, set the MenuBar property to a zero-length string ("").

You can also decide which view the form should take and whether to display the MinMax buttons and the scroll bars. You can use VBA code to set these preferences for the form:

```
Me.CurrentView = 1     'Opens the form in form view by default.
Me.MinMaxButtons = 0 'No MinMax buttons are visible
```

The preceding two statements include comments — the text following the apostrophe. Any text after the apostrophe is ignored by Access. This is an easy way to document your code and is an excellent habit to form.

Other MinMaxButtons property settings include 1 (Min button only), 2 (Max button only), and 3 (both buttons, the default setting).

```
Me.ScrollBars = 0     'No scroll bars
```

The other settings for the Scrollbars property settings include 1 (H only), 2 (V only), and 3 (both, the default setting).

Form Object Methods

Table 5-1 shows the eight methods that you can use to manipulate the form.

TABLE 5-1 FORM OBJECT METHODS

GoToPage	Moves to the first control on the specified page.
Move	Moves the form to coordinates in the window with respect to the left and top margins and sets the height and width.
Recalc	Recomputes all the calculated controls on the form.
Refresh	Updates the underlying record source with the changes you made in the form.
Repaint	Performs complete screen updates.
Requery	Updates data in the form from the data source.
SetFocus	Moves focus to a form control on the active form. Can be used with GoToPage to move to a specific control on a specific page.
Undo	Resets all changes you have made to the current record in the form.

The first example of form methods checks to see if the form is movable. If the form is movable, the procedure moves the form to the upper-left corner of the screen and sets the height and width. If the form is not moveable, a message is displayed to that effect:

```
If Forms!Volunteers.Moveable Then
    Forms!Volunteers.Move _
        Left:=0, Top:=0, Width:=300, Height:=3500
Else
    MsgBox "You can't move the form."
End If
```

The next example updates the data in the form when it opens (activates). The Refresh method reflects the changes made in the control sources for all the controls on the form:

```
Sub Form_Activate()
    Me.Refresh
End Sub
```

This code moves to Page 3 in the Volunteers form and sets focus on the Cell Phone text box control. The GoToPage method applies to forms in which you have added page breaks to separate different categories of data.

```
Forms!Volunteers.GoToPage 3
Forms!Volunteers![Cell Phone].SetFocus
```

Control Object Properties

Different types of controls have varying collections of properties and methods. In the following examples, we concentrate on text box and combo box controls in a form and how to manage them with VBA.

The first examples show how to change the text box properties with VBA code. Start with making the PhoneNumber field invisible in the form; you can place this statement so that the field doesn't show when you open the form.

```
Me!PhoneNumber.Visible = False
```

If you want to customize the alignment of values in a text box control, set the TextAlign property. The TextAlign property can set the alignment for all types of values, as shown in Table 5-2.

TABLE 5–2 SETTINGS FOR THE TEXTALIGN PROPERTY

Setting	Result
0	Aligns text on the left, numbers and dates on the right.
1	Aligns all values on the left.
2	Aligns all values in the center.
3	Aligns all values on the right.
4	Distributes text, numbers and dates evenly.

This statement centers the value in the Info control.

```
Me!Info.TextAlign = 2
```

The next statement changes the row height of the LastName control and the column width of the Address control in the form. The row height is set to 450 twips. A *twip* is $1/20$ of a point; 567 twips equals 1 centimeter. The –2 setting for the column width property changes the width to fit the visible text in the control.

```
Me!LastName.RowHeight = 450
Me!Address!ColumnWidth = -2
```

To change the appearance of a text box control, work with the Formatting properties. This example uses the `ForeColor`, `BackColor`, and `BorderColor` properties:

```
Me!LastName.ForeColor = RGB(255,0,0)
Me!LastName.BackColor = RGB(255,255,0)
Me!LastName.BorderColor = RGB(0,0,0)
```

A quicker way to set several control properties at once is to use the With...End With structure. For example, the preceding example would look like this:

```
With LastName
     .ForeColor = RGB(255,0,0)
     .BackColor = RGB(255,255,0)
     .BorderColor = RGB(0,0,0)
End With
```

You'll see more of these shortcuts in Chapter 9.

Control Object Methods

Control objects have several of the same methods as the form object: `Move`, `Requery`, `SetFocus`, and `Undo`. All work the same with controls as with forms. Other control object methods include:

- `Dropdown`: Forces a combo box to drop-down the list of values when the control gets focus. You don't have to click the down arrow to see the list.

- `SizeToFit`: Changes the size of the control so that it fits the text or image in it. This method can be used only in the Form view.

Specific types of controls use a lot more methods. See the Help topic for other controls to see which methods apply to them.

The following is an example of using the `Dropdown` property with the `LastName` combo box control. The combo box displays a list of volunteers' last names in the DARs form when you click on the control or reach it by pressing the Tab key.

```
Me.Controls!LastName.Dropdown
```

The `Requery` method helps to ensure that you are seeing the most current data in the form. This method does a complete job of updating the data in a form, a control, and the underlying data source by doing the following:

- Rerunning the query that serves as the basis for the form or control.

- Displaying new or changed records and removing deleted ones from the underlying table.

- Updating records displayed if any changes have been made to the form's `Filter` property.

The following statement updates the `Miles` value in the DARs form with any changes that have been made to the DARs table:

```
Forms!DARs!Miles.Requery
```

Now that you have a taste of how you can use VBA to create just the application that you need, let's take a look at the tool you will use to do that — the Visual Basic Editor.

Introducing the Visual BASIC Editor

The Visual BASIC Editor provides an ideal workplace for writing, running, and debugging your VBA code. You can open the VB Editor window anytime while working with Access. The VB Editor actually includes four windows, but we'll focus on the main Code window for now.

Opening the Code window

All code writing is done in the Code window and how you open it depends on what you want to do:

- There are a couple of ways to start a new module object:
  - Click the Modules tab in the database window and click New.
  - Choose Module on the Insert menu.
- If you just want to make changes to an existing module object, choose the module in the Database window and click Design.
- If you want to create or edit code used in a form or report, use either of these steps:

- Open the form or report in Design view and point to Macro in the Tools menu, then click Visual BASIC Editor from the submenu.

- If you don't want to open the form or report first, just select it in the Database window and click the Code toolbar button.

◆ If you want to write a new event procedure for a form or report or one of the controls in it, open the form or report in Design view and open the Property sheet for the form, report, or control. Then click the Build (...) button next to the relevant event property and choose Code Builder from the Choose Builder dialog box.

If no class module exists for the form or report yet, the VB Editor window opens with only the two Option statements.

All of these actions open the VB Editor window. Whether code is already showing or it is virtually empty depends on how you opened it and the presence of any existing code. Figure 5-5 shows the VB Editor window opened by clicking the Code toolbar button while in Design view of the DARs form. The VB Editor Standard toolbar and menu bar provide all the commands that you need to create and run code. Look at the first toolbar button – View Microsoft Access; click this button to return to the Access window that you came from. The VB Editor window remains open and you can return to it by clicking the Code toolbar button or by choosing from the taskbar at the bottom of your screen.

The other buttons are detailed in Chapter 7, where you will get a complete tour of the VB Editor window and how to use all the features.

Two important features to see in the VB Editor window are the two list boxes beneath the toolbar.

The Object list box shown in Figure 5-6 contains a list of all the objects in the form design. To write a procedure that applies to another object — for example, the Car_Wash control — select it in the list and the VB Editor begins a new procedure for you.

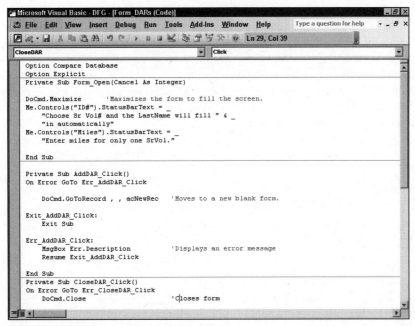

Figure 5-5: Opening the VBE window.

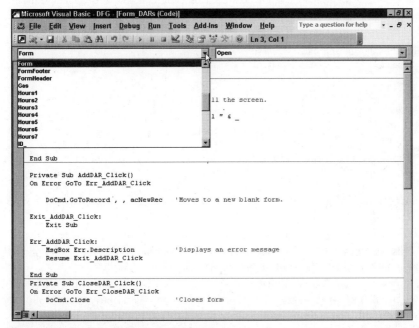

Figure 5-6: The list of objects in the form.

The other list box shown in Figure 5-7 displays a complete list of procedures that can be performed on the object chosen in the Object list box. When you choose an object, the default procedure appears in the Procedure list box. For example, if you choose Form, you will see the Open procedure; if you choose a command button control, the Click procedure shows up. If an object already has an associated procedure, that procedure name appears in bold in the Procedure list when you choose that object.

Three procedures appear in Figure 5-8.

◆ `Form_Open` executes when the form opens and contains a single statement:

`DoCmd.Maximize`

So when the DARs form opens, it immediately fills the screen.

◆ The Command Button Wizard created the second procedure, `AddDAR`. When you click that button, the `AddDAR_Click` procedure executes. This statement was discussed earlier in this chapter. See "About Properties."

Of interest in this procedure is the error handling provision inserted by the wizard. The following statement after the `Sub` statement branches to the segment that displays the built-in error message.

`On Error GoTo Err_AddDAR_Click`

The statement then goes back and exits the procedure.

 You'll see a lot more about how to deal with all kinds of errors in Chapters 8 and 10.

◆ The third visible (but incomplete) procedure closes the form when you click the Close Form command button. The wizard also created this procedure.

Ways to build a procedure

You've seen a couple of examples of the code created by the Command Button Wizard. This is an easy and quick way to build a procedure. You can always open it and make changes, but the wizard gives you a start.

Another way to build a procedure is to convert a macro that you created in Access. Figure 5-8 shows a form created to locate a specific activity code and display its description. The user enters the activity code number and clicks the OK button to display the record extracted by the `LookUpCode` query. The OK button has a macro that passes the value entered in the Code field to the query. The Cancel button closes the form without looking for an activity code.

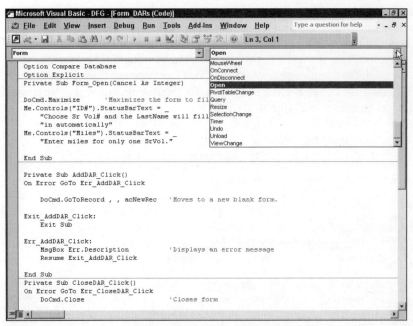

Figure 5-7: The list of procedures related to the selected object.

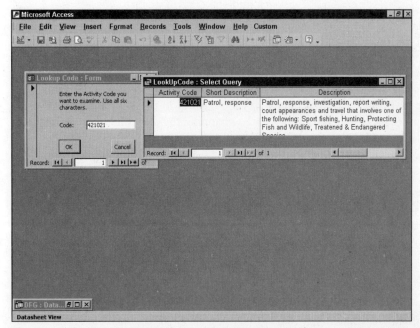

Figure 5-8: Entering an activity code to display its description.

You have a couple of ways to convert macros. If a form or report contains the macros, open the form or report in Design view and choose Macro in the Tools menu. Then click Convert Form's (or Report's) Macros to Visual BASIC. If you don't want to open the form or report first, select the macro name in the Macros tab of the Database window and choose Macro on the Tools menu. Then click Convert Macros to Visual BASIC. Either way, you will see a dialog box offering you a couple of options, as shown in Figure 5-9:

◆ **Add error handling:** Throws in the On Error set of statements.

◆ **Include macro comments:** Copies any comments that you added to the macro actions. Comments are always welcome in code.

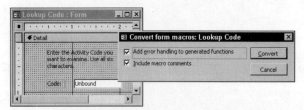

Figure 5-9: Converting a macro to a procedure

Figure 5-10 shows the two procedures that resulted from converting the macros that were attached to the command buttons in the Lookup Code form. If you look at the two buttons' OnClick event properties, you will see that the new procedures have replaced the macros.

A third, and very easy, way to build a procedure is to cruise the VBA Help files and locate some code that matches what you want to do. Select the code in the Help window and copy it to the Clipboard. Then paste it in the VB Editor window and make any changes that you need, such as changing the object names to match your application.

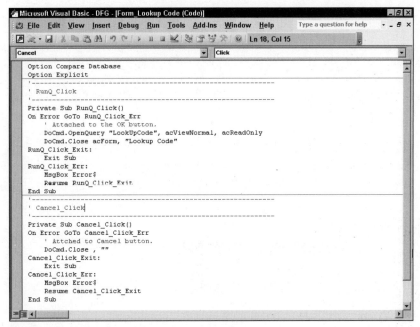

Figure 5-10: A procedure from a converted macro.

Summary

In this chapter, I gave you a glimpse into the basics of objects and methods used in the Visual BASIC for Applications language with some examples of what you can do with the language. I also gave a brief introduction into the Visual BASIC Editor. The next chapter contains more details about what comprises the VBA language and how the parts fit together smoothly.

Chapter 6

VBA Programming Fundamentals

IN THIS CHAPTER

◆ Understanding the elements that make up VBA, including modules and procedures

◆ Declaring variables, constants and arrays

◆ Using built-in functions

◆ Manipulating objects and collections

◆ Controlling execution by branching and looping

THIS CHAPTER INTRODUCES THE VBA language elements and illustrates how they fit into VBA programming.

VBA Language Elements

The basic element of the VBA language is the *module*. There are two module types:

◆ **Standard module:** Stored as a named Access object. It is a collection of *declarations, procedures,* and *functions.*

◆ **Class module:** Stored with its host object. In Access 97 and later, you can create a class module independent of a form or report. These are also listed on the Modules tab in the database window. A class module contains all the *code* related to a *form* or *report* object.

A module can contain two kinds of procedures:

◆ **Function procedure:** Returns a value that works in an expression.

For example, this function returns the full name of volunteer and displays it with the `MsgBox` function:

```
Private Function FullName() As String
'Concatenates the first and last names with a space between.
```

```
      FullName = FirstName & " " & LastName
      MsgBox "The volunteer's name is " & Fullname
End Function
```

◆ **Sub procedure:** Performs a specific operation but does not return a value. For example, a procedure that responds to the click of a command button is a sub procedure, also called an *event procedure*.

The following sub procedure prompts the user to enter a number representing the desired color for a label, as shown in Figure 6-1. In the event of an error, the message in Figure 6-2 appears.

```
Private Sub Set_Color_Click()
'Change the color of the label named Label0.
Dim intColor As Integer
intColor = InputBox("Enter a number between 1 and 4, _
    "Set Color")
Label0.BackStyle = Normal    'Change from Transparent
'Then set the desired color
Select Case intColor
    Case 1                    'Sets to red
        Label0.Color.BackColor = 255
    Case 2                    'Sets to green
        Label0.Color.BackColor = 845388
    Case 3                    'Sets to blue
        Label0.Color.BackColor = 16711680
    Case 4                    'Returns color to gray
        Label0.Color.BackColor = 12632256
    Case Else                 'Number entered not 1, 2, 3, or 4
        MsgBox ("Invalid number. Please enter 1-4")
End Select

End Sub
```

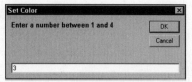

Figure 6-1: InputBox function prompts for color number.

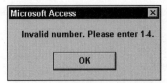

Figure 6-2: MsgBox displays error message.

The preceding sub procedure shows several of the important features you can use in VBA.

◆ The InputBox function prompts for a value that is used in the Select Case structure. (The InputBox function is explained elsewhere in this chapter.)

◆ Each entered value causes execution to branch to a different set of statements. These statements set the back color property of the label. If the user fails to enter one of the required numbers, a message is displayed requesting a valid number.

◆ Each of the lines of text you see preceded by an apostrophe is a comment and is ignored by VBA.

 Comments are a very important part of your code. Use them generously.

A module has a couple of other statements automatically placed before any of the procedures in the module. These are the Option statements:

```
Option Compare Database
Option Explicit
```

The Option Compare statement determines how Access compares character strings in the module.

◆ Database: This setting, shown in the code above, uses the same sort order as the database itself.

◆ Binary: This setting sorts based on internally stored binary values in which all upper case letters come first, followed by the lower case letters. Use the statement:

```
Option Compare Binary
```

◆ **Text:** This setting is case-sensitive and is based on your local language. Use the statement:

```
Option Compare Text
```

The `Option Explicit` statement requires you to explicitly declare all the variables you intend to use.

 `Option Explicit` prevents you from misspelling the variable names when you use them in the code.

Writing a VBA Procedure

A procedure is simply a group of statements. Each statement is a complete instruction to VBA. Statements are made up of *keywords, operators, variables, constants,* and *expressions.* The three statement types are:

◆ **Declaration statements:** Name variables, constants, or other procedures that you use in the procedure.

◆ **Assignment statements:** Set one of the variables or constants equal to a value or expression.

◆ **Executable statements:** Cause some action to take place, such as

■ Running a method or function

■ Looping through a block of code

■ Branching to a different location in the procedure

All procedures begin with a statement that

◆ Specifies the name and type of procedure

◆ Ends with an `End` statement

Adding frequent comments to the code is important. This helps you figure out what the code was designed to do even weeks after you have moved on to another project. Any text that follows an apostrophe on a line is ignored by VBA. You can place a comment on a line by itself or on the same line with a statement:

```
'This comment is on a separate line.
intA = 10  'This comment shares a line with an instruction.
```

When you add a comment to a line of code, tab over once or twice to separate the comment from the statement. You can still use the old method of preceding the comment with the Rem designation if it is on a separate line, but the apostrophe is easier. Comments appear in the Code window in a different color from the code statements. These colors and many other features of the Code window can be changed with the VBE options.

 When you are testing a procedure and you want to skip an instruction or two, you can *rem* a statement out (add an apostrophe at the beginning of the line so VBA thinks it is a comment). Remove the apostrophe when you are ready to move on.

Get into good code habits

You have some leeway in how you format your code. One way stretches the code out so every statement occupies a single line, another way compacts it into fewer lines. A third way enables you to write a single long statement on more than one line.

When you enter instructions and other statements in a procedure, you usually place each one on a separate line. The code is easier to read this way.

```
Sub TryIt()
Dim intA As Integer, intB As Integer, intC As Integer
    intA = 10
    intB = 15
    intC = 20
    MsgBox intA + intB + intC

End Sub
```

If you have a number of short instructions and don't want to use up the space, you can place two or more on a single line, separated by colons:

```
Sub TryIt()
Dim intA As Integer, intB As Integer, IntC As Integer
    intA=10: intB = 15: intC = 20: MsgBox intA + intB + intC

End Sub
```

Continued

Get into good code habits *(Continued)*

One disadvantage of stacking several instructions on one line is that if one of them causes an error, the debugger stops at the whole line. It's up to you to figure out which instruction is wrong.

You can continue a single instruction on multiple lines by adding a space and an underline character to the end of the line. It's a good idea to indent the continuations so you can recognize them easily.

```
Function LabelAddress() As String
'Uses ASCII characters to cause a carriage return and line
feed.
Dim strLineFeed As String
strLineFeed = Chr(13) & Chr(10)
LabelAddress = FullName & strLineFeed & _
    Address & strLineFeed & ", " & _
    State & " " & ZipCode

End Function
```

As you enter code, the VB Editor makes a few adjustments to make the code even easier to read. For example, the Editor often inserts spaces and adjusts the case of keywords.

Using variables and constants in a procedure

After you have decided what you want a procedure to do, you must provide the data for it to work with. A lot of Access data is stored in tables; other items must be provided at runtime.

VBA code has two kinds of data:

♦ **Variable:** Contains a value that can change during execution. It is a uniquely named item. You can specify the type of data you expect the variable to contain.

After you have named the variables, you can use expressions in the code to assign values to them, like this:

```
Dim curTax As Currency, dteSold As Date, intAge As Integer
    curTax = Sale*.075
    dteSold = #12/31/2002#
    intAge = 21
```

♦ **Constant:** Retains the value you assign it throughout the procedure. It is a uniquely named item. A constant can be either

- A string or number value

- Another constant

- An expression that combines string or number values with arithmetic or logical operators

Guidelines for assigning names

When you name a VBA procedure, constant, variable, or argument, it is important to give it a meaningful name. That way you can easily understand its purpose. After you decide what to call it, follow the VBA naming rules:

- The name can contain up to 255 characters.

- The first character must be a letter.

- You can include letters, numbers, and underscore characters (_).

- Don't include any punctuation characters or spaces.

- Be careful not to use a VBA key word such as If, Loop or Abs.

- Don't give two variables the same name in one procedure.

Most programmers get into the habit of adding a prefix to the name that indicates the type of item or the data type of a variable. For example, I like to use these prefixes with variables:

- "dbs" for a database

- "rst" for a recordset

- "con" for a constant

- "int" for an integer

- "bln" for Boolean

- "dte" for a date

- "str" for a string

Use these prefixes when you declare the variables:

```
Dim strLastName As String
Dim intAge As Integer
Dim dteDateHired As Date
Dim blnChoice As Boolean
```

When you assign a name, you don't have to worry about case. VBA is not case sensitive and "fgh" looks just the same to it as "FGH." However, whatever capitalization you assign to a variable or constant name is preserved in later instances.

If a list of values refers to the same variable or constant, you can use an *array* (a list of values with the same name). Arrays are explained in this chapter.

Deciding on a data type

You give your variables and constants a data type in one of the following ways:

◆ Specify the data type for your variables and constants manually when you declare them.

◆ Let Access use the default Variant data type.

 To help the procedure run as fast as possible, minimize the space needed by selecting the data type with the lowest storage requirements that matches your data.

Table 6-1 lists the built-in VBA data types you can assign to variables and constants and the data they usually store.

TABLE 6-1 VBA DATA TYPES

Data Type	Stores
Boolean	True or False
Byte	Positive integers between 0 and 255
Integer	2-byte integers between –32K and +32K
Long	4-byte integers between –2 billion and +2 billion
Currency	+ and – currency values with 4 decimal places
Single	4-byte decimal values
Double	8-byte decimal values
Date	Dates between 1/1/0100 and 12/31/9999
String (variable length)	Up to 2 billion characters
String (fixed length)	Up to 65K characters
Object	Named Access object
Variant (with numbers)	Up to the same range as Double numeric data type
Variant (with characters)	Up to 2 billion characters

What's a variant?

A variant sounds like something you would find sleeping along the railroad tracks but in VBA it is actually a very flexible and adaptive data type. You can store numeric, string, date/time, or Boolean values in variables declared as Variant. If you leave the data type out of a `Dim` statement, VBA automatically assigns it as a Variant. When you give the variable a value, VBA reassigns a matching data type to the variable. For example, the second statement in the following example automatically defines `varGetVal` as a Date/Time data type:

```
Dim varGetVal
varGetVal = #7/31/2002#
```

This statement redefines the Variant variable as a String variable:

```
varGetVal = "Regular"
```

You can create your own data types using the `Type` VBA statement. User-defined data types are explained elsewhere in this chapter.

Declaring variables

If you have included the `Option Explicit` statement, you must declare all the variables you plan to use in the procedure. To declare a variable with VB, you usually use the `Dim` statement. Where you place the `Dim` statement determines the *scope* of the variable.

◆ If you put the `Dim` statement after the two module `Option` statements, but before the first `Sub` or `Function` opening statement, the variable is available to all the procedures in the module.

◆ If you place the `Dim` statement after the `Sub` or `Function` statement, the variable is available only within that procedure.

The scope of a variable refers to its availability to other procedures. When the variable is no longer available it loses its value and name. If you understand how the scope affects the use of a variable, you can avoid naming conflicts.

Three *levels of availability* apply to variables:

♦ **Procedure level:** Available only within the procedure. The variable is declared with the Dim statement in the procedure placed immediately after the Sub or Function statement, like this example:

```
Sub MyProc()
Dim dteStPat As Date
```

♦ **Module level:** Available to all the procedures in the module. The variable is declared with a Private statement in the declarations section of the module. This is the same as placing the Dim statement at the module level, like this example:

```
Option Compare Database
Option Explicit
Private strMySSN As String
Sub MyProc()
```

♦ **Public level:** Available to all procedures in the entire application or project. The variable is declared with a Public statement in the declarations section of the module, like this example:

```
Option Compare Database
Option Explicit
Public strEMail As String
Sub MyProc()
```

The Static statement creates a variable that retains its value between calls to the host procedure from within the module.

```
Option Compare Database
Option Explicit
Static intNum As Integer
Sub MyProc()
```

You can declare each variable in a separate statement or save space by declaring several at once. Here are some examples:

♦ You can use several Dim statements, like this:

```
Dim intA As Integer
Dim intB As Integer
Dim strName As String
```

♦ If you are declaring multiple variables with the same Dim statement, you must specify the data type for each, even if they are all the same, like this:

```
Dim intA As Integer, intB As Integer, strName As String
```

◆ The following `Dim` statement makes the `intC` variable an integer; the others are variant data type:

```
Dim intA, intB, intC As Integer
```

 Use the appropriate data type when declaring variables and constants. This saves time and memory. If you don't specify a data type, VBA assigns the variant, which takes up a lot of memory.

Declaring constants

Use the `Const` statement to declare constants instead of the `Dim` statement. You assign the constant a name, data type, and a value with the `Const` statement. A constant can be of any data type except object. If you declare more than one constant in a single statement, separate them by commas and be sure to include the data type for each constant in the declaration.

Here are a couple of examples of declaring constants:

```
Const conMonth As Integer = 9
Const conDate As Date = #12/31/2003#
Const conPrice As Currency = 950, conModel As String = "Reg"
```

 It is common practice to use the "con" prefix with constants instead of a prefix that implies the data type.

The lifetime of variables

The *lifetime* of a variable is the period of time during which it has a value. The value may change during the lifetime but the variable still has a value. All variables are initialized with a default value when the procedure begins and is assigned other values as the procedure executes. For example, a numeric variable starts out as 0 while a string variable is initialized as a zero-length string.

If a procedure calls yet another procedure during execution, the values of the variables are retained. The variables lose their value only when the host procedure ends.

Declaring a constant has advantages. For example, when you are calculating sales totals that include sales tax and shipping/handling costs. These add-on costs are fixed for now but inevitably change in the future. Declare them as constants with the current values; don't hard-code them into the expressions in the procedure. Then when costs go up, you need only change the constant assignment instead of plowing through the code to find every instance of the cost.

To make the constant available to other procedures in the module, precede the `Const` keyword with `Public`.

```
Public Const conPrice As Currency = 4200
Public Const conTax As Single = .075
Public Const conQty As Integer = 12
```

Built-in constants

In addition to the constants you create with the Const statement, you have access to many *intrinsic constants* for a procedure. These constants work with particular functions, methods, or properties. You can get intrinsic constants from such sources as Access, VBA, Access Data Objects (ADO), and Data Access Objects (DAO). When you get into the VB Editor window, you can prowl around in the Object Explorer to see lists of these intrinsic constants and find out when they are applicable, as shown in the following figure.

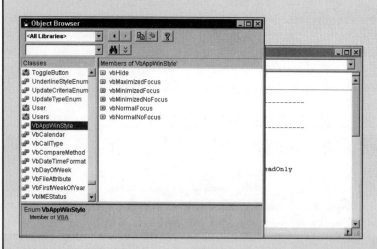

The intrinsic constant names usually include a two-character prefix that gives you a clue where they come from. For example:

◆ `acCurViewDatasheet` is an Access constant that sets the form's current view to datasheet.

◆ `acStart` is a member of the Access AcFindMatch object and sets the search to look at the start of the field for a match.

◆ `dbDescending` is a DAO constant that applies to the sort order.

◆ `dbEditAdd` is a DAO constant that sets the Allow Edit and Allow Add properties of a form or datasheet.

◆ `adAddNew` is an ADO constant that sets the Allow Additions property of a form to Yes or No (True or False in VBA speak).

◆ `adDelete` is an ADO constant that sets the Allow Deletions property of a form.

◆ `vbDatabaseCompare` is a VBA constant that sets the Option Compare Database statement for a module.

◆ `vbSunday` is a VBA constant that assigns the value 1 to a firstdayoftheweek argument.

Using intrinsic constants can provide some stability to your procedures. Even if the underlying values change in later versions of Access, the constant names remain the same.

Declaring arrays

An *array* is a list of values of the same data type that have the same name. To declare an array, use the `Dim` declaration and specify the data type, just as with variables and constants.

Usually, you indicate the *size* or *dimensions* of the array:

◆ When you specify the size of the array, it is called a *fixed size array.*

◆ If you don't specify the array size, it is called a *dynamic array.*

ASSIGNING A FIXED SIZE ARRAY

For example, a list of the letters of the Greek alphabet could be represented by an array containing 24 string variables, each one having a single value of a letter in the Greek alphabet.

```
Dim strGreek(23) As String
```

Each element in the array is assigned an index number, beginning with 0.

◆ The first Greek letter, *alpha,* is represented as `strGreek(0)`.

◆ The twenty-fourth letter, *omega,* is represented as `strGreek(23)`.

To specify the lower index as 1 instead of 0, include it in the declaration. Alpha becomes strGreek(1):

```
Dim strGreek(1 to 24) As String
```

Using the Option Base 1 statement at the module level forces all arrays that you define in the module to begin indexing arrays at 1 instead of the default 0.

An array doesn't have to be a one-dimensional list. For example, you could create a two-dimensional array of the letters of the Greek alphabet with the accompanying equivalent in the English alphabet:

```
Dim strGreek(23,1) As String
```

Or, if `Option Base 1` is used:

```
Dim strGreek(24,2) As String
```

Real-life example of an array

Here's a real-life example of using arrays. I wrote a VBA program to determine the dates for volunteer schedules. Each volunteer signed up to work on, for example, the 2nd and 4th Mondays of each month. Another signed up for the 1st, 3rd, and 5th Tuesdays of each month.

To come up with the actual calendar dates, I created seven 5-element arrays, one for each day of the week:

```
Dim intSun(1 to 5) As Integer, intMon(1 to 5) As Integer
Dim intTue(1 to 5) As Integer, intWed(1 to 5) As Integer
Dim intThu(1 to 5) As Integer, intFri(1 to 5) As Integer
Dim intSat(1 to 5) As Integer
```

The procedure went on to prompt the scheduler to enter the desired month. Then, after determining how many days were in the month and which weekday was the first of the month, I used a nested series of Select Case segments to populate the arrays with the appropriate dates.

There's more of this example in Chapter 9.

To conserve RAM space, specify a data type for the array; otherwise, the array defaults to the variant data type. An integer array with 100 rows and 100 columns takes up 20,000 bytes of memory. An array of the variant data type with the same dimensions takes up at least 160,000 bytes.

You can also create three-dimensional arrays that would represent values laid out in a cubic solid.

The alternative to a fixed-sized array is a *dynamic* array that you can size during code execution. Declare the array without any index or size settings and use the ReDim statement to declare the array implicitly within the procedure.

```
Dim intArray() As Integer
..........
...........
ReDim intArray(10, 10)
```

When you use ReDim to change the dimensions of the array, all the values are lost. To redeclare the array and add values to the existing values, you need to use the Preserve keyword and add the new elements to the existing array:

```
ReDim Preserve intArray(UBound(intArray) + 20)
```

This statement keeps the existing values in the intArray and adds 20 more slots to the upper index boundary. You can't use the Preserve keyword to add another dimension to the array, just to increase the upper index boundary.

Declaring object variables

An object variable represents an Access object such as a recordset, a form, or even a complete database.

TIP

Declaring object variables can simplify your code by assigning a shortcut name to the object for executable statements.

Object variables are declared the same way you declare any other variable, except that you declare an object, not a data type. Some examples are:

```
Dim dbMyData As Database
Dim rstMyTable As Recordset
Dim frmMyForm As Form
Dim rptMyReport As Report
```

```
Dim fldMyField As Field
Dim ctlMyControl As Control
Dim txtMyTextBox As TextBox
```

After declaring the object variables, you can set them to specific objects in the database.

```
Set dbMyData = CurrentDb()
Set rstMyTable = dbMyData.OpenRecordset("Volunteers")
```

The Set statement comes with two optional keywords: New and Nothing. The New keyword actually creates a new instance of the object. (An *instance* is a temporary copy of an open object that can provide several copies of the same form on the screen at once.) Here's an example:

```
Set frmNew = New Form_Vols
```

After the object variable is set, the variable inherits the methods and properties of that object. You can set Colors, Visibilities, and even Event Procedures on a form object variable.

To see both the original and the copy of the form on the screen at once, set the form's visible property to True, like this:

```
Set frmNew.visible = True
```

The Nothing keyword breaks the connection between the object variable and any specific object. For example, when you are through with the copy, use the Nothing keyword to remove it:

```
Set frmNew = Nothing
```

Declaring user-defined data types

The term, "user-defined data type" is a little misleading because it can contain several elements of differing data types. This special data type is very useful as a shortcut to creating a data structure, such as a schedule or an address book.

To define a composite data type, use the Type statement at the module level. Once you have declared the user-defined data type, you can use it in procedures in any of the variable declaration statements: Dim, Private, Public, ReDim, or Static.

TIP A common use for user-defined data types in Access is to define a record structure in a database. The record can contain related elements of various data types.

The following example creates a data type that is used when building the duty schedule for the volunteers. When you declare an element as a fixed-length string, such as a field in a table definition, you must provide the number of characters, like this:

```
Type SVSched
    SVDate As Date
    SV# As String * 4        'a 4-character string
    SVName As String * 20    'a 20-character string
    Duty As String * 50      'a 50-chracter string
End Type
```

Then when you prepare the schedule for the coming month, you can use the user-defined type to declare a fixed array that you can populate with the upcoming schedule for the 30 volunteers, like this:

```
Sub CreateSchedule()
Dim udtVolSched (1 To 30) As SVSched

udtVolSched(1).SVDate = #1/1/2003#
udtVolSched(1).SV# = "V18"
udtVolSched(1).SVName = "Andersen"
udtDuty(1) = "Deliver citations to court houses."

End Sub
```

Assigning values to variables

An *assignment* statement is an instruction that sets a variable equal to a value or to an expression that evaluates to a value. The expression can contain

- ◆ Key words
- ◆ Operators
- ◆ Other variables
- ◆ Constants

When the expression is evaluated, it results in a string, number, or object that must match the data type of the declared variable.

Constants are assigned values when you declare them.

Assignment statements can be as simple as setting an integer counter to 1 or as complex as setting and activating a filter for records in a form. Many assignment statements use functions in the expression to create the value. (There's more about the built-in functions in this chapter.)

Expressions often contain operators. The *operators* fall into three categories:

◆ *Arithmetic operators* include *addition (+), subtraction (-), multiplication (*), division (/), exponentiation (^),* and a couple more that you may not have met up with in school:

  ■ The *modulo division* operator (Mod) returns the remainder left from a division operation, rounded to an integer.

    Its partner is the *integer division* operator (\) that returns the whole number part of the result with the fraction truncated.

  ■ The *concatenation operator* (&) adds two or more strings and other characters together into a single value.

    In some cases you can use the plus sign (+) to concatenate strings but it is safer to use the & operator.

Here are a few examples of assignment statements:

```
intA = 10
intA = 10+1
intSquare = 12^2
blnY = True
dteStartDate = Date() + 30  'Returns 30 days later than today.
strFullAddress = [Addr] & ", " & [City] & ", " & [State] & _
        " " & [PostalCode]
intPrice = Price\2          'Returns 17 if the Price is 35.
modPrice = Price Mod 2      'Returns 1 if the Price is 35.
Me.Option29.ControlTipText = "Choose to summarize hours by "
& _
"Activity Code"
```

The preceding line sets the ControlTipText for one of the options in an option group on a form. Additional statements could add such tips for the other options in the group.

◆ The *comparison operators* are the same as with Access query expressions. They test one value or expression against another and return the appropriate result. These operators include

- Equal to (=)

- Greater than (>)

- Less than (<)

- Greater than or equal to (>=)

- Less than or equal to (<=)

- Not equal to (<>).

◆ The *logical operators* examine two expressions and return a result depending on the True/False condition of the expressions and the type of logical action of the operator. Table 6-2 lists the logical operators used in VBA.

TABLE 6-2 LOGICAL OPERATORS

Operator	Description	Result
NOT	Negates the expression	True becomes False, False becomes True
AND	Logical conjunction of two expressions	True only if both are True
OR	Logical disjunction of two expressions	True if one or both are True
XOR	Logical exclusion of two expressions	False if both are the same value
EQU	Logical equivalence of two expressions	True if both True or both False
IMP	Logical implication of two expressions	False only if expression 1 is True and expression 2 is False

Logical operators can return unexpected results if one or both of the expressions evaluate to Null. Check the Help topic for that operator if you are not seeing what you expect.

The order of precedence with respect to these operators is the same as in Access but you can change that by adding parentheses. When an expression contains operators from more than one category, the arithmetic operators are evaluated first, followed by the comparison operators, then the logical operators last. If operators have equal precedence, they are evaluated in the left-to-right order in which they appear in the expression. One exception is the concatenation operator (&) which follows the arithmetic operators and precedes all the comparison operators.

Here are a few examples of using logical operators in VBA code.

◆ The Not operator toggles the pesky Office Assistant on and off:

```
Application.Assistant.Visible = NOT
Application.Assistant.Visible
```

◆ Two expressions using the And, Or, and Xor operators:

```
Sub LogicComp()
Dim curPrice As Currency, curCost As Currency
Dim blnEcon101 As Boolean
curPrice = 150
curCost = 35
'Both expressions are True.
blnEcon101 = curPrice > 100 AND curCost < 50      'Returns True
'First expression is True, the second is False.
blnEcon101 = curPrice > 100 OR curCost > 50       'Returns True
'Both expressions are False.
blnEcon101 = curPrice < 100 XOR curCost < 50      'Returns True
End Sub
```

Using Built-In Functions

When you were using the Expression builder in Access to help create expressions for calculated controls on forms and reports, you could choose from an extensive list of built-in functions as shown in Figure 6-3. These functions are also available in VBA through the VB Editor.

To see a complete list of functions for a VBA statement, start a new procedure and type VBA followed by a period. Then scroll down the alphabetized list to find the one you want (see Figure 6-4).

Some of the items in the list are preceded by a flying brick icon that indicates the item is a function. A property icon precedes others shown in the figure. The list also includes modules, enumerated constants, Global code, and VB constants. The preceding icon indicates the type of item.

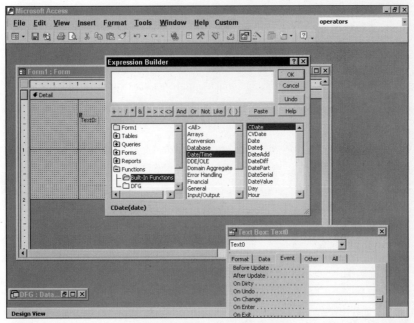

Figure 6-3: Choosing a function from the Expression builder.

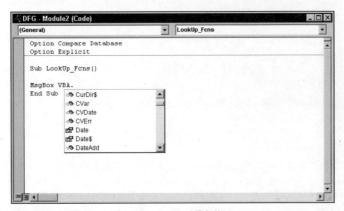

Figure 6-4: Finding a function in the VBA list.

The following bit of code displays two message boxes. The first displays the current system date. The second displays a date two months later.

```
Sub LookUp_Fcns()
MsgBox VBA.Date
MsgBox VBA.DateAdd("m", 2, Date)
End Sub
```

VBA Syntax Essentials

When you start using functions in VBA code, you must know how to read the syntax to provide the necessary arguments in the correct order. The VBA document convention shows you which items are keywords and which arguments are required and optional:

◆ Items that appear in bold with initial caps are keywords. For example, the **Sub**, **Print**, **If**, **True** and the function name itself.

◆ Items all lower case and in italics are placeholders for information you supply. For example, **object**, **varname**, **arglist**, and **condition**.

◆ Items lower case, in italics and enclosed in brackets are optional. For example, [statements] or [element].

◆ Choices of mandatory items appear in bold enclosed in braces separated by a vertical bar. For example, {**While | Until**}.

For example, the syntax for the DateAdd function in the Help topic is:

```
DateAdd(interval, number, date)
```

◆ **DateAdd** is the keyword

◆ All three arguments are required.

The **DatePart** function is a little more complicated:

```
DatePart(interval, date[, firstdayofweek[, firstweekofyear]])
```

◆ **DatePart** is the keyword .

◆ *interval* and *date* are required.

◆ *firstdayofweek* is optional and specifies which day is the first day of the week.

By default, VBA assumes Sunday is the first day of the week.

◆ *firstweekofyear* is optional and specifies the first week of the year.

By default, VBA assumes the week containing January 1 is the first week of the year.

Chapter 8 explains syntax in detail.

The DateAdd function requires arguments in a specific order to be able to evaluate the function. Each function has a clearly defined syntax that you must follow closely. The DateAdd function requires three arguments:

◆ A string argument representing the interval of time you want to add to the date. Refer to the date format settings for the string arguments. This example used "m" to indicate the month interval.

◆ A numeric expression that is the number of units of the specified time you want to add. Use a positive number to get dates in the future or a negative number to get dates in the past.

◆ The date variable or literal date value to which you want to add (or subtract) the interval of time.

Some helpful built-in functions

Let's take another look at the MsgBox function that is so useful for conversing with the user. It becomes a simple version of the custom dialog box and is also very useful during debugging by displaying intermediate values.

The advantage of a MsgBox function is that it both displays the message itself and returns the user's response. The simplest version only requires the user to click OK to close the modal box. Other button responses are coded so you can interpret the response and perform other operations based on the returned value.

The MsgBox function syntax shows only one required argument, the prompt, but there are four optional arguments:

```
MsgBox(prompt[, buttons][, title] [, helpfiles, context])
```

The *prompt* argument is a string containing the message to be displayed in the box. The buttons argument represents the combination of several different options:

◆ Buttons to display

◆ Default button

◆ Box modality

◆ Position of the message box on the screen

◆ Text alignment and reading direction

Each of these settings has an associated number; the *buttons* argument can be entered as the *sum of all the option numbers* or the list of the names of the settings. For example, if you want to see the Yes, No, and Cancel buttons (3), a Warning icon (48), and have the second button (No) as the default (256), you could use the *sum* of those three settings, 307, as the argument. The *title* argument is the text you want to appear in the box's title bar. The *helpfiles* and *context* arguments refer to the information that you want displayed when the user clicks the Help button.

To make use of the user response, you can set a variable to the value returned by the button click. For example,

```
Resp = MsgBox("Delete this record?",307, "Respond")
```

Instead of using the sum of the numeric codes for the button options, you could spell out the constant names for the *buttons* argument:

```
vbYesNoCancel + vbExclamation + vbDefaultButton2
```

The returned value ranges from 1 to 7, depending on which button the user clicked. For example, OK = 1 and No = 7. Then you can use the response in an If Then...Else or Select Case structure to carry out the desired action.

The InputBox function is almost the mirror image of the MsgBox function. It is more versatile at getting information but less helpful dispensing information. You saw an example of the InputBox function at the beginning of this chapter.

I can't resist exposing you to one more of my favorite build-in functions, IIf, the "immediate if" function. The IIf function provides a one-line alternative to the more complex If...Then...Else structure. The IIf syntax is:

```
IIf(expr, truepart, falsepart)
```

All three arguments are required:

- ◆ expr is the expression to be evaluated.

- ◆ truepart is the value to return if the expression evaluates to True.

- ◆ falsepart is the value to return if the expression evaluates to False.

For example, you want to create a signature code using the volunteer's initials but some of them don't use a middle initial. You can use the IsNull function in the expr argument to test for a blank MI value. Enter a zero-length string as the truepart argument and use the MI field for the falsepart argument:

```
IIf(IsNull([MI], "", [MI])
```

Combine that with the Left function that extracts characters from the left end of the string and concatenate with the first and last name values:

```
Sig = Left([FirstName],1) & Left(IIf(IsNull([MI]), "", [MI]),1) _
    & Left([LastName],1)
```

Both arguments are evaluated even though only one is returned. So you can't use the IIf function to test for division by 0 because that causes an error.

Chapter 9 shows how to use the IIf function with the Nz function to handle Null values.

Manipulating Objects and Collections

The whole purpose of Access is to store and retrieve information in an efficient and effective manner. Many of the VBA features help make this job quick and easy. For example, you can use the With...End With construct to work with a single object and the For Each...Next construct to work with a collection of related objects.

The with...end with structure

The With statement is handy for performing a series of statements on a single object without repeating the object reference in each statement. For example, the following series of statements can change the appearance of a label in the current form:

```
Sub ChangeLabel()
Me.Label0.Height = 100
Me.Label0.Width = 200
Me.Label0.Caption = "My Label"
Me.Label0.Font.Color = 255
Me.Label0.Font.Bold = True
Me.Label0.Font.Italic = True
Me.Label0.Fint.Size = 16
End Sub
```

If you use the With...End With structure, you can save a lot of code entry time. The With syntax requires only one argument: the object you want to work on. This can be a named object or a user-defined type.

```
With object
   [statements]
End With
```

The statements between the With and End With statements all refer to the same object. You can't change objects within the block. To work on another object, you open another With block. For example, the following code changes the label size and caption:

```
With Label0
   .Height = 100
```

```
   .Width = 200
   .Caption = "My Label"
End With
```

In this case, I left out the font settings. To work with another object that is a member of the first object, you can nest the With statements by placing one group within the other. While you are in the inner With block, the object in the outer block is masked until you reach the inner End With statement. Here's how nesting With blocks works:

```
With Label0
      .Height = 100
   .Width = 200
   .Caption = "My Label"
   With .Font
       .Color = 255
       .Bold = True
       .Italic = True
   End With
End With
```

Never jump into or out of a loop structure without completing the block. You can add code that jumps to the last statement, usually an End statement, if you need to terminate the process but never jump out from one of the internal statements. This caution applies to all the looping constructs in VBA.

The for each...next structure

The For Each...Next structure repeats a block of code for each item in an array of objects in a collection. (A collection refers to a group of objects usually of the same type.) For example, all the controls on a form or report form a collection. You can use For Each...Next to perform the same action on every member of the collection or jump to the end of the loop if you want to.

The For Each...Next syntax includes two required arguments and one type of optional argument.

```
For Each element In group
    [statements]
    [Exit For]
    [statements]
Next [element]
```

The required *element* argument is the variable used to move through the items in the collection or array. In an array, the element must be a Variant variable. In a collection, the element can also be a generic object variable such as a form or report, or any specific object variable, such as the DARs form.

The required *group* argument is the name of the object collection or array. The optional *statements* arguments are executed on each item in the group.

If there is at least one item in the group, the block is entered and all the statements are executed on the first element. If there are more elements, the statements are repeated for each element. When the list is exhausted, execution drops to the statement following the Next statement.

This loop structure has an escape hatch. You can use the Exit For statement anywhere in the loop, more than once, if necessary. You can use this statement to exit the loop under specific conditions. Execution then continues with the statement immediately following the Next statement.

This example of the For Each...Next loop changes the fore color and the font size of all the command buttons in the form when the form opens. It operates on all the command buttons until it reaches the Cancel button when it exits the loop.

```
Private Sub Form_Open(Cancel As Integer)
Dim btn As Object
For Each btn In Me.Controls
    If btn.ControlType = 104 Then    'It is a command button
        btn.ForeColor = 255
btn.FontBold = True
If btn.Name = "Cancel" Then
            Exit For
            End If
        btn.Caption = "My Button"
    End If
Next
End Sub
```

As an example of using the For Each...Next loop with an array, the next code declares an array with 10 elements and the Item element argument both as Variant data type. The counter element, i, is declared as an integer. Then populates the array with numbers that are the product of the index i by 2.5. In the For Each...Next loop, the numbers are all changed to negative numbers. The Debug.Print statement displays the results of the procedure in the Immediate window. Chapter 7 further explains the Immediate window and other features of the VBA.

```
Sub ForEach()
Dim varArray(10), Item
Dim i As Integer
For i = 1 To 10
    varArray(i) = 2.5 * i
```

```
Next i
For Each Item In varArray
    Item = Item * (-1)
    Debug.Print Item
Next Item
End Sub
```

Controlling Execution

You may want to run some operations from start to finish without interruption. But one of the most important features of event-driven programming is the ability to control the process. VBA offers several ways you can influence the program flow:

◆ Branch to another location in the procedure.

◆ Carry out an action based on a specific condition.

◆ Choose from a list of options based on the value of a variable.

◆ Repeat a sequence of statements a specified number of times or until a certain condition is met.

◆ Pause during execution or exit the procedure.

This chapter presents some simple examples of these types of execution control statements. Chapters 8 and 9 contain more advanced examples.

Branching statements

VBA code normally executes one statement at a time in the order they appear in the procedure. There are often times when you want to execute a different block of code instead of the next sequential statements. Branching statements change the execution sequence to a different path.

Branching statements come in five different flavors. Some branch unconditionally and others branch only if a certain condition is met.

GOTO

The most basic branching statement is the GoTo statement:

```
GoTo line
```

The *line* argument is required and can be either of these values:

◆ **Line number:** Any combination of digits that is unique within the module.

◆ **Line label:** Any combination of up to 40 characters followed by a colon (:).

Place the line number or label in the first position of the statement line.

The following example branches unconditionally to line number 67 then later to the line labeled "Line1."

```
GoTo 67
[statements]
67     Exit Sub
[statements]
GoTo Line1
[statements]
Line1:
Exit Sub
```

 Using a lot of unconditional GoTos can result in confusing code. Use it only when necessary. Structured program control statements, such as For...Next and If...Then...Else, are a lot easier to follow and debug in a procedure.

GOSUB...RETURN

The GoSub...Return statement structure branches to a subroutine within the same procedure and returns to the statement immediately following the most recently executed GoSub statement. This effectively embeds a labeled subroutine within the procedure:

```
GoSub line
    .....
    line
    .....
    Return
```

The Return statement is actually the last statement in the subroutine. If the subroutine is more than a few statements, you achieve a more structured program if you create a separate procedure.

ON...GOSUB AND ON...GOTO

The On...GoSub and On...GoTo statements branch to one of several lines, depending on the value returned by the expression.

```
On expression GoSub destinationlist
On expression GoTo destinationlist
```

Both of these statements require a list of line numbers or labels separated by commas and an *expression* that determines which line in the *destinationlist* is to be the target.

The *expression* must be a numeric expression that evaluates to a whole number between 0 and 255, inclusive. The first line is *1*. If the expression evaluates to other than a whole number, the value is rounded.

These actions are determined by the expression:

- If the *expression* evaluates to either 0 or more than the number of lines in the list, control drops to the statement following the On statement.

- If the *expression* evaluates to either a negative number or greater than 255, an error occurs.

 TIP   On...GoSub and On...GoTo have been generally replaced by more flexible Select Case branching.

ON ERROR

The On Error statement can branch to an error-handling routine when a run-time error occurs. The statement comes in three versions:

- ◆ On Error GoTo *line:* Branches to a specific line in the same procedure when a run-time error occurs.

- ◆ On Error Resume Next: Sends control to the statement following the one in which the run-time error occurred.

- ◆ On Error GoTo 0: Disables any error-handling within the procedure.

Chapter 9 presents much more about building error-handling techniques.

Decision-making

VBA provides two important structures for decision-making. These structures are used to execute a block of code only under certain circumstances. One of them evaluates a condition that is either true or false then executes a set of statements depending on the outcome. The other structure includes a group of code blocks and executes one of them depending on the value returned by the expression. Both of these extremely flexible structures are used extensively in applications. Code created by an Access Wizard has many examples of these structures.

THE IF...THEN...ELSE STRUCTURE

The If...Then...Else structure executes a block of code conditionally, depending on the outcome of an expression. You can prepare for both outcomes:

◆ Specify the code to run if the expression is true, then skip to the statement following the End If statement.

◆ Provide an additional block of code to execute if the expression evaluates to False.

The If...Then...Else syntax looks like this:

```
If condition Then [statements] [Else elsestatements]
[statements]
[ElseIf condition-n Then
    [elseifstatements]...
[Else
    [elsestatements]]
End If
```

The only required argument is the *condition*. This is a numeric or string expression that evaluates to True or False. If it is Null, it is considered to be False. It doesn't make much sense to make all the statements optional but they are. The following example returns a discount value if the sale total exceeds $1000.

```
Function GetDiscount(Sale As Single) As Single
GetDiscount = 0        'Sets discount to default 0
If Sale>1000 Then
    GetDiscount = .85 'Returns an 85% discount
End If
End Function
```

If the decision is a simple one, you can use the single-line version of the If...Then...Else statement. In this case, one statement is required if no Else clause is included.

```
If condition Then [statements] [Else statements]
```

```
If Sale>1000 Then GetDiscount = .85
```

You can nest additional If clauses within the original clause to make other choices. For example, if there is also a discount for sales over $100. If the Sale value is less than $100, the GetDiscount variable is set to 0.

```
Function GetDiscount(Sale As Single) As Single
If Sale>1000 Then
    GetDiscount = .85      'Returns 85% discount
    ElseIf Sale > 100 Then
        GetDiscount = .90  'Returns 90% discount
    Else
    GetDiscount = 0
End If
End Function
```

The sequence of these nested If statements is important. Check for the larger price value first. If reversed, sales over $1000 would also get the 90% price discount.

If several possible outcomes of the expression require different actions, it is more efficient to use the Select Case structure.

THE SELECT CASE STRUCTURE

The Select Case structure is a better alternative when you have at least three values or conditions to choose from. You both include a group of statements for each expected value and specify a block of code to execute when the test expression doesn't evaluate to any of the specified values in the list.

The Select Case syntax shows only one required argument although at least one Case expressionlist-n is required to carry out the process.

Select Case *testexpression*

    [Case *expressionlist-n*]

    [statements-n]

    [Case Else

    [statements]]
End Select

The *testexpression* argument can be any string or numeric expression that evaluates to one of a list of values. The *expressionlist-n* argument represents the delimited list of values that can result from the *testexpression*. You include a Case statement for each of those values. When the expression results in one of those values, the statements following the Case statement for that value are executed.

If the *testexpression* doesn't match any of the values in the list, the block of code following the Case Else statement is executed. If you have not added the Case Else, execution jumps to the statement following the End Select statement.

The Select Case structure is ideal for choosing the code to run after making a selection from an option group. This example opens a report in Print Preview when you click the Preview button on the form shown in Figure 6-5. The report that is previewed depends on the option that was selected before clicking the button.

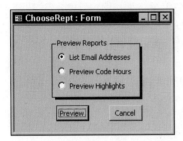

Figure 6-5: Selecting a report from the option group.

The procedure is attached to the On Click event property of the Preview command button and includes the following Select Case structure:

```
Private Sub Preview_Click()
    Select Case [Preview Reports]
        Case 1
        DoCmd.OpenReport "emails", acViewPreview, "", "", _
acNormal

        Case 2
        DoCmd.OpenReport "CdHrs", acViewPreview, "", "", _
        acNormal

        Case 3
            DoCmd.OpenReport "HiLites", acViewPreview, "", "", _
acNormal
    End Select
End Sub
```

There is no need for the Case Else statement in the above example because the *testexpression* depended on the fixed list of options in the option group.

You can use multiple expressions or ranges of values in any of the Case statements. For example,

```
Case 1 to 5              'executes the block if the value is 1,2,3,4
                         'or 5
Case "cats" To "dogs"    'strings that fall within the alphabetic
                         'range between cats and dogs.
Case 10 To 20, Is > 500  'values from 10 to 20, inclusive, or
                         'greater than 500
```

You can also nest Select Case structures but each Select Case statement must have a corresponding End Select statement.

Looping structures

Looping means repeating a block of statements. Some loops are repeated a specific number of times while other loops continue until a specified condition is met. VBA offers three types of looping structures:

- ◆ The Do...Loop statement

- ◆ The While...Wend statement

- ◆ The For...Next statement

THE DO...LOOP STRUCTURE

The Do...Loop looping structure has two ways to loop through the code:

- ◆ *While* the specified condition remains True.

- ◆ *Until* the specified condition becomes True.

The syntax is as follows:

```
Do [{While | Until} condition]
    [statements]
    [Exit Do]
    [statements]
Loop
```

The *condition* argument is required but it may appear with the Do statement or with the Loop statement. If it appears with the Do statement, the condition is evaluated before the block of code is executed. If it appears with the Loop statement, it is evaluated after the code is executed but before control is passed to the beginning of the loop.

The *condition* argument is a string or numeric expression that evaluates to True or False. If it is Null, it is considered False. You can use the Exit Do statement anywhere in the block of code to leave the loop under a specified condition. Control moves to the statement immediately following the Loop statement.

The following example, repeats the MsgBox statement and displays the current value of the intNum variable until the intNum variable reaches 10.

```
Dim intNum As Integer
intNum = 0
Do While intNum < 10
    MsgBox intNum
    intNum = intNum + 1
Loop
```

Using the next statement shows the same results:

```
Do Until intNum = 10
```

You can turn this around and place the {While | Until} clause at the bottom with the Loop statement but it may not give you the same results. For example, this next loop would execute 11 times because the condition is evaluated after the statements were executed.

```
Dim intNum As Integer
intNum = 0
Do
    MsgBox intNum
    intNum = intNum + 1
Loop While intNum < 10
```

Always increment (or decrement) the counter variable within the loop. If you forget, the loop executes forever or until your system times out and you will think your computer has crashed.

THE WHILE...WEND STRUCTURE

The While...Wend structure repeats the block of code as long as the *condition* expression remains True. It is similar to the Do While...Loop structure. While...Wend follows this pattern:

```
While condition
    [statements]
Wend
```

The `Do While...Loop` structure is a little more flexible because it offers a way to leave the loop with the `Exit Do` statement. This example of using the `While...Wend` structure subtracts 2 from the counter and stops execution when the counter becomes negative.

```
Dim intNum As Integer
intNum = 20
While intNum > 0
    MsgBox intNum
    intNum = intNum - 2
Wend
```

THE FOR ...NEXT STRUCTURE

The `For...Next` structure repeats a block of code a specified number of times. The loop uses a counter variable that you specify in the `For` statement. The syntax is:

```
For counter = start To end [Step step]
    [statements]
    [Exit For]
    [statements]
Next [counter]
```

The `counter`, `start`, and `end` arguments are required because they specify the range of the loop. The `step` argument is optional.

- ◆ The `counter` is a number variable, usually an integer.

- ◆ The `start` and `end` arguments define the initial and final values of the *counter*.

- ◆ A `step` argument determines the amount by which the `counter` is changed each time through the loop.

  The `step` argument can be either positive or negative. The default value is 1. The `step` value is added to the counter each time all statements in the loop are executed.

TIP Unlike the Do...Loop, you must not manually change the value of the counter within the loop. Let the For...Next structure do that.

Here is an example of using the `For...Next` structure. The counter starts at 20 and adds its value to intTotal, then counts down by 1 with each repetition. The message box displays the value 40 after the loop is completed.

```
Dim I As Integer, intTotal As Integer
intTotal = 0
For I = 20 To 1 Step -1
    intTotal = intTotal + 2
Next
MsgBox intTotal
```

If you don't include the *step* argument in the `Next` statement, it is implied as 1 anyway. You can also nest these `For...Next` structures just like other loops. Each loop must have a unique name for its counter argument and each `For` statement must have a corresponding `Next` statement.

Pausing or exiting statements

The `Exit` statement leaves a block of code such as a loop or a called procedure and transfers control back to the statement following the end of the loop or to the statement following the statement that called the procedure.

Don't confuse the `Exit` statement with the `End` statement. `Exit` does not define the end of the procedure, just transfers control out of it.

The statement comes in five different forms:

- Exit Do is used inside a Do...Loop. Transfers control to the statement that follows the Loop statement.

- Exit For is used in a For...Next or For Each...Next loop. Transfers control to the statement that follows the Next statement.

- Exit Function exits the function and transfers control to the statement following the one that called the function.

- Exit Property exits the property procedure and transfers control to the statement that called the property procedure.

- Exit Sub exits the sub procedure in which it appears. Control transfers to the statement following the one that called the sub procedure.

The End statements establish the end of a procedure or a block of code. The End statement executes the following tasks:

◆ Stops execution immediately.

◆ Closes any open files opened by the Open statement.

◆ Resets all the *module-level* variables and all the *static local* variables in all modules.

The End syntax also comes in different forms:

◆ End Function **ends a function procedure.**

◆ End If **ends the** If...Then...Else **structure.**

◆ End Property **ends a property procedure.**

◆ End Select **ends the** Select Case **statement.**

◆ End Sub **ends a sub procedure.**

◆ End Type **ends a user-defined type definition.**

◆ End With **ends the** With **structure.**

Summary

In this chapter, we have presented the fundamental components of the VBA language and how they can help with Access application development. We have just scratched the surface and have a lot more to dig into.

We show you more about working in the Visual Basic Editor windows in the next chapter then move on to Chapter 8 in which we describe more details of the VBA language with many practical examples.

Chapter 7

The Visual Basic Editor

IN THIS CHAPTER

◆ Starting and working with the Visual Basic Editor

◆ Making use of the Project Explorer and the Properties windows

◆ Exploring Access objects and collections with the Object Browser

◆ Entering and editing VBA code

◆ Customizing the VBE environment

◆ Getting help with VBA

THE VISUAL BASIC EDITOR (VBE) provides a flexible environment in which to enter, run, and debug VBA code. This chapter explores the VBE and most of its features and options.

 Chapter 10 explains running and debugging VBA code.

Starting the Visual Basic Editor

You have several ways to reach the Visual Basic Editor. Which one you use depends on what you are doing and what you want to do.

No matter where you are in Access, you can always open the VBE window by using one of the following methods:

◆ Pointing to Macro on the Tools menu and choosing Visual Basic Editor

◆ Pressing Alt+F11

Some other ways to start the VBE from the database window are as follows:

♦ **Create a new module:** Choose New on the Modules page in the database window.

♦ **Edit an existing module:** Select the module in the database window, and click Design.

♦ **Edit code that is stored with a specific form or report:** Select the form or report in the database window, and click the Code toolbar button.

♦ **Edit in an event property:** Use the Build (...) button in one of the event properties of a form, report, or control. Follow these steps:

1. Open the Event tab of the property sheet and click in the event property of interest.

2. Click the Build button at the right of the property box.

3. Choose Code Builder from the Choose Builder dialog box. You can also move to the VBE from a form or report design view by using either of the following methods:

   ■ Clicking the Code toolbar button

   ■ Choosing Code from the View menu

What you see in the VBE window when it opens depends on how you opened it:

♦ If there is code related to the object you have selected, the code appears in the VBE window.

♦ If you are writing a new module, the window is blank, except for the following two Option statements:

```
Option Compare Database
Option Explicit
```

Figure 7-1 shows the VBE window with the code from the Choose Report form.

Option Compare Database, Option Explicit, and the Choose Report form are covered in Chapter 6.

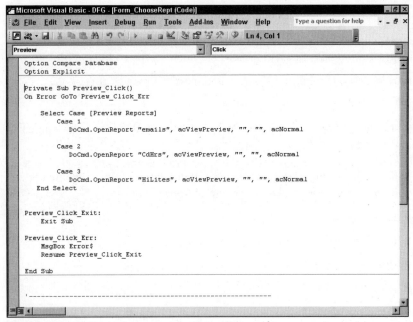

Figure 7-1: The Visual Basic Editor window with code.

The window that you first see is the Code window. You can use the following other windows when you are working with VBA code:

◆ **Project Explorer window:** Displays a hierarchical list of the current projects, with all the items in the projects and the references that are used by the projects.

◆ **Properties window:** Displays the design-time properties of selected objects and controls and their current settings. You can use the Properties window to change the settings for any of the objects in the project. The Properties window is explained elsewhere in this chapter.

◆ **Immediate window:** Testing and debugging tool; covered in Chapter 10.

◆ **Watch window:** Testing and debugging tool; covered in Chapter 10.

◆ **Locals window:** Testing and debugging tool; covered in Chapter 10.

Touring the VBE window

You spend most of your coding time in the Code window. The code that is displayed in Figure 7-1 is the event procedure that executes when you click the Preview button in the Choose Report form.

At the top of the code window, you can see two combo box controls that contain important lists:

◆ **Object combo box:** Shows Preview, the name of the command button

◆ **Procedure combo box:** Shows Click, the event to which it responds

MENUS

The VBE menu bar contains familiar menus and commands, but some commands are not shown in the built-in Access Menu bar:

◆ **Edit menu:** Contains traditional editorial commands, plus commands that quickly activate the following editing options:

- List Properties

- List Constants

- Quick Info

- Parameter Info

- Complete Word

These commands are also available on the Edit toolbar. The preceding options are further explained in the section "Entering VBA Code," later in this chapter.

◆ **View menu:** Includes the following commands:

- **Code:** Displays the code for the object that is current in the Access window, if the window is blank

- **Object:** Switches you to the Access window with the current object

- **Definition:** Opens the Object Browser window with the currently selected code object highlighted

◆ **Tools menu:** Includes the following commands:

- **References:** Opens the References dialog box, where you can choose additional Dynamic Link Library (DLL) references.

- **Macros:** Opens a dialog box with a list of macros in the current database that you can run or edit.

- **Options:** Controls the editor's appearance and behavior. You can find more information about setting the VBE options in the section "Customizing the VBE Environment," later in this chapter.

◆ **Windows menu:** Switches to any open Access window.

◆ **Help menu:** Includes *MSDN on the Web,* which links you to the Microsoft Developer's Network on the Web. (VBA help is covered in section, "Getting Help with VBA," later in this chapter.)

The Debug and Run menus are covered in Chapter 10.

You can choose a command from the shortcut menu in the Code window. Right-click anywhere in the window, and you see the list of commands that are shown in Figure 7-2.

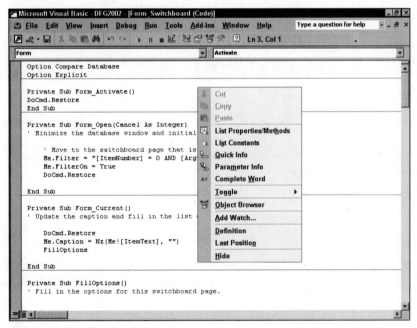

Figure 7-2: The VBE shortcut menu.

TOOLBARS

The Standard toolbar has many buttons that offer shortcuts to the menu commands that you use most often. You can call up two other toolbars when necessary: Edit and Debug. Both of these are floating by default, but you can also dock them.

 The UserForm toolbar is on the toolbar list when you right-click in an empty space on the toolbar. This toolbar is not relevant in Access. It is available because other Microsoft Office programs, such as Excel, apply UserForms through VBE.

STANDARD TOOLBAR BUTTONS   Many of the Standard toolbar buttons are also found on the Access toolbars but there are some buttons found only in VBE.

◆ **View Microsoft Access:** This first button on the Standard toolbar returns you to the Access window in which you were working before activating the VBE.

 You can also return to Access by clicking in the taskbar at the bottom of the screen.

◆ **Insert:** This button displays a list of the following items, which you can add to the current code:

- Module
- Procedure
- Class Module

 The icon on the button represents the last object that you added.

The area at the right end of the Standard toolbar indicates the current line and column location of the cursor within the code. For example, in Figure 7-2, the cursor was on line 7 in column 41 when I right-clicked in the Code window.

EDIT TOOLBAR BUTTONS   The Edit toolbar contains 14 buttons that provide many of the same code-editing commands that are found in the Edit menu. Some of the buttons display helpful lists of properties, methods, and constants that are relevant to the code.

DEBUG TOOLBAR BUTTONS   The Debug toolbar contains shortcuts to many commonly used items on the Debug menu.

Chapters 9 and Chapter 10 show Debug testing new sub procedures.

OTHER BUTTONS   In the lower-left corner of the Code window, you find two additional buttons. Click these buttons, described as follows, to change the amount of code that is visible in the Code window:

♦ **Left button:** Displays only the current procedure

♦ **Right button:** Shows code from all the procedures in the module

CUSTOMIZING   You can move the toolbars and customize them, just as you can with Access toolbars. Open the Customize dialog box using one of the following methods:

♦ Right-click an empty space on a toolbar, and choose Customize.

♦ Choose View→Customize.

Using the Project Explorer

You can use the Project Explorer to navigate among the Access objects in your project. The Project Explorer lists all loaded projects and all the items that are included in each project. To open the Project Explorer window, choose View→Project Explorer (or press Ctrl+R). The window is docked on the left of the screen by default, as shown in Figure 7-3.

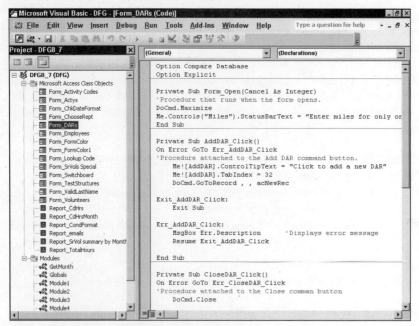

Figure 7-3: Opening the Project Explorer window.

The following three buttons are located on the Project Explorer toolbar:

◆ **View Code:** Opens the Code window for the selected object

◆ **View Object:** Opens an Access window that displays the selected object

◆ **Toggle Folders:** Switches between views of the folders, as follows:

■ **Folder view:** Shows all the objects in the database, listed as class objects attached to forms or reports or as modules.

Figure 7-3 shows the Project Explorer in folder view.

■ **Folder contents view:** Displays all objects in alphabetic order by name, regardless of object type.

The plus (+) and minus (–) signs expand and collapse the branches of the tree. The Project Explorer list indicates the type of item by adding an icon to each item name. The list can include the following items:

◆ Forms

◆ Reports

◆ Modules

◆ Documents

◆ Class modules not stored with a form or report

◆ ActiveX designer (.dsr) files

◆ References

Figure 7-3 shows forms, reports, and modules in the list.

When you first open the Project Explorer, the highlighted object is not necessarily the owner of the code in the Code window.

You can see the code for a specific object in the following two ways:

◆ Select the object in the Project Explorer, and click the View Code button.

◆ Double-click the object.

To see longer object names, you can widen the Project Explorer window by
dragging the left border.

ADDING AND REMOVING MODULES

You saw how to add a new procedure to the VBE window by checking the Insert
toolbar button. You can also add and remove procedures with the Project Explorer.

◆ **Add a new module to the project:** You can add a new module to the project from the Project Explorer by using one of the following methods:

■ Select the project name, and choose Insert→Module.

■ Right-click in the Project Explorer window, choose Insert from the
shortcut menu that appears, and choose Module or Class Module (as
shown in Figure 7-4).

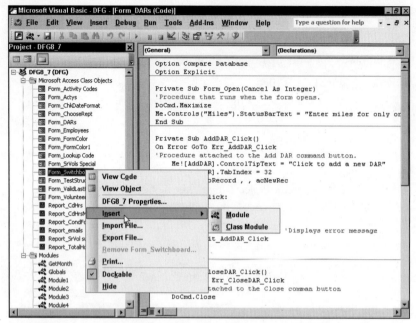

Figure 7-4: Inserting a module or class module into an existing module.

◆ **Delete a module from the project:** Select the module, and choose File→Remove <*modulename*>. You are asked if you want to export the module before removing it. If you respond Yes, the Export File dialog box opens; here, you can choose the destination and enter a filename. The module is removed from the Project Explorer using this method.

◆ **Export a copy of the module:** Use the Export command.

Exporting does not delete the original module from the project.

The Remove option is not available for Access class objects.

IMPORTING AND EXPORTING OBJECTS

Working within the Project Explorer, you can also import and export files.

◆ **Import a file into your project with the Project Explorer:** Follow these steps:

1. Choose File→Import File, or right-click and select Import File from the shortcut menu that appears.

2. In the Import File dialog box, locate the VB file that you want and then click Import.

    VB files have the file extensions .frm, .bas, and .cls.

◆ **Export a file from your project:** Follow these steps:

1. Choose File→Export File, or right-click and select Export File from the shortcut menu that appears.

2. In the Export File dialog box, find the destination for the file, give the file a name, and then click Export.

    Filenaming depends on the type of file:

    ■ **Access class module files:** Saved as files with a .cls extension

    ■ **Module files:** Saved as files with a .bas extension

    Unlike choosing to export the file before you delete it, exporting accomplishes the following items:

    ■ Creates a copy in the new location

    ■ Keeps the original in your project

◆ **Close the Project Explorer window:** Click the Close button (X) on the window's toolbar.

Using the Properties window

The Properties window displays a list of all the design-time properties that you have set for selected objects. You can change any of these properties if you are in Design mode.

Design mode is the time during which no code in the project is running and no events occur in the host object or project. To set the VBE to Design mode, choose either Run→Design Mode or click the Design Mode button on the Standard toolbar. Repeat the choice to exit Design mode.

To open the Properties window, choose View→Properties Window or press F4. All the controls and properties of the currently selected object are listed in the Properties list. Figure 7-5 shows the Properties window with the Preview command button selected in the Object box.

To select another control, click the down arrow in the Object box and choose from the list of objects and controls in the current project as shown in Figure 7-6.

The tabs in the Properties list are as follows:

- ◆ **Alphabetic:** Shows all the properties for the selected object that can be changed at design time and indicates their current settings. To change a property setting, select the property name and take one of the following actions:

  - Select from the list of settings

  - Type a new setting

- ◆ **Categorized:** Similar to the groupings that you find in the Access property sheet tabs. For example, the Preview button has properties in the Data, Event, Format, and Other categories, as shown in Figure 7-7. If you scroll down the list, you can see the list of Other properties.

The list of properties in each group can be expanded or collapsed by clicking the plus or minus sign, respectively.

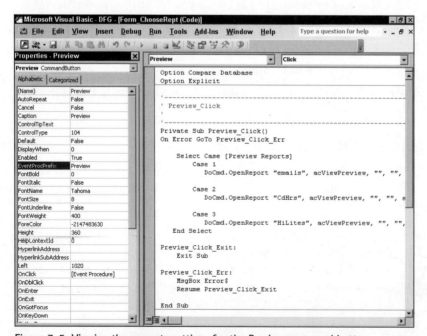

Figure 7-5: Viewing the property settings for the Preview command button.

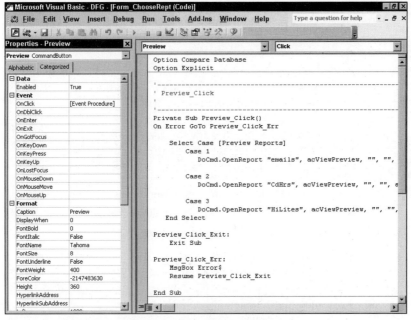

Figure 7-6: Choosing another control in the Properties window.

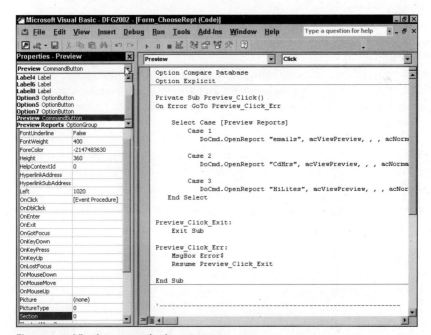

Figure 7-7: Viewing properties by category.

The categories are alphabetized, unlike the sequence of tabs in the Access property sheets.

To remove the Properties window, click the Close button.

As with the property sheets in Access, if you select multiple controls while in the Access design view, only those properties that are common to all the controls are displayed in the VBE Properties window. Also, no control name appears in the Object box in the Properties window in VBE.

Working with the Object Browser

The Object Browser is a valuable tool for working in the VBE window. With it you can look through lists of all the objects and their properties, methods, and events and the constants that are available in Access and other applications that support VBA. You can scroll through the lists. When you locate the method or property that you need, copy and paste it into the module that you are working on in the Code window.

To open the Object Browser, press F2 or click the Object Browser button on the VBE Standard toolbar. Figure 7-8 shows the Object Browser with the Switchboard Form class selected.

Any class or member of a class that has any VBA code associated with it appears in bold. In Figure 7-8, the Switchboard form and several of its members appear in boldface. The Switchboard Manager created the switchboard and included the following procedures:

- FillOptions **sub procedure:** Does most of the work building the switchboard by filling in the options that you specify when you use the Switchboard Manager

- Form_Activate **event procedure:** Executes when the form is activated and restores the switchboard form to its previous size

- Form_Current **event procedure:** Executes when the form gets focus, sets the form caption, and calls the FillOptions procedure

- Form_Open **event procedure:** Executes when the form opens, minimizes the database window, and opens the Switchboard form

- HandleButtonClick **function:** Executes when a selection is made in the form and returns the value of the selection for use in a Select Case structure

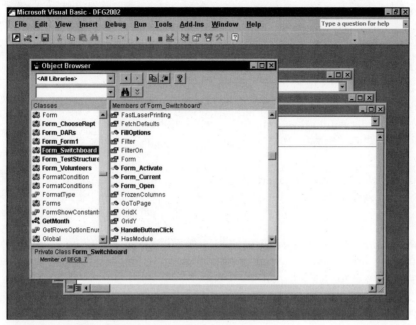

Figure 7-8: Looking at classes in the Object Browser.

 The procedures are listed in alphabetical order, not in order of logical execution.

TOURING THE OBJECT BROWSER

At the top of the Object Browser window is the Project/Libraries box, where you can select from the list of available libraries or current projects. The default is <All Libraries> but you can select a specific library from the list. Libraries are explained in detail in the section "Choosing a Project or Library" in this chapter.

The Object Browser window has the following main list panes:

◆ **Classes:** Displays all the available classes in the library or project that is currently selected in the Project/Libraries box.

  ■ The first item in the Classes list is always <globals> (the group of globally accessible members of all types).

  ■ If you have written code for a class, that class name appears in bold-face, as shown in Figure 7-7.

- Several forms from the Senior Volunteers project are listed in boldface in the Classes list. Their event members also appear in boldface in the Members of list.

◆ **Members of:** Displays all the elements of the class that you have selected in the Classes list in either of the following orders:

- **Elements of the same group type together:** Elements are in alphabetical order within the group. To switch to this arrangement, right-click in the Object Browser and choose Group Members from the shortcut menu that appears.

- **All elements in alphabetical order:** This is the default. To switch to this view, right-click in the Object Browser and remove the check mark from the Group Members option in the shortcut menu that appears.

At the bottom of the Object Browser window, the Details pane displays a definition of the currently selected class or member. You can find a link in these definitions that jumps to the parent class or library. For example, Figure 7-9 shows the class `ColorConstants` with the `vbMagenta` member selected. The Details pane shows the value of the constant and links to VBA and ColorConstants.

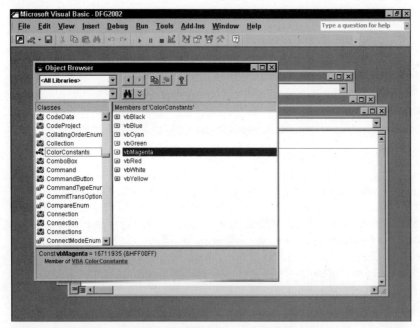

Figure 7-9: Defining a member of a class.

◆ If you click on the ColorConstants link, it jumps to the VBA host class.

◆ If you click on the VBA link, the library name and the complete path and file name appear in the Details pane as follows

```
Library VBA
                    C:\Program    Files\Common    Files\Microsoft
Shared\VBA\VBA6\VBE6.DLL
      Visual Basic For Applications
```

 Each of the three panes in the Object Browser can be resized to give you more room. Drag the split bar to resize a pane.

The Object Browser has the following toolbar buttons to make browsing easier:

◆ **Go Back and Go Forward:** Move through items that you have previously selected. These buttons work just like the ones in the Help window.

◆ **Copy to Clipboard:** Copies the selected item from the Members of list or the Details pane to the clipboard.

◆ **View Definition:** Opens a Code window and displays the selected user-defined sub or function procedure.

For example, choose Form_Switchboard in the Classes list and click the View Definition button to see the class module for the form.

◆ **Help:** Displays the online help topic for the selected item in either list.

◆ **Search:** Starts a search for the text that you typed in the Search Text box at the left of the button.

◆ **Show/Hide Search Results:** Opens and closes the Search Results pane.

CHOOSING A PROJECT OR LIBRARY

The default setting in the Project/Library box is <All Libraries>. You can choose to limit your module to a single library or project by choosing from the drop-down list shown in Figure 7-10.

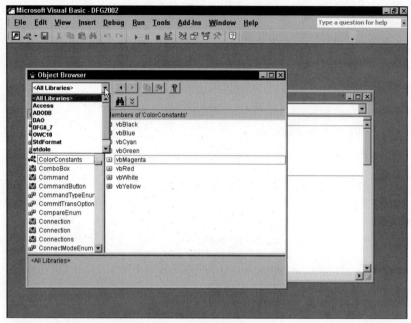

Figure 7-10: Choosing a different library or project.

To use objects from another library that is not on the list, set a reference to that library by following these steps:

1. Choose References from either of the following menus:

   ■ Tools

   ■ Shortcut

2. Select the library that you need, and then click OK.

Figure 7-11 shows the choice of the Microsoft Office 11.0 Object Library. The next time you look at the Project/Library list, that library will be in the list.

SEARCHING IN THE OBJECT BROWSER
The Object Browser Search feature can locate a certain word or part of a word in the Classes and Members of lists. Follow these steps to perform a search:

1. Enter the string that you are looking for in the Search Text box.

   Any standard wildcard character can be used in the search string.

2. Start the search with either of the following actions:

- Click the Search button.

- Press Enter.

Figure 7-12 shows the result of searching for the word *constants*. The word is found in several libraries.

The results of the search include the library, class, and member names in each item in the list, preceded by an icon that indicates the type of object. Go to the online help topic "Icons Used in the Object Browser and Code Windows" to see what each icon represents. Scroll down the list to find the item that you need. To close the results pane, click the Show/Hide Search button.

TIP The Search Text box retains the search strings that you entered until you close Access. You can return to any of them by choosing the string from the drop-down list in the box.

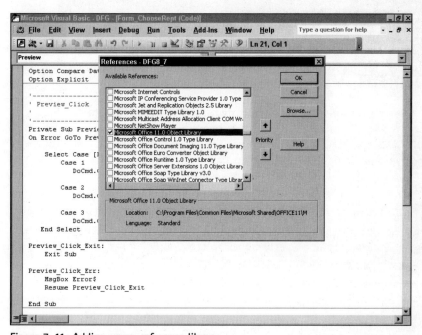

Figure 7-11: Adding a new reference library.

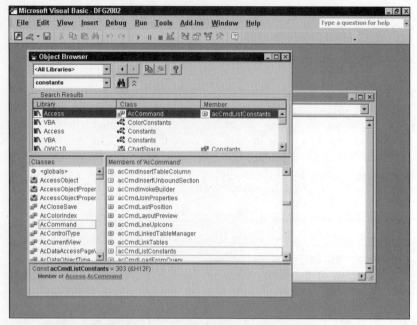

Figure 7-12: The results of searching for the word constants.

Entering VBA Code

Before you can start entering code, you need the framework to hold it. All code is contained within a procedure, either a sub procedure or a function procedure. Procedures are contained in modules. A module can contain as many procedures as you need to do the job.

Chapter 9 presents information about creating and using the property procedure that can create and manipulate custom properties. You can choose from the following types of property procedures: `Property Let`, `Property Get`, and `Property Set`.

To start a new procedure in an existing module, perform one of the following processes:

 ◆ Type **Sub** or **Function** and the procedure name below the module Option statements. The editor automatically adds the parentheses and the `End` statement for you. Now enter the procedure code between the Sub statement and the End statement, starting with the declarations.

This is the easiest way to start a new sub procedure or function.

◆ Open the Add Procedure dialog box (see Figure 7-13) with either of the following steps:

- Open the module in the Code window, and choose Insert→Procedure.

- Click the Insert button on the Standard toolbar, and choose Procedure from the list that appears.

In the Add Procedure dialog box, specify the following for the procedure:

- Name

- Type

- Scope

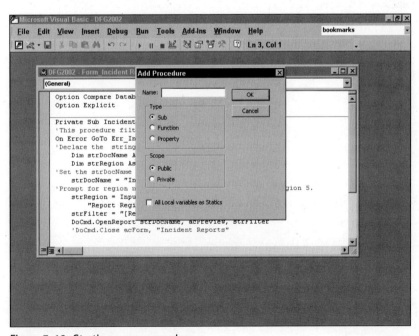

Figure 7-13: Starting a new procedure.

Checking the All Local Variables as Statics option ensures that all variables declared in the procedure retain their values after the procedure ends.

You can enter the code statements in the following ways:

◆ **Type one line at a time.** All the common word processing tools work with the text, and you have all the help from the VBE options.

This is the simplest way, and often the easiest.

◆ **Start with a wizard.** Let the wizard write the code, and then make any changes you need.

The following example is the On Click event procedure for a button on a form. The Command Button Wizard wrote the following code to open the designated report in Print Preview and show all the records in the underlying Incidents table:

```
Private Sub Incident_Reports_Click()
On Error GoTo Err_Incident_Reports_Click
    Dim stDocName As String
    stDocName = "Incident Report"
    DoCmd.OpenReport stDocName, acPreview
Exit_Incident_Reports_Click:
    Exit Sub
Err_Incident_Reports_Click:
    MsgBox Err.Description
    Resume Exit_Incident_Reports_Click
End Sub
```

To limit the records that are included in the report, you can add code to apply a filter. First display an InputBox function that prompts for the Region number. Then build a filter to use when the report opens. (It's a good idea to add comments as you modify the code.)

The following code is shown after you add the InputBox function and the filter:

```
Private Sub Incident_Reports_Click()
'This procedure filters incident reports by region.
On Error GoTo Err_Incident_Reports_Click

'Declare the string variables
    Dim strDocName As String, strFilter As String
    Dim strRegion As String

'Set the strDocName to the Incident Report
    strDocName = "Incident Report"

'Prompt for region number to use as filter. Default is
Region 5.
    strRegion = InputBox("Enter Region number", _
        "Report Region", "Region 5")
    strFilter = "[Region #] = '" & strRegion & "'"
    DoCmd.OpenReport strDocName, acPreview, , strFilter
    DoCmd.Close acForm, "Incident Reports"

Exit_Incident_Reports_Click:      'User clicked Cancel
    Exit Sub

Err_Incident_Reports_Click:
    MsgBox Err.Description
    Resume Exit_Incident_Reports_Click

End Sub
```

If you have written a macro to carry out a series of actions, you can convert the macro to code. If the macro were designed to execute based on a form, report, or any of the controls, the new code is stored in the class module for that object. For example, the macro shown in Figure 7-14 is attached to the LostFocus event property of the ZipCode text box in a form that is used for entering incident report information. When focus moves to the Region # text box, the macro automatically enters the Region # that corresponds to the ZipCode in the report. If the ZipCode is not in the list, the Region # shows Unk.

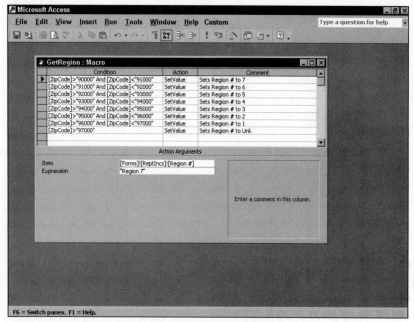

Figure 7-14: A macro that automatically enters the Region #.

To convert the macro to VBA, follow these steps:

1. Open the form in Design view, and choose Tools→Macro.

2. Click Convert Form's Macros to Visual Basic.

   You see a box that includes options for adding error handling and including the macro comments. Keep these options.

3. Click Convert.

The following VBA code is an example of the result:

```
'----------------------------------------------------------------
' ZipCode_LostFocus
'----------------------------------------------------------------
Private Sub ZipCode_LostFocus()
On Error GoTo ZipCode_LostFocus_Err

    If (ZipCode > "90000" And ZipCode < "91000") Then
        ' Sets Region # to 7
        Forms!ReptIncs![Region #] = "Region 7"
    End If
    If (ZipCode > "91000" And ZipCode < "92000") Then
```

```
        ' Sets Region # to 6
        Forms!ReptIncs![Region #] = "Region 6"
    End If
    If (ZipCode > "92000" And ZipCode < "93000") Then
        ' Sets Region # to 5
        Forms!ReptIncs![Region #] = "Region 5"
    End If
    If (ZipCode > "93000" And ZipCode < "94000") Then
        ' Sets Region # to 4
        Forms!ReptIncs![Region #] = "Region 4"
    End If
    If (ZipCode > "94000" And ZipCode < "95000") Then
        ' Sets Region # to 3
        Forms!ReptIncs![Region #] = "Region 3"
    End If
    If (ZipCode > "95000" And ZipCode < "96000") Then
        ' Sets Region # to 2
        Forms!ReptIncs![Region #] = "Region 2"
    End If
    If (ZipCode > "96000" And ZipCode < "97000") Then
        ' Sets Region # to 1
        Forms!ReptIncs![Region #] = "Region 1"
    End If
    If (ZipCode > "97000") Then
' Displays "Unk"
        Forms!ReptIncs![Region #] = "Unk"
    End If
ZipCode_LostFocus_Exit:
    Exit Sub
ZipCode_LostFocus_Err:
    MsgBox Error$
    Resume ZipCode_LostFocus_Exit
End Sub
```

The online help topics include a lot of useful but anonymous code. You can copy code and paste it into your module. Then change the variable names and values to ones that fit your application.

As you are entering code, you often see the lists of relevant objects, properties, and methods that apply to what you are entering. For instance, if you type **DoCmd** followed by a period, you see the list of methods that work with the DoCmd object. You have the following ways to enter the selected item in the list into the current line of code:

◆ **Double-click:** Enters the item

◆ **Press Tab:** Enters the item

◆ **Press the spacebar:** Enters the item and adds a space

◆ **Press Enter:** Enters the item and moves to a new blank line

 TIP For this to work, you must check the Auto List Members option in the Options dialog box. The following section explains customizing the VBE environment for this and other options.

Editing VBA code

Between the Edit menu and the Edit toolbar, you have many tools to help you write correct and effective VBA code.

EDIT MENU

The Edit menu in the VBE window has most of the common text-processing tools that you need; these include Cut, Copy and Paste, and Find and Replace. The following additional commands are especially designed for working in the Code window:

◆ **Indent and Outdent:** Move code lines left or right one tab space.

 TIP Pressing Tab or Shift+Tab is faster than choosing from the Edit menu.

◆ **List Properties/Methods:** Shows a list of properties and methods available to the object that was entered just before the period.

 NOTE This is the same as the Auto List Members option.

◆ **List Constants:** Shows a list of the constants that are valid for the property that you entered before the equals sign.

◆ **Quick Info:** Displays syntax for the function, method, or procedure when you place the mouse pointer on its name.

This is the same as the Auto List Members option.

- **Parameter Info:** Displays information about the parameters of the function on which you are resting the mouse pointer.

- **Complete Word:** Automatically completes the word that you are typing.

- **Bookmarks submenu:** Controls bookmarks in a form in the following ways:
    - Toggles a bookmark on or off
    - Moves focus to the next or previous bookmark
    - Removes all bookmarks from the form

Several of these menu commands are also available by right-clicking and choosing from the shortcut menu that appears.

EDIT TOOLBAR

The Edit toolbar contains buttons that carry out the most common editing functions plus a few special buttons:

- **Toggle Breakpoint:** Turns on and off a breakpoint in the code. This command is also in the Debug menu.

- **Comment Block:** Excludes a selected block of code from execution.

    The VBE adds apostrophes to the beginning of every line of code in the selected block.

- **Uncomment Block:** Removes comment apostrophes from the selected block of code, as shown in Figure 7-15.

When you are editing code, whether it is your own or was created by a wizard, you can get back to the automatic drop-down lists of members and quick info by deleting the last few characters of the keyword. When you enter the characters again, you activate the lists and syntax information.

Figure 7-15: Removing the comment characters from code.

Saving VBA code

Saving your new or edited code is easy. You have the following choices:

♦ If you were working on a class module, you are prompted to save the changes when you close the form or report.

♦ If you were working on a module object, you are prompted to save the changes when you close Access.

♦ If you have changed several modules, you can choose which changes you want to keep.

Figure 7-16 shows the list of recent changes when closing Access.

All the changed modules are selected, so choose Yes to save them all. To keep one and discard the rest, deselect the ones that you don't want and choose Yes to save the remainder.

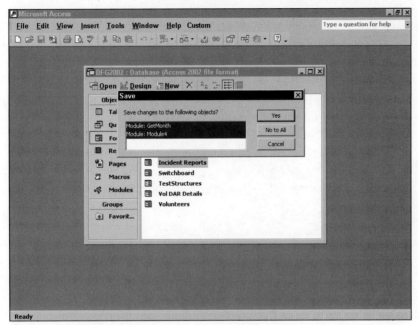

Figure 7-16: Access prompts you to save changes in code.

Customizing the VBE Environment

In an effort to provide just the workplace that its users want, Microsoft has provided a means to change the VBE environment. Many of the options relate to the appearance of the code in the Code window; others affect the behavior of the editor while you are entering code. Several useful features automatically help you complete a statement or display information about functions and their arguments as you type.

To reach the Options dialog box, choose Tools→Options. The Options dialog box contains four tabs, as shown in Figure 7-17.

Setting the Editor options

The options on the Editor tab specify the Code window settings.

AUTO SYNTAX CHECK

If you check the Auto Syntax Check option, VBE automatically checks each line of code as you move to the next statement. The editor automatically corrects some of the obvious errors such as a missing closing quotation mark; you must fix other errors yourself. If an error exists in the syntax, a dialog box displays an explanation of the problem. The message is usually clear enough that you can figure out where you went wrong. Figure 7-18 shows a message indicating that the closing parenthesis is missing.

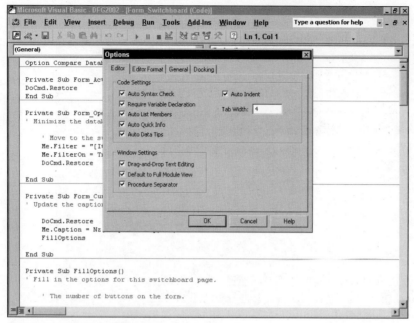

Figure 7-17: Setting VBE options.

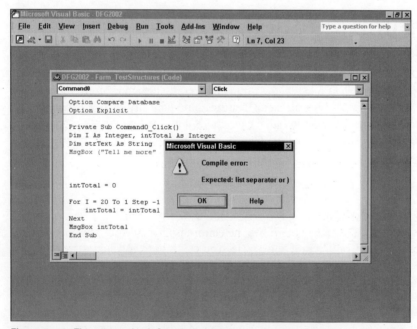

Figure 7-18: The syntax check found an error.

This type of error is called a *compile* error; *run-time* errors occur when the procedure executes. Chapter 9 covers run-time errors.

If this option is not checked, the code that contains the syntax error appears in a different color in the Code window without the explanation. It is up to you to decide how to fix it.

This is a good option if you are new to VBA. When you have more experience, you may find the pop-up boxes to be a nuisance.

REQUIRE VARIABLE DECLARATION

When checked, the Require Variable Declaration option requires that you declare all the variables that you use in the module. With this option checked, every new module includes the `Option Explicit` statement.

This is a good option to keep for the following reasons:

◆ It can prevent misspellings in the code. If you misspell a variable, you see an error message.

◆ If you don't declare your variables, they are all variant data type, which takes more space.

This option works only on new modules that you create. The modules that were in place before you set this option are not affected, but you can go back and add the `Option Explicit` statement.

AUTO LIST MEMBERS

With the Auto List Members option set, the editor displays a list of relevant objects, properties, and methods as you enter code. You can select the appropriate constant from the list instead of typing in the name. Figure 7-19 shows the list of members of the `DoCmd` object that begin with *Open*. You can scroll down the list or type the first few characters to reach the member that you need. This option saves a lot of time.

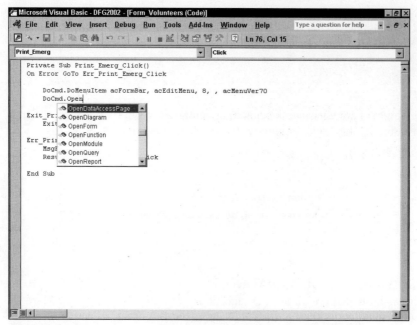

Figure 7-19: Selecting from the auto list of members.

AUTO QUICK INFO

The Auto Quick Info option displays all the syntax information about functions and their arguments as you type. The argument that is currently called for appears in boldface as you work through the statement. Figure 7-20 shows the syntax for the `OpenReport` method, with the report name as the first argument to be specified.

AUTO DATA TIPS

The Auto Data Tips option automatically displays the current value of a variable when you move the mouse pointer over it. This helpful tool works only in Break mode during debugging. Figure 7-21 shows the value of the `intTotal` variable after the procedure loops three times.

When you reach a constant argument, such as the next one in the `OpenReport` method `View As AcView`, a list of members pops up if you have checked the Auto List Members option.

AUTO INDENT

Indenting lines of code makes them easier to read and illustrates the structured logic. With this option set, once you indent a line of code, the editor automatically indents the next line to match. Press Tab to indent and Ctrl+Tab to outdent.

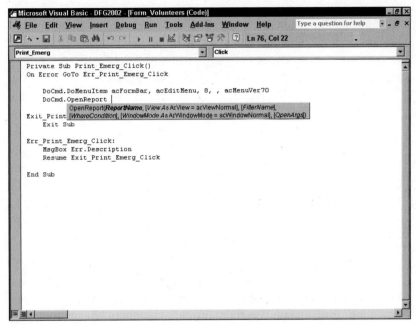

Figure 7-20: The required syntax for the `OpenReport` method.

Figure 7-21: Checking the `intTotal` variable value during debugging.

TAB WIDTH

Setting the Tab Width option specifies the number of characters to indent when you press Tab.

 The default of 4 characters is fine.

DRAG AND DROP IN TEXT EDITING

The Drag-and-Drop Text Editing option allows the traditional word processing drag-and-drop method of editing. This can move code elements to the Immediate or Watch window.

DEFAULT TO FULL MODULE VIEW

The Default to Full Module View option displays all the procedures in the current module as a single, scrollable list. With this option turned off, you see only one procedure at a time. You can still use the buttons at the lower-left corner of the Code window to change the view manually.

PROCEDURE SEPARATOR

The Procedure Separator option draws a line across the screen between procedures.

 This can be a big help if you have several procedures in the module and you are viewing the full module.

Setting Editor Format options

The Editor Format tab allows you to specify the appearance of the VBE screen (see Figure 7-22).

CODE COLORS

The Code Colors list box shows ten different categories of text that you find in the VBE window. For any category, you can specify the following colors:

- ◆ Foreground text color
- ◆ Background text color
- ◆ Color of the indicator that appears in the left indicator margin

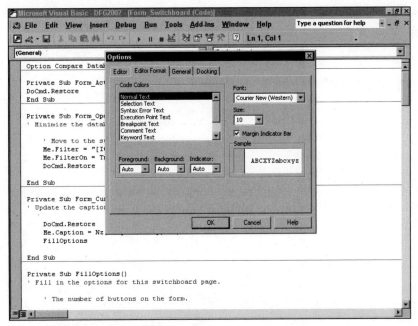

Figure 7-22: Setting Editor Format options.

To set the colors, follow these steps:

1. Select the category in the Code Colors list.

2. Click the down arrow next to the item that you want to change.

3. Use one of the following steps to pick a color:

   - Select the color that you want from the palette.

   - Choose Auto to keep the default color.

As you consider the various colors, the Sample pane shows how they will look.

FONT AND FONT SIZE

The default font settings work fine, but if you need a larger font for better visibility, choose one in the Font or Size option box. You should stay with a fixed-width font because the code lines up better vertically, making them easier to read.

MARGIN INDICATOR BAR

The margin indicator bar is the vertical margin at the left side of the Code window. The bar shows break points and other helpful indicators during debugging.

Setting General options

The General tab, shown in Figure 7-23, allows you to specify the form grid settings and some error-trapping and compilation options. User forms are not relevant to Access, so you don't need to worry about those settings. The default settings work fine under normal conditions.

 Chapter 9 explains error handling.

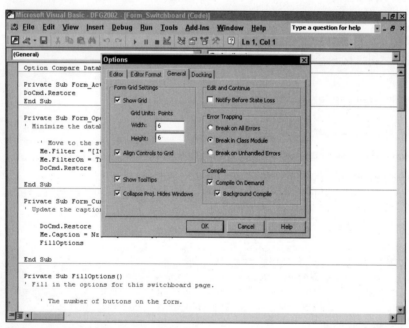

Figure 7-23: Setting the General options.

Setting Docking options

Figure 7-24 shows a list of all the windows in the VBE workplace, with check boxes for allowing each one to be docked. When one of the windows is docked, it appears anchored alongside the Code window or one of the other VBE windows. This can be helpful because you know where the window will appear, and it does not distract you by floating around the VBE window. By default, all the windows are dockable except the Object Browser; you can also make that one dockable by selecting its check box.

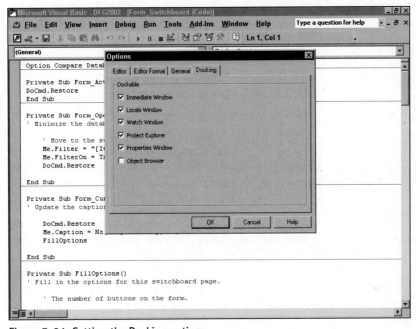

Figure 7-24: Setting the Docking options.

Getting Help with VBA

When you need more information about VBA, you have several ways of quickly getting the information that you need. The following actions all take you to the Microsoft Visual Basic Help window:

◆ Choosing Microsoft Visual Basic Help from the Help menu

◆ Pressing F1

◆ Clicking the Help button on the Standard toolbar

◆ Figure 7-25 shows the Help Table of Contents. Click a closed book icon to expand the list of subtopics. If you are currently connected to the Web, you will access the online Help Table of Contents.

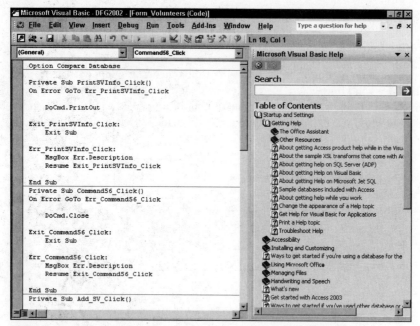

Figure 7-25: Opening the Microsoft Visual Basic Help Table of Contents.

If you have a specific question, you can type it in the Type a question for help box in the menu bar. This works just like Access Help. You can choose a topic from the list or retype the question.

Be as specific as possible with your question to help zero in on the answer.

If you are writing VBA code and need help with a specific keyword, place the cursor on the word and press F1. Figure 7-26 shows the Filter Property help topic that appears when you press F1 with the cursor on the Filter keyword.

The Help button in the Object Browser can provide information about objects, properties, methods, and constants when you are connected to the online Help source. Simply select the item in the Classes or Members of list, and click the Help button. Figure 7-27 shows the help topic for the Modify Method of the FormatCondition object.

After you have the Help window open, you can minimize it to keep it active. When you need to look something up, either press Alt+Tab or click the Help button in the taskbar.

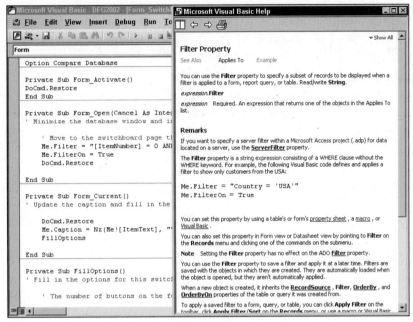

Figure 7-26: Getting help from the Code window.

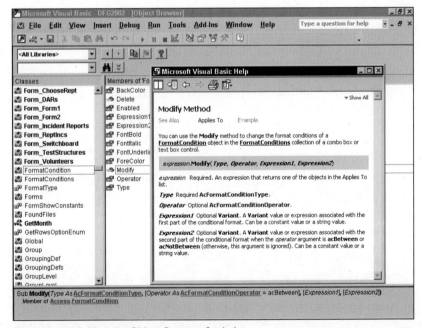

Figure 7-27: Asking the Object Browser for help.

Summary

In this chapter, we presented the environment of the Visual Basic Editor and showed you how to make it work for you. You can use many of the features, such as the Object Browser, the Project Explorer, and the Properties windows, to help build correct VBA code quickly and easily.

The next chapter presents examples of code that is useful for working with forms and reports and the controls they contain.

Chapter 8

Using VBA Language Elements

IN THE PRECEDING TWO CHAPTERS, we introduced you to the VBA language and escorted you through the Visual Basic Editor environment. Now it is time to get down to business and investigate the elements that make up the VBA language and how they fit together.

A Closer Look at VBA Elements

A procedure is made up of the following elements:

◆ **Procedure name and end statements**

◆ **Declaration statements:** Name and define all the words that you use in the procedure that VBA doesn't recognize as its own. These words can be any of the following items:

   ▪ Variables

   ▪ Constants

   ▪ Arrays

   ▪ Objects

Your declaration statements give VBA the custom pieces for the job.

◆ **Assignment statements:** Always contain an equal sign and give a value to an item that you have declared. You can use either of the following items:

  ■ A stated value

  ■ An expression that can be evaluated

◆ **Executable statements:** Tell VBA what to do with the pieces that you have defined, such as the following:

  ■ Carrying out a method or function

  ■ Looping through a block of code

  ■ Branching to another location in the procedure

◆ **Comments:** Document the logic and meaning behind the code.

If you are declaring a constant, you assign the value to it in the declaration statement so that you don't need a separate assignment statement for it.

Putting the VBA elements together

The following VBA elements work together in a procedure:

◆ **Object:** An element of the Access application. For example, tables, forms and reports, and the controls in forms and reports are all objects. You must identify the object that you want to work with before you can ask VBA to apply one of the methods to the object or make any changes to its properties.

VBA has some objects of its own, including the DoCmd object, which you use frequently when developing an application.

◆ **Method:** A process that an object can perform. For example, a combo box control can perform the AddItem method that adds a new item to the list of values. The following statement adds the name Jones to the combo box declared as ctrlComboBox and places the name at the top of the list.

```
ctrlComboBox.AddItem Item:="Jones", Index:=0
```

The AddItem method shown here has the following arguments:

- Item: The text of the new item. This argument is required.

- Index: Positions the new item in the list. This argument is optional.

The list is indexed beginning with 0, so the preceding statement would place Jones at the top of the drop-down list. If you choose not to include the Index argument, VBA places the new item at the end of the list.

Methods are like the actions that you used with macros. The name *method* avoids confusion and follows the object-oriented programming style.

◆ **Property:** A named attribute of an object, for example, the color of a text box control or the height of a command bar button. Other properties provide information about an Access object, such as whether a form was opened for read-only. For example, you could use the following statements in a With...Wend block to change the font to bold in all the text box labels on the form. The acLabel constant is a member of the AcControlType class and refers to text box label controls, as follows:

```
Dim btn As Object
If btn.ControlType = acLabel Then
    btn.FontBold = True
End If
```

You can also retrieve information about properties with VBA. For example, to see the name of the current form, use the following statements:

```
Dim strMyForm As String
strMyForm = Screen.ActiveForm.Caption
MsgBox strMyForm
```

◆ **Event:** A specific action that happens to or with a certain object. For example, the form opens, the command button is clicked, or you make a selection from a combo box control. Other events are caused by user actions, such as moving the cursor, or by the system, such as run-time errors caused by the code. Each object has a set of events that it is subject to. You can write code to respond to the events that you expect.

Chapter 16 explains events and the sequence in which they occur. You must attach a procedure to the right event if you want to achieve the outcome that you need.

DEFAULT EVENTS

A *default event* is the event that most commonly occurs with a particular object. The default event doesn't occur automatically, just most often. For example, the event that's usually associated with a command button is the Click event. The default event for a form is Load. Table 8-1 lists the default events for Access objects.

TABLE 8-1 DEFAULT EVENTS FOR ACCESS OBJECTS

Default Event	Objects
Before Update	Combo box, list box, option group, and text box
Click	Form detail section, check box, command button, image, label, and option button
Enter	Subform
Format	All report sections
Load	Form
Open	Report
Updated	Bound and unbound object frame and chart

To start a sub procedure or a function procedure for an object's default event in the Code window, choose the object in the Object box. The default event automatically shows up in the Procedure box. Figure 8-1 shows the startup of a new procedure for a combo box control named Hours1 on the DARs form. The procedure attaches to the Before Update event property. If you want the procedure to be attached to a different event, choose a different procedure in the Procedure box.

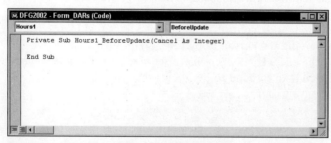

Figure 8-1: Starting a default event procedure.

The default event for the combo box control is `Before Update`. This event occurs after you have made a choice from the combo box list or entered a value but before you move to the next control on the form. When the combo box loses focus, the data in it is updated. This event is useful for confirming a change of data in the combo box or validating a new entry.

Another way to start a new procedure is to click the Build button (...) in the relevant event property in the object's property sheet and then choose Code Builder in the Choose Builder dialog box. This starts an event procedure that executes when the selected event occurs.

To see which events relate to an object, go to the VBE window and select the object name from the Object box. Then click the down-arrow next to the Procedure box to see the list of events. Figure 8-2 shows the list of events that can work with the Patrol Type combo box object in the DARs form.

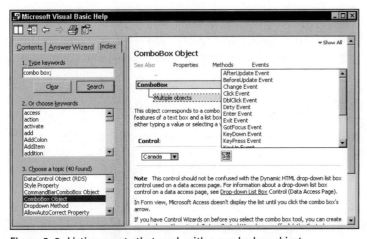

Figure 8-2: Listing events that work with a combo box object.

As you enter code in the VBE window, you get a lot of help from the editor. By setting the options mentioned in Chapter 7, you see lists of valid methods and constants and syntax details as you type.

More about Variables and Constants

You were introduced to variables and constants in Chapter 6 with some examples of declaring them in a procedure. To declare variables and constants of your own, you use a `Dim` or `Const` statement. The constants you define are called *symbolic constants*. There are many other useful types of constants that come with Access and VBA and other libraries such as DAO and ADO. We'll look at a few of these now.

Intrinsic constants

Intrinsic constants are automatically declared by Access for use in macros and VBA procedures. Access also provides access to many constants in other libraries. Functions, methods, and properties require specific intrinsic constants as arguments. The Object Explorer can show you the lists of intrinsic constants from all the libraries that your application references.

You can tell which object library owns the constant by its two-letter prefix, as follows:

- ◆ `ac` means Access

- ◆ `ad` indicates ADO

- ◆ `vb` refers to Visual Basic

ACCESS CONSTANTS

Just because you didn't define the constant doesn't mean that you can't use it just like your own. You can use intrinsic constants anywhere that you can use symbolic or user-defined constants. As an example of using Access constants, the following statement opens the DARs form in normal form view but in read-only mode.

```
DoCmd.OpenForm "DARs", acNormal, , , acFormReadOnly
```

Figure 8-3 shows the syntax for the `OpenForm` method in the Quick Info ScreenTip.

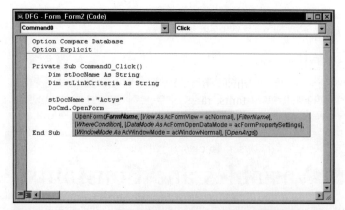

Figure 8-3: Checking the syntax for the `OpenForm` method.

The only required argument for the `OpenForm` method is the form name. The rest of the arguments are optional, but if you are using an argument that appears later in the syntax line, you must add the comma placeholders so that Access can tell which arguments you are providing. The `acNormal` constant is a member of the `AcFormView` class and is used here as the `View` argument. The `acFormReadOnly` constant is a member of the `AcFormOpenDataMode` class of constants and is used here as the `DataMode` argument. If you use the `acFormReadOnly` constant to open a form, the New Record button in the navigation bar is grayed out, and many of the editing menu commands and toolbar buttons are unavailable. You can't edit records or add new ones.

The current style for intrinsic Access constants is a mixture of uppercase and lowercase letters. In previous versions of Access, the parts of the constant names were separated by underscore characters, not by concatenating them into a single name. For example, what is now `acNext` used to be `A_NEXT` with a value of 1. Figure 8-4 shows the constant in the Object Browser window. All of these old intrinsic constants are listed as members of the `OldConstants` class. Even though these constants are no longer used, Access is backward compatible and still works with them without creating errors.

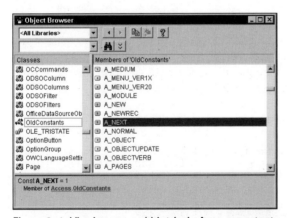

Figure 8-4: Viewing some old intrinsic Access constants.

VISUAL BASIC CONSTANTS

VBA is host to literally hundreds of intrinsic constants. The Visual Basic Constants help topic shows 23 categories of constants, ranging from `Calendar` constants to `VarType` constants. VBA claims that these constants work anywhere in your code in place of actual values. Figure 8-5 shows the list of Visual Basic constants displayed with the help of the Object Browser. To display this list, do the following:

1. Open the Object Browser and enter Constants in the Search Text box and click Search.

2. Select VBA Constants in the Search Results box and click the Help button.

3. In the Help topic for Constants (Object Browser) click the See Also link.

4. Select Visual Basic Constants in the Topics Found dialog box and click Display.

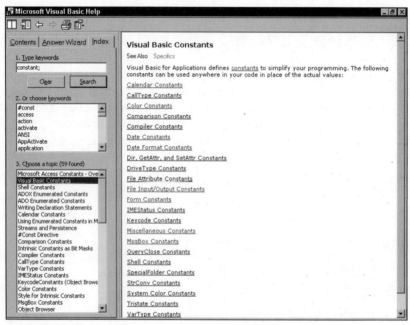

Figure 8-5: Viewing the list of Visual Basic constants.

For example, the following example determines whether the DARDate field is displayed in long or short date format in the form. This example executes when the form loads and displays a message box stating the current format of the DARDate field (as shown in Figure 8-6).

```
Private Sub Form_Load()

If Me!DARDate.Format = "Long Date" Then
    MsgBox "DARDate appears in long date format"
Else
    MsgBox "DARDate appears in short date format"
End If

End Sub
```

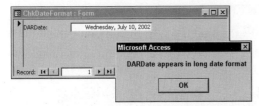

Figure 8-6: Displaying the current date format for the DARDate field.

You can insert several execution statements to change the date format if it is not what you want. Figure 8-7 shows the results of changing the date format to short date format if it is currently in long date format.

```
If Me!DARDate.Format = "Long Date" Then
    'Convert to Short Date format.
    Me!DARDate.Format = "Short Date"
    MsgBox "DARDate now appears in short date format"
Else
    MsgBox "DARDate already appears in short date format"
End If
```

Figure 8-7: Changing the date format with VBA.

One useful type of Visual Basic constant is the Keycode constant, which can identify which key was pressed to pass the key code to a VBA statement. For example, the vbKeyPageDown constant represents pressing Page Down.

SYSTEM-DEFINED CONSTANTS

System-defined constants are keywords that have a special meaning to Access. The constants True, False, and Null work anywhere in Access, including VBA, to create a conditional expression or to set a True/False property. Several other VBA functions test for the Null condition and perform specific actions if found to be true.

About enumerated constants

In previous versions of Access, the intrinsic constants stood alone, but starting with Access 2002, they are grouped in sets, called *enumerated constants*. You see these constants in the following instances:

◆ In drop-down lists as you enter code in the Code window (if you have checked the Auto List Members option in the Editor Options dialog box)

◆ When you are viewing the syntax line for a method, function, or property

As you reach an argument in the syntax, the list of enumerated constants appears. You must check the Auto Quick Info option for this feature to work.

The Object Browser lists the names of the sets of enumerated constants in the Class box. When you select a set, the list of members of that set appears in the Members of box. The following figure shows the set of AcCurrentView enumerated constants in the Object Browser window.

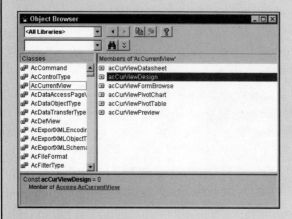

The figure illustrates the following important features:

◆ The Details pane at the bottom of the Object Browser window describes the class and the selected member; the class type is Enum and it is a member of the Access library.

◆ In the icons that accompany the class and member names, the single tablet icon represents an enumerated constant and the double tablet icon indicates a set of enumerated constants.

The old versions of these constants still work in most cases. If you were permitted to leave an argument blank in the earlier version, Access 2003 automatically inserts the default constant. You may have a problem if you run VB code by using Automation; in this case, a blank argument causes an error. This problem does not occur if you run the code directly in Access.

Common Procedures for Forms

Forms are active workplaces; VBA can speed your work. You can build sub and function procedures to accomplish the following tasks:

◆ Add a value to a combo box list

◆ Make decisions and act upon them

◆ Move around the form

◆ Filter records

◆ Set form and control properties

We present examples of what VBA can do for you in the following sections.

Adding an item to a combo box list

Combo box controls are a popular way of saving time while entering data. You simply choose a value from the drop-down list and move on. But what if the value that you want to put in that control is not on the list? If you have set the Limit To List property to Yes, the NotInList event occurs, and you see an error message about the value not being in the list.

This event can allow users to add an item to the list on the fly for temporary use in the current session. The NotInList event procedure is slightly different from those you've seen so far.

The procedure declaration statement names the procedure and declares the following two arguments:

◆ NewData is the string value that you entered in the combo box.

◆ Response is based on the integer constant that is returned by the MsgBox function. The value that is assigned to the Response argument determines how the event plays out.

The following procedure allows the user to add a new font size to a combo box control.

```
Private Sub FontSize_NotInList(NewData As String, _
Response As Integer)
Dim ctlComboBox As ComboBox
'Assign the ctlComboBox as the FontSize property.
Set ctlComboBox = Me!FontSize
'Prompt user to verify the added value.
If MsgBox("This value is not on the list. Add it?", _
    vbOKCancel) = vbOK Then
```

```
    'Set the Response argument to show item is added.
    Response = acDataErrAdded
    'Add the entered value to the row source with a semicolon.
    ctlComboBox.RowSource = ctlComboBox.RowSource & ";" & NewData
Else
    'User chooses Cancel, suppress error message and undo change.
    Response = acDataErrContinue
    ctlComboBox.Undo
End If
End Sub
```

Figure 8-8 shows the results of entering 15 in the FontSize combo box and pressing Enter. (The list does not include the value 15.)

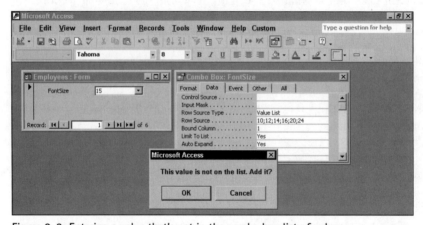

Figure 8-8: Entering a value that's not in the combo box list of values.

The MsgBox function syntax, displayed as follows, shows how this works:

```
MsgBox(prompt[, buttons] [, title][, helpfile, context])
```

In the MsgBox statement, only two of the arguments are used: prompt and buttons. The buttons constant, vbOKCancel, places only two buttons in the message box: OK and Cancel. The If...Then...Else statement tests for which button was clicked. If it was the vbOK button, the Response argument is set to acDataErrAdded. Then a semicolon and the NewData value are added to the RowSource property.

```
ctlComboBox.RowSource = ctlComboBox.RowSource & ";" & NewData
```

Figure 8-9 shows the value that was added to the RowSource property for the FontSize combo box.

If the Cancel button was clicked, the `Else` clause takes over and sets the `Response` argument to `acDataErrContinue`, and the value is not added to the list. The assignment of the `ctlComboBox` variable is also negated with the `Undo` method.

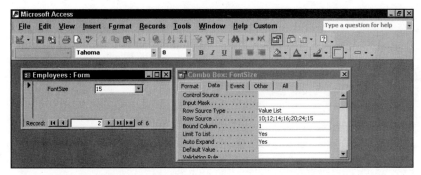

Figure 8-9: A new value has been added to the `RowSource` property.

The third Response constant, `acDataErrDisplay`, displays the default error message, and the user does not have the choice of adding the value to the list. If you're not going to allow additions to the value list, you don't need this event procedure. Just let the user see the default `NotInList` error message, as shown in Figure 8-10.

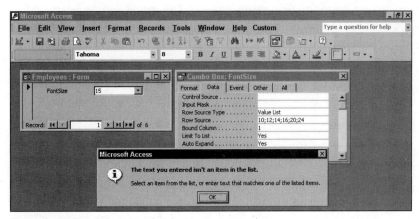

Figure 8-10: The default `NotInList` error message.

Any value that you add to the list in this manner is only temporary. When you close and reopen the form, the new value is no longer in the following lists:

◆ The Row Source list

◆ The combo box drop-down list

To add the value permanently, add it to the lookup list in the table definition or to the combo box's RowSource property.

If you have set the RowSource property to a separate table as the source of the values, you can use the NotInList event procedure to add new values to that table.

 The preceding example applies to unbound combo boxes. To add an item to a bound combo box, you are actually adding a value to a field in the underlying record source. This can cause a problem if other required fields or a primary key also needs to be added to a new record. The best approach is to prompt the user for all the required data, save the new record, and then requery the combo box.

Moving around a form

VBA can move among the controls in a form or display other records in the form. You can also create a filter to limit the records that you want to see or to find a specific record.

MOVING AMONG CONTROLS
The GoToControl method of the DoCmd object is the best way to move around from one control to another on a form in form view. The following statement moves focus to the LastName text box control:

```
DoCmd.GoToControl "LastName"
```

You can accomplish the same thing by using the following code:

```
Dim ctlMyControl As Control
Set ctlMyControl = Forms!DARs!LastName
DoCmd.GoToControl ctlMyControl.Name
```

To make the movement conditional, you can add an If...Then...Else structure. The following code looks at the Insurance Co. field, and if it shows None, focus skips the other insurance-related information controls and moves to the More Info memo field.

```
Dim strIns As String
Set strIns = [Insurance Co.]
'If there is no insurance company listed, move on.
If strIns = "None" Then
    DoCmd.GoToControl "More Info"
End If
```

To move focus to either another control on the form or to another form, you can use the SetFocus method instead. Use this statement to place the cursor on a specific control when the form opens or is updated with new records.

```
Forms!Volunteers!LastName.Setfocus
```

FINDING RECORDS

You have the following ways of finding records in a form or datasheet:

- ◆ Look for a record with the same value as appears in the current selection or control.

- ◆ Look for a specific value in a field or control, as follows:

  - ■ In datasheet or form view, use the Filter By Selection tool to find other records with the same values in that field or control.

  - ■ To locate a record with a specific value, choose Edit→Find.

Now you can carry out these searches with VBA by using either the FindRecord or GoToRecord method.

For example, the following code maximizes the DARs form when it opens and moves to the 10th record in the form:

```
Sub Private Sub Form_Open(Cancel As Integer)
DoCmd.Maximize
DoCmd.GoToRecord acDataForm, "DARs", acGoTo, 10
End Sub
```

The GoToRecord syntax requires only one expression, the object: DoCmd. All the other arguments are optional. For example, if you used the following code in the DARs form Open event, you would get the same result because the first argument is assumed to be the default acActiveData argument and the active form is the DARs form. The acGoTo argument is implied when you include the offset argument (10, in this case). Be sure to include the comma placeholders for the missing arguments, as follows:

```
DoCmd.GoToRecord, , , 10
```

The next block of code also maximizes the form upon opening. It then sets focus on the Code1 control and moves to the first record in the DARs form that has the value 424511 in the Code1 field. You could also add code to prompt the user for the search value.

```
Private Sub Form_Open(Cancel As Integer)
```

```
DoCmd.Maximize
Me.Code1.SetFocus
DoCmd.FindRecord "424511"
End Sub
```

The FindRecord method also has interesting syntax that mirrors the settings that you can specify in the Find and Replace dialog box, as follows:

```
Expression.FindRecord(FindWhat, Match, MatchCase, Search, _
    SearchAsFormatted, OnlyCurrentField, FindFirst)
```

The required expression is again the DoCmd object, and FindWhat (424511 in the preceding private sub routine) is the only required argument. The other arguments accomplish the following tasks:

- Match: Specifies where to find the data in the field, as follows:
  - Anywhere in the field
  - The whole field (this is the default)
  - The beginning of the field
- Matchcase: Determines whether the search is case sensitive. The default is False.
- Search: Specifies the search direction and length, as follows:
  - From the current record up to the first record
  - From the current record down to the last record
  - All records (this is the default)
- SearchAsFormatted: Determines whether the search matches the values that are displayed, not what is stored. The default is False.
- OnlyCurrentField: Determines whether the search is limited to the current field instead of including all the fields in each record. The default is True.
- FindFirst: Determines whether the search starts at the first record instead of the current record. The default is True.

FILTERING RECORDS

To see only the records that contain information about a certain subject, you can prompt the user to enter the relevant value and then use VBA code to set the filter. For example, the following code asks the user for the activity code that she is interested in and then applies the filter:

```
Private Sub Command6_Click()
Dim strCode As String
strCode = " [Activity Code] = " _
```

```
        & InputBox("Enter the activity code", "Filter records")
Me.Filter = strCode
Me.FilterOn = True
End Sub
```

 To be safe, add the statement `strCode = " "` to start with a blank filter. This ensures that nothing is carried over from another procedure.

Figure 8-11 shows the Input Box that requests the filter string, and Figure 8-12 shows the form with only the records that relate to the entered Activity Code value.

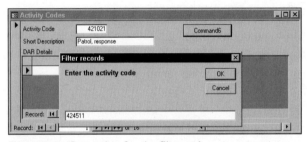

Figure 8-11: Prompting for the filter string.

Figure 8-12: The results of filtering the records in the form.

After viewing the filtered records in the form, the user can simply click the Remove Filter toolbar button to get all the records back.

Allowing edits in a read-only form

You may have a form that contains relatively static data, such as employee information that is used mostly as a lookup form. To guard against unwanted data changes, you have set the form's `Allow Edits` property to No. But occasionally, some of the data changes. For example, an employee changes her home phone number to avoid the dinnertime solicitors or gets married and changes her last name. So you decide to edit the data while you have the form open, but the property setting prevents you from editing the data.

You could switch to form design view, change the property to Yes, make the changes, and restore the property to No. It is easier to add a command button that changes the property on the fly and keeps it that way until you are finished changing the record. Then, when you save the record, the property reverts to No (or False in VBA speak).

Add a new command button without the help of the Command Button Wizard, and attach the following code to the button's On Click event property:

```
Private Sub Edit_Record_Click()
'Sets the Allow Edits property to Yes
Me.AllowEdits = True
'Moves the cursor to the first text box field.
LastName.SetFocus
End Sub
```

When you finish editing the current record, you want the read-only mode to be reset. The form's After Update event occurs when you save the record, either by moving to another record or by choosing Records→Save Record. So you can attach an event procedure to the On After Update event property that restores the ban on editing, as follows:

```
Private Sub Form_AfterUpdate()
'Resets the read-only property
Me.AllowEdits = False
'Displays message that edit is completed.
MsgBox "Edit complete."
End Sub
```

Figure 8-13 shows the result of using the new Edit command button to make changes in a record in the Volunteers form that is set to prevent editing. After the record is saved, you see a message to that effect.

The only problem with this is that you may not have made any changes in the data after all, so this event doesn't occur. You still want to reset the read-only restriction, so attach a similar procedure to the form's On Current property. This time, omit the MsgBox function, or you see the message every time you open the form. Use the following code:

```
Private Sub Form_Current()
'Resets the read-only property
Me.AllowEdits = False
End Sub
```

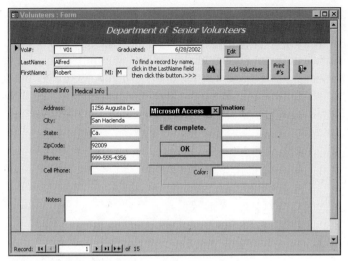

Figure 8-13: Editing data in a read-only form.

Entering and validati3ng data

The list of procedures that are used to guarantee that complete and error-free data is entered into the database is very long and limited only by your imagination. In addition to the properties that you can set to validate data, you can use VBA to help in the following ways:

◆ Make sure that you enter complete information into a record on the form. You can attach the following code to the LostFocus event of a required text box control, Field2 in this example. If Field1 has the value ABC, Field2 must also contain a value.

```
Private Sub Field2_OnLostFocus()
Dim strMsg As String, strKey as String
Dim ctlField As Control
strMsg = "You must enter a Field2 value for an ABC
transaction."
strKey = [Field1]                 'Set the value of the key to
the Field1 value.
ctlField = Me!Field1
If [Field1] = "ABC" And  [Field2] = "" Then
    MsgBox = strMsg               'Display the error message
    DoCmd.GoToControl ctlField    'Move back to Field1
    DoCmd.FindRecord strKey       'Find the record
    Me.Field2.SetFocus            'Return focus to Field2
End If
End Sub
```

◆ Make sure that you enter a field value in a bound text box control. If you had not set the field's `Required` property in the table design to Yes, the following code can make sure that the entry is made. Use the `IsNull` function to test the contents of the field. Attach the procedure to the form's `Before Update` event so that it executes when you try to save the record and move on to the next one.

```
Private Sub Form_BeforeUpdate(Cancel As Integer)
If IsNull(LastName) Then
    MsgBox "LastName is required"
    DoCmd.GoToRecord , , acLast 'Move back to previous record
    LastName.SetFocus     'Move cursor back toLastName field.
End If
End Sub
```

Figure 8-14 shows the result of trying to leave the `LastName` field blank.

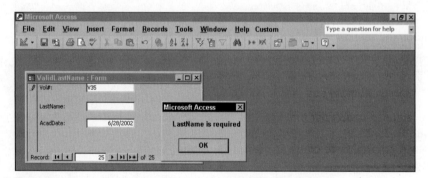

Figure 8-14: A message appears if the `LastName` field is left blank.

When you are looking for blank fields, there is a difference between zero-length strings and Null values. If the user skips the field, the result is Null. If the user presses the spacebar, the result is a zero-length string. So, in this case, use the `IsNull` function to test for a blank field.

Setting form and control properties

The following examples set properties with VBA.

The following three statements set the tab properties for three of the text box controls on the current form. These statements can be included in the form's `OnCurrent` event procedure:

◆ `TabStop` **property:** Determines whether you can reach a control by pressing Tab. When set to False, you can still reach it by clicking in the control.

```
Me!LastName.TabStop = False
Me!FirstName.TabIndex = 5
Me!Address.AutoTab = False
```

♦ TabIndex **property:** Determines the control's place in the tab order. This statement places the FirstName control in 6th place (the tab order index starts with 0).

♦ AutoTab **property:** Keeps the cursor from automatically moving to the next field in the tab order when the last character in the Input Mask property for the Address field is entered.

The following is an example of changing form properties at the same time as control properties:

```
Private Sub Form_Open(Cancel As Integer)
'Removes both scrollbars and adds the record selector.
'Adds a caption and a ScreenTip to the command button.
'Adds a status bar message for the Activity Code control.
Me.RecordSelectors = True
Me.ScrollBars = 0
Me.Caption = "DAR Activity Codes"
Me!Command6.Caption = "&Find Code"
Me!Command6.ControlTipText = "Click to find activity code"
Me![Activity Code].StatusBarText = "Enter Acty code"
End Sub
```

TIP Some properties can't be set in VBA. Check with the Help index to find out from which view to set the property. For example, BorderStyle can only be set in the form design view.

Common Procedures Used with Reports

Reports are more static than forms because they are relatively inactive. You can still use VBA to set properties and options for previewing and printing reports, as described in the following items:

♦ If you are preparing an important business report and want certain data to stand out, you can add conditional formatting to the design.

♦ You can cancel printing automatically if the report contains no data.

◆ You can suppress printing of one or more sections of the report.

For example, you have created a report with most of the important information in the report footer, and you want to save space by omitting all the information in the detail section.

◆ You can force a new page when a certain condition arises.

The next sections describe the code that applies in these situations.

Applying conditional formatting

You can create a simple procedure that tests the value of one of the text box controls in the report and, based on that value, change the appearance of the data before previewing or printing the report.

The following example looks at the DueDate value in the underlying data source; if the date is earlier than the current system date, the control colors change, as follows:

```
Private Sub Detail_Format(Cancel As Integer, FormatCount As Integer)
'Set the font weight constants
Const conHeavy = 900
Const conNormal = 400
'Test the DueDate value, if earlier than today, make changes.
If DueDate < Date Then
    DueDate.BackColor = vbYellow
    DueDate.ForeColor = vbBlack
    DueDate.FontWeight = conHeavy
Else
    DueDate.BackColor = vbBlack
    DueDate.ForeColor = vbWhite
    DueDate.FontWeight = conNormal
End If
End Sub
```

The procedure executes when the detail section is formatted for preview. Figure 8-15 shows the result of previewing the report with these format changes.

Controlling printing

If the underlying record source of the report contains no data, the NoData event can cancel printing a blank report. The NoData event applies to the entire report object, not an individual section, as follows:

```
Private Sub Report_NoData(Cancel As Integer)
MsgBox "No data in recordset. Printing cancelled."
End Sub
```

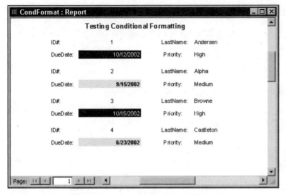

Figure 8-15: Formatting a report conditionally.

There are ways to keep a section from showing up in preview or print:

◆ Set the section's visible property to False.

◆ Attach the following statement to the section's `Format` event:

```
Private Sub PageHeaderSection_Format(Cancel As Integer,
FormatCount As Integer)
Me.PrintSection = False
End Sub
```

A couple of other properties are handy when printing reports that can vary in size. The `Can Grow` and `Can Shrink` properties adjust the height of a form or report section to fit all the data that the section contains. The following statements set both of these properties for the detail section of the current report:

```
Me.Section(acDetail).CanGrow = True
Me.Section(acDetail).CanShrink = true
```

The `ForceNewPage` property is more complicated. This property has the following settings:

◆ **None** (0 in VBA): Prints the current section on the current page. This is the default.

◆ **Before Section** (1 in VBA): Prints the current section at the top of a new page.

◆ **After Section** (2 in VBA): Prints the section immediately following the current section at the top of a new page.

◆ **Before & After** (3 in VBA): Prints the following sections:

- Prints the current section at the top of a new page.

- Prints the following section at the top of another new page.

For example, if you want to have the company title and watermark printed on the first page and the rest of the report to begin on the next page, attach the following statements to the Format event of the report header section:

```
Me.Section(acHeader).ForceNewPage = 2
```

You can also test for the settings of many of these properties by setting a constant to the property. For example, to see the current setting of the report header section's ForceNewPage property, use the following statements:

```
Dim intSeeVal As Integer
intSeeVal = Reports![MyReport].Section(acHeader).ForceNewPage
MsgBox intSeeVal
```

Working with Tables and Queries

Many VBA methods can be used to work with tables and queries. You can run a query to find specific information based on the user's input or use the popular DLookup function to accomplish the same type of search. When your database grows beyond its practical size, you can run an action SQL query to archive or delete the outdated records.

The following example can run in a function to display the description for the activity code 423610:

```
Dim dbs As Database
Dim rst As Recordset
Dim strSQL As String

strSQL = "SELECT [Activity Codes].[Description] FROM " _
& "[Activity Codes] " _
& "WHERE [Activity Codes].[Activity Code] " _
& "= 423610"

Set dbs = CurrentDb
Set rst = dbs.OpenRecordset(strSQL)
MsgBox rst!Description
```

To see the activity code with the description in the message box, use the following text for the MsgBox statement:

```
MsgBox "423610: " &Chr(10) & Chr(13) & rst!Description
```

The Chr(10) and Chr(13) ASCII character codes add a carriage return and line feed to the message that appears in the message box, creating a two-line message. Don't enclose the whole expression in quotation marks, or it all appears in the message.

If you want the user to be able to enter the activity code and find the description, use the DLookup function as follows:

```
Public Function FindACDescription()
'This function brings up the description of any
'activity code that the user enters into the input box.

Dim lngActivityCode As Long

strActivityCode = "[Activity Code] = " _
& InputBox("Enter an activity code")
MsgBox DLookup("Description", "Activity Codes", strActivityCode)

End Function
```

The RunSQL method is used with the DoCmd object to run an action query such as Append, Delete, or MakeTable. If you simply want to query a database, create a query definition object using a SELECT SQL statement.

Creating queries is discussed in Chapter 9.

The following example uses the RunSQL method to delete outdated DAR reports:

```
Dim strSQL As String
'This example deletes any DARs that are older than
'74 days.

strSQL = "DELETE DARs.*, DARs.DARDate  FROM DARs " _
    & "WHERE (((DARs.DARDate)<=Date()-75));"
DoCmd.RunSQL strSQL
```

This block of code can work in a function with a similar block of code that stores the old records in an archive table, as discussed in the next section.

Requesting User Information

If the user wants to be able to decide which records are to be saved, you can create a procedure that prompts for the parameters to be used.

The following example uses the InputBox function to gather the starting and ending dates for the range of records to remove from the table:

```
Private Sub ArchiveDARsBetweenDates()

'This procedure appends a set of records from the DARs table
'where the dates are between the time range input by the user.
Dim dbs As Database
Dim rst As Recordset
Dim strSQL As String
Dim dteSDate As Date
Dim dteEDate As Date
'Turn off the warning about deleting records.
DoCmd.SetWarnings False

dteSDate = InputBox("Enter Start Date")
dteEDate = InputBox("Enter End Date")

strSQL = "INSERT INTO DARArchive SELECT DARs.* " _
& "FROM DARs WHERE (((DARs.DARDate) Between " _
& "#" & dteSDate & "# And #" & dteEDate & "#));"

DoCmd.RunSQL strSQL
'Restore the warning window.
DoCmd.SetWarnings True
End Sub
```

You can attach this procedure to a command button that the user can click when he wants to archive some of the older records.

To protect against a missing date, you can add an If...Then...Else statement with the Len function to cover the situation where the user doesn't enter one or both date values. The Len function returns the number of characters in a string. For this, change the date variables from the date data type to the variant type so that you can check for a zero-length string. If a date is missing, display a message to the user and end the function by using the following code:

```
Private Sub ArchiveDARsBetweenDates()
Dim dbs As Database
Dim rst As Recordset
Dim strSQL As String
Dim varSDate As Variant
Dim varEDate As Variant

DoCmd.SetWarnings False
varSDate = InputBox("Enter Start Date")
varEDate = InputBox("Enter End Date")

'Check for dates in both entries.
If Len(varSDate) = 0 Or Len(varEDate) = 0 Then
    MsgBox ("Skipped for now. Need both dates.")
    Exit Sub
End If

strSQL = "INSERT INTO DARArchive SELECT DARs.* " _
    & "FROM DARs WHERE (((DARs.DARDate) Between " _
    & "#" & varSDate & "# And #" & varEDate & "#));"

DoCmd.RunSQL strSQL
DoCmd.SetWarnings True
End Sub
```

TIP Use quotation marks carefully in the SQL statement. One way to make sure that the statement is correct is to create a query that creates the same result in query design view and then look at the SQL view of the query. You can copy and paste the SQL statement into the VBA code.

Summary

In this chapter, we have given you a closer look at some of the ways that VBA code can work with forms and reports. This chapter has also described some of the ways that you can get information from the users and help prevent errors from creeping into your database. In the next chapter, we put all the pieces together and show you how to create complete, useful, and innovative procedures for your application.

Chapter 9

Building a Sub Procedure

IN THIS CHAPTER

- ◆ Declaring and scoping sub procedures
- ◆ Planning what you need in the procedures
- ◆ Running sub procedures
- ◆ Examples of code for Access objects
- ◆ Handling run-time errors
- ◆ Improving performance

A PROCEDURE IS A BLOCK OF VBA statements that carries out a specific task. A procedure can be as short as a single statement or can contain several hundred statements. Two VBA statement types exist: sub procedures and function procedures. The main difference is that a function procedure returns a value while a sub procedure does not. This chapter concentrates on sub procedures. (Chapter 11 focuses on making function procedures work for you.)

Declaring a Sub Procedure

The declaration statement requires the following elements:

- ◆ Sub keyword
- ◆ Procedure name
- ◆ End Sub statement

The Sub declaration syntax shows several optional elements, as follows:

```
[Private | Public | Friend] [Static] Sub name ([arglist])
```

TIP When you name a new procedure, give it a name that explicitly describes its purpose, for example, `AddDAR`, `PrintSVInfo`, or `FindSV`. If you need to use more than a single word, connect them with underscore characters, for example, `Sort_DARs` or `Print_Smry`.

A sub procedure declaration has the following optional elements:

- `Private`: Limits the procedure to other procedures within the same module.

- `Public`: Makes the procedure available to all the other procedures and modules in the current project.

- `Friend`: Makes the procedure callable from modules outside the class but part of the project within which the class is defined.

  This element is used only with form and class modules, not standard modules.

- `Static`: Preserves the value of the local variables between procedure calls. This option applies only to variables created in this procedure, not to those used by this procedure but created in another procedure.

- `arglist`: The list of variables that are passed to the procedure when it executes. The names are separated by commas, and the list is enclosed in parentheses. If no arguments are needed, just use the empty parentheses.

- `statements`: VBA code to be carried out by the procedure.

- `Exit Sub`: Forces an abnormal exit from the procedure before reaching the normal End Sub statement.

  If the procedure were called by another procedure, processing resumes at the statement following the one that called the procedure; otherwise the procedure just stops. More than one `Exit Sub` statement can be used; in several conditions, you would want to exit the procedure.

Looking at the arguments

Some procedures need information from you to run. These arguments are passed to the procedure when it executes. For example, in Chapter 8, the `FontSize_NotInList` sub procedure received the argument `NewData` when it executed in response to an unrecognized font size entry. `NewData` assumes the characters that are entered in the combo box control.

```
Sub FontSize_NotInList(NewData As String, Response As Integer)
```

The procedure requested an OK or Cancel from the user and then set the `Response` argument accordingly, either to add the value to the combo box list or to abandon it and display a message to the user that the addition was canceled. These arguments are both used internally by the procedure and not returned to the user.

The argument list has the following structure and syntax:

```
[Optional][ByVal|ByRef][ParamArray] varname [()][As
type][=defaultvalue]
```

The only required element is the name of the argument, `varname`. The optional elements are as follows:

- ◆ `Optional`: Indicates that the listed argument is not mandatory; the procedure can run without it. If more than one argument is passed, all subsequent arguments are also declared optional. This option doesn't work for ParamArray arguments.

- ◆ `ByVal`: Indicates that the value of the argument is passed.

- ◆ `ByRef`: Indicates that the argument is passed by referring to the address of another variable to use as the argument.

- ◆ `ParamArray`: Indicates that the argument in the list is an array of Variant elements. This type of argument can pass a varying number of arguments. If you use this, it must be the last element in the argument list, and it can't be used with `ByVal` or `ByRef`.

- ◆ `varname`: The name that represents the argument to be used in the procedure. If the argument is an array, you must specify the dimensions of the array in parentheses.

- ◆ `type`: Indicates the data type of the argument. This option uses the same elements as a variable declaration statement.

- ◆ `=defaultvalue`: Any constant or expression that evaluates to a constant to be used as the default value for an optional argument.

 TIP By default, arguments are passed by reference (which takes only 4 bytes of space). If you include the `ByVal` keyword, the original variable is copied; this can take more space depending on the data type. So, it is more efficient to pass arguments, especially string and variant types, by reference.

Scoping a sub procedure

You can set the scope for individual procedures within the module. The scope of a procedure determines whether other procedures can call it.

The following keyword elements of the Sub statement specify the scope of the procedure:

♦ Public: The procedure can be called by a procedure in any module in the current project. Both of the following procedures are declared as public:

```
Sub Form_Load()
    [statements]
End Sub

Public Sub Command6()
    [statements]
End Sub
```

♦ Private: Limits procedure calls to the current module. An example is as follows:

```
Private Sub Form_AfterUpdate()
```

 TIP Keeping procedures private within a module can help prevent errors that can occur when one procedure changes the value of a variable whose name is also used by another procedure.

You can use the Private keyword at the module level to force all the procedures and functions within it to be private. Then, even if you declare a sub as public, it is still private. Simply add the following statement before the first Sub or Function statement in the module:

```
Option Private Module
```

Planning a Sub Procedure

Thinking ahead is always a good idea. This concept also applies when you are building VBA procedures. When you are starting a new application, split it into small increments, each performing a specific task. It is easier to debug and maintain an application if it is not a complex web of intertwined actions.

The example we present here is a real-world situation. The Senior Volunteer organization spends a lot of time helping regular law enforcement personnel by providing nonconfrontational services. The volunteers visit protected sites and make sure that the fences and gates are intact. They deliver documents to courthouses throughout the county and provide public services, such as dispensing public safety information and responding to telephone calls.

Each volunteer is required to fill out a Daily Activity Report (DAR), which lists the hours spent on each activity and provides details of each activity. The chief wants to be kept informed about the work that the volunteers are doing, so we are to provide, among other reports, a summary of the hours spent on each activity. Figure 9-1 shows the data-entry form where all the volunteer activities are logged.

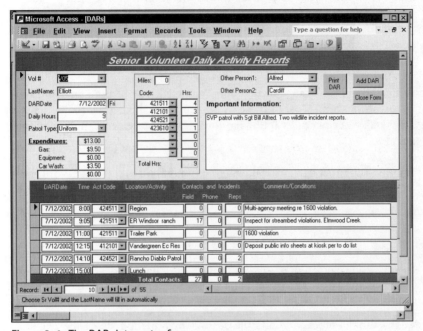

Figure 9-1: The DAR data-entry form.

This special form is based on a query that links two tables: the DAR table and the DAR Details table. We use this form to enter all the DAR data and to view specific DAR information. The entered data goes directly into the two underlying tables. The following special features in this form are not VBA related, but they are interesting nevertheless:

◆ The Vol # control is a 2-column combo box that shows both the volunteer ID number and the last name when you click the down arrow. When you choose Vol # from the list, the last name is automatically entered into the LastName control. The Row Source property for the combo box is SELECT SrVols.[Vol#],SrVols.LastName FROM SrVols;.

◆ When you enter the DAR date, the corresponding day of the week appears automatically in the unbound control to the right of the DARDate control. The WeekDay control Data property is =Format([DARDate], "ddd"). The date is also automatically entered into the DARDate control in the subform.

◆ As you add expenditures for gas, car washes, etc., the total appears in the top row of the group. The Expenditures control Data property is =[Gas]+[Equipment]+[Car Wash]+[Other].

♦ As you add hours in each of the Hrs controls, they are totaled and displayed in the Total Hrs control. The Total Hours Data property is an
expression that adds all the Hrs entries (1 through 7).

♦ In the subform, as you enter the number of contacts and reports for each
activity, they are totaled and displayed in the Total Contacts controls in
the subform footer section. These summary controls use the Sum() function. For example, the Total Field Contacts Data property is =Sum([#
Physical Contacts]).

Several small blocks of code execute when you click one of the command buttons at the top of the form. Most of these commands were created by the Command
Button Wizard, as you can see by following the OnError statements that the wizard
always includes:

♦ The first sub procedure, as follows, simply maximizes the form to fill the
window when it opens:

```
Private Sub Form_Open(Cancel As Integer)
DoCmd.Maximize
End Sub
```

♦ The next procedures, described as follows, respond to clicking the AddDAR,
CloseDAR, and PrintDAR command buttons (I added the comments to the
code):

■ The AddDAR procedure uses the GoToRecord method, using the
acNewRecord intrinsic constant to move to a new blank form.

■ The CloseDAR procedure simply closes the form and returns to the
database window.

■ The PrintDAR procedure prints the current DAR form and the form
remains open.

```
Private Sub AddDAR_Click()
'Moves to new empty form.
On Error GoTo Err_AddDAR_Click
    DoCmd.GoToRecord , , acNewRec
Exit_AddDAR_Click:
    Exit Sub
Err_AddDAR_Click:
    MsgBox Err.Description
    Resume Exit_AddDAR_Click
End Sub
```

```
Private Sub CloseDAR_Click()
'Closes DARs form.
On Error GoTo Err_CloseDAR_Click
    DoCmd.Close
Exit_CloseDAR_Click:
    Exit Sub
Err_CloseDAR_Click:
    MsgBox Err.Description
    Resume Exit_CloseDAR_Click
End Sub

Private Sub PrintDAR_Click()
'Prints the current DAR form
On Error GoTo Err_PrintDAR_Click
    DoCmd.DoMenuItem acFormBar, acEditMenu, 8, , acMenuVer70
    DoCmd.PrintOut acSelection
Exit_PrintDAR_Click:
    Exit Sub
Err_PrintDAR_Click:
    MsgBox Err.Description
    Resume Exit_PrintDAR_Click
End Sub
```

◆ The last block of code is slightly different because it uses the DoMenuItem method to call upon a command in the Edit menu on the Form View command bar; the command should be Select Record. However, Select Record is the 11th command in the Access 2003 Edit menu. You can change that element to the intrinsic constant acSelectRecord to ensure that it is the right command. The final argument in the DoCmd.DoMenuItem statement is the intrinsic constant acMenuVer70. This method was written for Access 95 databases and is still used in the wizard's code.

In Access 97, the DoMenuItem method was replaced by the RunCommand method. DoMenuItem is still included for compatibility with earlier versions of Access. If you were writing the code yourself, you would probably use the latter RunCommand method of the DoCmd object, as follows:

```
DoCmd.RunCommand acCmdSelectRecord
```

TIP

Use the Object Browser in the VBA window to find just the right intrinsic constant for the method.

Facing the programming problem

The problem that we face is how to summarize data that appears in different fields in the underlying query. Specifically, we want to sum the hours that are spent on each activity over all the volunteers. Unfortunately, the hours are listed in seven different fields because the volunteers may do up to seven different jobs per day, and each must be documented separately. When a volunteer reports her day's activities, several different activity codes are available, each with a number of hours attributed to it, as shown previously in Figure 9-1.

If we put all the pairs of activity codes and associated hours from all the DARs in a separate table, it is easy to build a query to summarize the hours per activity code. So, we built a ghost table named CodeHrs with only two fields: Activity Code and Hours.

As we worked on the solution, we decided to add a primary key ID# field with the AutoNumber data type (just to keep Access from bugging us about not having a primary key) and the DARDate field so that we could summarize by month if necessary. Figure 9-2 is an table to collect activity code hours.

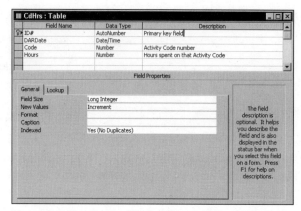

Figure 9-2: Creating a table to collect activity code hours.

Next, we created a series of Append queries to extract the Code and Hrs fields from the DARs table and place them in the new CdHrs table. This required an Append query for each of the seven sets of codes and hours in the DAR. The sub procedure runs when the CdHrs report opens. The report itself is based on a query that links the CdHrs table with the Activity Codes table to get the description of the code. The query also summarizes the hours by code.

After declaring the strSQL string variable, the first statement turns off the warning messages so that the user doesn't panic at the warning message indicating that records are about to be deleted. Then, the action query deletes all the records from the CdHrs table so that it is empty before inserting the new Activity Code and Hours values. The append query SQL statement adds the record only if the hours are not equal to 0. The last statement before End Sub restores the warning messages.

Here is the sub procedure that is attached to the On Open event property of the Activity Code Summary report. The procedure adds up the hours spent on each activity on a daily basis.

```
Private Sub Report_Open(Cancel As Integer)
'A Delete query removes all records from the CdHrs table then
'Populates the CdHrs table using a series of append queries.
'The seven append queries place the seven sets of Activity Codes
'and corresponding Hours from the DAR into a single table.

Dim strSQL As String
'The next statement turns off the warning messages.
DoCmd.SetWarnings False

'The query deletes all records from the CdHrs table.
strSQL = "DELETE CdHrs.* FROM CdHrs;"
DoCmd.RunSQL strSQL

'The next seven append queries populate the CdHrs table.
strSQL = "INSERT INTO CdHrs ( DARDate, Code, Hours ) " & _
    "SELECT DARs.DARDate, DARs.Code1, DARs.Hours1" & _
    "FROM DARs " & _
    "WHERE (((DARs.Hours1)<>0));"
DoCmd.RunSQL strSQL
strSQL = "INSERT INTO CdHrs ( DARDate, Code, Hours )" & _
    "SELECT DARs.DARDate, DARs.Code2, DARs.Hours2 " & _
    "FROM DARs WHERE (((DARs.Hours2)<>0));"
DoCmd.RunSQL strSQL

strSQL = "INSERT INTO CdHrs ( DARDate, Code, Hours )" & _
    "SELECT DARs.DARDate, DARs.Code3, DARs.Hours3 " & _
    "FROM DARs WHERE (((DARs.Hours3)<>0));"
DoCmd.RunSQL strSQL

strSQL = "INSERT INTO CdHrs ( DARDate, Code, Hours )" & _
    "SELECT DARs.DARDate, DARs.Code4, DARs.Hours4 " & _
    "FROM DARs WHERE (((DARs.Hours4)<>0));"
DoCmd.RunSQL strSQL

strSQL = "INSERT INTO CdHrs ( DARDate, Code, Hours )" & _
    "SELECT DARs.DARDate, DARs.Code5, DARs.Hours5 " & _
    "FROM DARs WHERE (((DARs.Hours5)<>0));"
DoCmd.RunSQL strSQL
```

```
strSQL = "INSERT INTO CdHrs ( DARDate, Code, Hours )" & _
    "SELECT DARs.DARDate, DARs.Code6, DARs.Hours6 " & _
    "FROM DARs WHERE (((DARs.Hours6)<>0));"
DoCmd.RunSQL strSQL

strSQL = "INSERT INTO CdHrs ( DARDate, Code, Hours )" & _
    "SELECT DARs.DARDate, DARs.Code7, DARs.Hours7 " & _
    "FROM DARs WHERE (((DARs.Hours7)<>0));"
DoCmd.RunSQL strSQL

DoCmd.SetWarnings True

End Sub
```

Figure 9-3 shows the result of running this Append query procedure. Notice that the status bar displays the description of the selected field, Hours1.

ID#	DARDate	Code	Hours
3564	7/10/2002	423110	1
3509	7/10/2002	421021	7
3528	7/10/2002	424511	4
3508	7/10/2002	421021	7
3563	7/10/2002	423110	1
3606	7/11/2002	421511	2
3566	7/11/2002	421021	1
3565	7/11/2002	421021	1
3605	7/11/2002	421511	2
3513	7/11/2002	423110	5
3512	7/11/2002	423110	5
3511	7/11/2002	423110	5
3510	7/11/2002	423110	5
3581	7/12/2002	421021	6
3582	7/12/2002	412101	3
3607	7/12/2002	423110	1
3532	7/12/2002	424511	2
3616	7/12/2002	424521	1
3584	7/12/2002	424521	6
3619	7/12/2002	423610	1
3529	7/12/2002	424521	2
3530	7/12/2002	421511	4
3567	7/12/2002	424521	3
3514	7/12/2002	421511	4

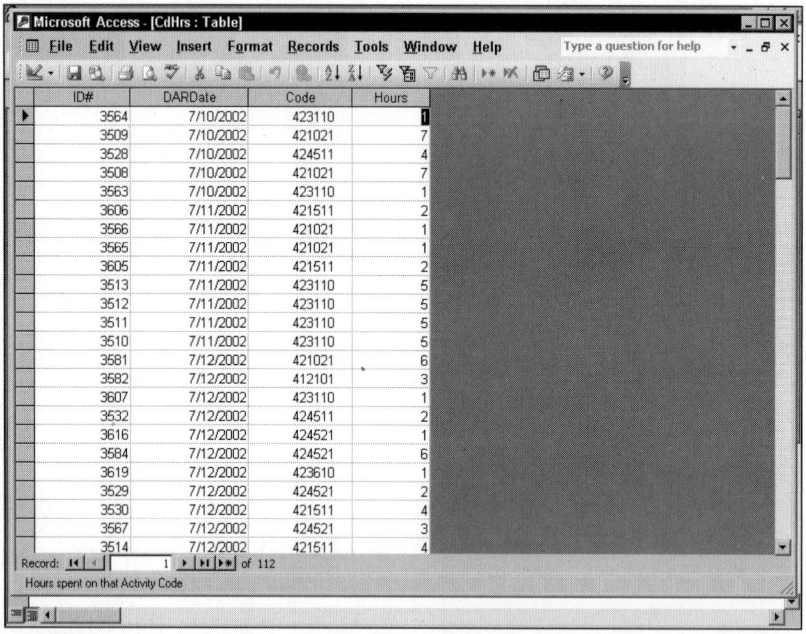

Figure 9-3: Filling the CdHrs table for the summary report

NOTE: The RunSQL method works only with action queries or data definition queries. To run a simple select query in VBA, create the query design in Access and then open the form or report based on that query in a procedure.

The select query that provides the record source for the report performs the following tasks:

◆ Groups the records by code.

◆ Totals the hours for each code.

◆ Sorts the results in descending order by total hours. (The activity that received the most attention is first in the list.)

Figure 9-4 shows the query design, and Figure 9-5 previews the resulting CdHrs report.

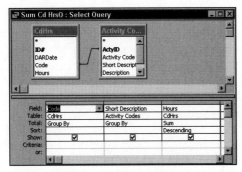

Figure 9-4: The summarizing query.

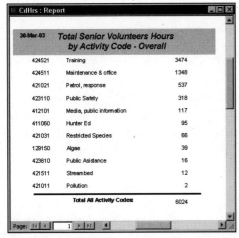

Figure 9-5: The resulting Activity Code Hours report.

More planning strategies

As you work with your client and discover how he works and what he wants out of the application, you can add more features to the project, such as the following:

◆ Visual and audio features to keep the user focused and prevent random key presses

◆ Customized help in the form of screen tips and status bar messages

◆ Compiled help topics that appear when the user clicks the What's This? button

ADDING SENSORY FEATURES

When a procedure, such as a complex transaction process, takes a while to execute, no visual or audio indications tell you that the procedure is still running. The user may think that the system has stopped working and begin pressing keys at random. It is a good idea to provide some evidence that all is well.

Changing the default cursor to an animated hourglass icon can convince the user that the procedure is still running properly. When the lengthy process is over, convert the cursor back to the default icon by using the following code:

```
DoCmd.HourGlass True     'Changes the cursor to the hourglass
    [long process]
DoCmd.HourGlass False    'Converts back to default
```

You can combine the visual evidence of an ongoing process with a sound that indicates its completion. Use the Beep command or the Beep method to send a sound through the system speaker. Both DoCmd.Beep and simply Beep can create the sound.

TIP Beeps can be a big help during debugging. Place the DoCmd.Beep statement in several places within the code. If you count the number of beeps that occurred, you can tell how far the procedure went before encountering an error.

REQUESTING USER INPUT

As you have seen in previous examples, you can use several built-in functions to get user input. The MsgBox function is primarily intended to deliver information, but it can also accept the response from the user and pass it on. The dialog box is modal (it remains open, waiting for a response). When the user clicks one of the buttons, an integer is returned to the code. For example, the MsgBox dialog box shown in Figure 9-6 appears when you save a new record and either moves to a new blank record in the form or closes the form.

```
Response = MsgBox("Record saved. Do you want to add another?", _
    vbQuestion + vbYesNo, "More Data?")
If Response = vbYes Then
    DoCmd.GoToRecord, , acNew
Else
    DoCmd.Close
End If
```

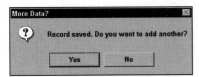

Figure 9-6: Getting a response with a MsgBox function.

The InputBox function also displays a prompt and waits for a response from the user. The response could be entering a value in the text box or clicking one of the buttons. The InputBox function returns the string value of what is entered in the text box. For example, the InputBox dialog box shown in Figure 9-7 prompts for the Region Number to be used as a filter for records in a report. The default Region Number is set to 5.

```
Dim strRegion As String
Dim strFilter As String
strRegion = InputBox("Enter Region Number.", "Region Review","5")
strFilter = "[Region]= """ & strRegion & """"
```

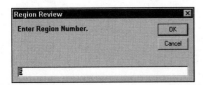

Figure 9-7: Using the InputBox function to get user input.

Chapter 12 contains more information about using the MsgBox and InputBox functions.

PLANNING FOR ERRORS

The Microsoft Access message that you see when an error occurs is not always as informative as it could be. When you are designing an application, consider the errors that can happen and try to create more useful messages, even with helpful remedies for the problem.

For example, if the user tries to save a file to a disk and the disk is not in the proper drive, you can trap that error and display a custom message. The Disk not ready error is #71, so you can add the following code to the procedure:

```
On Error GoTo Error_Handler
    [statements]
Exit Sub    'Branches to End Sub so won't run the error
            'handler every time the procedure executes.
Error_Handler:
    If Err = 71 Then
        MsgBox "Disk is not ready. Check drive and try again"
    Else            'Display built-in error message
MsgBox "Error number " & Err.Number & ": " & _
Err.Description
    End If
Resume Next
End Sub
```

You can find more about trapping and handling run-time errors in the section "Dealing with Errors," later in this chapter.

Chapter 10 explains how to locate and fix code and syntax errors.

INCLUDING CUSTOM HELP

You have the following ways to help the end user become acquainted with a new application:

◆ **ControlTips:** Quickly display the purpose of a control on a form in form view. If you don't specify the text in the item's Properties menu, you can set it with VBA code.

For example, the following statement sets the ControlTip property for the FindSV button:

```
Forms("Volunteers").Controls("FindSV").ControlTipText = _
    "Click to look for Senior Volunteer"
```

◆ **Status bar information:** Automatically prints messages. To display a message in the status bar, set the `StatusBarText` property to a string expression. The following statement places a message in the status bar when the `ID#` text box control in the DARs form gets focus. You place the statement in the form's `Open` event procedure, as follows:

```
Private Sub Form_Open(Cancel As Integer)
DoCmd.Maximize
DoCmd.GoToRecord acDataForm, "DARs", acGoTo, 10
Forms("DARs").Controls("ID#").StatusBarText = _
    "Choose the Sr Vol# and the LastName will fill in
automatically"
End Sub
```

Figure 9-8 shows the message in the status bar of the DARs form.

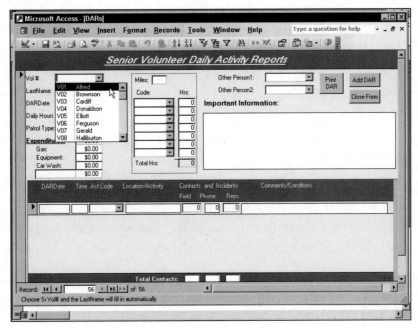

Figure 9-8: Displaying a message in the form status bar.

◆ **Compiled custom help topics:** Deliver help that is focused on the current application. You can create help text for the `What'sThis?` control on the command bar of a form.

Custom help files contain numbered blocks of text that are individually referred to as the *HelpContextID* property. Set the property to the number of the block that contains the relevant information.

Chapter 20 explains the details of creating custom help files.

Running a Sub Procedure

The most important reason to execute a procedure on demand is to make sure that it runs properly and provides the correct results. Once you have evaluated the procedure, it runs when the event occurs ("event-driven," remember?) or when it is called by another procedure.

You have several ways to run a procedure, depending on whether you are debugging it during development or whether it is complete and must execute when the relevant event occurs.

Running during development

While you are writing VBA code, the Visual Basic Editor offers the following ways to run all or part of the procedure:

◆ If the procedure requires no arguments, the easiest way to run the procedure is to place the cursor within the code and choose Run→Run Sub/ User Form.

◆ If the procedure requires an argument, you can cause the underlying event to occur or even attach the procedure to a temporary button click event. Make sure that all the necessary arguments are available and that you are running the procedure in the right setting, for example, with a form open in form view.

Chapter 10 explains running code during debugging.

Calling from another procedure

To make one procedure call another procedure, enter the name of the called procedure with values for all the required arguments. When you have a group of procedures that must be executed in a specific order, an easy way to organize the execution is to call them all from a host sub procedure. The following example includes the Host procedure, which calls two others, CountTo and AllDone. The Limit argument value, 10, is passed with the call to the CountTo procedure. The final message is shown in Figure 9-9.

```
Public Sub Host()
    CountTo 10
    AllDone
End Sub

Public Sub CountTo(Limit)
Dim intCount As Integer
Dim intTotal As Integer
intTotal = 0
For intCount = 1 To Limit
    intTotal = intTotal + 1
Next intCount
MsgBox intTotal    'Displays the final count, 10.
End Sub

Public Sub AllDone()
MsgBox "Ran through all loops"
End Sub
```

Figure 9-9: The final message from the group of procedures.

You can even call a procedure from another module. For example, if you add the following code to a different module in the database and run that module, you see the same result:

```
Public Sub CallHost()
Host
End Sub
```

These are all public procedures and are therefore available to any module in the project.

Running when an event occurs

In addition to the behind-the-scenes events, such as a form loading or a report formatting, you can use other events to run the procedure:

◆ The following visible events can trigger a procedure:

■ Clicking a command button on a form

■ Entering a value in a text box control and pressing Tab

■ Opening a report in print preview

All of these events can have VBA code attached to them to accomplish a specific purpose.

◆ Custom menus and toolbar buttons can trigger a procedure.

For example, to save time, you can add a toolbar button to the Senior Volunteers Database toolbar that immediately opens the DARs form for adding new records.

Chapter 4 adds a Custom menu to the Standard menu bar. The Custom menu displays a text message that depends on the current weekday.

The following example adds a toolbar button to the Database toolbar; that button runs the Host procedure:

1. Use the Customize dialog box to add the button.

2. Right-click the new button, and change the name to RunHost.

3. Choose Properties from the shortcut menu that appears, and enter Host in the On Action box (see Figure 9-10).

When you click the new button in the database window, you see the same result as when you ran the procedure in the Module window.

Figure 9-10: Calling a procedure by clicking a toolbar button.

Passing arguments

Arguments are more commonly used with function procedures, but you occasionally need to pass one or more arguments to a sub procedure. You include the arguments in the Sub statement. For example, the following statement passes the LastName string, the HireDate date, and Supervisor string arguments to the UseArg sub procedure:

```
Sub UseArg(LastName As String, HireDate As Date, _
Supervisor As String)
```

When you call the procedure, you specify the argument values in the calling statement. The argument values should appear in the same order as in the Sub statement, as follows:

```
UseArg "Jones", #12/20/92#, "Morgan"
```

Another way to pass the values is by including the argument name. Then you don't need to be explicit about the order of the arguments in the passed list, as follows:

```
UseArg Supervisor: = "Morgan", HireDate:=#12/20/92#, _
LastName:="Jones"
```

It is sometimes easier to declare the arguments as public variables. Then you don't need to pass the values with the calling statement. The procedure already has access to them.

Chapter 11 covers passing arguments in greater detail.

More Code Examples

There are no limits to the ways you can use VBA to customize the Access database to suit your needs. Here we present a few examples that may be of interest and can give you an idea of VBA's capabilities and inspire you to explore more ways you can put VBA to use.

For tables and queries

You don't normally think of using VBA code when working with the basic tables and queries in Access. However, sometimes you need to make changes at run time, and this requires writing some procedures. The following are examples of how VBA can help you create a helpful application.

BUILDING NEW TABLE AND QUERY DEFINITIONS

The DAO structure includes the `TableDef` and `QueryDef` objects, which can create new tables or queries in the database. You can also use VBA methods to make changes in existing tables and queries. This can be especially useful if you want to create a temporary table or query rather than store the object with the database.

CREATING A NEW TABLE STRUCTURE   You use the `CreateTableDef` method to build a new table that is complete with fields, field properties, and indexes. Once defined, you can append the new table to the database. If the table were intended to be temporary, you can delete it from the collection or simply not append it to the collection in the first place.

The following example performs two actions:

◆ Creates a new table definition to contain information about the department region offices.

◆ Specifies the `RegionNo` field as the primary key by setting the field's `Primary` property to True.

You must define at least one field for the `TableDef` object before you can add it to the database, as follows:

```
Sub NewTblDef()

Dim dbsDFG11 As Database
Dim tdfNewTbl As TableDef
Dim idxNew As Index

Set dbsDFG11 = CurrentDb

'Build a new table definition.
Set tdfNewTbl = dbsDFG11.CreateTableDef("Regions")

With tdfNewTbl
    'Define the table fields and add them to the new table.
    .Fields.Append .CreateField("RegionNo", dbLong, 20)
    .Fields.Append .CreateField("Region", dbText, 25)
    .Fields.Append .CreateField("Title", dbText, 20)
    .Fields.Append .CreateField("Manager", dbText, 20)
    .Fields.Append .CreateField("Phone", dbText, 20)
    .Fields.Append .CreateField("Range", dbMemo)

     'Create new index object and add to the Indexes collection.
    Set idxNew = .CreateIndex("RegNoIndex")
    idxNew.Fields.Append idxNew.CreateField("RegionNo", dbLong, 2)
    idxNew.Primary = True
    .Indexes.Append idxNew

End With

'Append the new Regions table to the DFG11 database.
dbsDFG11.TableDefs.Append tdfNewTbl

End Sub
```

Figure 9-11 shows the new table that results from the `NewTblDef` procedure; the `RegionNo` field is designated as the primary key.

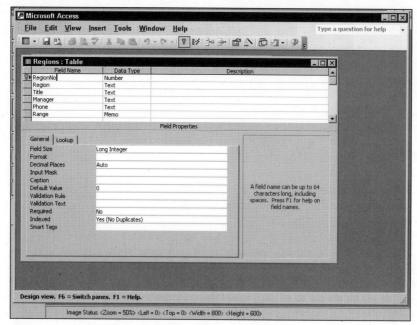

Figure 9-11: Creating a new table definition with VBA code.

CREATING AND RUNNING A NEW QUERY DEFINITION   The `CreateQueryDef` method works with SQL statements to create the query you want. You can take either of the following actions:

◆ Append the new query to the `QueryDefs` collection

◆ Run the query in place without saving it as a database object

At times, you may want to run a query on the fly and work with the resulting snapshot. The NewQryDef procedure creates a new query that prints a list of all volunteers that have e-mail addresses.

```
Sub NewQryDef()
Dim dbsDFG11 As Database
Dim qdfE-mail As QueryDef
Dim rstTemp As Recordset

Set dbsDFG11 = CurrentDb
With dbsDFG11
    'Create a new query definition.
    Set qdfE-mail = .CreateQueryDef("GetE-mailList", _
        "SELECT * FROM SrVols WHERE e-mail Is Not Null")
```

```
    'Open recordset and print report.
    With qdfE-mail
        Debug.Print .Name
        Debug.Print "   " & .SQL
        Set rstTemp = .OpenRecordset(dbOpenSnapshot)
        With rstTemp
            .MoveLast
            Debug.Print " Number of records = " & .RecordCount
            Debug.Print
            .Close
        End With
    End With
    End With
End Sub
```

If you expect to create and print the results of several query definitions, you can place the code that opens the record set and prints the results into a function. There, the action is available to any query definitions that you create.

To delete the new query definition after viewing the results, add the following statements before the final End With statement:

```
.QueryDefs.Delete qdfE-mail.Name
.Close
```

CREATING NEW INDEXES

You usually set indexes for a table in the table design window, but you can also do this with VBA. The NewIndex procedure uses the CreateIndex method to build two new indexes for the SrVols table definition and adds them to the Indexes collection for the database, as follows:

```
Public Sub NewIndex()
Dim dbsDFG As Database
Dim tdfVols As TableDef
Dim idxCity As Index, idxZipCode As Index

Set dbsDFG = CurrentDb
Set tdfVols = dbsDFG!SrVols

With tdfVols
    'Create an index object then add fields to it.
    'then add the index to the index collection.
    Set idxCity = .CreateIndex("City")
    With idxCity
        .Fields.Append .CreateField("City")
        .Fields.Append .CreateField("LastName")
```

```
    End With
    .Indexes.Append idxCity

    'Create another index based on the ZipCode field.
    Set idxZipCode = .CreateIndex
    With idxZipCode
        .Name = "ZipCode"
        .Fields.Append .CreateField("ZipCode")
        .Fields.Append .CreateField("LastName")
    End With
    .Indexes.Append idxZipCode
'Refresh the indexes collection.
.Indexes.Refresh
End With
End Sub
```

Figure 9-12 shows the SrVols table open in design view with the Indexes dialog box open. The two new indexes are included in the list.

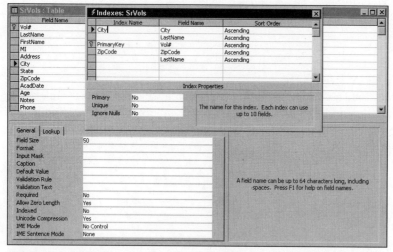

Figure 9-12: Adding new indexes with VBA code.

VBA code can remove indexes from a table definition as well. The following code deletes the City index from the SrVols table definition. Both of these public procedures are included in a standard module on the Modules page of the database window.

```
Public Sub DeleteIndex()
Dim dbsDFG As Database
```

```
Dim tdfVols As TableDef
Dim idxCity As Index, idxZipCode As Index

Set dbsDFG = CurrentDb
Set tdfVols = dbsDFG!SrVols
With tdfVols
    .Indexes.Delete ("City")
End With
End Sub
```

When you build a new index in the table definition, you can specify that Null values be ignored. You can do the same with indexes that you create with VBA. The following block of code prompts the user for the decision about setting the Ignore Null values with the new index:

```
' Set the IgnoreNulls property of the City Index object
' based on the user's input.
Select Case MsgBox("Do you want to set IgnoreNulls to True?", _
        vbYesNoCancel)
    Case vbYes
        idxCity.IgnoreNulls = True
    Case vbNo
        idxCity.IgnoreNulls = False
    Case Else
        dbsDFG.Close
    End
End Select
```

ARCHIVING RECORDS

If a database keeps adding records without having a method of getting rid of any, the database eventually grows very large. Regularly removing the outdated data is essential. To keep the information for historical purposes, you can archive it in a table and keep that table in the background, or you can place the data on a floppy disk or CD instead of on your hard drive.

The following procedure executes when the user clicks the Archive command button on the Applicant form. It prompts the user to confirm the removal of the records, and if the returned value is 7 (Yes), the procedure continues. If the value returned by the InputBox function is anything other than 7, the procedure exits.

```
Private Sub Archive_Click()
'Archives inactive Applicant Data to ArchiveAppl Data table
Dim strSQLArchive As String, strSQLDelete As String
Dim intChoice As Integer
```

```
intChoice = MsgBox("Do you want to archive inactive data now? ", _
    vbYesNo + vbQuestion, "Archive?")
If intChoice = 7 Then     'If not Yes, exit procedure.
    GoTo Exit_Archive_Click
Else
    strSQLArchive = "INSERT INTO [ArchiveAppl Data]" & _
        "SELECT [Applicant Data].* FROM [Applicant Data]" & _
        "WHERE ((([Applicant Data].[Deceased?]) = True) " & _
        "OR ((([Applicant Data].[Moved Out State]) = True) " & _
        "OR ((([Applicant Data].[Returned-Not want]) = True);"
    DoCmd.RunSQL (strSQLArchive)

'Delete the same records from the Applicant Data table.
strSQLDelete = "DELETE [Applicant Data].* _
 "FROM [Applicant Data]" & _
        "WHERE ((([Applicant Data].[Deceased?]) = True) " & _
        "OR ((([Applicant Data].[Moved Out State]) = True) " & _
        "OR ((([Applicant Data].[Returned-Not want]) = True);"
    DoCmd.RunSQL (strSQLDelete)
End If

Exit_Archive_Click:
    Exit Sub
End Sub
```

 We have left the warning messages turned on so that we could verify that the same number of records are inserted into the archive as are deleted from the Applicant Data table.

EXTRACTING E-MAIL ADDRESSES

An interesting example of creating queries with VBA is one that extracts specific e-mail addresses. Once the query runs, you can copy the addresses to an e-mail message and send the message to all the addressees at once.

The following example looks at the list of volunteers who read newspapers and other material to visually impaired listeners. The database includes information about the readers, the material they read, and the current reading schedule. This information is stored in several related tables, two of which are as follows:

- ◆ The Volunteers table includes the volunteers' name, address, e-mail address, and other information.

- ◆ The Schedule table includes the newspaper or other material and the dates and times that the volunteers read to listeners.

The goal is to extract specific groups of volunteer e-mail addresses to send information regarding the schedule or the material and to send the message to all selected volunteers at once. A form enables the manager to choose the relevant material. The set of options in the form is not contained in an option group because the manager should be able to select more than one type of material. Option group controls contain a list of mutually exclusive options. Figure 9-13 shows the form from which the manager chooses the materials.

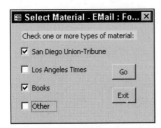

Figure 9-13: Selecting the e-mail recipients.

The following procedure executes when the user clicks the Go button on the form after making her selections. The procedure builds a series of SQL strings and queries the underlying tables based on the selections made in the form. The form then closes, and the e-mail list dynaset that was created by the combined `DoCmd.RunSql` statements is displayed. If the user clicks the Exit button without making a selection, the form closes and displays the last set of e-mail addresses that were extracted by the procedure.

```
Private Sub Go_Click()
'This procedure creates a list of e-mail addresses for readers of
'selected material.
Dim strSQLE-mail As String, strEmptyT As String
strEmptyT = "DELETE [E-mail List].* FROM [E-mail List];"
DoCmd.SetWarnings False
DoCmd.RunSQL strEmptyT

If SDUT = True Then        'Material is SD Union
   strSQLE-mail = "INSERT INTO [E-mail List] ( [Last Name], " & _
  "[First Name], e-mail, Material, SchedDay )" & _
       "SELECT Volunteers.[Last Name], " & _
  "Volunteers.[First Name], Volunteers.e-mail, " & _
  "Schedule.Material, Schedule.SchedDay " & _
       "FROM Volunteers INNER JOIN Schedule " & _
       "ON (Volunteers.[First Name] = Schedule.[First Name]) " & _
       "AND (Volunteers.[Last Name] = Schedule.[Last Name]) " & _
       "WHERE (((Volunteers.e-mail) Is Not Null) AND " & _
```

```
                    "((Schedule.Material) Like 'SD Union*'));"
        DoCmd.RunSQL strSQLE-mail
    End If

    If LAT = True Then          'Material is LA Times
    strSQLE-mail = "INSERT INTO [E-mail List] ( [Last Name], " & _
        "[First Name], e-mail, Material, SchedDay )" & _
            "SELECT Volunteers.[Last Name], " & _
     "Volunteers.[First Name], Volunteers.e-mail, " & _
    "Schedule.Material, Schedule.SchedDay " & _
            "FROM Volunteers INNER JOIN Schedule " & _
            "ON (Volunteers.[First Name] = Schedule.[First Name]) " & _
            "AND (Volunteers.[Last Name] = Schedule.[Last Name]) " & _
            "WHERE (((Volunteers.e-mail) Is Not Null) AND " & _
            "((Schedule.Material) Like 'Los Angeles*'));"
        DoCmd.RunSQL strSQLE-mail
    End If

    If Books = True Then          'Material is books
    strSQLE-mail = "INSERT INTO [E-mail List] ( [Last Name], " & _
        "[First Name], e-mail, Material, SchedDay )" & _
            "SELECT Volunteers.[Last Name], " & _
     "Volunteers.[First Name], Volunteers.e-mail, " & _
    "Schedule.Material, Schedule.SchedDay " & _
            "FROM Volunteers INNER JOIN Schedule " & _
            "ON (Volunteers.[First Name] = Schedule.[First Name]) " & _
            "AND (Volunteers.[Last Name] = Schedule.[Last Name]) " & _
            "WHERE (((Volunteers.e-mail) Is Not Null) AND " & _
            "((Schedule.Material) Like 'Books'));"
        DoCmd.RunSQL strSQLE-mail
    End If

    If Other = True Then          'Any other material
    strSQLE-mail = "INSERT INTO [E-mail List] ( [Last Name], " & _
        "[First Name], e-mail, Material, SchedDay )" & _
            "SELECT Volunteers.[Last Name], " & _
     "Volunteers.[First Name], Volunteers.e-mail, " & _
    "Schedule.Material, Schedule.SchedDay " & _
            "FROM Volunteers INNER JOIN Schedule " & _
            "ON (Volunteers.[First Name] = Schedule.[First Name]) " & _
            "AND (Volunteers.[Last Name] = Schedule.[Last Name]) " & _
            "WHERE (((Volunteers.e-mail) Is Not Null) AND " & _
            "((Schedule.Material) Like 'Other'));"
        DoCmd.RunSQL strSQLE-mail
    End If
```

```
DoCmd.SetWarnings True
DoCmd.Close
End Sub
```

For forms and reports

Forms are the most active objects in an Access application because they deal directly with the user. Wizards can create the following items:

♦ Command button controls that can, for example, accomplish the following tasks:

   ■ Open other forms

   ■ Print reports

   ■ Edit data

♦ Reports and subreports that contain detailed data and a wide variety of summary information

After you have the skeleton of the form or report, you can customize it with VBA to perform many run-time actions that the wizards can't do for you in advance, such as the following:

♦ Change form, report, or control properties at run time, based on certain values, such as total sales, an expiration date, or a filter to name just a few

♦ Filter records before previewing the report

♦ Suppress printing sections based on current information

VALIDATING DATA

When you create a new table, you can set validation rules for individual fields and for a complete record. You can do the same thing with VBA code and attach it to the data-entry form. You supply the following items:

♦ The validation rule

♦ The message to display if an entry violates the rule

For example, the senior volunteer program requires that any new member must be at least 50 years old. So, you can set a validation rule for the Age text box control in the data-entry form to verify that the age requirement is met. The following code sets this rule when the form opens. Figure 9-14 shows what happens when you enter an age under 50 in the Volunteers form.

```
Private Sub Form_Open(Cancel As Integer)
'This procedure sets the validation rule and text for the
```

```
'Age text box control in the Volunteers form.
Dim strRule As String, strText As String

strRule = ">=50"
strText = "You must be 50 or over to be a senior volunteer"

Me!Age.ValidationRule = strRule
Me!Age.ValidationText = strText

End Sub
```

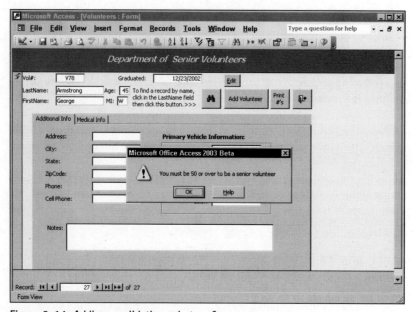

Figure 9-14: Adding a validation rule to a form.

This method adds the rule to the control on the form. Any data that is entered in datasheet view (as opposed to form view) isn't checked. To add the rule to the table itself, use the following public sub procedure. It does not add the rule and text to the table definition in the table design view, but it does apply the rule when entering data in the datasheet view.

```
Public Sub ValidAge()
Dim dbs As Database, tdf As TableDef
Dim fld As Field

Set dbs = CurrentDb
Set tdf = dbs.TableDefs("SrVols")
```

```
Set fld = tdf.Fields("Age")
fld.ValidationRule = ">=50"
fld.ValidationText = "Senior Vols must be at least 50"

End Sub
```

The same technique can apply record-level validation rules. For example, if the table has two date fields and one must be earlier than the other, a record-level validation rule would ensure the compliance of the data.

FILTERING RECORDS

A select query expression can limit the records that are displayed in a form. You can also build a filter expression to use when you open the form. The following procedure executes when you click the OpenForm button that appears on a switchboard form:

```
Private Sub OpenForm_Click()
'This procedure opens the DARs form and filters
'for DARs from Senior Volunteer Elliott.
    Dim strDocName As String
    Dim strFilter As String

    strDocName = "DARs"
    strfilter = "LastName = 'Elliott'"
    DoCmd.OpenForm strDocName, , , strFilter
End Sub
```

If you want the user to be able to select the volunteer's name to use in the filter, use the following code instead. Be careful to include the complete sets of double quotation marks that enclose the single quotation marks in the resulting filter expression. To check the filter string while you are creating the code, you can add a MsgBox statement to display the result of the statement. Figure 9-15 shows the correct filter string for displaying only records for Volunteer Elliott after the user enters that name in the InputBox dialog box.

```
Private Sub OpenForm_Click()
'This procedure prompts the user for the volunteer's last name
'then filters the records that appear in the DAR form.
    Dim strDocName As String
    Dim strFilter As String, strName As String

    strName = InputBox("Enter Sr Vol last Name", "Last Name")
    strFilter = "LastName = " & "'" & strName & "'"
    strDocName = "DARs"
    DoCmd.OpenForm strDocName, , , strFilter
End Sub
```

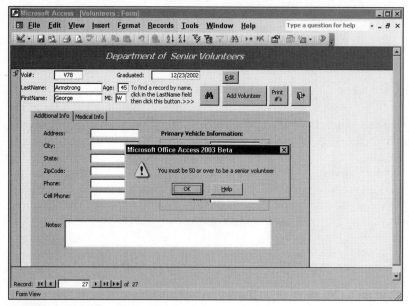

Figure 9-15: Verifying the filter string.

 You can use all double quotation marks in the filter expression, but it is easier to read the expression if you use both single and double quotation marks.

It is important to prevent errors from entering the database; many procedures are focused on that effort. For example, to make sure that you have a complete address for the volunteers, check to see if all the components are present. If a street address is entered, the record must also contain a ZipCode value. The following procedure can make sure that the data is complete before moving to the next record. The IsNull function tests for Null values in the field. The If Not IsNull expression returns True if the Address field contains data. Combine that with testing for Null in the ZipCode field to complete the test. If the ZipCode value is missing, the cursor returns to the ZipCode text box control. Attach the procedure to the form's BeforeUpdate event. Figure 9-16 shows the validation text message when the record includes an address but the ZipCode field is blank.

```
Private Sub Form_BeforeUpdate(Cancel As Integer)
'If the record includes an address, look for the ZipCode.

If Not IsNull(Address) And IsNull(ZipCode) Then
    MsgBox "Please enter the ZipCode", vbExclamation
    ZipCode.SetFocus          'Return to the ZipCode control
```

```
    Cancel = True              'Cancel saving the record
End If
End Sub
```

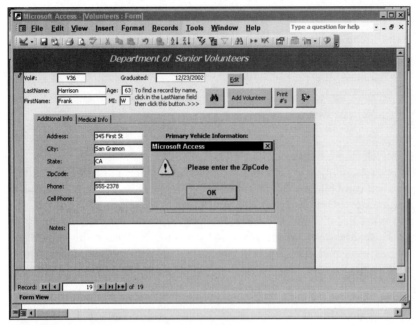

Figure 9-16: Requesting a zip code for the address.

DISPLAYING DATA

If some confusion exists about how data is to be entered in a form, you can create input masks for text box controls. Input masks have the following benefits:

♦ Data entry is easier

♦ Inconsistent values can be blocked

The following procedure sets the input mask properties for the Phone and ZipCode text box controls in the form. Figure 9-17 shows the mask that appears when the cursor is in the Phone text box.

```
Private Sub Form_Load()
'This procedure adds input masks to the Phone and Zipcode fields.
Forms![SrVols Special]!Phone.InputMask = "(###) ###-####"
Forms![SrVols Special]!ZipCode.InputMask = "00000-9999"
End Sub
```

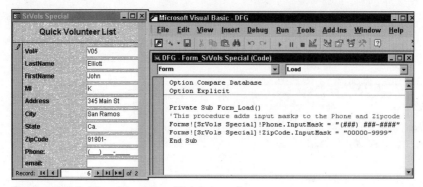

Figure 9-17: Guiding data entry with input masks.

SUPPRESSING BLANK FIELD LABELS

When you print a report, it looks more professional if labels don't appear next to blank fields. You can build a short code block that checks for data in a field and, if none exists, suppresses printing the label for that field. The following code tests for a blank Important Info field and, if it is blank, sets the control's label visible property to False. The Boolean variable blnInfo is set to True if the Important Info field has a value and False if it is blank. Then, the label's visible property is set to the blnInfo value.

```
Private Sub Detail_Format(Cancel As Integer, FormatCount As Integer)
'If the Important Info field is blank, don't show the label.

Dim blnInfo As Boolean
'Check for blank Info field.
blnInfo = Not IsNull(Important_Info)
'Set the Visible property for the label
Label3.Visible = blnInfo
End Sub
```

TIP

Be sure to use the label's correct name, not the text that it shows in the report preview. Check the Name property on the Other tab of the label's property sheet.

PRINTING SELECTED LABELS

When you are ready to send information to clients, you may want to send it only to certain ones in a specific state, for example. The following procedure prompts the user for the desired state and then opens the Print Preview window of the label report showing only those labels. If the user does not enter a state, all the labels appear. Figure 9-18 shows the InputBox window.

```
Private Sub Report_Open(Cancel As Integer)
'This procedure filters the labels by state, if desired.
Dim strState As String
Dim strFilter As String
'Prompts for state abbreviation
strState = InputBox("Enter 2-character state code, e.g. CA")

'If no state entered, shows all labels.
If strState = "" Then
    DoCmd.OpenReport "Labels Volunteers", acViewPreview
Else
    strFilter = "[State] = """ & strState & """"
    DoCmd.OpenReport "Labels Volunteers", acViewPreview, , strFilter
End If
End Sub
```

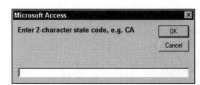

Figure 9-18: Prompting for the state value.

We used all double quotation marks in this filter expression.

CENTERING A TITLE

An easy way to center a title on the title page of a report is to set the location as the report header section is being formatted. First set the header's `Height` property to the full height of the page, minus the top and bottom margin widths. Then, use the following code to force the title to a horizontal and vertical location on the page. Figure 9-19 shows the result of previewing the report.

```
Private Sub ReportHeader_Format(Cancel As Integer, FormatCount As
Integer)
Dim rpt As Report
Dim strTitle As String
Dim intHSize As Integer, intVSize As Integer
Set rpt = Me
strTitle = "Senior Volunteers - 2003"
'Set the report scale to pixels and the font properties.
```

```
With rpt
    .ScaleMode = 3
    .FontName = "Courier"
    .FontSize = 24
    .FontBold = True
End With
'Compute the height and width of the text.
intVSize = rpt.TextHeight(strTitle)
intHSize = rpt.TextWidth(strTitle)

'Compute the location for the text.
rpt.CurrentX = (rpt.ScaleWidth / 2) - (intHSize / 2)
rpt.CurrentY = (rpt.ScaleHeight / 3) - (intVSize / 2)
'Print the title.
rpt.Print strTitle
End Sub
```

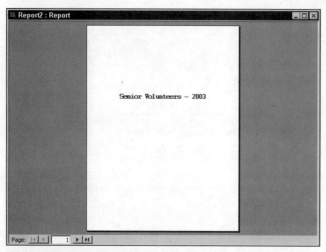

Figure 9-19: Centering the title page.

 The original equation for the `CurrentY` setting divided the `rpt.ScaleHeight` property by 2 to center the text vertically. To show the report title slightly above the center of the page, we changed the expression to divide the page height by 3. You may need to adjust the margins to get the text centered horizontally.

Dealing with Errors

You can encounter the following types of errors when you write and run VBA procedures for an Access application:

♦ **Syntax and other grammatical errors:** These errors are the easiest to fix because the VB editor helps you find them and often suggests corrections or corrects the error automatically, as follows:

  ■ The VB editor spots some syntax errors when you complete a line of code and try to move to the next line, for example, if you forget an equals sign or misspell an intrinsic constant.

  ■ Other syntax errors are detected when you try to run the procedure, for example, undeclared variables or properties that don't match the object.

Chapter 10 shows you ways to detect and correct syntax and grammatical bugs in your code.

♦ **Run-time errors:** These errors can't be detected until you run the procedure in its intended environment. You can anticipate many of these errors and make provisions for dealing with them. We include a few examples of run-time errors and their remedies next.

♦ **Logic errors:** These errors just give you the wrong answer. The procedure does just what you told it to, but you still come up with the wrong result. You must find and fix this type of error. When creating a new application, always run the procedure with a simple example of the data to see that the application produces the correct result at least some of the time. This eliminates gross errors, but it does not check functionality over the entire range of possible input data values.

Handling run-time errors

When an error occurs, the procedure stops and displays a message box with the error number and a description of what occurred. Instead of making the user interpret the sometimes obscure message and handle the error, it is good practice to trap any errors and handle them internally (or at least present a clearer explanation to the user). Figure 9-20 shows a typical error message that occurs when you encounter the `Loop` statement without having executed the `For` statement, and Figure 9-21 shows a more friendly error message that you can use instead.

Figure 9-20: A typical built-in error message.

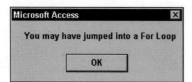

Figure 9-21: A more user-friendly message.

> **TIP** In the VBE window, choose Tools→Options. Then click the General tab and check the Break on Unhandled Errors option so that the procedure stops for errors that you have not trapped. If you use the Break On All Errors option, the procedure stops at all errors and ignores your error-handling code.

You have probably noticed that all the code created by an Access wizard includes the OnError GoTo statement, which jumps to another location in the procedure. The On Error statement comes in the following versions:

◆ OnError GoTo label enables the error-handing routine and branches to the block of code that begins at the specified line in the same procedure. Control jumps to that line if a run-time error occurs.

◆ On Error Resume Next sends control back to the statement immediately following the one that caused the error without interrupting the execution. This statement is handy during debugging if you want to use code to check the properties of the Err object. You then correct the error within the code, not with an error handler.

◆ On Error GoTo 0 disables the error handler that was enabled earlier in the current procedure.

> **NOTE** Even without the On Error GoTo 0 statement, the error handler is automatically disabled when the procedure has finished. The properties of the Err object are also cleared.

Within the error handling routine, the `Resume` statement can direct execution back to the procedure. The `Resume` statement comes in the following variations, depending on where you want to go:

- `Resume` or `Resume 0` goes back to the statement that caused the error. This is helpful when the user is prompted to enter a value but enters an invalid one and causes the error. You can have the error handler display an explanation and return to the prompt to give the user a second chance.

- `Resume Next` is used if the error handler has fixed the error or you just want to continue execution at the line following the one that caused the error.

- `Resume label` returns control to a specified line in the current procedure.

At times, you want to exit the procedure when an error occurs. In that case, use the `Exit Sub` or `Exit Function` statement in the error handler. You can also label a line that precedes the `Exit` statement within the normal block of code and then have the error handler branch to that location after dealing with the error.

 To label a line, enter a name followed by a colon (:). Place the first character or number in the first space of the code line. Begin the executable code on the next line.

When you write an error-handling routine in a procedure, be sure to include a way to leave the procedure. Also place the `Exit Sub` or `Exit Function` statement in the procedure before the error-handling routine, or you execute the handler every time you run the procedure. The following is an example of error-handling code:

```
Sub LookFor()
'Start the error handler
On Error GoTo Error_LookFor
    [statements that may cause an error]
Exit_LookFor:
    Exit Sub
Error_LookFor:
    [error handing code]
    Resume Exit_LookFor
End Sub
```

After an error has occurred, you need to find out what kind of error it is and handle it. Looking at the VBA `Err` object is one way to interpret the problem. The `Err` object captures information about the most recent error and stores it in its

Number and Description properties. In the error-handling routine, you can compare the Err number with likely error codes and, if you find a match, display a clear message about the error.

 TIP The Raise method can generate a VBA error that hasn't occurred. To look up Access, ADO, or DAO errors, use the AccessError method. See the help topics for more details.

The following example prompts the user to enter the name of a volunteer to delete the record from the table. When the warning message appears that the record is about to be deleted, the user has the option of canceling the deletion.

```
Public Sub DelRecord(strName As String)
On Error GoTo DelRecordErr:
Dim strSQL As String

'This procedure deletes records from a table where the
'last name equals the argument passed by the user.
strSQL = "Delete * FROM Volunteers Where " & _
        "LastName = '" & strLName & "'"

DoCmd.RunSQL strSQL
'A warning message is displayed.
'If the user cancels the action, error # 2501 occurs.
Exit_DelRecord:
    Exit Sub
DelRecordErr:
    If Err.Number = 0 Then
        Exit Function
    ElseIf Err.Number = 2501 Then
MsgBox "The delete action was canceled by the user.", vbInformation,
"Delete Action"
    Else
 MsgBox Err.Number & ": " & Err.Description, vbCritical, "Delete
Action"
    End If
    Resume Exit_DelRecord
End Sub
```

The following example shows you how to create your own run-time error messages using the Raise method with the Err object. This allows you to assign your own message and error number to an error. The VBA type mismatch error is number 13.

```
Public Sub CheckDateFormat()
On Error GoTo CheckDateFormatErr
Dim intNumberToInsert As Integer
Const conDataMismatch As Integer = 13
Const errErrThisIsATest = "The value entered was not a valid " _
        & " number."
intNumberToInsert = InputBox("Enter a number to insert.", _
"Date Input Example")
Exit_CheckDateFormat:
Exit Sub

CheckDateFormatErr:
If Err = 0 Then
Exit Sub
        ElseIf Err = 13 Then
        ' Regenerate original error.
        Dim intErrNum As Integer
        intErrNum = Err
        Err.Clear
        Err.Raise intErrNum + 514, , errErrThisIsATest
    Else
        ErrRaiseErr.Number, , Err.Description
End If
Resume Exit_CheckDateFormat
End Sub
```

Appendix C provides a list of the VBA error codes. Look in the help topic "ErrorValueEnum" for a list of numbered ADO error messages. The help topic "Trappable Microsoft Jet Errors" lists the DAO errors.

Improving VBA Code Performance

A few nanoseconds may not seem like a lot of wasted time, but efficient code always pays off. You can save time and memory by following some basic guidelines. Always make sure that your code is compiled. Compiling the code at run time takes extra time. If you have changed the name of the database, you should recompile the code.

Some other tips to improve code performance include declaring variables and searching efficiently for specific records.

Declaring variables

Always explicitly declare the variables that you use in the procedure, and use the most specific type of variable possible. For example, if you are declaring a variable to represent a report, declare it as a Report type instead of an Object or Variant type.

If you refer to a specific value of a property or control in a form, create a variable instead of using the complete identifier. In addition, when you are referring to a control or property in an event procedure, use the Me keyword in the code instead of the complete identifier.

When you are using mathematical variables, use the Integer or Long data types, depending on whether the variable assumes an integer or decimal value. These data types are more memory efficient.

If you are working with arrays of values, declare a dynamic array. When you are finished with the array, be sure to use the Erase or ReDim statement to release the memory that was reserved for the array.

Searching for records

Scrolling through a large table of records can take a lot of time. The following are ways to zip to the information that you need:

◆ If you often return to a specific record, use a bookmark instead of using the `FindRecord` or `FindNext` method.

◆ If you plan to use the `FindRecord` or `FindNext` method, be sure that you have indexed the field that contains the value you are looking for.

The Me Keyword

The Me keyword can serve a number of purposes. It is often used to implicitly refer to an open form or to report controls collection. It is much faster to type **Me** than to type the entire explicit object reference to the control.

`Me!LastName.SetFocus` refers to the text box control that is bound to the `LastName` field in the currently open form and moves the cursor to that control. The explicit reference is `Forms!Volunteers!LastName.SetFocus`. If the name of the form or control contains a space, enclose the name in brackets.

The Me keyword is available to every procedure in the class module. This also makes it useful for passing information about one instance of the form to another module. It can also be used as a command to return to the currently active form.

Streamlining code

When your code calls a procedure in another module, the entire module is loaded into memory. This takes time and uses up space, so follow these two guidelines:

- Place all the related procedures in the same module so that the code runs more efficiently.

- Delete procedures that you don't need and declared variables that are no longer referenced.

The handy IIf (Immediate If) function is a tempting shortcut in place of the If...Then...Else structure. But if either of the return expressions takes a while to evaluate, it is better to use the If...Then...Else structure.

Summary

In this chapter, we have demonstrated some of the ways that you can use VBA procedures in an application. We addressed the task from the ground up, planning and scoping the project to adding user interaction and error handling.

In the next chapter, we dig into the process of producing error-free code.

Chapter 10

Running and Debugging VBA Code

IN THIS CHAPTER

◆ Examining types of code errors and knowing when they occur

◆ Using the VBE debugging tools

◆ Executing a test run on a procedure

◆ Controlling execution during debugging

◆ Setting breakpoints and checking progress

AFTER YOU WRITE A VBA PROCEDURE to carry out an activity, you must try it out. You need to test drive it to be sure that no programming errors exist in the code. But you also need to find out if the procedure accomplishes the purpose that you had in mind. Does the sub procedure perform the right operation, and does the function return the correct result?

VBA Language Errors

The Visual Basic Editor does as much as possible to help you write error-free code and even corrects some mistakes automatically. Some errors occur within a single statement and are detected when you press Enter to move to the next statement. For example, you may have an expression that is incomplete or you may have omitted a closing quotation mark. We call these *syntax* or *code-entry* errors even though the error message is `Compile error`.

You won't notice other errors until you try to run the procedure; for example, the `End If` statement may be missing from the `If...Then...Else` structure. This type of error is also called a *compile error* because the code must first be compiled before running.

◆ Break a complex program into single-purpose sub or function procedures.

◆ Be generous with comments so that you know exactly what each block of code should do.

◆ Explicitly declare all variables that you use in the procedure to avoid mis-spelling, which causes a compile error.

◆ Use a comfortable naming convention so that you can quickly recognize the purpose of the variables.

Common errors can occur when writing and compiling VBA code. Some of these errors are discussed in the following sections.

Code entry errors

When you commit a syntax error, the editor displays a message when you try to move to the next statement. The code line text appears in red, and the error is high-lighted in dark blue.

 You can change these code colors by selecting from the Editor Format tab of the Options dialog box.

For example, the following statement causes an error because the Or operator must have complete expressions on both sides:

```
If Me.Vol_ = "VO1" Or = "VO2" Then
```

Figure 10-1 shows the resulting error message. The pound sign (#) in the Vol# field name is an underscore because the pound sign is a reserved character in VBA.

In many cases, the editor adds a closing quotation mark or parenthesis, but other times, it can't find a clear solution. For example, if you omit the closing quotation mark within a statement instead of at the end of a statement, you see an error message. Figure 10-2 shows the message that does not exactly pinpoint what is wrong with the statement, but it's close. The statement is missing the closing quotation mark after Ferguson, so the Then keyword is considered part of the string expression. The string expression should close with a quotation mark.

Preventing Errors

Once errors get into your code, you can spend a lot of time hunting them down and fixing them. It is better to avoid them if possible. The following techniques can help you keep errors to a minimum:

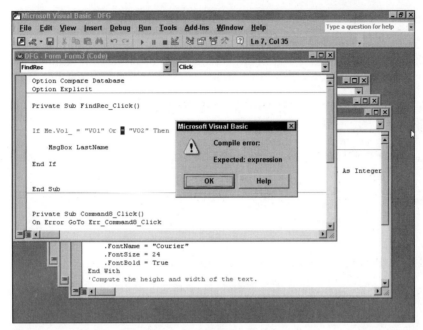

Figure 10-1: An error caused by an incomplete expression.

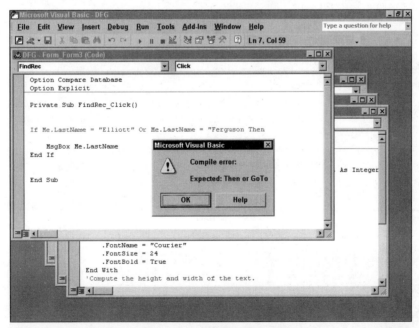

Figure 10-2: A missing quotation mark within the statement.

Compile-time errors

When you try to run a procedure and the editor detects a problem with fitting the statements together, execution stops and you are returned to the code window for the explanation. The following sections provide a few examples of compile-time errors.

INCORRECT LINE LABEL

You are trying to branch to a different location in the procedure, but you have mis-spelled the line label. Figure 10-3 shows the message that is caused by the mis-spelled line label, as follows:

◆ The `Resume` statement refers to the line labeled `Exit_FindRec_Click`.

◆ The `Exit Sub` statement follows the line labeled `Exit_FindMyRec_Click`.

To fix this error, follow these steps:

1. Click OK.

2. Correct either the line label or the reference in the `Resume` statement so that they match.

3. Return to the Access window, and try to run the procedure again.

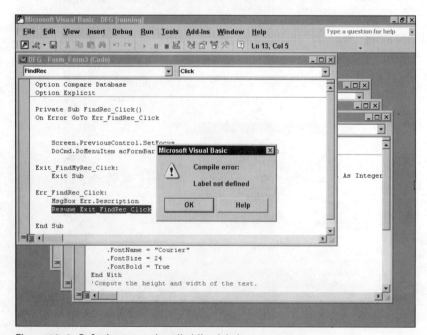

Figure 10-3: Referring to a misspelled line label.

What Is Compilation?

Compiling a procedure is like planning and getting ready to pack for a long camping trip. During the compilation process, Access reads the entire procedure and translates the human-readable statements into machine-readable form.

As part of the compilation process, the compiler checks for the following items:

- ◆ Complete logic structures

- ◆ Variable declarations

- ◆ Misspelled keywords

- ◆ Mismatched objects for methods or properties

- ◆ Many grammatical errors

After compiling, the package is passed on to the linker that runs the code.

UNDEFINED VARIABLES

A compilation error may refer to an undefined variable, which is usually caused by one of the following items:

- ◆ Misspelling the variable

- ◆ Failing to declare the variable

In the case shown in Figure 10-4, the SrVol reference was intended to refer to a control in the form, but that field was not included in the form design.

To correct this error, click OK and return to the Access window to find the correct field name.

MISSING ARGUMENT

Sometimes the editor catches a missing required argument at compile time. Figure 10-5 shows the error message that was triggered by the lack of the required report name argument in the DoCmd.OpenReport method syntax.

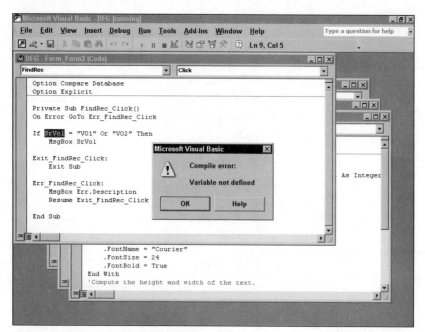

Figure 10-4: The variable is not defined.

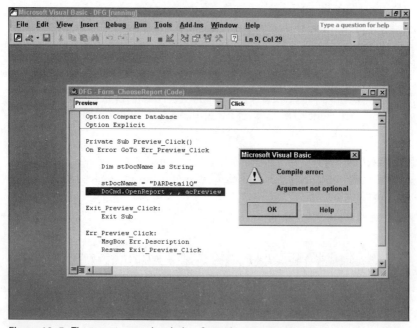

Figure 10-5: The report name is missing from the statement.

Take the following actions to fix this error:

♦ Click OK, and then replace the first comma with the name of the variable that represents the report name, stDocName in this case.

Remove the first comma. Otherwise, the acPreview argument moves out of its proper sequence, and you will print the report instead of preview it.

♦ Reconstruct the correct syntax by deleting all the text beyond the OpenReport method and working with the AutoQuick Info display.

MISSING CLOSING STATEMENTS

Failing to include an End If, End With, or End Select statement is a common error. All of these closing statements are required in these code structures. Figure 10-6 shows a message about a missing End If statement. To correct this, simply add the statement before the End Sub statement.

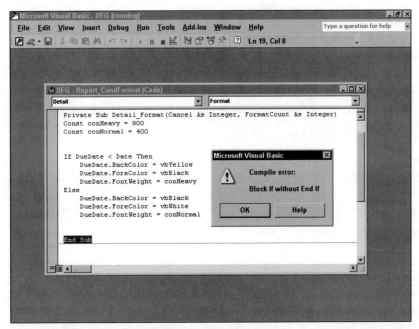

Figure 10-6: The End If statement is missing.

Testing

No matter how carefully you write VBA code, you can't be sure it does what you intended unless you try it out. Sub procedures and functions require slightly different triggering actions. The following sections describe how to test run these procedures.

Procedure testing

After you have written a new procedure, you must check it out by running it. Use one of the following steps to do so:

◆ To test an event procedure, such as one that runs when you click a command button, you can cause the event to occur by clicking the button. For example, the following code responds to clicking the SeeMore command button.

```
Private Sub SeeMore_Click()
'This procedure displays a message then performs some arithmetic
'and displays the result.

Dim I As Integer, intTotal As Integer
Dim strText As String

MsgBox ("Tell me more")
    intTotal = 0
    For I = 20 To 1 Step -1
        intTotal = intTotal + 2
    Next
MsgBox intTotal
End Sub
```

◆ You can run a procedure that requires no arguments from the Code window by clicking the Run Sub/User Form button on the Standard toolbar. For example, the GetName procedure can run from the Code window.

```
Private Sub GetName()
'This procedure requests a name, then opens a form with records
'filtered to that name.

Dim strDocName As String
Dim strFilter As String, strName As String
```

```
strName = InputBox("Enter Sr Vol last name", "Last Name")
strFilter = "LastName = " & "'" & strName & "'"
strDocName = "DARs"
MsgBox strFilter
DoCmd.OpenForm strDocName, , , strFilter

End Sub
```

◆ For a procedure that requires an argument, such as the value of a control on a form, first open the underlying object in design view and then click the Run Sub/User Form button. To pass arguments to the sub procedure `TellMore(Arg1, Arg2, Arg3)`, simply list them with the procedure call, as follows:

```
TellMore abc, def, ghi
```

If you use the `Call` statement, enclose the arguments in parentheses, as follows:

```
Call TellMore(abc, def, ghi)
```

Another way to run a new sub procedure is to call it from another procedure. For example, the following code runs two sub procedures from one main procedure. The main sub procedure calls the two other sub procedures, `TellMore` and `GetName`.

```
Private Sub RunSubs_Click()
    SeeMore
    GetName
End Sub
```

You can switch between procedures by choosing from the Window menu. When you choose Window, you see a list of all the class modules in the project and the standard modules that opened during the current session. Select the one that you want to work on.

Function testing

To test a function you must take one of the following actions:

◆ Use the function in an expression in a sub procedure.

◆ Use the `RunCode` macro action.

A Brief History Lesson

Developers of large computer programs realized that it was nearly impossible to remove all the bugs from the code, so they devised a way to estimate the number of bugs that remain. They intentionally injected a large number of various types of bugs into the system and then tried to detect and correct as many as possible. For example, if they had trapped 88% of the bugs they introduced, they could estimate that they had also removed 88% of the errors that they didn't plant. Thus, the developers could claim a "virtually error-free" program.

Subsequent versions of the program would remove more bugs as users reported them; the developers could then claim "new, improved" software.

Chapter 11 explains running and debugging functions.

If you have included error-trapping features in the procedure, you should disable error trapping before trying to run the procedure so that you can focus on the statement that causes the error. To disable error trapping, follow these steps in the VBE Code window:

1. Choose Tools→Options.

2. Click the General tab.

3. In the Error Trapping group, select Break On All Errors.

Now, when an error occurs, you automatically switch to Break mode, with the statement that caused the error being highlighted.

Using VBE Debugging Tools

You don't have to depend on the VB editor to track down your code errors. Several tools are quite useful for finding errors in your logic, that is, not in the VBA code grammar and structure. These tools can detect and fix errors and track the values of variables in the code as they change. The following tools help ensure that although you may not be causing any VB errors, you are reaching the correct values in your logic:

◆ Toolbars for code development actions

◆ Windows in which you can monitor your progress

Code development toolbars

These toolbars can be displayed in the VBE window. Both are available by right-clicking in an empty space in the Standard toolbar and choosing from the list. These toolbars float by default; you can also dock them to a side of the Code window.

In the next section of this chapter, we discuss how all these buttons can help you with your VBA code.

DEBUG TOOLBAR

The Debug toolbar presents the following buttons. All of these functions are also available from menus:

◆ **Design Mode:** Toggles design mode on and off (Run menu)

◆ **Run Sub/UserForm:** Runs the current procedure if the cursor is somewhere within the procedure (Run menu)

◆ **Break:** Stops execution while program is running and switches to Break mode (Run menu)

◆ **Reset:** Clears module-level variables and the execution stack and resets the project (Run menu)

◆ **Toggle Breakpoint:** Sets or removes a breakpoint at the current line (Debug menu and Edit toolbar)

◆ **Step Into:** Executes statements one at a time (Debug menu)

◆ **Step Over:** Runs a called procedure without stepping through and then returns to the next statement in the calling procedure (Debug menu)

◆ **Step Out:** Executes the remaining lines of the current procedure (Debug menu)

◆ **Locals Window:** Opens the Locals window (View menu)

◆ **Immediate Window:** Opens the Immediate window (View menu)

◆ **Watch Window:** Opens the Watch window (View menu)

◆ **Quick Watch:** Shows the Quick Watch window with the current value of the selected expression (Debug menu)

◆ **Call Stack:** Displays the Calls dialog box, which lists the currently active procedure calls (View menu)

EDIT TOOLBAR

The Edit toolbar presents the following buttons. Most of these functions also are available from menus:

- ◆ **List Properties/Methods:** Opens the list of properties and methods that are available for the object that precedes the period (Edit menu)

- ◆ **List Constants:** Shows the constants that are valid choices for the property that precedes the equals sign (Edit menu)

- ◆ **Quick Info:** Shows syntax for the variable, function, method, or procedure that contains the cursor (Edit menu)

- ◆ **Parameter Info:** Shows information about the parameters of the function that contains the cursor (Edit menu)

- ◆ **Complete Word:** Accepts the characters that VBA adds to the word that you are entering (Edit menu)

- ◆ **Indent:** Shifts all lines in the selection to the next tab stop (Edit menu)

- ◆ **Outdent:** Shifts all lines in the selection to the previous tab stop (Edit menu)

- ◆ **Toggle Breakpoint:** Sets or removes a breakpoint at the current line of code (Debug menu and Debug toolbar)

- ◆ **Comment Block:** Places the comment character at the beginning of each line in the selected block of code (not on menus)

- ◆ **Uncomment Block:** Removes the comment characters from the lines in the selected block of code (not on menus)

- ◆ **Toggle Bookmark:** Turns bookmarks on or off for the active line (Edit menu→Bookmarks submenu)

- ◆ **Next Bookmark:** Moves to the next bookmark in the stack (Edit menu→Bookmarks submenu)

- ◆ **Previous Bookmark:** Moves to the previous bookmark in the stack (Edit menu→Bookmarks submenu)

- ◆ **Clear All Bookmarks:** Removes all bookmarks (Edit menu→Bookmarks submenu)

Using Bookmarks

You can place bookmarks in your VBA code in a similar manner to placing them in a recordset. The bookmarks act as placeholders that you can return to later instead of scrolling through the code. Use the Edit toolbar buttons to set bookmarks on and off or to move to the next or previous bookmark, just as you would with bookmarks in Access objects. When you add a bookmark, an aqua rectangular icon appears in the margin indicator at the left of the statement.

TIP The Comment Block and Uncomment Block toolbar buttons are especially handy during debugging. To skip over a statement while you are debugging code, you can place an apostrophe at the start of any line. To omit a block of code, select the block of code and click the Comment Block button; Access adds all the apostrophes for you. This method can remove more than one block of code from execution. When you want the block of code back in the running, select it and click Uncomment Block.

Working in the Immediate window

The Immediate window is a versatile workplace where you can test code by taking the following actions:

- Displaying the results of a line of code, such as the following:
  - Values of controls, fields, or properties
  - An expression's result
- Assigning new values to controls, fields or properties and then rerunning the procedure with the new values

To open the Immediate window, follow these steps:

1. Suspend execution by either of the following actions:
   - Choose Run→Break.
   - Click the Break button on the Standard toolbar.

2. Open the Immediate window with either of the following actions:

    ■ Click the Immediate Window button on the Debug toolbar.

    ■ Choose View→Immediate Window.

After you have the Immediate window open, you can view current values, type a line of code, call another procedure, change the value of a variable or a property. The following describes some Immediate window uses that can help with debugging.

VIEWING CURRENT VALUES

Either of the following actions shows either an expression's results or a variable's current value:

◆ Use the `Debug.Print` method, as follows:

   `Debug.Me.LastName`

◆ Type `?` and the name of the variable, as follows:

   `?LastName`

To see the result of an expression, type the name of the variable the expression evaluates to. For example, if the expression is TotalSale = Price*(1.075), type ? TotalSale or Debug.Me.TotalSale in the Immediate window.

Figure 10-7 shows the Immediate window with the value of the `LastName` control in the current record. The record was visible in the DAR form when you clicked the Print DAR command button on the form. Click the Continue toolbar button to proceed to the next statement.

Using special keys

If you have selected the Use Access Special Keys option in the Startup dialog box, you can also open the Immediate window and the Code window by pressing Ctrl+G. The code for the currently open or selected Access object is shown in the Code window.

The Use Access Special Keys option also permits the following special key combinations:

◆ Brings the database window to the front (F11)

◆ Toggles between the built-in menu bar and a custom menu bar (Ctrl+F11)

◆ Starts the Visual Basic Editor (Alt+F11)

◆ Pauses receiving records from the server (Ctrl+Break)

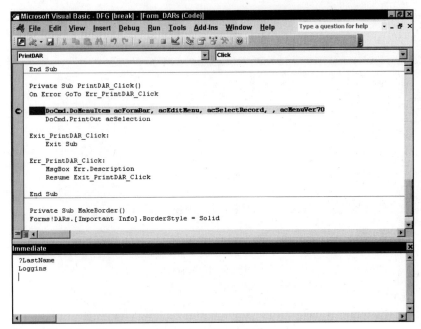

Figure 10-7: Checking the current value of a control.

RUN A PROCEDURE

The Immediate window can execute a procedure and show the result. To run the procedure, open it in the Code window and then type the procedure name in the Immediate window.

Figure 10-8 uses the GetWeekDay procedure to find the day of the week for a specific date.

EDIT A VARIABLE

You can change the value of a variable while you run the procedure in the Immediate window. Follow these steps:

1. Click in the margin indicator next to the statement following the statement that sets the value of the variable.

   This sets a breakpoint at the statement where you click. The procedure halts until you tell it to proceed.

2. Change the value of the variable in the Immediate window, and continue execution.

Breakpoints are explained elsewhere in this chapter.

Figure 10-9 shows the result of changing the SaleDate value and continuing execution.

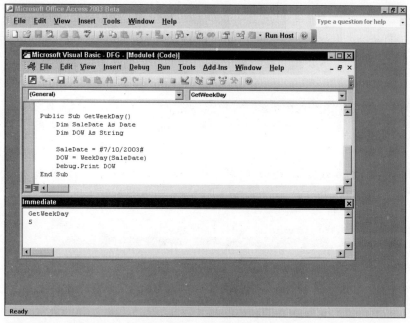

Figure 10-8: Running a procedure from the Immediate window.

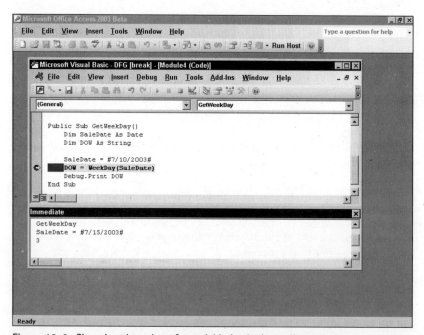

Figure 10-9: Changing the value of a variable in the Immediate window.

TIP You can repeat a line without retyping the name of the procedure. Just place the insertion point in the line, and press Enter.

WORKING WITH PROPERTIES

You can examine or change property settings with the Immediate window. Follow these steps:

1. Click in the margin indicator next to the statement following the statement that sets the value of the variable. This sets a breakpoint at the statement where you click.

   The procedure halts until you tell it to proceed.

2. When execution stops, type ? followed by the name of the property you want to check out. Then press Enter.

TIP For example, to see the ControlTipText for the AddDAR button, enter the following statement in the Immediate window and press Enter:

```
?Me.[AddDAR].ControlTipText
```

The window shows the following text which is the current Control Tip for the button.

```
Click to add a new DAR.
```

3. Repeat step 2 to view other property settings.

   For example, the following statement in the Immediate window displays the current value of the Tab Index:

   ```
   ?Me![AddDAR].TabIndex
   ```

   Figure 10-10 shows the results of using the Immediate window to view current settings of the ControlTipText and TabIndex properties for the AddDAR button..

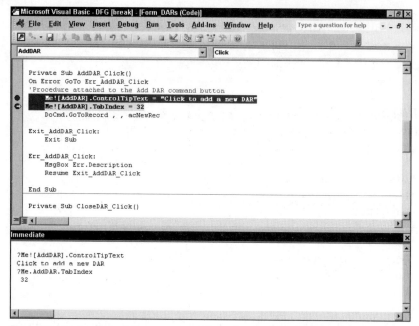

Figure 10-10: Looking at the property settings for the AddDAR command button.

To change one of the properties, enter the changes in the Immediate window; use the same syntax as you would in the Code window.

For example, to change the ControlTipText property and look at the results, enter the following code:

```
Me.AddDAR.ControlTipText = "Click to add DAR"
?Me.AddDAR.ControlTipText
Click to add DAR
```

The Immediate window supports many shortcut keys to help speed things along. The help topic "Immediate Window Keyboard Shortcuts" lists the shortcut key combinations.

Working in the Locals window

The Locals window automatically displays a list of all the objects and declared variables that are used in the current procedure. The window shows the name, current value, and type of all the items in the list. The values in the list update every time you suspend execution with a breakpoint or when you are stepping through code.

Figure 10-11 shows the Locals window for the event procedure that executes when you click the Set Color button on a form. The button opens an input box that prompts the user to enter a number between 1 and 4. Two breakpoints are set to capture the value of the intColor variable before and after the user enters the desired color code.

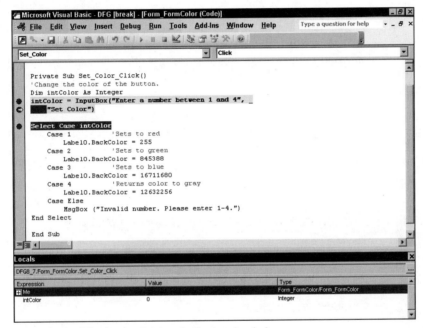

Figure 10-11: Viewing local values in the Locals window.

The window header shows the name of the current procedure. The main part of the window is divided into three columns:

◆ The first column in the Locals window, Expression, lists the names of the variables. The first item in the list is one of the following:

■ The module name, if the current module is a standard module

■ Me, if the procedure is part of a class module

◆ The second column lists the current values of the variables, which you can edit in place.

Click a value and make the change, and then press Enter or click elsewhere on the screen. If you have entered an illegal value, you remain in Edit mode and a message box explains the error. To cancel the edit, press Esc.

Numeric variables and properties must show a value. String variables can be blank.

◆ The third column indicates the type of variable or object.

 You can drag the column separators to change the width of a column.

After viewing the initial value in the Locals window, click Continue to move to the next breakpoint, the Select Case statement. Figure 10-12 shows the result of entering 1 in the input box.

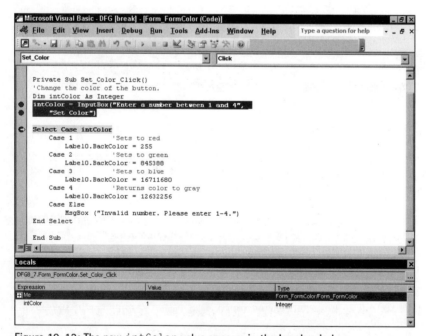

Figure 10-12: The new intColor value appears in the Locals window.

The Me variable can be expanded by clicking the plus sign (+) to show an alphabetized list of all the module-level variables and properties, with their current value and type. Figure 10-13 shows the expanded list for the Set_Color_Click module.

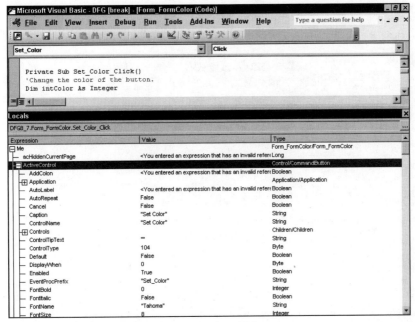

Figure 10-13: Expanding the list of Me-level variables.

Some variables, such as an array variable, may show the expand symbol. To change a variable in the expanded list, click the expand (+) icon, make the changes, and then click the collapse (–) icon.

Working in the Watch window

The Watch Window automatically displays a list of all the objects and declared variables used in the current procedure. Here are some of the things you can do with the Watch window.

◆ To add an item to the Watch list, select the item in the code that you want to monitor and then choose Debug→Add Watch. If you didn't select an item, you can type it in the Expression box (see Figure 10-14).

You can also add a Watch by dragging selected expressions from the Code window into the Watch window.

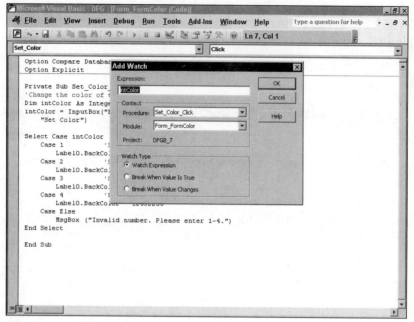

Figure 10-14: Adding an expression to the Watch list.

You can make the following adjustments in the Add Watch dialog box:

- Select the Procedure and Module to specify the range in which you want to have the expression evaluated.

- Choose the Watch Type to define how the system responds to the expression, as follows:

  - **Watch Expression:** Displays only the value.

  - **Break When Value Is True:** Pauses execution when the expression evaluates to True.

  - **Break When Value Changes:** Pauses execution when the value changes.

Figure 10-15 shows the Watch window after adding the InputBox and intColor expressions to the Watch list; breakpoints are set for both statements.

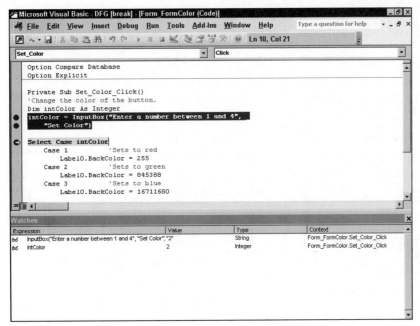

Figure 10-15: Viewing current values in the Watch window.

◆ To edit a watch expression, choose Debug→Edit Watch. Make the desired changes in the Edit Watch dialog box, which has most of the same options as the Add Watch dialog box.

◆ To delete the watch from the list, take either of the following actions:

- Choose Edit Watch, and click Delete.

- Select the expression in the Watch window, and press Delete.

◆ To check the current value of an expression that you haven't added to the Watch list, you can use the Quick Watch command. Select the expression in the Code window, and then take either of the following actions:

- Choose Debug→Quick Watch.

- Press Shift+F9.

◆ To add the expression to the Watch list, choose Add, as shown in Figure 10-16.

Choosing a Window

You should note the following significant differences between the Locals window and the Watch window:

◆ **Variables and expressions:** All appear in the Locals window, but only those you add to the Watch list appear in the Watch window.

◆ **Value updates:** Values in the Locals window change only when execution is suspended; the Watch window is updated while code is executing.

You can change the value of a variable in either window during a break.

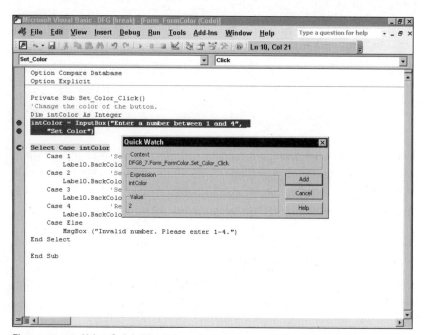

Figure 10-16: Using Quick Watch to see a value.

Controlling Execution During Debugging

When you run a procedure and an error occurs, either during execution or after completion, it is not always obvious where the error occurred. It is often helpful to execute the statements one at a time or in small increments. VBA offers the following ways to control the execution so that you can zero in on the cause of the error and fix it quickly:

◆ Step through the code one statement at a time

◆ Execute a specific statement

◆ Set breakpoints at specific statements where you can examine current values

◆ Add a `Stop` statement to halt execution

◆ Skip called procedures so that they are not executed one statement at a time

◆ Exit code and reset the variables and expressions to their original values.

Stepping through code

To step through your VBA code a little bit at a time, you need to suspend execution. Suspending execution keeps the code running but pauses between statements. While the code is suspended, you can check the current value of the variables. When you restart execution, you can choose to do the following:

◆ Execute a single statement at a time

◆ Jump to the next breakpoint

You can stop execution in the following ways:

◆ Add breakpoints at strategic locations, for example, just after an expression is evaluated or a value changes.

This is probably the best method of stopping execution.

◆ Stop execution manually by either of the following:

■ Click the Break button on the Standard toolbar

■ Choose Run→Break.

After you have suspended execution, you can move through the code and focus on specific statements.

◆ To step through the code one statement at a time and into the code of a called procedure, click the Step Into button on the Debug toolbar.

◆ To skip stepping through a procedure that is called from the current one, choose Step Over.

For example, you are debugging Procedure X, which includes a call statement to Procedure Y. You have already checked out Procedure Y, so you don't need to take the time to step through it. Procedure Y runs to completion, and then execution stops at the statement in Procedure X that follows the statement that called Procedure Y.

Once you start stepping through Procedure Y, you don't need to step through the whole thing. You can run Procedure Y to completion and return to Procedure X by choosing Step Out on the Debug toolbar.

◆ When you are sure that a block of code is complete and error-free, you can skip it and continue stepping through the code further down. While you are stepping through the code, place the cursor in the statement where you want to stop and choose Debug→Run To Cursor. When execution reaches the statement with the cursor, step-through resumes.

SETTING BREAKPOINTS

You can set breakpoints only on executable statements, not on declarations or comments. To specify a statement as a breakpoint, place the insertion point in the line of code and do one of the following:

◆ Click Toggle Breakpoint on the Debug toolbar.

◆ Choose Debug→Toggle Breakpoint.

◆ Right-click, and choose Toggle→Breakpoint on the shortcut menu that appears.

◆ Press F9.

TIP The easiest way to set the breakpoint at a certain statement is to click in the left margin bar next to the statement.

All of these actions place a dot in the left margin and change the color of the entire statement. Figure 10-17 shows a procedure with three breakpoints.

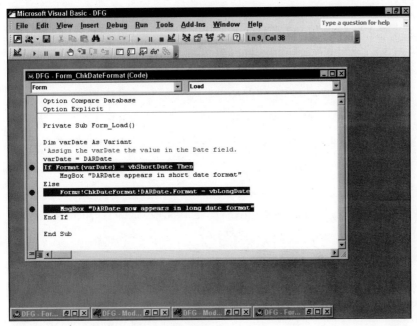

Figure 10-17: Setting breakpoints in code.

After you have set the breakpoints, you can do a lot of debugging, such as the following:

◆ While the code is suspended, you can do the following:

■ Check for intermediate values, and run the subsequent code one line at a time.

■ Change the value of variables in the Immediate or Locals window.

■ Resume execution at a statement that you want next without running the code in between.

◆ To resume execution at the next statement after the breakpoint, do one of the following:

■ Choose Run→Continue.

■ Click the Continue button on the Standard toolbar.

◆ To jump to another statement, follow these steps:

1. Place the insertion point anywhere in the statement.

2. Choose Debug→Set Next Statement.

3. Drag the yellow arrow in the margin indicator down to the statement that you want to run next.

4. Click the Run Sub/UserForm button.

◆ To remove a breakpoint after debugging, repeat the same action that you used to set the breakpoint as described earlier.

◆ To clear all the breakpoints at once, do one of the following:

■ Choose Debug→Clear All Breakpoints.

■ Press Ctrl+Shift+F9.

 Breakpoints are not saved with the code. If you need them again to continue debugging at a later session, you must reset them.

ADDING STOP STATEMENTS

You can suspend execution by adding Stop statements at strategic points. You can place Stop statements anywhere in your procedure to pause execution while you examine the results of the statements. Unlike breakpoints, the Stop statements remain with the procedure until you delete them.

 You can add a reminder to remove the Stop statements. Add a Debug.Print "There is a Stop here" statement just before each Stop statement. Then you can delete both statements and continue with execution.

Tracing calls

We recommend breaking complex operations into smaller, more reliable procedures that can be called when needed. Although modularized code is slightly less efficient than code in a single block because of the extra Call and Return statements, it is easier to debug and maintain. This structure results in a nested hierarchy of called procedures called a *stack*. All uncompleted procedures are listed in the stack. At the top of the list is the most recently called procedure, followed by the one called before that, and so on. This is called *FILO* (first in, last out).

A bit of computer humor: One system was classified as FISH — First In Still Here.

While you are debugging a project, you may need to see which procedures started and are still active. You can view the list while in Break mode by choosing View→Call Stack. If you have the Locals window open, you can also display the Call Stack dialog box by clicking the Calls button (...) that appears at the right side of the Procedure box.

Exiting and resetting

When you are finished running the procedure, you can simply close the VBE window and return to the Access window.

To reset the project and clear the stack and module-level variables, click the Reset button on the Debug toolbar.

There may be times when you try to make a change in a procedure during a break that causes VB to reset the project. In that case, you get a warning (as shown in Figure 10-18); you can proceed with the action or choose not to proceed.

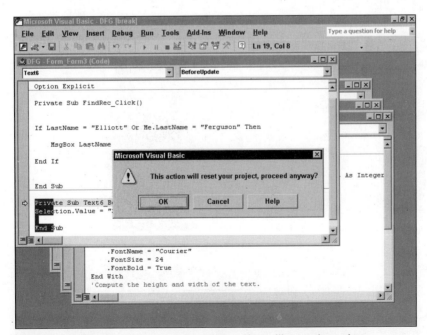

Figure 10-18: You have tried to make a change that will reset the project.

When you have finished evaluating a procedure, you can quickly move to another procedure by selecting the Window menu and choosing from the list. The list contains all the procedures that have been active during the current session (as shown in Figure 10-19).

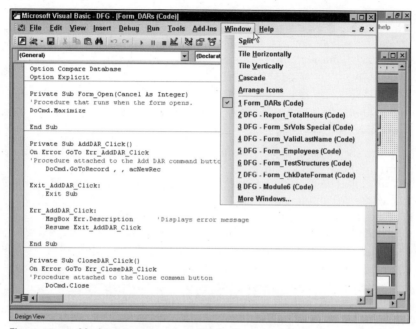

Figure 10-19: Moving to another procedure in the current project.

Summary

In this chapter, we have explored some of the tools VBA provides to help you create error-free code. Tools such as the toolbars and extra windows provide quick access to debugging features. You saw how to control execution by stepping through statements and setting specific breakpoints.

In the next chapter, we look at how creating VBA functions differs from writing sub procedures.

Chapter 11

Creating Function Procedures

IN THIS CHAPTER

- ◆ Understanding the difference between sub procedures and function procedures
- ◆ Making use of built-in functions
- ◆ Passing arguments
- ◆ Writing custom functions
- ◆ Running and debugging functions

Now that you know all about sub procedures and how to create, debug, and use them, you now find out how useful function procedures can be.

What's the Difference?

Both sub and function procedures can take arguments, execute a series of statements, and change the values of the arguments that are passed to them. However, only function procedures can do the following:

- ◆ Derive a value
- ◆ Return a value to the project

  The returned value bears the name of the function itself and you can use it to do the following:

  - As a variable in other code statements

On the right side of an expression like a built-in intrinsic function. Many built-in functions, such as the following, are used while developing Access databases:

- ◆ `Date`: Returns the current system date
- ◆ `Rtrim`: Truncates trailing spaces from a text field
- ◆ `MsgBox` and `InputBox`: Provide user interaction

The value that is returned from a function depends on the result of the expression it evaluates, as follows:

◆ Yes or No (True or False).

For example, the IsNull function returns Yes (True) if the expression is Null and No (False) if it is not.

◆ Value.

For example, the statement DatePart("d", Date()) returns the numeric value of the weekday of the current system date; this function includes a second function within the expression.

TIP To see all built-in Access and VBA functions, open the Expression Builder, double-click the Functions folder expansion button, and then click Built-in Functions. You can either scroll down the entire list at once or choose to see only a specific group of functions.

You can place functions in class modules that are stored with the form or report.

TIP If you often call a function from other procedures, place the function in one of the standard modules on the Modules page of the Database window.

Using Built-in Functions

To put a function to use, you can do the following:

◆ Call it from a sub procedure

When you call the function from a sub procedure, you create an expression using the function to return a value. For example, the following expression returns the current system date:

```
dteToday = Date()
```

◆ Use it as a control source

- ◆ Attach it to an event property

- ◆ Run it from a macro

The `Format` function can customize the date display to what you want to see. For example, the following statements return a more readable format (see Figure 11-1):

```
myDate = #1/15/2004#
strDate = Format(myDate, "dddd, mmm d yyyy")
MsgBox "My next birthday is " & strDate
```

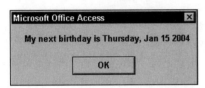

Figure 11-1: Using built-in functions to customize the display.

Passing arguments

Arguments are bits of information that a function needs for its job. Not all arguments are required; some are optional.

All arguments are passed by reference unless otherwise specified. This means that you pass the names of the arguments as shown in the following code:

```
Function MyProc(Arg1 As String, Arg2 As String) As String
```

This method is efficient because only 4-byte pointers are passed to the function, not a mixture of various-length values. These arguments are treated as variables and can be changed during the execution of the function.

You can pass an actual copy of the value. To do this, you must add the `ByVal` keyword, as follows:

```
Function MyProc(ByVal Arg1 As String, ByVal Arg2 As String) As String
```

Arguments passed by value cannot be changed during the execution of the function or the procedure that called the function.

If the function does not return a value, you don't need to enclose the arguments in parentheses. The following code is an example of using a function that doesn't return a value:

```
strResponse = MsgBox "All finished"
```

If you expect a response, you must use the parentheses, as follows:

```
strResponse = MsgBox("Are you finished?", 4, "Status")
```

In the preceding example, the second argument, 4, displays Yes and No buttons in the dialog box, and the function returns value of the button that the user clicked.

When you call the function, be sure to pass the arguments in the same order that they appear in the Function statement. For example, the Pmt function syntax is as follows:

```
Pmt(rate, nper, pv[, fv[, type]])
```

The terms in this code are described as follows:

- ◆ rate: Annual percentage rate
- ◆ nper: Number of payment periods
- ◆ pv: Present value
- ◆ fv: Future value
- ◆ type: Payments due at either the beginning or end of the payment period

If you want to know how much to save each month to accumulate $50,000 by the time your newborn daughter reaches college age, you can use the Pmt function to make this determination. Figure 11-2 shows the result of running the GetTuition sub procedure, which calls the Pmt function, as follows:

```
Sub GetTuition()
    Dim varTu
ition As Variant, varAge As Variant
    Dim varAPR As Variant, varPresVal As Variant
    Dim Savings As Variant, Fmt As String
varTuition = 50000
varAge = 18
varAPR = .065
varPresVal = 0
Fmt = "$###,##0.00"
```

```
Savings = Pmt(varAPR/12, varAge*12, varPresVal, varTuition)
MsgBox("You must save at least " & Format(Savings, Fmt) _
 & "each month")
End Sub
```

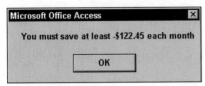

Figure 11-2: Calculating what you need to save for college tuition.

 Why does this figure show a negative amount to save for tuition? In accounting terms, that is exactly what that is: a deduction from your regular income.

More built-in functions

Here are some more popular built-in functions you can use in your code or in control properties.

THE DATEPART FUNCTION

To show the day of the week automatically when you enter the date, use the `DatePart` built-in function as the Control Source property for the control (see Figure 11-3).

THE DLOOKUP FUNCTION

The `DLookup` domain function returns the value of a particular field from a specified set of records that are defined by a table, query, or SQL expression.

The function has the following two required arguments and one optional argument:

```
DLookup(expr, domain[, criteria])
```

You can use the `DLookup` function to find the Senior Volunteer ID number, for example, as follows:

```
Dim varSrVolID As Variant
varSrVolID = DLookup("[Vol#]", "SrVols", "[LastName] = "Elliott"")
```

`Vol#` is the `expr` argument, the `SrVols` table is the `domain` argument, and `"[LastName] = "Elliott""` represents the optional `criteria` argument.

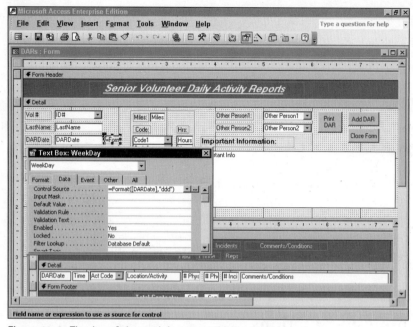

Figure 11–3: The day of the week is automatically entered.

THE MSGBOX AND INPUTBOX FUNCTIONS

The `MsgBox` and `InputBox` functions are popular user-interactive functions. Both of them have a wide variety of settings that can customize the display.

Chapter 12 further explains how you can use the `MsgBox` and `InputBox` functions in your application.

MSGBOX   The `MsgBox` function is designed primarily as a distributor of information, but it also accepts the user's button click response and acts on that. For example, you can set the `MsgBox` to return a value or not, give it a special name, and specify preferred graphics and an arrangement of buttons.

The `MsgBox` syntax includes the following five arguments; only one is required.

```
MsgBox(prompt[, buttons] [, title] [, helpfile, context]
```

The `prompt` argument is the only required `MsgBox` argument. It is a string expression that is displayed in the dialog box. You can use up to 1024 characters, depending on the font you are using.

You can use the vbCrLf (carriage return/line feed) constant to format a multiple-line message.

MsgBox has the following four optional arguments:

♦ buttons: Represents the total of the codes for the buttons, the icon, and other specifics of the dialog box appearance.

♦ title: Places custom text in the title bar of the dialog box. (The default is "Microsoft Access.")

♦ helpfile and context: Refer to compiled help file items.

INPUTBOX The InputBox function is designed specifically for user input. The dialog box performs the following tasks:

♦ Prompts the user for information

♦ Returns a string that contains the response

The InputBox function syntax is similar to that of the MsgBox function, as follows:

```
InputBox(prompt[, title] [, default] [, xpos] [, ypos] [, helpfile, context])
```

Like the MsgBox function, the prompt argument is the only required InputBox argument. It is a string expression that is displayed in the dialog box. You can use up to 1024 characters, depending on the font you are using.

InputBox has the following arguments that are different from MsgBox:

♦ default: A string expression that is displayed in the text box as a default response. If you don't include one, the text box is empty.

♦ xpos and ypos: Numeric expressions that specify the horizontal and vertical location of the dialog box on the screen.

The following optional InputBox arguments are the same as for MsgBox:

♦ title: Places custom text in the title bar of the dialog box. (The default is "Microsoft Access.")

♦ helpfile and context: Refer to compiled help file items.

CODE FROM THE SWITCHBOARD MANAGER

One of the most complex and versatile, albeit lengthy, functions that was created for an Access database processes the choice that you make in a switchboard. The Switchboard Manager creates the form based on the information that you enter during the process. The data is stored in a table called Switchboard Items; the table includes the following:

- Switchboard ID number
- Data for each switchboard item, as follows:
  - Item number
  - Text
  - Command
  - Argument

Figures 11-4 and 11-5 show an example of a switchboard together with the Switchboard Items table that was created by the Switchboard Manager.

Figure 11-4: A typical switchboard.

Switchboard Items : Table

SwitchboardID	ItemNumber	ItemText	Command	Argument
1	0	Main Switchboard		Default
1	1	Enter/Edit Senior Volunteers	3	Volunteers
1	2	Review DARs	3	DARs
1	3	Preview Reports	1	2
1	4	Lookup Email Addresses	4	emails
1	5	Exit This Database	6	
2	0	Preview Reports	0	
2	1	Senior Volunteer Summary	4	SrVol Summary
2	2	Volunteer Summary by Month	4	SrVol summary by Month
2	3	Activity Code Hours	4	CdHrs
2	4	Activity Code Hours by Month	4	CdHrsMonth
2	5	Return to Main Switchboard	1	1
	0			

Record: 1 of 12

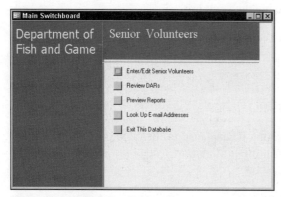

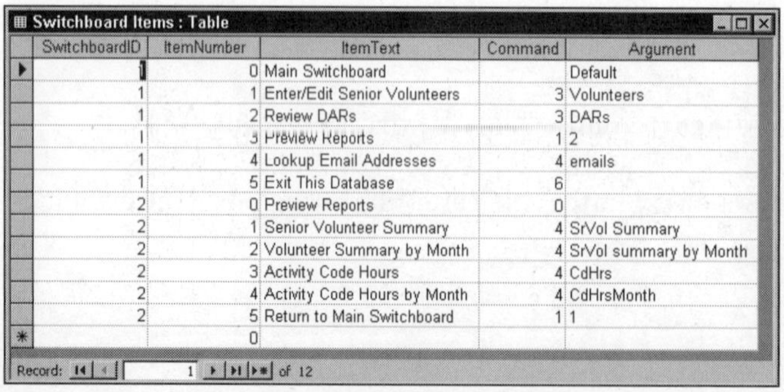

Figure 11-5: The Switchboard Items table created by the Switchboard Manager.

When you open the switchboard form, the following sub procedures run:

◆ Form_Activate with a single command, DoCmd.Restore.

◆ Form_Current performs the following actions:

  ■ Minimizes the database window

  ■ Initializes the form

  ■ Moves to the switchboard page named as the default in the startup options.

◆ The FillOptions procedure is called from the Form_Current procedure and fills in the options for each of the buttons from the Switchboard Items table.

◆ The HandleButtonClick function is the last procedure in the module; this function responds to the choice made by the user.

Figure 11-6 shows the function that is attached to the On Click event property of the first button on the switchboard form. (The argument 1 is passed to the function, indicating that button number 1 was clicked. Clicking the second button would pass 2 to the function.)

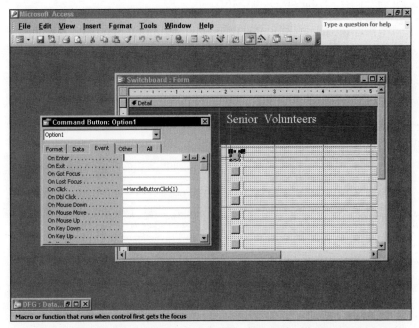

Figure 11-6: The HandleButtonClick function is attached to an event property.

The first block of code in the `HandleButtonClick` function declares constants and variables to be used in the function. Some error-handling is also included. For example, if no item in the Switchboard Items table matches, an error message is displayed, the variables are cleared and the function exits.

```
Private Function HandleButtonClick(intBtn As Integer)
' This function is called when a button is clicked.
' The intBtn argument indicates which button was clicked.

    ' Constants for the commands that can be executed.
    Const conCmdGotoSwitchboard = 1
    Const conCmdOpenFormAdd = 2
    Const conCmdOpenFormBrowse = 3
    Const conCmdOpenReport = 4
    Const conCmdCustomizeSwitchboard = 5
    Const conCmdExitApplication = 6
    Const conCmdRunMacro = 7
    Const conCmdRunCode = 8
    Const conCmdOpenPage = 9

    ' An error that is special cased.
    Const conErrDoCmdCancelled = 2501

    Dim con As Object
    Dim rs As Object
    Dim stSql As String

On Error GoTo HandleButtonClick_Err

    ' Find the item in the Switchboard Items table
    ' that corresponds to the button that was clicked.
    Set con = Application.CurrentProject.Connection
    Set rs = CreateObject("ADODB.Recordset")
    stSql = "SELECT * FROM [Switchboard Items] "
    stSql = stSql & "WHERE [SwitchboardID]=" & _
        Me![SwitchboardID] & " AND [ItemNumber]=" & intBtn
    rs.Open stSql, con, 1     ' 1 = adOpenKeyset

    ' If no item matches, report the error and exit the function.
    If (rs.EOF) Then
        MsgBox "There was an error reading the " & _
            "Switchboard Items table."
        rs.Close
        Set rs = Nothing
        Set con = Nothing
```

```
        Exit Function
    End If
```

The following Case structure examines the Command value passed to it and compares it with the declared constants.

```
Select Case rs![Command]

  'Go to another switchboard.
Case conCmdGotoSwitchboard
    Me.Filter = "[ItemNumber] = 0 AND [SwitchboardID]=" &_
        rs![Argument]

' Open a form in Add mode.
Case conCmdOpenFormAdd
    DoCmd.OpenForm rs![Argument], , , , acAdd

' Open a form.
Case conCmdOpenFormBrowse
    DoCmd.OpenForm rs![Argument]

' Open a report.
Case conCmdOpenReport
    DoCmd.OpenReport rs![Argument], acPreview

' Customize the Switchboard.
Case conCmdCustomizeSwitchboard
    ' Handle the case where the Switchboard Manager
    ' is not installed (e.g. Minimal Install).
    On Error Resume Next
    Application.Run "ACWZMAIN.sbm_Entry"
    If (Err <> 0) Then MsgBox "Command not available."
    On Error GoTo 0
    ' Update the form.
    Me.Filter = "[ItemNumber] = 0 AND [Argument] = 'Default' "
    Me.Caption = Nz(Me![ItemText], "")
    FillOptions

' Exit the application.
Case conCmdExitApplication
    CloseCurrentDatabase

' Run a macro.
Case conCmdRunMacro
    DoCmd.RunMacro rs![Argument]
```

```
' Run code.
Case conCmdRunCode
    Application.Run rs![Argument]

' Open a Data Access Page
Case conCmdOpenPage
    DoCmd.OpenDataAccessPage rs![Argument]

' Any other command is unrecognized.
Case Else
    MsgBox "Unknown option."

End Select
```

◆ The function finishes by closing the Switchboard Items recordset and exiting the function after clearing the variables. The following error-handling code blocks complete the function:

```
' Close the recordset and the database.
rs.Close

HandleButtonClick_Exit:
On Error Resume Next
    Set rs = Nothing
    Set con = Nothing
    Exit Function

HandleButtonClick_Err:
    ' If the action was cancelled by the user for
    ' some reason, don't display an error message.
    ' Instead, resume on the next line.
    If (Err = conErrDoCmdCancelled) Then
        Resume Next
    Else
        MsgBox "There was an error executing the command.", &

        vbCritical
        Resume HandleButtonClick_Exit
    End If

End Function
```

Do You Want Strings?

Many built-in functions come in the following versions:

- ◆ One that returns the default variant data type

- ◆ One that returns a string version of the result

Each has its advantages, as follows:

- ◆ The variant version can be more convenient, because it can handle different data types without a problem.

- ◆ The string version can be more efficient because it uses less memory.

To decide which version of the function to use, consider using the string version in the following cases:

- ◆ An extensive program that includes many variables.

- ◆ You enter data directly into random-access files.

The string version of a function is easily recognizable by the $ character at the end of the function name. For example:

- ◆ Chr is the variant version, and Chr$ is the string version.

- ◆ Format returns a variant, while Format$ returns a string.

The same help topic explanation applies to both versions.

 Chapter 13 covers custom dialog boxes and switchboards in detail.

Writing Custom Function Procedures

Creating custom functions is similar to writing sub procedures. You can place a function in either of the following:

- ◆ A class module that is attached to a form or report

- ◆ A standard module

Creating the function

To start a new function, do one of the following:

- In the database window, click Modules in the Objects group, and then click New.

- To open an existing standard module or unassociated class module, select the module in the Modules page and click Design.

- To open a class module, open the form or report in design view, and click the Code button on the toolbar.

- To start a new class module that is not associated with a form or report, choose Insert→Class Module while in the Database window.

Declaring the function

The first statement in a function procedure is the one that does the following:

- Names the function

- Lists the arguments (if any)

The `Function` statement has the following syntax:

```
[Public | Private | Friend] [ Static] Function name [(arglist)] [As type]
    [statements]
    [name = expression]
    [Exit Function]
    [statements]
    [name = expression]
End Function
```

The elements of the `Function` statement are the same as those in `Sub` statement.

 Chapter 9 describes the function elements and the argument list components.

The only required elements are as follows:

- `Function` keyword
- Name

If you pass arguments with the optional `arglist`, you need provide only the names of the arguments.

The `Exit Function` statement causes an immediate exit from the function, and execution resumes at the statement following the one that called the function. You can place `Exit Function` statements anywhere in the code.

Determining the scope

The `Public` and `Private` elements of the `Function` statement determine the function's range of accessibility. If you don't specify the scope, Access uses the default `Public` setting. The function can then be called from a procedure in any module in the current project.

Returning a value

The function doesn't have to return a value, but if it does, assign the value to the name of the function. You can place any number of these assignments in the procedure.

Examples of useful functions

To call a function from several sources, you need to build the function in a standard module. Follow these steps:

1. Click the Modules button in the database window, and choose New.

2. In the VBE window, use one of the following actions to choose Procedure:

   ■ Choose Insert→Procedure.

   ■ Click Insert on the Standard toolbar, and choose Procedure from the drop-down list that appears.

3. In the Add Procedure dialog box (shown in Figure 11-7), enter the name of the function and choose Function as the procedure type.

Function Default Values

If you don't assign a value to the function name, the default value depends on how you declared the type of the function, as follows:

◆ Numeric functions: 0

◆ String functions: a zero-length string (`" "`)

◆ Variant functions: `Empty`

4. Click OK.

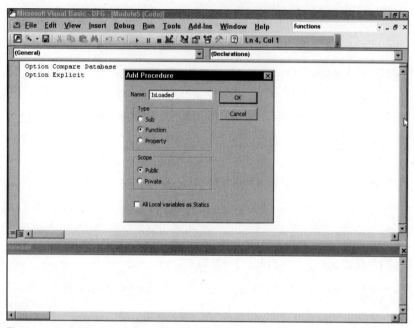

Figure 11-7: Adding a new function procedure to a module.

IN THE HUMAN RESOURCES DEPARTMENT

The Human Resources department is responsible for maintaining complete and accurate employee information. In addition, the department must be able to retrieve information and answer questions from management, such as the following:

◆ Finding the name of an employee's supervisor.

◆ Determining an employee's current status.

◆ Looking up the employee's supervisor's phone extension.

◆ Building an employee's complete name.

The following are functions that carry out these activities.

LOOKING UP THE SUPERVISOR'S EXTENSION This function requires an argument for the employee's company number. Then the function builds an SQL string around the EmpCN argument and filters the employee records to find the one that matches.

```
Public Function GetSupervisor(EmpCN As Long) As String
'This function uses the Employee Company Number to find and return
'the full name of the employee's supervisor.

On Error GoTo GetSupervisor_Err

Dim rst As Recordset
Dim strSQL As String

strSQL = "SELECT * FROM tblEmployee WHERE tblEmployee.EmpCN = "

'The next statement concatenates the EmpCN argument value
'with the SQL string and opens the recordset with that criterion.
'Then GetSupervisor is set to the value of the Supervisor
'field in the resulting record.

Set rst = CurrentDb.OpenRecordset(strSQL & EmpCN)
GetSupervisor = rst!Supervisor

GetSupervisor_Exit:
    Exit function

GetSupervisor_Err:
    If Err.Number <> 0 then
  MsgBox Err.Number & " " & Error.Description
    End If
End Function
```

DETERMINING AN EMPLOYEE'S CURRENT STATUS   This function also uses a SQL statement to return an employee's current status.

```
Public Function GetEmpStatus(EmpStatus As Long) As String
On Error GoTo GetEmpStatus_Err

Dim rst As Recordset
Dim strSQL As String

    strSQL = "SELECT * FROM EmpStatus WHERE EmpStatus.StatusID = "
    Set rst = CurrentDb.OpenRecordset(strSQL & EmpStatus)

    GetEmpStatus = EmpStatus!Status

GetEmpStatus_Exit:
    Exit Function
```

```
GetEmpStatus_Err:
   If Err.No <> 0 then
         MsgBox = Err.Number & " " & Err.Description
   End If
   End Function
```

USING THE DLOOKUP FUNCTION This function uses the DLookup built-in function to return the following:

- The name of an employee's supervisor

- The supervisor's phone extension number

This function uses the DLookup statement twice, as follows:

- In the first DLookup statement, Supervisor is the expression argument and tblEmployees is the domain argument. The criteria argument is the concatenation of the string "EmployeeName = " with the strSupName variable.

- The second DLookup statement repeats the process to find the supervisor's phone extension number.

The function returns the GetSupervisorExt string, which contains both the name and extension, as follows:

```
Public Function GetSupervisorExt(strEmployee As String) As String
'This is a simple example of a function that sends
'the employee's name as the argument, and returns
'the employee's supervisor name and contact extension.
On Error GoTo GetSupervisorExt_Err

Dim strSupName As String
Dim strPhoneNo As String

strSupName = DLookup("Supervisor", "tblEmployees", _
                  "EmployeeName ='" & strEmployee & "'")
strPhoneExt = DLookup("WorkPhone", "tblPhoneList", _
                  "EmployeeName ='" & strSupName & "'")
GetSupervisorExt = "This employees supervisor is " & strSupName _
& " and can be reached at extension:" & _ strPhoneExt
GetSupervisorExt_Exit:
    Exit Function
```

```
GetSupervisorExt_Err:
   If Err.No <> 0 then
       MsgBox = Err.Number & " " & Err.Description
   End If
End Function
```

BUILDING A FULL NAME   A very useful function builds a complete name out of the three fields in a table or form (see Figure 11-8).

Write the function as a new module, and then attach it to the `Control Source` property of an unbound text box control in the form. To accomplish this, use the following code:

```
Public Function GetFullName(FirstName As String, MI As String, _
LastName As String) As String
'This function concatenates the first name with the middle initial
'and last name.
'If there is no middle initial, the first and last names close up.

GetFullName = FirstName & " " & IIf(IsNull([MI]), "", [MI]) & _
    " " & LastName

End Function
```

Figure 11-8: Using a function to build a complete volunteer name.

After you have created and tested the function, you need to assign it to the control's Control Source property as follows:

1. Select the control in the form design.

2. Open the Property sheet and click the Data tab.

3. Then do either of the following:

    a. Enter the following expression:

        ```
        =GetFullName([FirstName],[MI],[LastName])
        ```

    b. Click the Build button (...) to open the Expression Builder and select the function name from the list of available functions as shown in Figure 11-9.

You can use the following steps to attach the function to the control's event property:

Select the name of the function from the DFG function list, as shown in Figure 11-9.

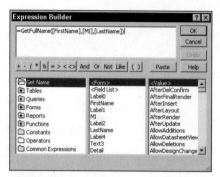

Figure 11-9: Selecting a custom function from the Expression Builder.

The GetFullName function uses the IIf and IsNull functions to check for a blank middle initial field.

USE A FUNCTION TO SYNCHRONIZE DATA IN TWO FORMS

A popular (but not built-in) function is the IsLoaded function, which tests the current state of a form, as follows:

- ◆ If the form is open in either form view or datasheet view, the function returns True.

- ◆ If the form is in design view or is closed, the function returns False. (The function is declared as Integer because the VBA value of True is –1 and False is 0.)

The following code determines whether a form is open. The form name is passed as an argument to the IsLoaded function. The two Const declarations clear the values of the form's ObjectState and CurrentView properties by setting them to 0.

```
Public Function IsLoaded(ByVal strFormName As String) As Integer
'This function returns True If the named form is open in Form View
'or Datasheet View. False if not.

Const conObjStateClosed = 0
Const conDesignView = 0
```

```
If SysCmd(acSysCmdGetObjectState, acForm, strFormName) <> _
    conObjStateClosed Then
    If Forms(strFormName).CurrentView <> conDesignView Then
        IsLoaded = True
    End If
End If
End Function
```

Two important form properties are used in this code and their values determine the current state of the form, as follows:

♦ The `ObjectState` property value depends on the current state of the form, as follows:

0: Form is closed

1: Form is open

2: Form is new

3: Form is changed but not saved (dirty)

♦ The `DesignView` property value depends on the current view of the form, as follows:

0: Design view

1: Datasheet view

2: Form view

The `SysCmd` method in the `If` statement returns the state of the form. The `SysCmd` syntax includes the following arguments:

■ The `Action` argument specifies the type of information that you want about the object. This argument is always required with `SysCmd`.

■ An intrinsic constant represents the object, `acForm` in this example.

■ The object is identified by name, which was passed by value to the `IsLoaded` function.

 The intrinsic constant and object name are only required for `SysCmd` with the `acSysCmdGetObjectState` action, which this example uses.

♦ The nested `If` statements follow these steps:

1. Check whether the form is not closed.

If the form is closed, the function ends. If the form is not closed, the function continues.

2. If the form is not closed, the next If statement checks whether the form is not in design view.

3. If both If statements are True (the form is not closed and not in design view), the function returns True.

TIP The IsLoaded function can prevent unauthorized changes to a form design.

One use for the IsLoaded function is to synchronize data in two unrelated forms. For example, the Activity Codes form contains a button that you can click to see a more detailed description of the code.

◆ When you click the button, the Actys pop-up form opens, with more information about the code that is currently showing in the Activity Codes form, as shown in Figure 11-10.

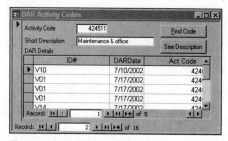

Figure 11-10: Synchronizing data in two forms.

◆ When you move to another record in the Activity Codes form, the Actys form does not move to the record that matches the Activity Code in the main form. You need to click the button again to refresh the information in the Actys form.

The IsLoaded function comes in handy if you want to synchronize the data in both forms. After you have built the IsLoaded function, follow these steps:

1. Create a macro, such as that shown in Figure 11-11, that runs the function if the Actys form is already open.

If the form is open, the macro filters the records to show the description that matches the record that is currently in the Activity Codes form.

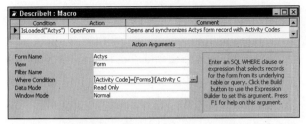

Figure 11-11: Using a macro to filter records if the form is active.

Be sure to use the complete identifier in the Where Condition text box in the Action Arguments pane of the macro design, as follows:

```
[Activity Code] = [Forms]![Activity Codes]![Activity Code]
```

If you need help with the identifier, click the Build button (...) next to the Where Condition argument and use the Expression Builder.

2. Set the Data Mode to Read Only and the Window Mode to Normal.

3. Save and name the macro, and then attach it to the On Current event property of the main form, the Activity Codes form.

Figure 11-12 shows the selection of the macro name from the list of available macros in the On Current event property box.

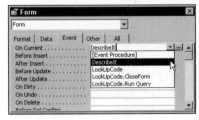

Figure 11-12: Setting the On Current property to the macro.

CHECK FIELDS FOR DATA TYPE

The FieldType function is a useful custom function that does the following items:

◆ Searches a table structure for the field that is used as the Control Source property for a control on a form

◆ Returns the data type of that field

The parent sub procedure is attached to the On Got Focus event property, and once it locates the field in the table structure, the procedure calls the FieldType function to identify the data type. You can copy the sub procedure for other controls in the form. These controls share the FieldType function, because they are all in the same class module.

This procedure refers to a database, a table definition, and fields as DAO (Data Access Objects).

The following code examines controls in a form and returns the control's name and data type:

```
Private Sub Field7_GotFocus()


    On Error GoTo Field7_Err:
    'Declare all the objects and variables used in the procedure.
    Dim tdf As DAO.TableDef
    Dim dbs As DAO.Database
    Dim fld As DAO.Field
    Dim ctlName As Control
    Dim srcType As Integer
    Dim srcTypeName As String

    Set db = CurrentDb
    Set tdf = db.TableDefs(Me.RecordSource)
    Set ctlName = Me.ActiveControl
    Debug.Print Me.ActiveControl

    'Step through the list of fields in the table to find the
    'control source for the field in question.
    'Set the srcType variable to the integer value of the data type.

    For Each fld In tdf.Fields
        If fld.Name = ctlName.ControlSource Then
            srcType = fld.Properties("Type")
        End If
    Next fld
    Debug.Print srcType
    'Call the FieldType function and pass the srcType argument.
    srcTypeName = FieldType(srcType)
```

```
    MsgBox ctlName.ControlSource & " is " & srcTypeName & _
" data type."
Field7_Exit:
    Exit Sub

Field7_Err:
    If Err.Number <> 0 Then
        MsgBox Err.Number & " " & Err.Description
    End If

End Sub

Function FieldType(fldType As Integer) As String
'Uses the passed integer field type to find the text definition.
On Error GoTo FieldType_Err:

    Select Case fldType
        Case 1
            FieldType = "Boolean"
        Case 2
            FieldType = "Byte"
        Case 3
            FieldType = "Integer"
        Case 4
            FieldType = "Long"
        Case 5
            FieldType = "Currency"
        Case 6
            FieldType = "Single"
        Case 7
            FieldType = "Double"
        Case 8
            FieldType = "Date"
        Case 10
            FieldType = "Text"
        Case 11
            FieldType = "OLE"
        Case 12
            FieldType = "Memo"
        Case 15
            FieldType = "GUID (Replication-ID)"
    End Select
    Debug.Print FieldType

FieldType_Exit:
    Exit Function
```

```
FieldType_Err:
    If Err.No <> 0 then
        MsgBox = Err.Number & " " & Err.Description
    End If
End Function
```

When you run the function, the MsgBox dialog box shows the name and data type of the DARDate field, as shown in Figure 11-13.

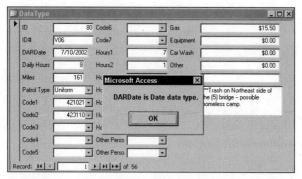

Figure 11-13: Inspecting the data type of a control in a form.

Running and Debugging a Function

Testing a new function is similar to testing a new sub procedure, except you can't just run the function in the Code window. You must take one of the following actions:

◆ Call the function from a sub procedure

◆ Run the function with a macro using the RunCode action

You can use all the VBE debugging tools to check the progress of the function. In the preceding code example, we have added three Debug.Print statements to check the following values:

◆ Name of the active control

◆ Number corresponding to the data type

◆ Name of the corresponding data type

If you set breakpoints in the code, you can see the values in the Immediate window when the code pauses (see Figure 11-14). Without breakpoints, you can return to the VBE code window and check the values.

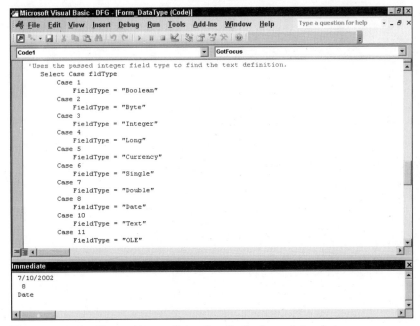

Figure 11-14: Looking at intermediate values in the Immediate window.

 NOTE If you call a function from a procedure that you are stepping through, when you get to the function, you can step through the function as well.

Summary

In this chapter, we have looked at several useful functions of Access and VBA. We also demonstrated how to create and make use of custom functions to carry out special activities. Writing and testing function procedures are similar to creating sub procedures, but functions are useful because they can return a value to your project.

In the next chapter, we look more closely into requesting user input and responding to the results.

Part III

Programming User Interactions with VBA

Chapter 12

Building User Interaction

IN THIS CHAPTER

◆ Creating a `MsgBox` macro

◆ Using a `MsgBox` function as an error trap

◆ Using `InputBox` functions

◆ Creating a dialog box and setting properties

◆ Adding controls to a dialog box

◆ Processing user input

◆ Creating a form from a template

◆ Adding the human touch

THE APPLICATIONS THAT YOU BUILD with Access are essentially interactive. Access is an event-driven program. It does not take any action until something happens. The user can click a button, move the mouse pointer, or close a form or report preview. The system can also encounter an error or request an argument to complete a command. It is a give-and-take scenario. In this chapter, we discuss some of the ways that you can make these interactions work for your users.

Requesting User Input

The `MsgBox` and `InputBox` functions create predefined dialog boxes that stay open until you respond to the message that's displayed. Both functions can return a response from the user. Your choice depends on your needs, as follows:

◆ The `MsgBox` function is focused more on presenting information to the user. It can return a value based on the user's action.

◆ The `InputBox` function is designed to gather a value from the user to complete an action.

Chapter 6 introduces the MsgBox and InputBox functions.

The MsgBox function

The MsgBox function displays information and waits for a response. It is a good way to impart information and get a simple answer in return. When the user clicks one of the buttons in the dialog box, the function returns the value of the response and quickly closes the box. The VBA procedure that you have written can then use the response to continue execution. You can use either a simple Yes or No, or you can assign a variable to the value that is returned by the MsgBox function and use the response in a Select Case or other branching structure.

You can use the MsgBox function in a macro if you are looking for a simple response. For example, you would like the user to be able to cancel the deletion of a record if it should in fact be saved. To do so, start a new macro and select CancelEvent as the action. Then click the Conditions button on the Macro Design toolbar to add the Condition column. Enter the following expression in the Condition column:

```
MsgBox("Do you mean to delete this SrVol?", 291, "Delete SrVol")<>6
```

The first string in the function is the message that is to be displayed in the box, the number 291 specifies the buttons and icon to display, and the second string appears as the title of the box. The 291 argument is the numeric sum of the Yes/No/Cancel button combination (3), the Warning Query icon (32), and the assignment of the second button (No) as the default (256). Because this is a condition, if the user's response is not 6 (Yes), the delete action is indeed canceled and the record is saved. Next, attach the macro to the Before Del Confirm event property of the form itself.

Figure 12-1 shows the macro and the message that is displayed when the user tries to delete a record.

If you would prefer that the operation be carried out by a procedure, convert the macro to a VBA function. Select the macro in the Macro window, and choose Tools→Macro→Convert Macros to Visual Basic.

Both of the following options in the Convert Macro dialog box are helpful, so keep them checked:

♦ Add error handling to generated functions

♦ Include macro comments

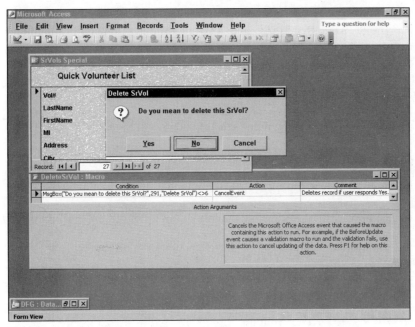

Figure 12-1: A macro that uses the `MsgBox` function to get a response.

The following function is a result of converting the `DeleteSrVol` macro:

```
'------------------------------------------------------------
' DeleteSrVol
'
'------------------------------------------------------------
Function DeleteSrVol()
On Error GoTo DeleteSrVol_Err

    If (MsgBox("Do you mean to delete this SrVol?", 291, _
"Delete SrVol")) Then
        ' Deletes the record if user responds Yes.
        DoCmd.CancelEvent
    End If

DeleteSrVol_Exit:
    Exit Function

DeleteSrVol_Err:
    MsgBox Error$
    Resume DeleteSrVol_Exit

End Function
```

The MsgBox function and its syntax were introduced in Chapter 6. The prompt argument is the only one that is required. This message is displayed in the dialog box. The prompt argument can contain up to 1024 characters, depending on the width of the font. To display the message in more than one line, concatenate the VBA constant vbCrLf within the message. The constant combines the ASCII carriage return character, Chr(13), with the line feed character, Chr(10). Figure 12-2 shows the results of the following sub procedure:

```
Private Sub Command0_Click()
MsgBox "This is the first line, " & vbCrLf & _
    "this is the second line, " & vbCrLf & _
    "and this completes the message.", _
    vbOKOnly + vbInformation, "Three-line message"
End Sub
```

Figure 12-2: Creating a multiple-line message.

The optional buttons argument can assume one of two formats, as follows:

- A numeric expression that represents the sum of the following:

  - The type of buttons to display.

  - The icon style to use.

  - The identity of the default button.

    This is illustrated in Figure 12-1 above where the buttons argument total is 291.

- A set of VBA constants that represent the button settings.

Table 12-1 describes the choices for the button settings, icon style, and default button assignment.

Table 12-1 MSGBOX FUNCTION BUTTONS ARGUMENT SETTINGS

VBA Constant	Value	Description
vbOKOnly	0	Displays the OK button only
vbOKCancel	1	Displays OK and Cancel buttons
vbAbortRetryIgnore	2	Displays Abort, Retry, and Ignore buttons
vbYesNoCancel	3	Displays Yes, No, and Cancel buttons
vbYesNo	4	Displays Yes and No buttons
vbRetryCancel	5	Displays Retry and Cancel buttons
vbCritical	16	Displays Critical Message icon
vbQuestion	32	Displays Warning query icon
vbExclamation	48	Display Warning Message icon
vbInformation	64	Displays Information Message icon
vbDefaultButton1	0	First button is default
vbDefaultButton2	256	Second button is default
vbDefaultButton3	512	Third button is default
vbDefaultButton4	768	Fourth button is default
vbApplicationModal	0	Modal; user must respond before continuing
vbSystemModal	4096	All applications are suspended until user responds
vbMsgBoxHelpButton	16384	Includes Help button
vbMsgBoxSetForeground	65536	Sets message box window in the foreground
vbMsgBoxRight	524288	Right-aligns text
vbMsgBoxRtlReading	1048576	Text appears as right-to-left reading on Hebrew and Arabic systems

You can use the sum of all the settings that you want to implement, or you can list the constants in the argument. It is easier to understand the choices if you use the constants, as shown in the following example:

```
MsgBox "Here we go again!", 563, "Test Case"

MsgBox "Here we go again!", vbYesNoCancel + vbExclamation + _
    vbDefaultButton4, "Test Case"
```

 To have some fun with numbers, try to build two combinations of the `buttons` argument values that result in the same total.

If you omit the `buttons` argument, it is assumed to be 0, the combined values of the `vbOKOnly`, `vbDefaultButton1`, and `vbApplicationModal` constants. This results in showing only the OK button; the message box stays on the screen until you click the OK button. But, if you omit the `buttons` argument and want to add a custom title to the message box, you must still include the comma placeholder.

The `title` argument specifies the text to display in the box's title bar in place of the default "Microsoft Access." In the preceding example, the message box would show Test Case in the title bar. The `helpfile` and `context` arguments identify the help file that can provide context-sensitive help with this dialog box. The `helpfile` argument is a string, while the `context` argument is a numeric expression.

You can use the value that is returned by the `MsgBox` function to fuel a `Select Case` or `If...Then...Else` structure. If you set a variable to the value that is returned by the `MsgBox` function, enclose all the arguments in parentheses, as follows:

```
strResponse = MsgBox("Please enter your ZIP code", vbOKOnly)
```

Table 12-2 lists the values that are returned by the `MsgBox` function when the user responds.

TABLE 12-2 VALUES RETURNED BASED ON USER RESPONSE

Constant	Value	Button Clicked
vbOK	1	OK
vbCancel	2	Cancel
vbAbort	3	Abort
vbRetry	4	Retry
vbIgnore	5	Ignore

Constant	Value	Button Clicked
vbYes	6	Yes
vbNo	7	No

The following example is an event procedure that executes before the form updates with the newly entered record data. It senses that no e-mail address exists although there is a last name, and it asks the user to check the address.

◆ If the user responds Cancel, focus is returned to the email control.

◆ If the user responds OK, the record is saved without an e-mail address.

Figure 12-3 shows the message box that results from the following code:

```
Private Sub Form_BeforeUpdate(Cancel As Integer)
Dim strMsg As String
Dim bytResponse As Byte
'Test both LastName and email values for blanks.

If Not IsNull(LastName) And IsNull(email) Then
    strMsg = "Are you sure there is no e-mail address?"
    bytResponse = MsgBox(strMsg, vbQuestion + vbOKCancel, _
    "No E-mail?")
    If bytResponse = vbCancel Then
    'You have clicked the Cancel button.
        email.SetFocus        'Return to the email control
        Cancel = True         'Cancel saving the record
    End If
End If
End Sub
```

If you have provided a customized help file for the application, you can pass the helpfile and context arguments with the MsgBox function. The user can press F1 to see the text that corresponds to the context numeric value.

You can include a Help button on the dialog box by adding the vbMsgBoxHelpButton constant to the list in buttons argument. Clicking the Help button opens the context-sensitive help of Microsoft Access. The message box remains open after you close the Help window, and no value is returned until you click one of the other MsgBox buttons.

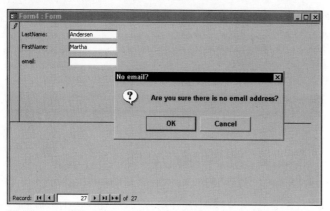

Figure 12-3: Using `MsgBox()` to check for e-mail addresses.

GETTING HELP FROM THE OBJECT BROWSER

When you are writing code that involves VBA constants, you can look them up in the Object Browser. In the VBA window, take one of the following actions:

♦ Click the Object Browser button on the Standard toolbar.

♦ Choose View→Object Browser.

TIP

If you choose the VBA Library from the Project/Library box, you don't have to scroll through all the other referenced library constants.

The VBA constants are grouped in many enumerations. The `VbMsgBoxStyle` enumeration contains constants that are used to specify the behavior of the `MsgBox` function. You use these constants to set the list of items for the `buttons` argument. Figure 12-4 shows the list of `MsgBoxStyle` constants.

When you select a constant in the Object Browser, you can see the equivalent numeric value in the taskbar. In Figure 12-4, you see that the value of the `vbOKCancel` button is set to 1. If you need more information about a constant, select the constant in the Members of pane and click the Help button in the Object Browser toolbar.

The `VbMsgBoxResult` enumeration lists the constants and the values that are returned by the `MsgBox` function after the user responds.

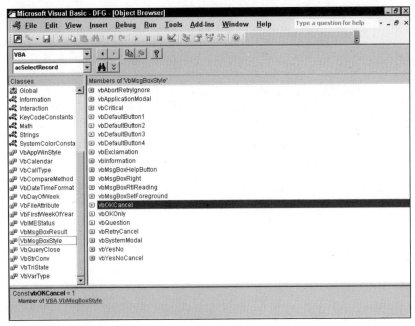

Figure 12-4: Looking up VBA constants in the Object Browser.

USING MSGBOX FOR ERROR HANDLING

If something goes wrong with a procedure, it is always helpful to see some additional information about what has happened over and above the standard error message. The following are some examples of putting the `MsgBox` function to work.

◆ Message boxes can interpret run-time errors when they happen.

◆ You can include more informative messages when an error occurs that the user can correct.

◆ You can create a custom list of numbered errors that relate specifically to your business.

The following function uses the `MsgBox` function to display custom error messages that are contained in the `tblErrors` table. With the function declared Public, it is available to any object in the project.

```
Public Function ErrorMessage(ErrorNo As Integer)
'This is a function that generates a message box with a
'custom error message. It uses a select case structure and
'a DLookup function to produce the text string description.
```

```
On Error GoTo ErrorMessage_Err:
Dim strErrDesc As String

Select Case ErrorNo              'Branches to custom error number

Case 3120
    strErrDesc = DLookup("ErrDesc", "tblErrors", & _
"ErrNumber =" & ErrorNo)

Case 3135
    strErrDesc = DLookup("ErrDesc", "tblErrors", & _
"ErrNumber =" & ErrorNo)

Case 3170
    strErrDesc = DLookup("ErrDesc", "tblErrors", _
"ErrNumber =" & ErrorNo)

Case 3320
    strErrDesc = DLookup("ErrDesc", "tblErrors", _
"ErrNumber =" & ErrorNo)

End Select

MsgBox "The following error Occurred " & ErrorNo & _
" " & strErrDesc , vbCritical, "Run-time error"

Exit_This_Function:
    Exit Function

ErrorMessage_Err:
    If Err.Number <> 0 Then
        MsgBox Err.Number & " " & Err.Description
    End If
    Resume Exit_This_Function

End Function
```

The InputBox function

The InputBox function creates a special message box that does the following:

♦ Displays a prompt for a single bit of information with an empty text box

♦ Waits for the user to enter text or click a button

♦ Returns the contents of the text box with the button response to the procedure that called the function

The `InputBox` syntax is as follows:

```
InputBox(prompt[, title] [, default] [, xpos] [, ypos] [, helpfile, context])
```

The `prompt` and `title` arguments and the `helpfile` and `context` arguments are the same as for the `MsgBox` function.

The optional `default` argument is the string expression to be displayed in the text box. If you omit this argument, the text box is empty.

The `xpos` and `ypos` arguments are numeric expressions that specify the location of the dialog box on the screen. The `xpos` argument determines the horizontal distance between the left edge of the box and the left edge of the screen. The `ypos` argument determines the vertical distance between the top of the dialog box and the top of the screen. Both are measured in twips. If these two arguments are omitted, the dialog box is centered horizontally and placed about one-third of the way down from the top of the screen.

 A *twip* is 1/20th of a point; there are 1440 twips in an inch. Therefore, if you want the `InputBox` 2 inches from the left side, set the `xpos` property to 2880.

COMBINING THE MSGBOX AND INPUTBOX FUNCTIONS

You can combine an `InputBox` function with the `MsgBox` function if you want to confirm the user's entry or display the entry in another context. For example, the following code displays a dialog box for entering your first name and then includes the entry in a message box. The `InputBox` shows a custom title, while the `MsgBox` shows the default "Microsoft Access." Figures 12-5 and 12-6 show how these two functions can work together.

```
Private Sub Form_Load()
Dim YourName As String
    YourName = InputBox("Please enter your first name", "Welcome")
    MsgBox "Welcome to the show, " & YourName & "!"
End Sub
```

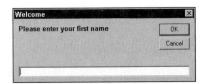

Figure 12-5: The `InputBox` prompts for your name.

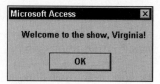

Figure 12-6: The MsgBox displays your response.

LOOKING UP A VALUE

If you are running a business and you need to keep current on your customers' outstanding balances, you can use the InputBox function to get the customer's ID number. The following example uses the InputBox response to query the database for the customer's invoices and sums all the items charged to the client that have not been paid for:

```
Public Function GetAmountOwed() As Currency

    On Error GoTo GetInvoiceNumber_Err:

    'This function allows a user to enter a client ID number
    'which looks up and adds the total amount of all invoices
    'owed to date.
    'The result is then returned.

    Dim dbs As Database
    Dim rst As Recordset
    Dim strInputString As String
    Dim strSQL As String

    strInputString = InputBox("Please enter the client's " _
                    & "ID number.", "Accounts Payable by client ID")

    strSQL = "SELECT Sum(tblTimeItemize.JobRate) AS SumOfJobRate " _
            & "FROM tblTimeItemize _
& "GROUP BY tblTimeItemize.ClientNo " _
            & "HAVING tblTimeItemize.ClientNo ='" _
& strInputString & "';"

    Set dbs = CurrentDb
    Set rst = dbs.OpenRecordset(strSQL)

    'The total amount is rounded to two decimal places.
    GetAmountOwed = Round(rst!SumOfJobRate, 2)
```

```
        rst.Close
        dbs.Close
Exit_This_Function:
    Exit Function

GetInvoiceNumber_Err:
    If Err.Number <> 0 Then
        MsgBox Err.Number & " " & Err.Description
    End If
    Resume Exit_This_Function

End Function
```

Preparing a Medium for User Input

You can use VBA to create a new form on the fly instead of building a form object and storing it in your project. For example, you can ask the user which report she would like to preview or which video to run. Once you have initiated a new form, you can set its properties to make it a dialog box in which the user makes a selection.

The following example is a form that displays the Senior Volunteers' names and e-mail addresses. When the form opens, you can select individual names to receive messages or select the complete list of e-mail addresses for distribution.

Starting the form design

As a wrapper procedure for this example, we have created a simple form with command buttons. One of them creates the Email Addresses form.

You use the `CreateForm` method of the `DoCmd` object to start a new form. The `CreateForm` method has no arguments, so the simple syntax is created as follows:

◆ Declare the variable to use in the procedure.

◆ Declare the form and control objects.

◆ Set the form to the `CreateForm` method.

◆ Specify the record source for the form.

The code that is used to create the new form is as follows:

```
Private Sub Build_Form_Click()
Dim frm As Form
Dim ctlField1 As Control, ctlField2 As Control, ctlField3 As Control
```

```
Set frm = CreateForm
frm.RecordSource = "SELECT SrVols.LastName, SrVols.FirstName, " & _
    "SrVols.email FROM SrVols WHERE (((SrVols.email) Is Not Null));"

DoCmd.Restore
```

Next, you set the form's properties.

Setting form properties

The form properties that you can set with VBA are the same as you find in the form's property sheet. However, the actual setting values may be different, because VBA uses intrinsic constants in many cases.

The following code uses a `With` structure to accomplish the following:

- ◆ Sets the form as a pop-up modal form, which doesn't close until the user responds

- ◆ Sets the default view as Continuous Form

- ◆ Turns off some features, such as the following:

    - ■ Dividing lines

    - ■ `MinMax` buttons

```
With frm
    .DefaultView = 1     'Continuous form view
    .Caption = "Email Addresses"
    .PopUp = True
    .Modal = True
    .AllowFormView = True
    .AllowDatasheetView = True
    .AllowPivotChartView = False
    .AllowPivotTableView = False
    .DividingLines = False
    .Width = 4600
    .AutoResize = True
    .AutoCenter = True
    .BorderStyle = 3
    .ControlBox = True
    .MinMaxButtons = 0
End With

frm.Section(acDetail).Height = 300
```

TIP Always provide at least one way for the user to close the form in case a problem occurs. This could be the Control Box button or the Close button.

Adding controls to the new form

Because this example focuses on names and e-mail addresses, we need to add these fields as controls to the new form using the CreateControl method. This method has a more complex syntax than the CreateForm method. The syntax is as follows:

```
CreateControl(formname, controltype[, section[, parent[,
columnname[, left[,top[,width[,height]]]]]]])
```

The CreateControl method has both required and optional arguments, as follows:

- ◆ The required arguments are as follows:

  - ■ formname: Identifies the open form where you want to place the new control.

  - ■ controltype: Identifies the control that you want to create. These are intrinsic constants, such as acCheckBox, acLabel, acTextBox, and acListBox.

    The CreateControl method Visual Basic help topic lists these intrinsic constants.

- ◆ The optional arguments are as follows:

  - ■ section: Specifies the section that contains the new control. Use intrinsic constants, such as acHeader or acFooter. If you omit the section argument, the detail section is the default.

  - ■ parent: Names the parent control of the attached control. This argument is a string expression. For example, if you are creating a label for a text box control, the name of the text box control is the parent.

  - ■ columnname: Identifies the field to which the control is to be bound (if it is a data-bound control).

  - ■ left and top: Specify the coordinates of the upper-left corner of the control, measured in twips. These arguments are numeric expressions.

  - ■ width and height: Specify the size of the control in twips.

Keep the comma placeholders if you skip some of the optional properties but use others that follow in the syntax. You don't need comma placeholders after the last optional property that you use.

The following statements add the `LastName`, `FirstName`, and `email` fields to the form as text boxes spaced across the form:

```
Set ctlField1 = CreateControl(frm.Name, acTextBox, acDetail, _
    "Last Name", "LastName", 100, 50, 2200)
Set ctlField2 = CreateControl(frm.Name, acTextBox, acDetail, _
    "First Name", "FirstName", 2880, 50, 2200)
Set ctlField3 = CreateControl(frm.Name, acTextBox, acDetail, _
    "Email Address", "email", 5760, 50, 2200)
DoCmd.Restore
DoCmd.OpenForm frm.Name, acNormal

End Sub
```

Figure 12-7 shows the new form as created by the preceding code. To see the form in datasheet view so that you could select a column of e-mail addresses to copy to your messaging system, you could set the `DefaultView` property to 2, the datasheet view. Figure 12-8 shows the same new form in datasheet view.

Email Addresses			
Alfred	Robert	rafathome@aol.com	
Brownson	Alice	abrown@greatone.org	
Cardiff	Bruce	cardiff@mcn.org	
Donaldson	Phillip	pdonald@webtv.net	
Elliott	John	jelliott@netzero.net	
Ferguson	Bertram	bferg@pacbell.net	
Gerald	Allen	agerald@worldnet.com	
Halliburton	Tracy	thall@cox.net	
Ireland	Ronald	rireland@aol.com	
Ferguson	Joseph	fergy@hotmail.com	

Record: I◄ ◄ [1] ► ►I ►* of 10

Figure 12-7: Creating a new form in continuous form view.

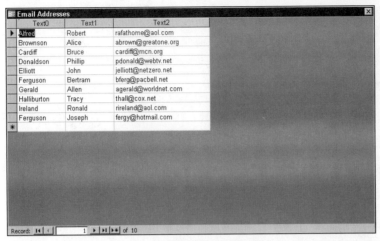

Figure 12-8: The same new form in datasheet view.

After you finish creating the basic parts of the form, you can add command buttons, labels, and other controls to carry out the rest of the desired activity. These items are easily added with the help of the wizards.

Creating a form that publishes a report

To be really automated, you can create a form that distributes selected information to selected recipients.

The next example distributes sales information and is based on a table. Two list boxes in the form enable the user to select names from one list to place in the other list, which contains the names of the intended recipients of the report. Once the recipients are selected, the Send button dispatches the report to the named recipients.

This example requires Microsoft Outlook–installed and –defined mail profiles.

This form includes the following procedures, one for each of the command buttons:

◆ Move

◆ Remove

◆ Send

Figure 12-9 shows the form in form view.

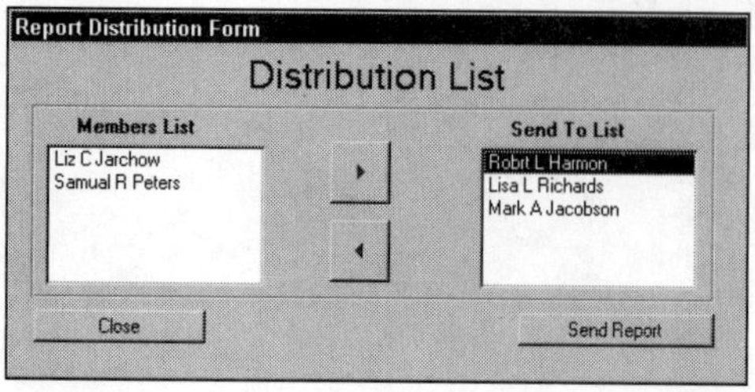

Figure 12-9: Using a form to select report recipients.

MOVE PROCEDURE

The first procedure responds to clicking the Move button after selecting a name in the Members List. If you have not selected a name, an error message is displayed. When the name is moved to the Send To List, it is removed from the Members List.

The following code moves the names from one list to the other:

```
Private Sub btnMove_Click()
'Moves selected name to the Sent list.
On Error GoTo btnMoveErr:

Dim dbs As Database
Dim rst As Recordset
Dim strSQL As String

'List3 is the name of the Members List list box control.
'List 14 is the name of the SendTo List list box control
strSQL = "SELECT * FROM EmployeeSalesSummary WHERE FullName = '" & _
    List3.Value & "'"

Set dbs = CurrentDb
Set rst = dbs.OpenRecordset(strSQL)

'Loop through the list and set the Selected property to True
With rst
    .Edit
    !Selected = True
    .Update
End With

'Update both lists.
Me.List14.Requery
Me.List3.Requery
```

```
btnMoveExit:
    Exit Sub

btnMoveErr:
If Err.Number <> 0 Then
    MsgBox Err.Number & " " & Err.Description
End If
Resume btnMoveExit

End Sub
```

REMOVE PROCEDURE

The Remove button has an event procedure that is attached to the On Click event property, like the preceding move procedure. When the name is removed from the Send To List, it is returned to the Members List.

   The following code works the opposite of the Move procedure by removing the name from the Send To List and placing it back in the Members.

```
Private Sub btnRemove_Click()
'Removes selected name from Send To list.

On Error GoTo btnRemoveErr:

Dim dbs As Database
Dim rst As Recordset
Dim strSQL As String

strSQL = "SELECT * FROM EmployeeSalesSummary WHERE FullName = '" & _
    List14.Value & "'"

Set dbs = CurrentDb
Set rst = dbs.OpenRecordset(strSQL)

With rst
    .Edit
    !Selected = False
    .Update
End With

'Update both list boxes.
Me.List14.Requery
Me.List3.Requery

btnRemoveExit:
    Exit Sub
```

```
btnRemoveErr:
If Err.Number <> 0 Then
    MsgBox Err.Number & " " & Err.Description
End If
Resume btnRemoveExit

End Sub
```

SEND SUB PROCEDURE

The Send sub procedure uses a Do Until... Loop structure to gather all the names in the Send To List and concatenate them into the strSendTo variable.

 The Send object only works when Microsoft Outlook is installed.

```
Private Sub btnSend_Click()

'This is a send button that sends the annual sales figures report
'to the people listed in the distribution box.

Dim rst As Recordset
Dim dbs As Database
Dim strSQL As String
Dim strSendTo As String
Dim strStatement As String

'Add all names that have been selected to the distribution list.

strSQL = "SELECT * FROM EmployeeSalesSummary WHERE Selected = True"
strStatement = "Here is the Sales Summary Report for the " & _
"annual sales figures"

'Set database and record set then empty the SendTo list
Set dbs = CurrentDb
Set rst = dbs.OpenRecordset(strSQL)
strSendTo = ""

'Loop until all distributions' emails have been listed.

Do Until rst.EOF
    strSendTo = strSendTo & rst!FName & rst!LName & _
"@OurSales.com; "
```

```
    rst.MoveNext
Loop

'Send report to employees of the list.

DoCmd.SendObject acSendReport, "Sales Summary", "HTML", _
    strSendTo, , , "Annual Sales Report", strStatement

End Sub
```

Creating a form from a template

If you like the form design, it can be a template to create forms with a similar appearance. Formatting properties, such as size and color, are transferred to the new form.

The `CreateForm` method syntax is as follows:

```
CreateForm([database[, formtemplate]])
```

For the `CreateForm` method syntax, both of the following arguments are optional:

◆ `database`: Names the database that contains the form that you want to use as a template.

If the template form is in the current database, you can skip this argument.

◆ `formtemplate`: The name of the form to be used as the template for the new form. If you don't provide a form template, Access uses the default template specified by the Forms/Reports tab of the Options dialog box (Tools→Options).

The following example creates a new form based on the `SrVols` form:

```
Private Sub Form_Template_Click()
Dim frm As Form

'Create a new form based on the SrVols form
Set frm = CreateForm(, "Volunteers")
DoCmd.Restore

'Set RecordSource property to SrVols table
frm.RecordSource = "SrVols"
End Sub
```

When you click the button that executes this procedure, the following actions take place:

- ◆ The new form appears on the screen in the same proportions and colors as the original form, as shown in Figure 12-10.

- ◆ The field list for the underlying record source of the original form is displayed, ready for adding fields to the new form design.

- ◆ The Toolbox is active and ready to go to work.

 If you specify a form as a template that doesn't exist in the database, Access uses the default template that is defined in the Form/Report tab of the Options dialog box.

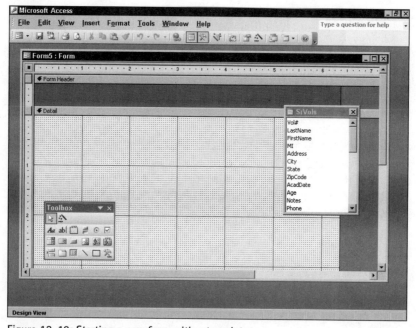

Figure 12-10: Starting a new form with a template.

Adding the Human Touch

Access sometimes assumes that its users are well versed in working with complex databases. One can always hope that is true, but it is better to provide some additional clues about what the program is doing. For example, some of the modal warnings can panic a new user and cause the wrong response. Other command buttons aren't intuitive.

Turning off warnings

Some of the Access automatic warnings can alarm a user. For example, the message "You are about to delete 9 record(s)." (see Figure 12-11) can cause an amateur user to be alarmed. The warning also says that if you delete the records, you can't undo the deletion and you will never see them again. If you respond No, the deletion is aborted, and that may not be what you wanted.

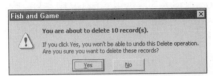

Figure 12-11: A warning message about deleting records.

You can turn off the pop-up warnings programmatically so that you can carry out an action that you are sure should be done. Then turn the warnings back on before exiting the procedure.

In Chapter 9, an example makes a list of volunteers who read specific material (selected in the form) and have e-mail addresses. We used the same datasheet to receive the records resulting from the query, so we had to delete the results of a previous query. We used the following statement to turn the warnings off:

```
DoCmd.SetWarnings False
```

Just before leaving the sub procedure, we added the following statement:

```
DoCmd.SetWarnings True
```

In contrast to this procedure, in the archiving example that preceded this one in Chapter 9, we left the warnings on so that the user could confirm that the same number of records were appended to the archive table as were deleted from the current table.

You can set the warnings on or off in either a function or a sub procedure.

Adding helpful hints

You have a couple of ways to help the user understand the contents of a field in a table or query or to identify the controls in a form. The following sections describe these tools.

ADDING DESCRIPTIONS

You have learned that adding descriptions to Access objects helps with database maintenance and distribution by reminding you about the purpose of the object. You can use VBA to add descriptions to tables, queries, and individual fields.

TABLES AND QUERIES   You can add descriptions to tables and queries that let the user know what the object contains or is used for. To add a description to a table or query, follow these steps:

1. Open the Properties dialog box with either of the following methods:

   - Right-click the table or query name in the Database window, and choose Properties from the shortcut menu that appears.

   - Choose View→Properties.

2. In the Properties box (as shown in Figure 12-12), enter up to 255 characters in the Description box.

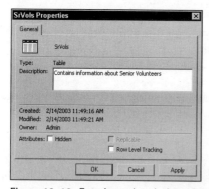

Figure 12-12: Entering a description of the SrVols table.

3. The information that you enter in the Description box appears in the Database window when you select the Details option for viewing database objects, as shown in Figure 12-13.

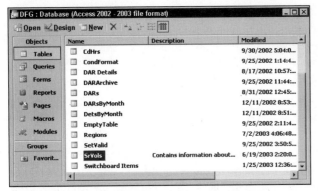

Figure 12-13: Viewing the description of table objects.

FIELDS You can add descriptions to fields in either tables or queries, as follows:

◆ For individual table fields, enter the description in the upper pane of the table design.

◆ To add descriptions to fields in a query design, open the field Properties sheet and enter the text in the Description box.

The description that you enter here appears in the status bar when you select the field in the table or query datasheet view.

ADDING OTHER CLUES

The Access window is another showcase for helpful hints. You can create ScreenTips to explain elements in the window and add text to the status bar.

SCREENTIPS ScreenTips are the bits of helpful information that pop up when you rest the mouse pointer on a control on a form. In VBA, you can use the ControlTipText property to create the text to display. Again, you can add up to 255 characters in the tip. You can provide tips for nearly all control types on a form except for lines, rectangles, subforms/reports, and tab controls.

For example, to set the ScreenTip for the LastName text box control, use the following statement:

```
Forms("Volunteers").Controls("LastName").ControlTipText = _
    "Enter Senior Volunteer's Last Name"
```

STATUS BAR DISPLAY The StatusBarText property specifies the text to display in the status bar when the control is selected. For example, to remind the Senior Volunteers not to include mileage for both members of the patrol unit (which would create double mileage statistics), add a message to the status bar. Place the following statement in the sub procedure that runs when the form opens:

```
Me.Controls("Miles").StatusBarText = "Enter miles for only one
SrVol."
```

Figure 12-14 shows the message that displays in the status bar when the Miles control gets focus.

HELPING DATA ENTRY

If you haven't added input masks to fields in the table design, you can place some input masks in a data-entry form to help users enter correct and complete data. These statements can be added to the procedure that executes when the form is loaded. When the user moves to the field to begin entering data, the input mask appears. Figure 12-15 shows an input mask in the ZipCode field in a form.

The following procedure applies input masks to the Phone and ZipCode controls in the SrVols Special form:

```
Private Sub Form_Load()
'This procedure adds input masks to the Phone and Zipcode fields.
Forms![SrVols Special]!Phone.InputMask = "(###) ###-####"
Forms![SrVols Special]!ZipCode.InputMask = "00000-9999"
End Sub
```

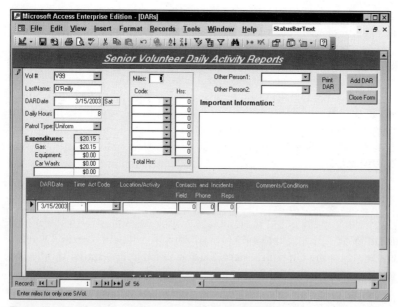

Figure 12-14: Displaying information in the status bar.

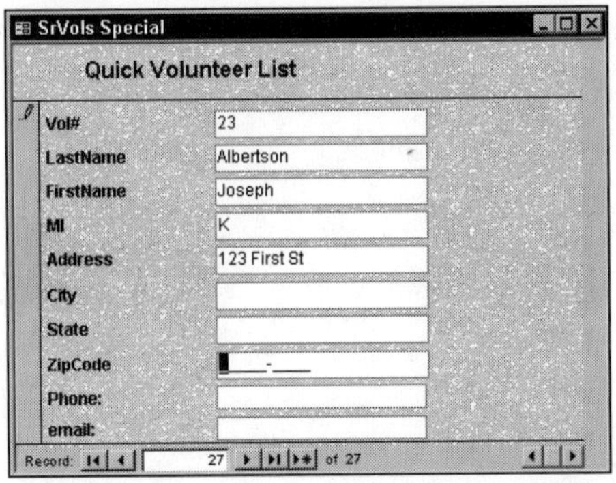

Figure 12-15: Input masks added with VBA code.

CUSTOMIZING COLORS IN A FORM

Customizing a data-entry form with your company's colors personalizes an otherwise impersonal business tool. For example, you can set the properties of each type of control in a form with VBA to a certain pattern of foreground and background colors, font size and type, and other visuals.

The following procedure sets colors and style for the form header, labels, and text box controls in the form:

```
Private Sub Form_Load()
Dim ctl As Control
Dim intNum As Integer, intEdit As Integer
Const conClear = 0
Const conBlue = 16711680
Const conWhite = 16777215
Const conRed = 255
Const conTransparent = 0
Const conDialog = 2
Const conYellow = 8454143


Me.FormHeader.BackColor = conYellow

For Each ctl In Me.Controls
    With ctl
            Select Case .ControlType
                Case acLabel
                    .SpecialEffect = acEffectShadow
                    .BorderStyle = conDialog
                    .BackColor = conBlue
                    .ForeColor = conRed
                    intEdit = True
                Case acTextBox
```

```
                        .SpecialEffect = acEffectNormal
                        .BackColor = conWhite
                        .ForeColor = conBlue
                        .BorderStyle = conTransparent
                        intEdit = True
                End Select
        End With
Next ctl

End Sub
```

Figure 12-16 shows a form that is customized with the preceding code.

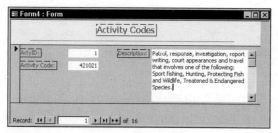

Figure 12-16: Customizing the appearance of an entry form.

Summary

In this chapter, we have described and demonstrated many of the ways you can use VBA to create and improve user interaction. We have discussed using two popular functions, MsgBox and InputBox, to impart and retrieve information. This chapter provides a firm basis for creating additional user assistance and customization.

In the next chapter, we delve further into the user interface by customizing menus and toolbars with VBA.

Chapter 13

Programming Menus and Toolbars

IN THIS CHAPTER

- ◆ Working with command bars
- ◆ Working with controls and their properties
- ◆ Working with menus and submenus
- ◆ Working with shortcut menus
- ◆ Attaching command bars to Access objects and controls
- ◆ Restoring built-in command bars

IN THIS CHAPTER, YOU DISCOVER how to customize command bars with VBA code. Not only can you change the behavior and appearance of built-in command bars, you can also create your own personalized command bars with special controls. After you create your own menus, toolbars, and shortcut menus, you can attach them to your Access objects and controls.

The CommandBars Collection

Command bars in Microsoft Access 2003 include all the menu bars and toolbars as well as all the shortcut menus in the application, both built-in and custom. While Access provides a wide variety of command bars, you may still want to create your own. In Chapter 4, we introduced you to the art of creating new custom command bars using the tools that Access provides. In this chapter, you find out how to use VBA to get even more inventive.

The `CommandBars` collection is contained in the `Applications` object. The command bar objects that form the `CommandBars` collection include toolbars, menu bars, and shortcut menus. All have been treated the same since Access 97. The collection also includes any custom command bars that you may have created using the Customize dialog box or VBA.

The built-in objects in the Access `CommandBars` collection include 178 command bars, as follows:

- ◆ 1 menu bar named, oddly enough, "Menu Bar"

- ◆ 51 toolbars

- ◆ 126 shortcut menus

 Of the 51 built-in toolbars in the collection, only 29 of them are available for customization in the Customize dialog box.

You can look at the current list of command bar objects with some simple VBA code. The following procedure displays the entire list of objects, including some custom ones, in the Immediate window in the Visual Basic Editor window (see Figure 13-1). The list shows the command bar index, name, and type and indicates whether it is currently displaying in the Access window. The figure shows that we checked several toolbars in the Customize dialog box to show in the Access window before running the procedure so that they would be listed as True in the result.

```
Sub ListCBars()
    Dim cbar As CommandBar
    Dim cbType As String
    For Each cbar In CommandBars
        Select Case cbar.Type
            Case msoBarTypeNormal
                cbType = "Toolbar"
            Case msoBarTypeMenuBar
                cbType = "Menu Bar"
            Case msoBarTypePopup
                cbType = "Shortcut"
        End Select
        Debug.Print cbar.Index, cbar.Name, cbType, cbar.Visible
    Next
End Sub
```

Setting options for all command bars

Several properties and options can be set that apply to all the command bars in your application. Others can be set individually for specific command bars. You can set these options either on the Options tab of the Customize dialog box (see Figure 13-2) or with VBA.

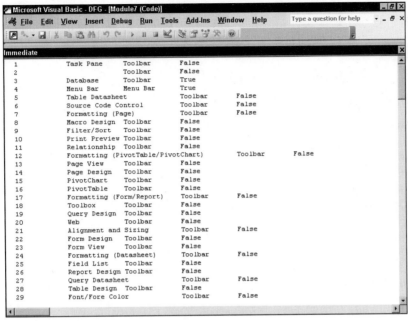

Figure 13-1: Listing the built-in Access 2003 command bars.

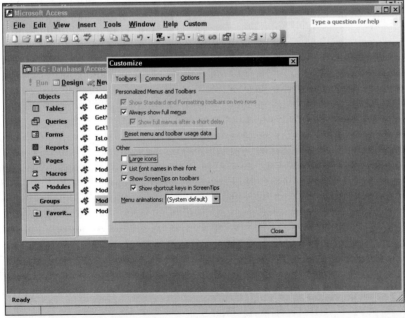

Figure 13-2: Setting options for the CommandBars collection with the Customize dialog box.

These settings affect all command bars in Microsoft Office, not just those that appear when you are running Access.

To set the options at run time, customize the options at the beginning and then return them to their defaults at the end of execution, using code such as the following:

```
'Set the command bar options.
With CommandBars
        .DisableCustomize = True      'Prevents changing settings
        .DisplayFonts = False         'Font names in system font
        .LargeButtons = True          'Displays large icon buttons
        .DisplayToolTips = False      'No ScreenTips
        .DisplayKeysInTooltips = False 'Excludes shortcut keys
        .MenuAnimationStyle = msoMenuAnimationSlide
'Menus slide on and off
End With
```

Most of the command bar options are set to True or False, but you have a choice of the following menu animation styles: None, Random, Slide, or Unfold. Each of these settings can be represented by its numeric value. For example, msoMenuAnimationSlide has the value of 3. The Options tab of the Customize dialog box also shows the Fade option in the drop-down list, but we didn't see it in the Office enumerated constants library. With the Boolean True/False options, True has the value of –1 and False has the value of 0.

At the end of the procedure, you can return the options to their default values, as shown in the following code:

```
'Return options to their default settings
With CommandBars
        .DisableCustomize = False
        .DisplayFonts = True
        .LargeButtons = False
        .DisplayToolTips = True
        .DisplayKeysInTooltips = True
        .MenuAnimationStyle = msoMenuAnimationNone
End With
```

Working with command bars

You can refer to an individual command bar in VBA code by using its index or title. For example, the Database toolbar has an index of 3, so you could refer to it with either of the following:

```
CommandBars(3)
CommandBars("Database")
```

The following code displays the name of the command bar with index 3 and the caption of the fifth toolbar button (see Figure 13-3):

```
Public Sub IndexA()
MsgBox CommandBars(3).Name & " Toolbar" & vbCrLf & _
    "Index is " & CommandBars(3).Index & vbCrLf & _
    CommandBars(3).Controls(5).Caption & _
    " Button number is " & CommandBars(3).Controls(5).Index
End Sub
```

Figure 13-3: Displaying the toolbar name and button caption.

You can also display the toolbar name and button caption using the command bar and control names, as follows:

```
Public Sub IndexB()
MsgBox CommandBars("Database").Name & " Toolbar" & vbCrLf & _
    "Index is " & CommandBars("Database").Index & vbCrLf & _
    CommandBars("Database").Controls("Print").Caption & _
    " Button number is " &
CommandBars("Database").Controls("Print").Index
End Sub
```

PREVIEWING COMMAND BAR PROPERTIES

All three types of command bars have several properties that you can set with VBA. Many can also be applied through the Customize dialog box. All command bar properties can be referred to either by their name or by their numeric equivalent.

Every command bar has a unique name that displays in the title bar. You can set the Name property when you create a new toolbar or change the name later, but you can't change the name of a built-in command bar.

When the command bar's Visible property is set to True, the command bar can be seen in the Access window.

SETTING THE COMMAND BAR TYPE   The msoBarType property is an enumerated constant that specifies the type of command bar, as follows:

- msoBarTypeNormal creates a toolbar. The numeric value is 0.

- msoBarTypeMenuBar creates a menu bar. The numeric value is 1.

- msoBarTypePopup creates a shortcut menu. The numeric value is 2.

We used this integer value earlier in the Select Case structure in the code that listed the command bars to return the type name instead of the numeric value.

POSITIONING THE COMMAND BAR   You can specify the precise location of the command bar on-screen with the Left and Top properties. These two properties define (in pixels) the placement of the upper-left corner of the command bar.

To specify whether the command bar is docked and if so where, use one of the following positioning properties:

- msoBarLeft (value 0) docks the command bar vertically on the left of the screen.

- msoBarTop (value 1) docks the command bar at the top of the screen.

- msoBarRight (value 2) docks the command bar vertically on the right of the screen.

- msoBarBottom (value 3) docks the command bar at the bottom of the screen.

- msoBarFloating (value 4) specifies that the command bar is not docked.

- msoBarPopup (value 5) creates a shortcut menu.

PROTECTING THE COMMAND BAR   You can keep others from moving, resizing, modifying, docking, or hiding your custom command bars by choosing from the Protection properties. Right-click a toolbar, and choose Customize from the short-cut menu that appears. Select a toolbar on the Toolbars tab, and click Properties (see Figure 13-4). You can also set all of these properties at run time with VBA.

Figure 13-4: Using the Customize tool to protect custom command bars.

As with other properties, Protection properties can be set using their names or their numeric values. The Protection properties are numbered, like other properties, but in a slightly different way. The property numbers are all powers of 2, with the additional value of 0, so that you can either list the names of the properties or add the values to form one value. With this exponential numbering system, no ambiguity in the result can occur. Each grouping of the properties results in a unique value.

The Protection properties are described in Table 13-1.

TABLE 13-1 PROTECTION PROPERTIES

Property	Numeric Value	Description
msoBarNoProtection	0	Permits the user to customize, resize, or move the command bar (default).
msoNoCustomize	1	Prevents any customization by the user.
msoNoResize	2	Prevents resizing by the user.
msoNoMove	4	Prevents the user from moving the command bar from its original location.
msoNoChangeVisible	8	Prevents the user from changing the visibility state. If hidden, remains hidden; if visible, remains visible.
msoNoChangeDock	16	Prevents the user from docking the bar in a different location.
msoNoVerticalDock	32	Prevents the user from docking the bar at the right or left edge of the screen.
msoNoHorizontalDock	64	Prevents the user from docking the bar at the top or bottom of the screen.

Setting one of these properties is equivalent to either clearing the check mark from the option or changing the docking choice in the Toolbar Properties dialog box.

CREATING A NEW COMMAND BAR

To build a new command bar with VBA, you use the Add method to add it to the CommandBars collection. The Add method syntax requires only the *expression* argument that returns a `CommandBars` object. The other arguments are optional. The `Add` method syntax is as follows:

```
Expression.Add(Name, Position, MenuBar, Temporary)
```

The optional arguments pass additional information as follows:

◆ If you omit the *Name* argument, a generic name is assigned.

◆ The *Position* argument specifies the location (left, top, right, or bottom) and the type of command bar (floating or pop-up shortcut menu, as described earlier).

◆ Set the *MenuBar* argument to True if you want the new command bar to replace the active menu bar.

◆ Set the *Temporary* argument to True if you want the new command bar to be deleted when the container application closes.

After defining the command bar itself, add the controls that you need. This also uses the `Add` method, with a slightly different syntax, which we describe in more detail in a later section.

The following code creates a new floating toolbar named MyReport with seven buttons (see Figure 13-5). Each added button is copied from an existing toolbar. This is a basic, no-frills command bar. You see how to add more personal touches later in this chapter.

```
Public Sub NewCB()
Dim repBar As CommandBar
Dim newBtn As CommandBarButton
'Add an error routine in case the command bar already exists
On Error Resume Next
CommandBars("MyReport").Delete
On Error GoTo 0

'Add the new command bar to the collection
Set repBar = CommandBars.Add("MyReport", msoBarFloating)
'Add buttons to the floating toolbar
Set newBtn = repBar.Controls _
    .Add(msoControlButton, CommandBars("Print Preview") _
    .Controls("One Page").ID)
Set newBtn = repBar.Controls _
    .Add(msoControlButton, CommandBars("Print Preview") _
    .Controls("Two Pages").ID)
```

```
Set newBtn = repBar.Controls _
    .Add(msoControlButton, CommandBars("Print Preview") _
    .Controls("Zoom").ID)
Set newBtn = repBar.Controls _
    .Add(msoControlButton, CommandBars("Database") _
    .Controls("Save").ID)
Set newBtn = repBar.Controls _
    .Add(msoControlButton, CommandBars("Database") _
    .Controls("Cut").ID)
Set newBtn = repBar.Controls _
    .Add(msoControlButton, CommandBars("Database") _
    .Controls("Copy").ID)
Set newBtn = repBar.Controls _
    .Add(msoControlButton, CommandBars("Database") _
    .Controls("Paste").ID)
repBar.Visible = True
End Sub
```

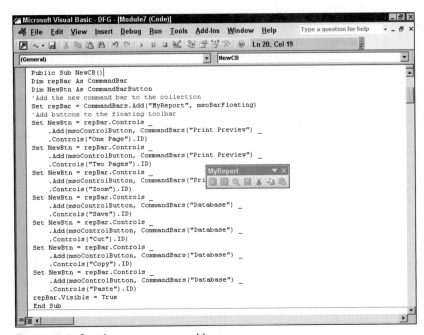

Figure 13-5: Creating a new command bar.

TIP As you create new command bars, you will probably not be satisfied with the first rendition of the bar or the controls on the bar. If you try to re-create the command bar without deleting it first, you get an error message. This can be frustrating. (Believe us; we know!) The easiest way to prevent this is to delete the command bar before trying to rebuild it. The first On Error statement responds to the error that you get when you try to create an object that already exists. This statement deletes the command bar. The second On Error statement simply proceeds with the rest of the code.

To display a specific custom command bar, you can use the ShowToolbar method. The following code displays the MyReport toolbar in all active Access windows:

```
DoCmd.ShowToolbar "MyReport", acToolbarYes
```

DELETING OR DISABLING A COMMAND BAR

You have created a custom command bar that is no longer needed. It is just taking up space, so you decide to delete it. However, you need to know its name or its index to delete it. Use the following statement to delete the command bar:

```
CommandBars("Not Needed").Delete
```

If you have used the wrong name or the command bar has already been deleted, you see an error message. To eliminate that interruption (if it is already gone, who cares about a warning?), add an On Error statement that just stops execution if the procedure can't find the command bar:

```
On Error Resume Next
CommandBars("Not Needed").Delete
On Error Go To 0
```

You can't delete built-in command bars, but you can modify them to suit your needs, as you see later in this chapter.

To simply keep the user from displaying the command bar, you can set its Enabled property to False. When the command bar is disabled, it is not available from the toolbars shortcut menu or from the Customize dialog box. The following code disables the MyReport command bar, displays a message box to that effect, and then re-enables it.

```
Public Sub Disable()
'This procedure disables the command bar and reenables it.
CommandBars("MyReport").Enabled = False
MsgBox "MyReport command bar is disabled"
```

```
CommandBars("MyReport").Enabled = True
MsgBox "MyReport command bar is enabled"

End Sub
```

Working with command bar controls

Now we discuss the individual controls on a command bar. The controls are members of the `CommandBar` class and can be of the following types:

◆ Standard toolbar buttons, such as Cut, Copy, and Paste

◆ Edit boxes, such as the Search text box in the Getting Started task pane

◆ Drop-down lists, such as the Font control, from which you can select a different font

◆ Combo boxes, such as the Top Values button on the Query Design toolbar

◆ Button pop-ups, which are actually menu items on a menu bar that open a list of individual menu choices, such as the File menu on the Database menu bar

To see what controls are on a command bar, use the following code to list them, together with their captions and control type (see Figure 13-6):

```
Public Sub FormButtons()
Dim cBar As CommandBar
Dim ctrl As CommandBarControl
Set cBar = CommandBars("Form Design")
For Each ctrl In cBar.Controls
    Debug.Print ctrl.Caption, ctrl.Type, ctrl.Index
Next ctrl
End Sub
```

 The ampersand character in the control caption designates the following character as the access key. This character appears underlined in the command bar and in the ToolTip.

You see that most of the controls on the Form Design toolbar are Type 1, the standard button. The Undo and Redo buttons are listed as Type 6, `msoControlSplitDropDown`, and the View button is Type 14, `msoControlSplitButtonPopup`. Use the Object Browser to scroll through the members of the `msoControlType` class (see Figure 13-7).

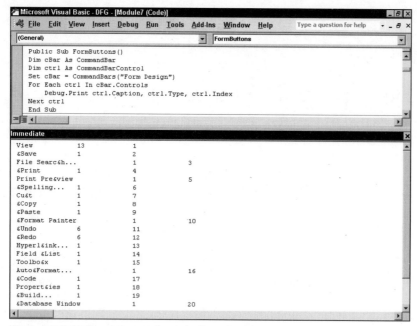

Figure 13-6: Listing the controls on the Form Design toolbar.

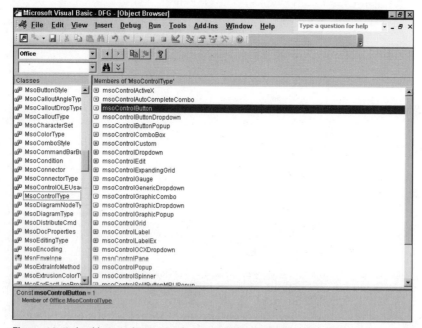

Figure 13-7: Looking at the types of command bar controls.

REFERRING TO COMMAND BAR CONTROLS

As you saw at the beginning of this chapter, you can refer to a command bar control by its caption or its index within the command bar. We prefer to use the caption, although that method is language-dependent.

The following statement displays a message box that shows the index of the Print button (4) on the Form Design toolbar. If you look at the toolbar, you see that Print is the fourth button.

```
MsgBox CommandBars("Form Design").Controls("Print").Index
```

LOOKING AT COMMAND BAR CONTROL PROPERTIES

Many of the command bar control properties apply to most of the types of controls. Others are geared to specific types. Table 13-2 shows some of the most commonly used control properties.

TABLE 13-2 COMMON CONTROL PROPERTIES

Property	Description
BeginGroup	True/False. Adds a separator bar above or to the left of the control.
BuiltIn	Read-only. Returns True if the command bar is an Access built-in command bar control.
Caption	Text that appears on the control. If the control shows only as an image, the caption text appears when the mouse pointer rests on the control.
Enabled	True/False. Permits the user to click the control and carry out the action.
Index	The numeric position of the control in the command bar.
OnAction	Names the VB procedure or macro to execute when the control is clicked.
ToolTipText	The text to display when the mouse pointer rests on the control.
Type	The numeric value that represents the type of control.
Visible	True/False. Displays or hides the control.

The Style property applies only to buttons and combo boxes. A few of these properties are also available with the Customize tool by right-clicking the control and choosing from the shortcut menu. The button styles are described in Table 13-3.

TABLE 13-3 BUTTON STYLES

Button Style	Value	Description
msoButtonAutomatic	0	Displays the default for that button type
msoButtonIcon	1	Displays only the image
msoButtonCaption	2	Displays only the text
msoButtonIconAndCaption	3	Displays both image and text
msoButtonIconAndWrapCaption	7	Displays both image and text side by side
msoButtonIconAndCaptionBelow	11	Displays the image above with text below
msoButtonIconWrapCaption	14	Displays only the text wrapped to fit the button
msoButtonIconAndWrapCaptionBelow	15	Displays both the image and text, with the text wrapped below the image

The following code results in the command bar shown in Figure 13-8:

```
Public Sub StyleButtons()
'Creates a toolbar with 7 buttons each with a different button style
Dim NewBtn As CommandBarButton
Dim NewBar As CommandBar

On Error Resume Next
CommandBars("StyleBar").Delete
On Error GoTo 0

Set NewBar = CommandBars.Add("StyleBar", msoBarFloating)
Set NewBtn = CommandBars("StyleBar").Controls.Add _
    (Type:=msoControlButton)
    With NewBtn
        .Caption = "New Style"
        .FaceId = 2
        .Style = msoButtonAutomatic
    End With
```

```
Set NewBtn = CommandBars("StyleBar").Controls.Add _
    (Type:=msoControlButton)
    With NewBtn
        .Caption = "New Style"
        .FaceId = 2
        .Style = msoButtonIcon
        .BeginGroup = True
    End With
Set NewBtn = CommandBars("StyleBar").Controls.Add _
    (Type:=msoControlButton)
    With NewBtn
        .Caption = "New Style"
        .FaceId = 2
        .Style = msoButtonCaption
        .BeginGroup = True
    End With
Set NewBtn = CommandBars("StyleBar").Controls.Add _
    (Type:=msoControlButton)
    With NewBtn
        .Caption = "New Style"
        .FaceId = 2
        .Style = msoButtonIconAndCaption
        .BeginGroup = True
    End With
Set NewBtn = CommandBars("StyleBar").Controls.Add _
    (Type:=msoControlButton)
    With NewBtn
    .Caption = "New Style"
        .FaceId = 2
        .Style = msoButtonIconAndWrapCaption
        .BeginGroup = True
    End With
Set NewBtn = CommandBars("StyleBar").Controls.Add _
    (Type:=msoControlButton)
    With NewBtn
        .Caption = "New Style"
        .FaceId = 2
        .Style = msoButtonIconAndCaptionBelow
        .BeginGroup = True
    End With
Set NewBtn = CommandBars("StyleBar").Controls.Add _
    (Type:=msoControlButton)
    With NewBtn
        .Caption = "New Style"
        .FaceId = 2
```

```
        .Style = msoButtonWrapCaption
        .BeginGroup = True
    End With
Set NewBtn = CommandBars("StyleBar").Controls.Add _
    (Type:=msoControlButton)
    With NewBtn
        .Caption = "New Style"
        .FaceId = 2
        .Style = msoButtonIconAndWrapCaptionBelow
        .BeginGroup = True
    End With

End Sub
```

Figure 13-8: Looking at different button styles.

You can use the following other button properties to customize your command bar buttons:

◆ FaceID: A number that specifies which graphic image to show on the button

◆ State: Returns the current state of the button (Down, Mixed, or Up)

Combo boxes also have some different properties because they contain a list of values to display when the user clicks the button. The msoComboStyle property has only the following two settings:

◆ msoComboLabel: Attaches a text label to the box

◆ msoComboNormal: Displays the combo box without a label

Other combo box properties are as follows:

◆ DropDownLines: The number of lines to display in the drop-down list

◆ DropDownWidth: The width of the displayed list

◆ List: An individual value in the list

◆ ListCount: The number of items in the list (read-only)

◆ ListHeaderCount: The number of columns in the list

◆ ListIndex: The index number of an item in the list

ADDING COMMAND BAR CONTROLS

You use the same Add method to place controls on a command bar that you used to create the command bar, but with some different arguments, as follows:

Expression.Add(*Type, Id, Parameter, Before, Temporary*)

The *Expression* argument is required and must return a CommandBarControls object. We usually just use CommandBarControls. All the arguments are optional.

The *Type* argument specifies which type of control you want to add. Even though over 20 types of command bar controls are listed in the Object Browser, you are limited to using the following ones:

◆ msoControlButton

◆ msoControlEdit

◆ msoControlDropDown

◆ msoControlComboBox

◆ msoControlPopup

The *Id* argument identifies a built-in control. If you leave it out or use 1, a blank control is added to the command bar.

The *Parameter* argument specifies information that is to be sent to a VBA procedure, or you can use it to store information about the control.

The *Before* argument is a number that points to a control that is already in the command bar. The new control is placed before the existing control. If you don't use this argument, the new control is placed at the end of the command bar.

Finally, the *Temporary* argument works the same as with adding a new command bar as discussed earlier. If set to True, the control is automatically deleted when the application closes.

ADDING BUTTON CONTROLS   The following code adds a blank button control to the MyReports toolbar and places it before button number 5 in the command bar:

```
CommandBars("MyReport").Controls.Add _
        (Type: = msoControlButton, Before: = 5)
```

Notice that the arguments are passed a little differently, by name and separated by commas. That way, you don't need to place them in an exact sequence and to remember to include commas in the right order if some of the arguments are not included.

The new button does nothing if you click it. You need to specify the OnAction property before it knows what to do. The following procedure places a group separator between the fourth and fifth button and then adds a new button at the end of the MyReports toolbar that executes a macro named ReptMacro:

```
Public Sub AddCtrl()
 Dim NewCtrl As CommandBarControl
 CommandBars("MyReport").Controls(5).BeginGroup = True
 Set NewCtrl = CommandBars("MyReport").Controls.Add _
    (Type:=msoControlButton)
With NewCtrl
    .FaceId = 46      'The Find button icon.
    .BeginGroup = True
    .OnAction = "ReptMacro"
    .Caption = "Click to find region report"
End With
End Sub
```

The FaceId property specifies the image to display on the button, and the Caption property displays a ToolTip when the mouse pointer rests on the button (see Figure 13-9).

Figure 13-9: Adding a new button to a command bar.

ADDING A COMBO BOX CONTROL   Combo box and drop-down controls are very useful in a command bar because they give you a set of choices to choose from instead of just clicking. When you choose from the list, the procedure or macro that you have named as the OnAction property executes with the value that you have selected. The following code adds a combo box control to the MyReport command bar, with a list of patrol regions from which to choose. Figure 13-10 shows the results of running this procedure.

```
Public Sub AddCombo()
'Declare the new control as a combo box
Dim newCombo As CommandBarComboBox
Set newCombo = CommandBars("MyReport").Controls.Add _
    (Type:=msoControlComboBox)
With newCombo
'Create the value list
    .AddItem "Region 1"
    .AddItem "Region 2"
    .AddItem "Region 3"
    .AddItem "Region 4"
    .AddItem "Region 5"
    .AddItem "Marine"
```

```
         .Caption = "Region"
         .Style = msoComboLabel          'Include a control label
         .OnAction = "AddFilter"          'Executes a macro
    End With
    End Sub
```

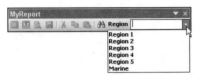

Figure 13-10: Adding a combo box control to
a custom command bar.

You can use some of the properties mentioned earlier to customize the combo box. The DropDownLines property limits the number of lines that you see when you click the drop-down arrow. The DropDownWidth property can be set to show the list as a different width than the entire control. This is handy if you have added a caption that adds to the overall width of the control.

You can use the ListCount property to return the number of items in the combo box list. If your application seems to be malfunctioning, the problem may be damage to a combo box. You can check the number that's returned against the number that you placed in it when you created it.

When you choose from the combo box list, the AddFilter macro applies a filter to the report to show only records from the selected region. If you use the same VBA code to add a drop-down control, the result is the same.

DELETING OR DISABLING COMMAND BAR CONTROLS

You can delete controls from built-in command bars or just disable or hide them using the following statements.

Use the Delete method to remove the control.

```
CommandBars("MyReport").Controls(5).Delete
```

Set the Visible property to False to hide the control, as follows:

```
Set ctrl = CommandBars("MyReport").Controls(1)
ctrl.Visible = False
```

Set the Enabled property to False to leave the control on the command bar but make it unavailable to the user, as follows:

```
Set ctrl = CommandBars("MyReport").Controls(1)
ctrl.Enabled = False
```

Working with Menus and Submenus

Customizing menu bars is a little more complicated than working with toolbars because most of the controls on a toolbar are designed to carry out a single operation. Some toolbar commands display a list of commands if they are defined as pop-up controls.

As discussed in Chapter 4, menu bars consist of menus, each of which displays a drop-down list of menu items or commands. Some of the items in the list are submenus that also show a list of menu commands.

You use the same Add method to add a new menu bar to the CommandBars collection. The Enabled, Position, Visible, and Protection properties work the same as for toolbars. The menu bar type is CommandBarPopup, and the menus on the bar are defined as msoControlPopup. The built-in Menu bar includes 16 controls, all of the control Type 10, msoControlPopup. Figure 13-11 shows the list of menus on the Menu bar.

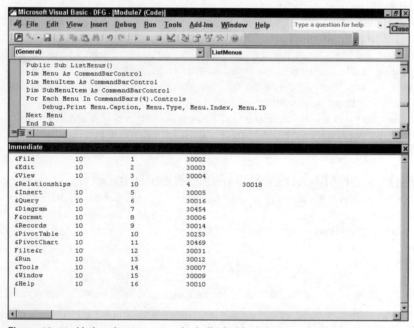

Figure 13-11: Listing the menus on the built-in Menu bar.

Adding a menu to the built-in Menu bar

The following code shows you how to add a new menu, Custom, to the Menu bar and place it just before the Help menu. Figure 13-12 shows the empty menu in the built-in Menu bar.

```
Public Sub AddMenu()
Dim NewMenu As CommandBarPopup
Dim NewItem As CommandBarControl
Dim NewSub As CommandBarPopup
Dim NewSubItem As CommandBarButton
'Add the new menu to the built-in Menu Bar, Index 4.
Set NewMenu = CommandBars(4).Controls _
    .Add(Type:=msoControlPopup, Temporary:=True, Before:=16)
NewMenu.Caption = "Custom"
```

Figure 13-12: Adding a menu to the Menu bar.

Next, we add menu items to the new menu with the following code. Figure 13-13 shows the Custom menu with the menu commands and a submenu.

```
Set newItem = NewMenu.Controls.Add _
    (Type:=msoControlButton)
    With newItem
        .Caption = "Item 1"
        .FaceId = 123
        .OnAction = "MacroA"
    End With
Set newItem = NewMenu.Controls.Add _
    (Type:=msoControlButton)
    With newItem
        .Caption = "Item 2"
        .FaceId = 234
        .OnAction = "MacroB"
    End With
Set newItem = NewMenu.Controls.Add _
    (Type:=msoControlButton)
    With newItem
        .Caption = "Item 3"
        .FaceId = 345
        .OnAction = "MacroC"
    End With
Set newItem = NewMenu.Controls.Add _
    (Type:=msoControlPopup)
    With newItem
        .Caption = "SubMenu"
        .BeginGroup = True
    End With
```

```
Set NewSubItem = newItem.Controls.Add _
    (Type:=msoControlButton)
    With NewSubItem
        .Caption = "Sub Item 1"
        .FaceId = 321
        .OnAction = "MacroD"
    End With
Set NewSubItem = newItem.Controls.Add _
    (Type:=msoControlButton)
    With NewSubItem
        .Caption = "Sub Item 2"
        .FaceId = 432
        .OnAction = "MacroE"
    End With
End Sub
```

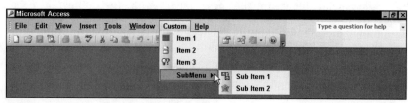

Figure 13-13: The completed Custom menu.

Adding a menu command to a built-in menu

If you don't need a complete new menu, you can just add a menu command to an existing menu. For example, the following code shows you how to add a menu command to the View menu. You can use this menu command to display a set of cat pictures. Figure 13-14 shows the new command in the View menu.

```
Public Sub AddItem()
Dim ViewMenu As CommandBarPopup
Dim newItem As CommandBarButton
'The View menu has the ID value of 30004.
'On Error routine executes if the control already exists.
On Error Resume Next
CommandBars(4).FindControl(ID:=30004) _
    .Controls("View Cat Pictures").Delete
On Error GoTo 0

Set ViewMenu = CommandBars(4).FindControl(ID:=30004)
Set newItem = ViewMenu.Controls.Add _
    (Type:=msoControlButton, Temporary:=True)
```

```
With newItem
    .Caption = "View Cat Pictures"
    .FaceId = 165
    .OnAction = "ViewCatPictures"
    .BeginGroup = True
End With
End Sub
```

Figure 13-14: Adding a menu command to an existing menu.

Creating a new menu bar

The following code creates a new menu bar to take the place of the built-in Menu bar. The new menu bar consists of three menus, the third of which shows the menu commands and a submenu with commands (see Figure 13-15).

```
Public Sub NewMenuBar()
Dim mBar As CommandBar
Dim mMenu As CommandBarControl
Dim mItem As CommandBarControl
Dim NewSubItem As CommandBarControl

'Delete the New Menu Bar if it already exists.
On Error Resume Next
CommandBars("New Menu Bar").Delete
On Error GoTo 0
```

```
Set mBar = CommandBars.Add(MenuBar:=True, _
    Position:=msoBarTop, Temporary:=True)
With mBar
    .Name = "New Menu Bar"
    .Visible = True
End With

Set mMenu = mBar.Controls.Add(Type:=msoControlPopup)
mMenu.Caption = "&First Menu"

Set mMenu = mBar.Controls.Add(Type:=msoControlPopup)
mMenu.Caption = "&Second Menu"

Set mMenu = mBar.Controls.Add(Type:=msoControlPopup)
mMenu.Caption = "&Third Menu"
Set mItem = mMenu.Controls.Add(Type:=msoControlButton)
With mItem
    .Caption = "F&irst Command"
    .FaceId = 356
    .OnAction = "Run First"
End With
Set mItem = mMenu.Controls.Add(Type:=msoControlButton)
With mItem
    .Caption = "&Second Command"
    .FaceId = 333
    .OnAction = "Run Second"
End With
Set mItem = mMenu.Controls.Add(Type:=msoControlPopup)
mItem.Caption = "SubMenu"

Set NewSubItem = mItem.Controls.Add _
    (Type:=msoControlButton)
    With NewSubItem
        .Caption = "Sub Item 1"
        .FaceId = 321
        .OnAction = "MacroD"
    End With
Set NewSubItem = mItem.Controls.Add _
    (Type:=msoControlButton)
    With NewSubItem
        .Caption = "Sub Item 2"
        .FaceId = 432
        .OnAction = "MacroE"
    End With

End Sub
```

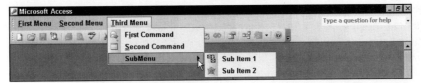

Figure 13-15: Creating a new menu bar.

Working with shortcut menus

Shortcut menus pop up when you right-click somewhere on the screen. The menu that you see depends on where you clicked and what's going on. Access provides 125 built-in shortcut menus for use in 12 different windows. You can use the following code to see a list of the built-in shortcut menus and the areas where they are active. Figure 13-16 shows the results of running this code.

```
Public Sub SCMMenus()
Dim cBar As CommandBar
For Each cBar In CommandBars
    If cBar.Type = msoBarTypePopup Then
        Debug.Print cBar.Index, cBar.Name
    End If
Next cBar
End Sub
```

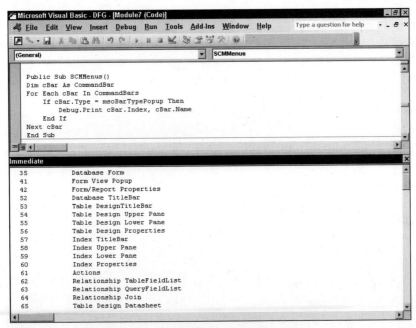

Figure 13-16: Looking at the list of built-in shortcut menus.

You can create you own shortcut menus to attach to a form or report by using the same Add method as you used to create new toolbars and menu bars. You can also make changes to built-in shortcut menus in much the same way as you would customize other command bars.

CREATING A NEW SHORTCUT MENU

The only difference between creating a new shortcut menu and a toolbar is that you must specify the *Position* argument as msoBarPopup instead of msoBarNormal.

The following code creates a new shortcut menu with four controls. Setting the Temporary control to True deletes the custom shortcut menu when the application terminates. This can be handy because it keeps the application from loading the system with extra menus. However, if you plan to attach the shortcut menu to a form, report, or control, don't make it temporary. The last statement in the following code displays the shortcut menu immediately in the VBA code window, as shown in Figure 13-17:

```
Public Sub CreateSCM()
Dim newSCM As CommandBar
Dim ctrl1 As CommandBarControl, ctrl2 As CommandBarControl
Dim ctrl3 As CommandBarControl, ctrl4 As CommandBarControl

'Delete the My Shortcut menu if it already exists.
On Error Resume Next
CommandBars("My Shortcut").Delete
On Error GoTo 0

Set newSCM = CommandBars.Add _
    (Name:="My Shortcut", Position:=msoBarPopup, Temporary:=True)
Set ctrl1 = newSCM.Controls.Add(Type:=msoControlButton)
With ctrl1
    .Caption = "Copy"
    .FaceId = 22
End With

Set ctrl2 = newSCM.Controls.Add(Type:=msoControlButton)
With ctrl2
    .Caption = "Check Spelling"
    .FaceId = 2
End With
```

```
Set ctrl3 = newSCM.Controls.Add(Type:=msoControlButton)
With ctrl3
    .Caption = "Print"
    .FaceId = 4
End With

Set ctrl4 = newSCM.Controls.Add(Type:=msoControlButton)
With ctrl4
    .Caption = "Find"
    .FaceId = 46
End With

newSCM.ShowPopup 200, 200
End Sub
```

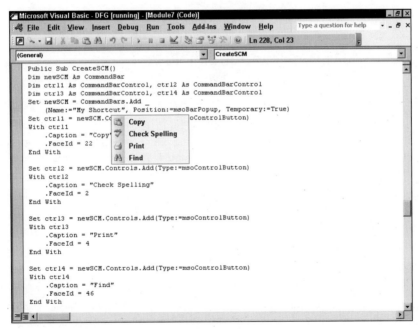

Figure 13-17: Creating a new shortcut menu.

Figure 13-18 shows the new shortcut menu attached to the Volunteers form.

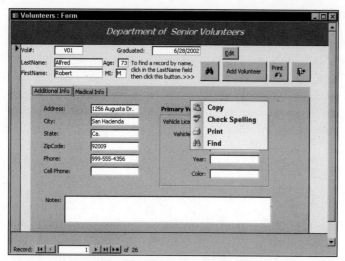

Figure 13-18: The new shortcut menu is attached to a form.

DISABLING OR DELETING SHORTCUT MENUS

To disable a shortcut menu, use the same property setting as with other command bars: Set the Enabled property to False.

Deleting a shortcut menu is a little more complicated. You must first change the type of command bar from a pop-up to a menu or toolbar. The only way to do this is by using the Customize tool. You can't change the bar type with VBA because it is a read-only property that's set when the bar is created. To delete a shortcut menu, follow these steps:

1. Right-click in a toolbar, and choose Customize from the shortcut menu.

2. On the Toolbars tab of the Customize dialog box, scroll down the list and select Shortcut Menus.

3. Click Properties.

4. Click the down arrow next to Selected Toolbar, and click the shortcut menu that you want to delete.

5. Click the Type down arrow, and choose Toolbar.

6. Click Close to return to the Toolbars tab, and locate the newly converted shortcut menu.

7. Select the menu, and click Delete.

8. Confirm the deletion.

Attaching command bars to Access objects and controls

You can specify the menu bar that you want to use for a database, form, or report. Set the MenuBar property to the name of the menu that you want to see. For example, the following statement attaches the My Report menu to the Senior Volunteer report:

```
Reports("Senior Volunteer").MenuBar = "My Report"
```

You can set the Toolbar property to the name of your custom toolbar. To attach a shortcut menu to a form or report, set the Short Menu property to True and assign the shortcut menu name to the ShortCutMenu property, as follows:

```
Forms(Volunteers").ShortcutMenu = True
Forms("Volunteers").ShortcutMenuBar = "My Shortcut"
```

If you want the assignments to be temporary, remove them at the end of the procedure, as follows:

```
Forms("Volunteers").ShortcutMenu = False
Forms("Volunteers").ShortcutMenuBar = ""
```

 If the object has the AllowShortcutMenus property set to False, you don't see any shortcut menus, even if you have attached one to the object.

Restoring built-in command bars

You can restore all or any part of a built-in command bar to the default settings. The easiest way to do this is to use the Customize dialog box. See Chapter 4 for the details of restoring and resetting command bars and their controls.

Summary

In this chapter, we have discussed the art of customizing command bars and attaching them to forms, reports, or controls. We have also shown how to work with shortcut menus.

In the next chapter, we discuss how to modify the Access workplace with VBA. We include setting startup properties and default database options as well as creating and appending new database and object properties.

Chapter 14

Changing the Workplace with VBA

IN THIS CHAPTER

- ◆ Setting startup properties with VBA

- ◆ Setting default database options

- ◆ Saving and restoring default options

- ◆ Creating and appending new properties

- ◆ Running an opening procedure

- ◆ Compiling code conditionally

NOT ALL USERS NEED OR WANT the same workplace environment. VBA offers many ways to modify the way that an application starts and to customize the default options that you can set manually with the Options dialog box. To change these options temporarily, you can save the original settings and restore them on database exit.

If the property collection doesn't include all the properties that you want, you can create new ones and add them to the collection. Many applications greet the user with a special screen. You can use VBA to decide which form to display at startup.

Finally, this chapter describes how to create compiled executable code for different operating environments.

Setting Startup Properties with VBA

Although you may have set the startup properties by using the Tools menu and the Options dialog box, you may want to change some of them at run time. For example, you may want to limit the user's freedom to make changes to database objects or you may want to replace the opening form with a specially tailored switchboard.

All the startup properties that you find in the Startup dialog box have VBA equivalents. For example, the Application Title property uses the name `AppTitle` in VBA, and the Display Database Window property uses the name `StartupShowDBWindow`. Some of the properties require True or False settings, while others use text values.

Figure 14-1 shows the Startup dialog box. Table 14-1 lists the VBA names that represent these properties in code.

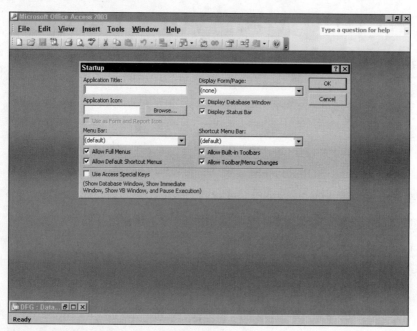

Figure 14-1: The database startup properties.

TABLE 14-1 STARTUP PROPERTIES AND THEIR VBA EQUIVALENTS

Startup Property	VBA Property Name	Value Type
Application title	AppTitle	Text
Application icon	AppIcon	Name of image
Display form/page	StartupForm	Name of form
Display database window	StartupShowDBWindow	True/False
Display status bar	StartupShowStatusBar	True/False
Menu bar	StartUpMenuBar	Name of menu bar
Shortcut menu bar	StartupShortcutMenuBar	Name of shortcut menu bar
Allow full menus	AllowFullMenus	True/False
Allow default shortcut menus	AllowShortcutMenus	True/False

Startup Property	VBA Property Name	Value Type
Allow built-in toolbars	AllowBuiltInToolbars	True/False
Allow toolbar/menu changes	AllowToolbarchanges	True/False
Allow viewing code after error	AllowBreakIntoCode	True/False
Use access special keys	AllowSpecialKeys	True/False

To set only two or three properties, use a sub procedure that sets the property and appends it to the application's Properties collection. You can build this procedure in a module that contains other utility public procedures as well. Then, when you want to change the properties, use the following steps:

1. Open the module in Design view.

2. Click in the sub procedure declaration.

3. Click the Run toolbar button.

The following sub procedure changes three of the startup properties:

```
Public Sub ChangeStartupProps()
Dim dbs As Object
Set dbs = CurrentDB
'The following displays a custom menu bar at startup,
'turns off the full menus and forbids toolbar changes.
dbs.Properties("StartupMenuBar") = "DFG Custom"
dbs.Properties("AllowFullMenus") = False
dbs.Properties("AllowToolbarChanges") = False
End Sub
```

Setting multiple startup properties

If you are planning to set a larger number of properties at once, it is more efficient to use a function that is called from the sub procedure to append each property as it is set.

In many cases, if the property is still in its default setting, it does not appear in the collection. Properties don't show up in the collection until they have been changed or set at least once. So, you can avoid run-time errors by including an error handler than runs if the referenced property is not found in the application's Properties collection.

The following example sets several of the startup properties using the ChangeProp function. The sub procedure ChangeStartUpProps calls the ChangeProp function and passes the following arguments to it:

- The name of the property

- The type of value used by the property: text or True/False

- The new value of the property

First, create the sub procedure that defines the properties and their new settings by doing the following:

- Declare the constants that represent the new setting values

- Call the ChangeProp function and pass the three arguments

```
Public Sub StartUpProps()
'Declare property value constants.
Const strt_Text As Long = 10      'For text values
Const strt_Boolean As Long = 1    'For True/False values

ChangeProp "AppTitle", strt_Text, "Fish and Game"
ChangeProp "StartupForm", strt_Text, "Welcome"
ChangeProp "StartupMenuBar", strt_Text, "DFG Custom"
ChangeProp "StartupShowDBWindow", strt_Boolean, False
ChangeProp "StartupShowStatusBar", strt_Boolean, False
ChangeProp "AllowBuiltInToolbars", strt_Boolean, False
ChangeProp "AllowFullMenus", strt_Boolean, False
ChangeProp "AllowBreakIntoCode", strt_Boolean, False
ChangeProp "AllowSpecialKeys", strt_Boolean, False
ChangeProp "AllowToolbarChanges", strt_Boolean, False
'Change the title bar text immediately.
Application.RefreshTitleBar

End Sub
```

Most changes in startup settings take place the next time that you open the database. Use the Application.RefreshTitleBar statement to change the text that appears in the database title bar immediately. The custom menu bar that you specify does not display until you close and reopen the database.

Next, build the called function that receives the arguments from the sub procedure and changes the settings. Include the On Error GoTo statement to handle the properties that are not yet members of the application's Properties collection. The error code for a property not found is 3270, which you can use to check for any missing properties. The error handler in the function uses the CreateProp method to build the missing property and then uses the Append method to add the missing property to the collection, as follows:

```
Set prp = dbs.CreateProperty(strPropName, _
    varPropType, varPropValue)
dbs.Properties.Append prp
```

The function also uses the Debug.Print command to display the names of the missing properties and to show the error number and description in the Immediate window, as follows:

```
Public Function ChangeProp(strPropName As String, _
    varPropType As Variant, varPropValue As Variant)
Dim dbs As Object
Dim prp As Variant
Const conPropNotFoundError = 3270
Set dbs = CurrentDb
On Error GoTo Change_Err
dbs.Properties(strPropName) = varPropValue
ChangeProp = True

Change_Exit:
    Exit Function

Change_Err:
    If Err = conPropNotFoundError Then   'property not found
      Debug.Print strPropName, Err.Number, Err.Description
        Set prp = dbs.CreateProperty(strPropName, _
            varPropType, varPropValue)
        dbs.Properties.Append prp
        Resume Next
    Else
        'Unknown error
        ChangeProp = False
        Resume Change_Exit
    End If

End Function
```

Figure 14-2 shows the VBE and Immediate windows after running the `ChangeStartupProps` procedure. Two of the properties were not in the collection and were added by the error handler in the `ChangeProp` function.

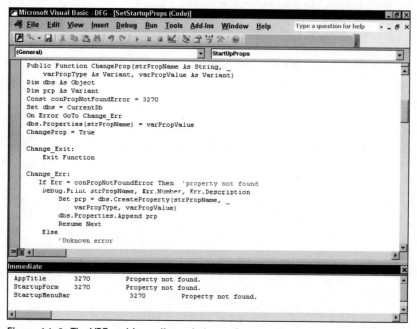

Figure 14-2: The VBE and Immediate windows after running the `ChangeStartupProps` procedure.

In Figure 14-3, you can see the new startup settings for the DFG database. The DFG Custom menu is not yet displayed in the database window. You need to close and reopen the database for that change to take effect.

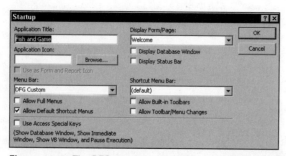

Figure 14-3: The DFG database with the new startup settings.

Resetting the default startup properties

To return the startup properties to their default settings, simply delete the custom settings from the Properties collection. The following code uses the `With...End With` structure to return several application properties to their default values:

```
Public Sub ResetProps()
Dim dbsDFG As Database

Set dbsDFG = CurrentDb
With dbsDFG
    .Properties.Delete "AppTitle"
    .Properties.Delete "StartupForm"
    .Properties.Delete "StartupMenuBar"
    .Properties.Delete "AllowFullMenus"
    .Properties.Delete "AllowBuiltInToolbars"
    .Properties.Delete "StartupShowDBWindow"
    .Properties.Delete "StartupShowStatusBar"
    .Properties.Delete "AllowToolbarChanges"
End With
Application.RefreshTitleBar
End Sub
```

When you open the Startup dialog box again, you see that these settings are restored to their default values.

Working with Environment Options

You have probably used the Options dialog box (by choosing Tools→Options) many times to set the default options for an application. The 12 tabs contain options for everything from choosing what to view in the database window to setting the default size for a text field in a table design. The options are classified as one of the following types:

◆ **True or False:** These are the check boxes that you see in the Options tabs.

◆ **String or number:** These are the text boxes into which you enter a text or numeric value.

◆ **Predefined options that are displayed in a list box, combo box, or option group:** You choose the one that you want from the value list or the option group. In many cases, you can also type in the value that you want.

VBA provides the following tools that you can use to set these option values and to view the current settings:

♦ The SetOption method sets or changes the current setting.

♦ The GetOption method returns the current value of the setting.

Both of these methods apply to the application object.

Setting option values

When you use VBA to set an option value, you need to know the name of the option but you don't need to refer to the Options dialog box tab where you can find the option. The SetOption method syntax is as follows:

```
expression.SetOption(OptionName, Setting)
```

The *expression* argument is simply Application, the only object that the method applies to. Both of the arguments are required. *OptionName* is the string name of the option. For example, to set the default width of the left print margin, use "Left Margin" as the option name (include the quotation marks).

 See the "Set Options from Visual Basic" help topic for a complete list of argument names that you can use when setting default options.

The *Setting* argument is the value that you want the option to acquire. The value that you use depends on the type of option that you want to set. Some options are simple check boxes, others can be chosen from a list, and still others require a string or numeric value to be entered.

If the option is a check box, you specify True or False as the setting. True has the value –1, and False has the value 0. For example, to set the Show Table Names setting in the Query Design pane of the Tables/Queries tab, use the following code:

```
Application.SetOption "Show Table Names", True
```

An example of entering a string argument is setting the default database folder on the General tab of the Options dialog box, as follows:

```
Application.SetOption "Default Database Directory", _
"C:\My Documents\Wiley"
```

If the option requires a numeric value, enter the value without the quotation marks. The following code sets the default column width on the Datasheet tab to 2 inches:

```
Application.SetOption "Default Column Width", 2
```

If the option setting is in an option group, you set the value by specifying its index. The first item in the group has the index number 0. The following code sets the cell effect on the Datasheet tab to Sunken, the third item in the list:

```
Application.SetOption "Cell Effect", 2
```

When you set the value of an option that appears as a combo box or list box, you specify the value by its index value in the list, just as you do for option groups. For example, the following code sets the default size for a number field (on the Table Design tab) to Decimal (the sixth item in the list):

```
Application.SetOption "Default Number field Size", 5
```

 The Help file indicates that items in a combo box list are specified in the SetOption method by their position in the list: first, second, third, and so on. However, experience shows that they are actually indexed in the list in the same way as options in an option group. The first has an index value of 0, the second, 1, and so on. Some options also don't respond as you would expect, so it is a good idea to experiment with the values and check out the results.

The following statements hide table names in query design, set a new default directory, change the datasheet column width to 2", change the number field size to Decimal, and set the cell effect in a datasheet to Sunken.

```
Public Sub ChangeOptions()
With Application
    .SetOption "Show Table Names", False
    .SetOption "Default Database Directory", "C:\My Documents\Wiley"
    .SetOption "Default Column Width", 2
    .SetOption "Default Number Field Size", 5
    .SetOption "Default Cell Effect", 2
End With
End Sub
```

Returning option settings

The `GetOption` method returns the current setting of one of the environment options. You can use this to test for specific settings and, based on the result, either accept the setting or change it with the `SetOption` method. The `GetOption` syntax, shown as follows, is simpler that the `SetOption` method:

```
expression.GetOption(OptionName)
```

Again, the *expression* argument is `Application`, and the required *OptionName* argument is a string that represents one of the options.

To directly examine an option setting, you can use the `GetOption` method as a `Debug.Print` statement, as follows:

```
Debug.Print Application.GetOption("Default Background Color")
```

The index number of the option is displayed in the Immediate window. If the background color is the default of white, the index is 15.

To use the result of the `GetOption` method elsewhere in your code, you can declare a variable and set it to the value that is returned by the method. The variable must be declared as a variant, because the value can be True (–1) or False (0), a string, or an index number.

For example, the following code returns True or False, depending on the current setting of the `Show Status Bar` property found on the View tab of the Options dialog box:

```
Dim varSet1 As Variant
varSet1 = Application.GetOption("Show Status Bar")
Debug.Print varSet1
```

If the option is checked, you see –1 (True) in the Immediate window. If not, you see 0 (False).

The following procedure examines the settings of the five options that were set in the preceding section and displays the results in the Immediate window.

```
Public Sub ReturnOptions()

Dim varSet1 As Variant, varSet2 As Variant
Dim varSet3 As Variant, varSet4 As Variant
Dim varSet5 As Variant

'Save current settings as variant variables
varSet1 = Application.GetOption("Show Table Names")
varSet2 = Application.GetOption("Default Database Directory")
varSet3 = Application.GetOption("Default Column Width")
```

```
varSet4 = Application.GetOption("Default Number Field Size")
varSet5 = Application.GetOption("Default Cell Effect")
Debug.Print "Show Table Names "; varSet1
Debug.Print "Default directory "; varSet2
Debug.Print "Default column width "; varSet3
Debug.Print "Default number field size "; varSet4
Debug.Print "Default datasheet cell effect "; varSet5

End Sub
```

Figure 14-4 shows the results of running the previous procedure.

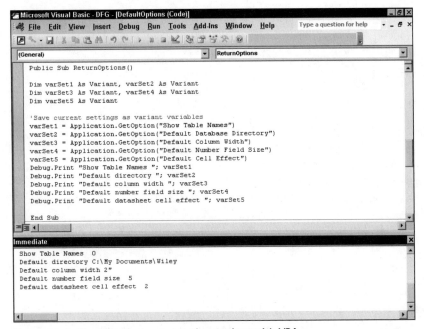

Figure 14-4: Checking the current option settings with VBA.

Saving and restoring original option settings

You may often want to change some of these settings temporarily and then restore them to the original settings when the user exits the application. You can combine the two option methods to accomplish that by using the following steps:

1. Use the GetOption method to set public variables equal to all the settings that you want to preserve. This function procedure runs when the application starts up.

2. Use the SetOption method to customize the environment.

3. Use the SetOption method in a sub procedure again to run when the application closes. This time the SetOption method uses the values that you saved as public variables to restore the original settings.

You can run the first step when the application starts by using an AutoExec macro with the action RunCode. The RunCode macro action requires a function argument. If you are using a sub procedure, as in this example, create a function that calls the sub procedure and use the function name as the AutoExec macro argument.

The following sub procedure saves some of the current default options settings to a set of public variables:

```
'First declare the public variables
Public varGridH As Variant, varGridV As Variant
Public varFontName As Variant, varFontSize As Variant
Public varEProcs As Variant, varSpell1 As Variant
Public varSpell2 As Variant

Public Sub SaveOptions()

'Save the current settings as the public variables.
varGridH = Application.GetOption("Default Gridlines Horizontal")
varGridV = Application.GetOption("Default Gridlines Vertical")
varFontName = Application.GetOption("Default Font Name")
varFontSize = Application.GetOption("Default Font Size")
varEProcs = Application.GetOption("Always Use Event Procedures")
varSpell1 = Application.GetOption("Spelling Ignore words in UPPERCASE")
varSpell2 = Application.GetOption("Spelling Ignore words with number)
End Sub
```

Figure 14-5 shows the VBE window with the SaveOptions procedure and with the saved values displayed in the Immediate window.

In the second step, you change the options for the current instance of the application. Follow these steps:

1. Create a sub procedure that customizes the options as desired. Use a series of SetOption methods, as shown in a preceding example.

2. Attach the procedure to the On Open event property of the form that you specified as Display Form/Page in the Startup dialog box or that you set with VBA.

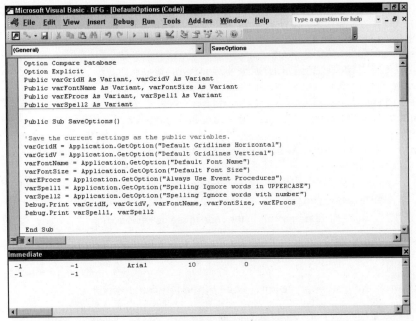

Figure 14–5: Saving the current options for later restoration.

It is important to understand the sequence of events that occur when an application starts. The `AutoExec` macro, if one exists, executes first. Then the startup settings take effect. So, the settings that are saved by the `AutoExec` macro are not disturbed by the changes that are made to the startup options by the `SetOption` methods.

The third step is to restore the options to their original values, which were saved in public variables, as follows:

1. Create the procedure that changes the options to the saved variable values.

2. Attach the restoration procedure to the `Close` event for a form or add to an existing exit procedure that runs when the user exits the application.

The following code restores the values to the specific options:

```
Public Sub RestoreOpts()
'Set the options to the values saved
'in the public variables
```

```
With Application
    .SetOption "Default Gridlines Horizontal", varGridH
    .SetOption "Default Gridlines Vertical", varGridV
    .SetOption "Default Font Name", varFontName
    .SetOption "Default Font Size", varFontSize
    .SetOption "Always Use Event Procedures", varEProcs
    .SetOption "Spelling Ignore Words in UPPERCASE", varSpell1
    .SetOption "Spelling Ignore Words with number", varSpell2
End With
End Sub
```

TIP While debugging this and any other code, it helps to insert a few
`Debug.Print` statements in the code to see how it is doing.

You can run the restore procedure in one of the following ways:

◆ If you have used the Switchboard Manager to create a main switchboard
for your application, the Switchboard Manager probably includes a choice
that exits the database.

◆ Attach the procedure to the `On Close` event property of the final user form.

Figure 14-6 shows the main switchboard that is used with the Senior Volunteers
database.

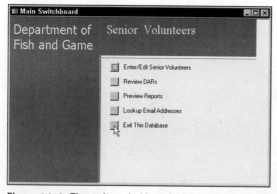

Figure 14-6: The main switchboard with an Exit This Database option.

To include the restoration procedure in the switchboard form's class module, use
the following steps:

1. Select the form in the database window.

2. Click the Code button.

3. Scroll down the VBE window to the `HandleButtonClick` function. You can then see the constants that are assigned to the choices in the switchboard at the beginning of the function.

   The Switchboard Wizard has assigned constants for the commands that can be executed. The command that exits the database has the value 6.

   ```
   ' Constants for the commands that can be executed.
   Const conCmdGotoSwitchboard = 1
   Const conCmdOpenFormAdd = 2
   Const conCmdOpenFormBrowse = 3
   Const conCmdOpenReport = 4
   Const conCmdCustomizeSwitchboard = 5
   Const conCmdExitApplication = 6
   Const conCmdRunMacro = 7
   Const conCmdRunCode = 8
   Const conCmdOpenPage = 9
   ```

4. Scroll down the code to the `Case` structure, and locate the `conCmdExitApplication` block.

5. Insert a statement that calls the `RestoreOptions` procedure, as follows:

   ```
   ' Exit the application.
   Case conCmdExitApplication
   Call RestoreOptions
          CloseCurrentDatabase
   ```

 If you have developed an application that runs in a language other than English, you still have to pass the arguments to both the `SetOption` and `GetOption` methods in English.

Creating and Appending New Properties

Earlier in this chapter, you saw how to use the `CreateProperty` and `AppendProperty` methods to help set startup options. If the property hadn't been changed lately, it was not a member of the Properties collection, so the `ChangeProp` function couldn't find it. In that case, the `ChangeProp` function just created the property and appended it to the collection.

You can use the same technique to create new properties for any object that the CreateProperty method applies to, including the following:

♦ Databases

♦ Documents

♦ Fields

♦ Indexes

♦ Query definitions

♦ Table definitions

The CreateProperty syntax, shown as follows, involves several arguments, and most of them are optional:

```
Set property = object.CreateProperty(name, type, value, DDL)
```

The various arguments of this syntax are as follows:

♦ The *property* argument is the variable that represents the property that you are creating. This argument is required.

♦ The *object* argument names the object for which you are adding the new property. This argument is also required.

♦ The optional *name* argument uniquely names the new property. If the name already exists in the collection, you get a run-time error when you try to append the property.

♦ The optional *type* argument specifies the data type that is used by the new property (for example, Text, Number, or True/False).

♦ The optional *value* argument determines the initial setting for the new property.

♦ The DDL argument indicates whether the property is a DDL object. The default setting is False.

The following code creates a new property with a text value and appends the property to the Properties collection of the DFG database:

```
Public Sub CreateProp()
Dim dbsDFG As Database
Dim prpNew As Property
Dim prpColl As Property

Set dbsDFG = CurrentDb
'Create and append new property
```

```
With dbsDFG
Set prpNew = .CreateProperty("MyProp", dbText, "Here it is!")
   .Properties.Append prpNew
End With
End Sub
```

NOTE You can also use the Append method to add new properties to the fields, indexes, query definition, and table definition Properties collections if the objects are in a Microsoft Jet workspace.

What is Conditional Compilation?

Conditional compilation is a tool that you can use to selectively choose the block of code that you want to be compiled and included in the deliverable code. For example, you may be creating an application that does the following:

♦ Is intended to run on different platforms, such as 16-bit or 32-bit Windows or Macintosh

♦ Uses different languages

♦ Uses different date and currency formats

You can write the code to suit each environment and separate the code into specific blocks. When you are ready to deliver the final product, you can compile only the appropriate block. The balance of the code is not included in the final executable compiled code.

Conditional compilation is also used during application development and debugging. You can approach a problem with different programming logic strategies and then run each solution separately to evaluate its speed and efficiency. You can also apply conditional compiling during testing to skip the debugging code and compile the rest of the code.

Starting conditional compilation

To begin conditional compilation, follow these steps:

1. Declare the conditional compiler constant #Const in the module that contains the alternative blocks of code.

2. Embed the code segments within the conditional compilation structure.

The #Const directive must be an expression that evaluates to True or False and can be used in the #If...Then...#Else directive. You can use a literal, another conditional compilation constant, or a combination that includes arithmetic or logical operators. You can use any operator except Is, but you can't use the standard constant declaration Const.

The #If...Then...#Else directive syntax is as follows:

```
#If expression Then
    statements
    #ElseIf  expression-n Then
        elseif statements
    #Else
        else statements
#End If
```

This structure works just like the regular If...Then...Else structure except that you can't place the whole structure on a single line, even if it is short. All the expressions that are used in the code must evaluate to True or False. All the expressions are evaluated, regardless of the outcome of the evaluation, so they must all be defined. If the #Const expression is not defined, it is evaluated as Empty instead of True or False, which can cause an error.

Compiling during debugging

By declaring the conditional compilation constant directive to a specific value, you can selectively run blocks of code in debugging mode while running other blocks as normal code. For example, the following statements run the first block of code if you are still debugging it so that it runs the debugging statements. The second block of code runs as normal code and skips any debugging statements.

```
'Declare your public compilation constant as part of the Declaration
'section. Then add each sub procedure to the module.
#Const conTryIt = 1

Sub CondComp()
    #If conTryIt = 1 Then
        'Run the code you want to debug.
        '
        '
    #Else
        'Run code normally without debugging statements.
        '
        '
    #End If
End Sub
```

Compiling with VBA constants

VBA provides some constants for use with the #If...Then...#Else directive that allow you to compile code for different platforms. These constants are global and apply to every member of the project. They are proprietary and can't be used to define your own constants.

The VBA compiler constants for a 16-bit platform are as follows:

♦ Win16 evaluates to True if the development environment is 16-bit Windows and False if not.

♦ Win32 evaluates to True if the development environment is 32-bit Windows and False if not.

The VBA constants that you can use in a 32-bit environment are as follows:

♦ Vba6 evaluates to True if you are using VBA Version 6.0 and False if not.

♦ Win16 evaluates to True if you are working in a 16-bit environment and False if not.

♦ Win32 evaluates to True if you are working in a 32-bit environment and False if not.

♦ Mac evaluates to True if you are working in a Macintosh environment and False if not.

You can nest the compiler directives to build the mix of environments that you need. The following example sets the public compiler constant euroLang to 1 and uses it to identify the block of code that is to be compiled for the European environment. It then nests this constant within the directive that compiles for different computer environments.

```
'Declare the public euroLang compiler constant
#Const euroLang = 1
'statements that fit all environments
'
'
#If Win32 Or Win16 Then
'statements exclusively written for the Windows environment
    '
    '
    #If euroLang = 1 then
        'statements written for the European environment
        'using Windows
```

```
    #Else
        'statements written for native language environment
        'using Windows
    #End If
#ElseIf Mac Then
    'Statements exclusively written for Macintosh environment.
    '
    '
    #If euroLang = 1 then
        'statements written for the European environment using
        'Macintosh systems
    #Else
'statements written for native language environment 'using Macintosh
systems
    #End If
#Else
    'Statements for any other platform.
    '
    '
    '
#End If
```

When you deliver the compiled code to the end user, only those statements that are meant for that environment are included in the executable code. You don't need to remove the other statements from the code.

Running an Opening Procedure

In the first section of this chapter, you saw how to set startup options, including the form to display when the database first opens. The Display Form/Page property is often set to display an opening form that welcomes the user to the application. This form remains on-screen for a few seconds and then changes to the main switchboard, which gives the user a choice of options. To accomplish this change, set the following properties for the Welcome form:

◆ Set the Timer property to 5000, a 5-second interval.

◆ Set the On Timer property to the name of the macro that closes the form and opens the switchboard (see Figure 14-7).

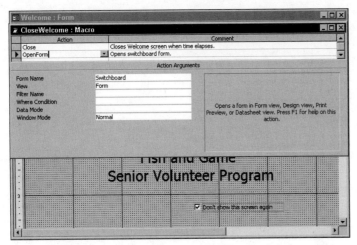

Figure 14-7: The macro that opens the switchboard after 5 seconds.

Changing the opening form

The Welcome form often has a check box that the user can select if she doesn't want to keep seeing it every time that she opens the database. You can write VBA code to do the following:

◆ Examines the value of the check box when the form closes.

◆ If Yes, changes the StartupForm property to the name of the main switchboard. The next time that the database opens, the Switchboard form appears instead of the Welcome form.

◆ If not checked, retains the Welcome form as the StartupForm property.

◆ If the StartupForm property has not been set to a custom form (that is, is not yet a member of the Properties collection), the function uses the error handler to create the property and set it to the Switchboard form.

The Northwind sample database includes this setup. The following code changes the opening form in the Senior Volunteers database:

```
Public Function HideWelcomeForm()
On Error GoTo HideWelcomeForm_Err

'Tests the HideWelcomeForm check box to determine if it was
'checked. If True, changes the database's Startup Form property.
'Attach it to the On Close event property of the Welcome form.
```

```
If Forms!Welcome!HideWelcomeForm Then
    'The check box is checked, so change the StartupForm
    'property to Switchboard. If not, leave as Welcome.
    CurrentDb.Properties("StartupForm") = "Switchboard"
Else
    CurrentDb.Properties("StartupForm") = "Welcome"
End If

Exit Function

HideWelcomeForm_Err:
    'If the property is not found in the collection,
    'create it and set it to the Switchboard form.
    'Then append the property to the collection.
    Const conPropertyNotFound = 3270
    If Err = conPropertyNotFound Then
        Dim dbs As Database
        Dim prop As Property
        Set dbs = CurrentDb()
        Set prop = dbs.CreateProperty("StartupForm", dbText, _
"Switchboard")
        dbs.Properties.Append prop
        Resume Next
    End If
End Function
```

After you have evaluated the function, attach it to the On Close event property of the Welcome form.

Summary

In this chapter, we have shown you many ways to customize your workplace environment – from changing the startup options to modifying the default database options and creating new properties. You have also seen how to create executable code for different operating environments.

In the next chapter, you find out how to connect your application to ActiveX Data Object libraries and work with ADO models.

Part IV

Advanced Access Programming Techniques with VBA

Chapter 15

Connecting to Databases with ADO

IN THIS CHAPTER

◆ Connecting your application to its data sources

◆ The ActiveX Data Object libraries

◆ The ADO object model

◆ The ADOX object model

THE DATA ACCESS OBJECT (DAO) model was appropriate and perfectly adequate back in the old days, when we were younger. Back then, applications dealt almost exclusively with data that was held in relational databases. Today, the majority of data sources that are accessed by applications are still relational databases, so DAO is still widely used, but nonrelational data sources are becoming more common. As a result, Access 2000 introduced a new way of connecting an Access application to a data source: using ActiveX Data Objects (ADOs). ADO technology is gradually displacing the older DAO technology, which was not as capable of handling diverse types of data sources. (DAO was designed to connect primarily to the Microsoft Jet database engine.) Any new development that you do should use ADO, not DAO, unless you have some compelling reason to use the older technology. The fact that you may be familiar with DAO and not with ADO probably does not fall into the category of a compelling reason. Keeping up with the advance of technology gives you a tangible rationale for lifelong learning.

Applications, Database Engines, and Data Sources

ADO works with OLE DB (Object Linking and Embedding Database) data providers to give your application access to a wide variety of data sources. Aside from Jet and SQL Server, you can directly access Oracle databases, and using ODBC (Open Database Connectivity), you can access many other relational databases as well. In addition, you can access data in such nontraditional data sources as Web pages and Windows 2000 directory services.

The ADODB, ADOX, and JRO Libraries

Access provides a multitude of useful libraries. Once you decide on libraries and specify them, you are ready to start using them to code your database and application.

Application libraries

The following Access libraries contain objects that you are most likely to need to build applications:

◆ ADODB

◆ ADOX

◆ JRO

For some tasks, you may need only one library. For other tasks, you may need objects from more than one library.

ADODB LIBRARY

Access installs the ADODB (ActiveX Data Object) library by default. It is a small library, whose objects provide the following:

◆ Basic functionality, such as the following:

  ▪ Making connections

  ▪ Issuing commands

  ▪ Retrieving recordsets

◆ The capability of navigating in a recordset

◆ Basic maintenance tasks that nearly all applications need to perform

Multiple versions of the ADODB library exist. You should choose your version based on the following criteria:

◆ If some of the machines that are to run your application are using Access 97, you should stay with version 2.1.

◆ If all your machines are running at least Access 2000, version 2.5 may be a better choice.

For many applications, ADODB may give you everything you need. If it does not, you must add references to either one or both of the ADOX and JRO libraries to make them available to your application.

ADOX LIBRARY

The ADOX (ADO Extensions for DDL and Security) library contains objects that accomplish the following:

◆ Enable you to create database objects, such as the following:

- Tables

- Indexes

- Keys

◆ Control security, such as granting and revoking access privileges

The ADOX library also contains tools to do the following:

◆ Establish referential integrity in a database

◆ Cascade updates and deletions

JRO LIBRARY

The JRO (Microsoft Jet and Replication Objects) library holds the tools that you need to replicate a Jet database.

 Replication allows each person on a network to operate on his or her own copy of a database. Changes made to each copy are later synchronized to keep all copies consistent.

Library installation

To make sure that the libraries you need are available to the database application you are building, specify the libraries from VBE. From the VBE main menu, select Tools→References and then place a check mark to the left of each library that you want your application to be able to access. Figure 15-1 shows the dialog box from which you can select appropriate libraries.

 Each library takes memory and thus reduces performance, so don't specify any libraries that you know your application doesn't need.

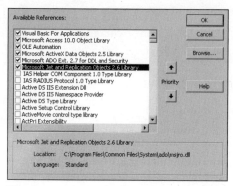

Figure 15-1: Choosing libraries from the References dialog box.

After you specify libraries, you are ready to start using them to code your database and application.

The ADO Object Model

To efficiently use code with ActiveX objects, you should understand the ADO object model, which gives structure to the objects that make up the model.

The ADO object model includes objects and collections of objects that are included in the ADODB library. An object may include another object or a collection of similar objects. Figure 15-2 shows the relationships among the various objects in the ADODB version 2.1 library.

In Figure 15-2, objects are shown in gray boxes with square corners and collections are shown in white boxes with rounded corners.

The ADODB library version 2.5 adds the following objects to the model:

◆ **Record object:** Contains the collection `Fields`, which in turn contains the object `Field`.

◆ **Stream objects:** Are useful for printing or reading the content of HTML or ASP files that are pointed to by a record. Stream objects are based on records.

The Connection object

The `Connection` object is the top object in the ADO hierarchy. Before you begin, you must have a connection to the data. The `Connection` object represents a single connection to an OLE DB data provider. As with any object, the `Connection` object encapsulates properties and methods. The `ConnectionString` property includes information about where the data source is located as well as a number of other specifications about the connection.

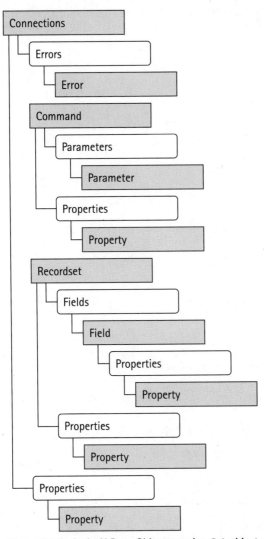

Figure 15-2: ActiveX Data Objects version 2.1 object model.

You can create a connection object with code similar to the following:

```
Sub ConnectOLS1()
Dim cnn1 As New Connection
Dim rst1 As Recordset

'Create the Connection
cnn1.Open "Provider=Microsoft.Jet.OLEDB.4.0;" & _
    "Data Source=C:\LunarSociety\OLS1.mdb;"
```

```
'Create a recordset reference, then set its properties
Set rst1 = New ADODB.Recordset
rst1.CursorType = adOpenKeyset
rst1.LockType = adLockOptimistic

'Open the recordset, and print several fields from a test record
rst1.Open "MEMBERS", cnn1
Debug.Print rst1.Fields(0).Value, rst1.Fields(1).Value, _
    rst1.Fields(2).Value, rst1.Fields(5).Value

'Clean up before exiting
rst1.Close
cnn1.Close
Set rst1 = Nothing
Set cnn1 = Nothing

End Sub
```

When executed, this code displays in VBE's Immediate window the contents of the requested fields from the first record in the MEMBERS table, as shown in the following example:

```
101          Bryce        Thoreau      (503) 555-8004
```

The preceding connection object code performs the following tasks:

- ◆ Creates a connection to the specified database
- ◆ Creates a recordset reference and sets its properties
- ◆ Opens the recordset
- ◆ Prints selected information from the recordset
- ◆ Closes the recordset and connection, and removes all traces of the recordset's brief existence from memory

 TIP Closing the connection and then the recordset, and then setting their values to Nothing helps to avoid memory leaks that can slow performance and even corrupt data.

To operate on an Access database that is already open, you can reference it without giving its full address, as follows:

```
Sub ConnectOLS1()
Dim rst1 As Recordset

'Create a recordset reference, then set its properties
Set rst1 = New ADODB.Recordset
rst1.CursorType = adOpenKeyset
rst1.LockType = adLockOptimistic

'Open the recordset, and print several fields from a test record
rst1.Open "MEMBERS", CurrentProject.Connection
Debug.Print rst1.Fields(0).Value, rst1.Fields(1).Value, _
    rst1.Fields(2).Value, rst1.Fields(5).Value

'Clean up after yourself
rst1.Close
Set rst1 = Nothing

End Sub
```

The preceding formulation may be preferable if you want to avoid hard-coding the location of the database, because you distribute the application to multiple sites.

The Recordset object

The Recordset object, like all objects, can be associated with properties, methods, and events.

This chapter explains several recordset object properties and methods.

Chapter 16 explains events in detail.

A couple of dozen properties may be associated with a recordset. Most of them are optional and aren't often needed.

ADO RECORDSET PROPERTIES

Although many recordset properties are not frequently used, a few are used fairly regularly. Among those are CursorType, LockType, and CursorLocation.

CURSORTYPE In Access, the cursor is the object that you use to move around within a recordset. It is a set of cached rows or row pointers from the database engine when you open a recordset.

 Cursor type is important in multiuser installations, where multiple people could be accessing the same recordset at the same time.

Four cursor types exist; however, in this case, *cursor* does not refer to your on-screen mouse arrow. The cursor types are described as follows:

◆ **Dynamic:** Shows all changes made by all users but is not fully supported by all data providers.

◆ **Keyset:** Shows changes made by other users but does not show new records added by other users

 Keyset prevents access to records that were deleted by other users.

◆ **Static:** A snapshot of the records at the time the recordset was created. Does not reflect changes made to the data.

◆ **Forward-only:** Faster than a static cursor but only scrolls forward through the records, never backward.

Starting with Access 2000, Forward-only is the default cursor type.

LOCKTYPE The LockType property specifies how data-access conflicts by multiple users are handled. Such conflicts could cause data corruption, or even a system lockup.

The four important lock types are as follows:

◆ **Read-only:** Allows only read access.

Read-only is the default lock type.

◆ **Pessimistic:** Locks a record as soon as a user starts editing it.

Pessimistic locking takes no chances on conflicts, but performance may suffer.

◆ **Optimistic:** Locks a record only when a user chooses to commit the edits that she has made.

Optimistic locking can have conflicts, but performance is high for the majority of cases when there is no conflict.

◆ **Batch optimistic:** Allows an entire batch of records to be updated before they are all sent at once to a remote database.

If any changed records conflict with changes made by another user, a problem could occur, but when no conflict exists, this lock type delivers high performance.

CURSORLOCATION   The `CursorLocation` property specifies the location of the current operation's cursor — either the client or the server (the server is the default cursor location).

If you are using Jet as your data source, leave the default value (server) intact. With Jet, the client is the server; everything happens on the local machine. If you specify the client as the server location, a copy of the cursor is cached on your machine; this wastes space.

Selecting LockType

Depending on the likelihood of conflicts and the value of performance on any given job, you should select the most appropriate lock type for the situation, as follows:

◆ If multiple users rarely simultaneously update the same database table, the performance of optimistic or batch optimistic locking may be worthwhile.

◆ If update conflicts are likely, pessimistic locking is the best choice.

◆ If only one station is likely to make updates, and any others will only view table contents, the read-only lock type gives the best performance.

Even if Jet is not your data source, it is usually best to use a server-side cursor unless you are performing operations for which a server-side cursor doesn't work. With Jet, sorting only works on the client machine. To perform a sort on a recordset, you must assign the adUseClient intrinsic constant to the recordset's CursorLocation property. Performing a seek, on the other hand, requires that you assign the adUseServer intrinsic constant to the recordset's CursorLocation property.

You can explicitly specify the cursor location when you are setting properties for a subprocedure, as shown in the following code:

```
rst.ActiveConnection = CurrentProject.Connection
rst.CursorType = adOpenKeyset
rst.LockType = adLockOptimistic
rst.CursorLocation = adUseServer
```

ADO RECORDSET PROPERTIES

Sort and Filter are two frequently used recordset properties.

SORT   The Sort property specifies the order of the rows. You can specify the sort order of a recordset with the ADO Sort property in either ascending or descending order. Remember, all you are sorting here is the recordset; the database is not affected.

> The ADO Sort property is like the SQL ORDER BY clause. If you create a recordset with an SQL statement, you can specify the order of the rows with an ORDER BY clause.

You can sort with the Access Sort property on just one field or on multiple fields, as shown in the following example:

```
rst.Sort = "Zip"           'Sorts records by Zip code (ascending)
rst.Sort = "Zip ASC"       'Sorts records by Zip code (ascending)
rst.Sort = "Zip DESC"      'Sorts records by Zip code (descending)
'Sort records first on Zip code descending, then on last name
'ascending
rst.Sort = "Zip DESC, LastName ASC"
```

FILTER   You can filter out unwanted rows from a recordset with the Filter property. For example, to restrict the records that are returned from the Oregon Lunar Society MEMBERS table to only those who actually live in Oregon, you could filter the recordset with the following statement:

```
rst.Filter = "Zip >= 97000 and Zip < 98000"
```

In SQL, a WHERE clause can restrict the rows that a recordset contains.

ADO RECORDSET METHODS

A couple of dozen methods are associated with the ADO Recordset object. You can find them in VBE's Object Browser, along with their syntax. The methods that are described in the following sections are those that are most frequently used.

MOVING IN A RECORDSET   One of the fundamental abilities you need, in order to operate on a recordset is the ability to move to specific records in the recordset.
   The following methods provide this ability:

◆ **MoveFirst:** Moves the cursor to the first record in the recordset

◆ **MoveLast:** Moves the cursor to the last record in the recordset

◆ **MovePrevious:** Moves the cursor from the current record to the previous record in the recordset

◆ **MoveNext:** Moves the cursor from the current record to the next record in the recordset

◆ **Move [N]:** Moves the cursor N records in either the positive or the negative direction from its current position. Movement in the positive direction is toward the last record in the recordset and movement in the negative direction is toward the first record.

Markers indicate the start and end of the recordset, as follows:

◆ **BOF:** Marker before the first record in a recordset.

   If you are at BOF and try to execute a MovePrevious method, an error is generated.

◆ **EOF:** Marker beyond the last record in a recordset.

   If you are at EOF and try to execute a MoveNext method, an error is generated.

 If you are in the middle of a 20-record recordset and execute a Move [40] method, the cursor is placed at EOF and no error is generated. If the cursor is already at EOF, that Move method would generate a runtime error. The same holds for a move in the negative direction that goes beyond BOF.

FIND   A recordset's `Find` method searches for the first record in the set that satisfies a specified search condition. For example, the following sub procedure finds a specific record in the OLS1 MEMBERS table:

```
Sub FindTom()
Dim rst1 As Recordset

'Create a recordset reference, then set its properties
Set rst1 = New ADODB.Recordset

'Open the recordset, Find Tom's record, then print several fields
'from his record
rst1.Open "MEMBERS", CurrentProject.Connection
rst1.Find "[FirstName] = 'Tom'"
Debug.Print rst1.Fields(0).Value, rst1.Fields(1).Value, _
    rst1.Fields(2).Value, rst1.Fields(5).Value

'Clean up after yourself
rst1.Close
Set rst1 = Nothing

End Sub
```

This code gives the following result in the Immediate window:

```
103           Tom            Charges        (503) 555-3211
```

Aside from the mandatory search criterion argument of the `Find` method (`"[FirstName] = 'Tom'"` in the preceding example), the `Find` method has three optional arguments that allow you to specify the following:

- How many rows to skip between the current cursor position and the record that you want
- The direction of movement (forward or backward)
- The position where you want to start if you do not want to start at the current cursor position

ADDNEW   It's easy to add a new row of data to a recordset in an Access table with a form or datasheet. However, you may also want to add data to a recordset from a program. The `AddNew` method is designed for such an operation.

When you are adding records to a recordset using the `AddNew` method, you must explicitly set the *cursor* type and the lock type.

The default values of the `CursorType` and `LockType` methods are forward-only and read-only, respectively. These settings do not allow you to make any changes to the recordset. You can't add, change, or delete anything.

The following code demonstrates adding a recordset row after having set the cursor type and lock type to values that permit you to add rows to the recordset:

```
Sub AddToMembers()
Dim rst1 As Recordset

'Create a recordset reference, then set its properties
Set rst1 = New ADODB.Recordset
rst1.CursorType = adOpenKeyset
rst1.LockType = adLockOptimistic

'Open the recordset
rst1.Open "MEMBERS", CurrentProject.Connection

'Add a new record
With rst1
    .AddNew
        .Fields("MemberID") = 106
        .Fields("FirstName") = "Bob"
        .Fields("LastName") = "Steinfeld"
        .Fields("Phone") = "(503) 555-9876"
    .Update
End With

'Clean up after yourself
rst1.Close
Set rst1 = Nothing

End Sub
```

In reality, you would probably not hard-code the addition of a person into the recordset, as was done for Bob Steinfeld in the preceding example. You are more likely to use variables that would allow you to add a batch of new records by looping through an array. However, this example illustrates the basic idea of how to add a new record by program.

The Field object

The `Recordset` object contains the `Fields` collection, which in turn contains the `Field` object. As of Access 2002, the `Record` object contains the `Fields` collection.

This broadening of scope expands the `Field` object out of the realm of pure relational databases to include parent/child relationships such as those between the following:

◆ Folders and subfolders

◆ Folders and the files contained in those folders

The `Field` object contains many properties and a couple of methods:

◆ **Properties:** Describe a field exhaustively, as follows:

   ■ `Value` is probably the most significant `Field` object property. It stores the field's data.

   ■ Other `Field` object properties contain metadata, such as `Name`, `DefinedSize`, `ActualSize`, and `Attributes`.

◆ **Methods:** Enable you to operate on the contents of large text or binary fields, one "chunk" at a time. The `Field` object has the following methods:

   ■ `GetChunk`

   ■ `AppendChunk`

TIP   VBE's Object Browser lists all the `Field` object's properties and methods.

The following code example retrieves the information in the record of the first member of the Oregon Lunar Society who is a Portland resident. The following procedure passes parameters in its call to a generic subprocedure that could retrieve a record from any table.

◆ The main procedure is as follows:

```
Sub CallFieldValues()
Dim str1 As String
Dim str2 As String
Dim str3 As String
Dim str4 As String

'Specify the data source for the member information
str1 = "Provider=Microsoft.Jet.OLEDB.4.0;" & _
    "Data Source=C:\LunarSociety\OLS1.mdb;"
```

```
'Specify a table within the record source
str2 = "MEMBERS"

'Specify a criterion for record retrieval
str3 = "City"
str4 = "Portland"

'Call the procedure to retrieve a Portland member

FieldValues str1, str2, str3, str4

End Sub
```

◆ The subprocedure is as follows:

```
'Generic procedure to construct a single-record recordset,
'and then display its contents
Sub FieldValues(str1 As String, str2 As String, _
    str3 As String, str4 As String)

Dim cnxn As ADODB.Connection
Dim rst1 As ADODB.Recordset
Dim str5 As String
Dim fld1 As ADODB.Field

'Open the Connection
Set cnxn = New ADODB.Connection
cnxn.Open str1

'Create recordset reference, and set its properties
Set rst1 = New ADODB.Recordset
rst1.ActiveConnection = cnxn
str5 = "SELECT * FROM " & str2 & " WHERE " & _
    str3 & " = '" & str4 & "'"

rst1.Open str5, , , , adCmdText

'Display field values for first qualifying record
For Each fld1 In rst1.Fields
    Debug.Print fld1.Name, fld1.Value
Next fld1

'Clean up before exiting
Set fld1 = Nothing
Set rst1 = Nothing

End Sub
```

In the preceding `rst1.Open` statement, `adCmdText` is an intrinsic constant that specifies a command type. It enables you to run a command based on an SQL statement that is stored as a text string. The SQL statement is the `SELECT` statement that is stored in `str5`. When you run this code, the `Name` and `Value` properties are displayed in the Immediate window, as follows:

```
MemberID      103
FirstName     Tom
LastName      Charges
OfficeHeld    Null
Email         waldo@magic.com
Phone         (503) 555-3211
Street        132 22nd St.
City          Portland
State         OR
Zip           97245
```

The Command object

The `Command` object is the primary actor in the ADODB library. You can do the following with this object:

♦ Perform a SELECT query to return a recordset

♦ Execute a parameter query that allows you to specify search conditions at run time

♦ Perform UPDATE, DELETE, and INSERT operations to change the contents of a data source

QUERYING A DATABASE TO RETRIEVE A RECORDSET

Perhaps the best way to show how to retrieve data from a data source using the `Command` object is to give an example. The following code retrieves the last names and e-mail addresses of all the people in the MEMBERS table of the OLS1 database:

```
Sub PrintTable()
Dim cmd1 As ADODB.Command
Dim rst1 As ADODB.Recordset
Dim str1 As String
Dim fld1 As ADODB.Field

'Specify a command, then execute it
Set cmd1 = New ADODB.Command
With cmd1
    .ActiveConnection = CurrentProject.Connection
    .CommandText = "SELECT FirstName, LastName, Email FROM MEMBERS"
```

```
        .CommandType = adCmdText
End With

'Set rst1 to the recordset returned by the command,
'then print the recordset
Set rst1 = cmd1.Execute
Do Until rst1.EOF
        str1 = ""
        For Each fld1 In rst1.Fields
                str1 = str1 & fld1.Value & vbTab
        Next fld1
        Debug.Print str1
        rst1.MoveNext
Loop

'Clean up before exiting
rst1.Close
Set fld1 = Nothing
Set rst1 = Nothing
Set cmd1 = Nothing

End Sub
```

The preceding example produces the following printout:

```
Bryce Thoreau moonman@coldmail.com
Cheryl Lancaster    starlass@cosmos.net
Tom Charges waldo@magic.com
Bob McGoing sparks@lightning.net
Gus Roderick    hotrod@davenport.net
Bob Steinfeld    tankmaster@gherkin.net
```

The cmd1 command that is located within the With...End With control structure causes the retrieval of a recordset. The contents of the recordset are then printed, one after another, within the Do Loop control structure.

The Parameter object

You can use parameters at run time to specify which records to retrieve.

The following example uses a Parameter object to retrieve only the records where the MemberID is 102:

```
Sub ParameterPrint()
Dim cmd1 As ADODB.Command
Dim rst1 As ADODB.Recordset
```

```vba
Dim str1 As String
Dim fld1 As ADODB.Field
Dim prm1 As ADODB.Parameter
Dim int1 As Integer

'Specify a command, then execute it
Set cmd1 = New ADODB.Command
With cmd1
    .ActiveConnection = CurrentProject.Connection
    .CommandText = "Parameters [IDNUM] Long;" & _
        "SELECT MemberID, FirstName, LastName, Email " & _
        "FROM MEMBERS " & _
        "WHERE MemberID = [IDNUM]"
    .CommandType = adCmdText
End With

'Create the parameter, and then accept user input
Set prm1 = cmd1.CreateParameter("[IDNUM]", _
    adInteger, adParamInput)
cmd1.Parameters.Append prm1
int1 = Trim(InputBox("Enter MemberID:"))
prm1.Value = int1

'Set rst1 to the recordset returned by the command,
'then print the recordset
Set rst1 = cmd1.Execute
Do Until rst1.EOF
    str1 = ""
    For Each fld1 In rst1.Fields
        str1 = str1 & fld1.Value & vbTab
    Next fld1
    Debug.Print str1
    rst1.MoveNext
Loop

'Clean up before exiting
rst1.Close
Set fld1 = Nothing
Set rst1 = Nothing
Set cmd1 = Nothing

End Sub
```

A dialog box pops up asking the user to enter the MemberID of the member whose record she wants to view. When the user enters 102, the following data is returned:

```
102 Cheryl  Lancaster    starlass@cosmos.net
```

The Record object

The Record object is new to ADODB library version 2.5. It is designed to point to

◆ Nonrelational objects, such as files in directories, accessing them via their Uniform Resource Locator (URL)

◆ The current row in a recordset

With the Record object you can, for example, retrieve and display the names of all the files and subfolders that are contained in a target folder on your local intranet server.

The Record object has quite a few properties and methods. Its methods include

◆ Open and Close

◆ MoveRecord

◆ CopyRecord

◆ DeleteRecord

TIP   Use the GetChildren method to retrieve the names of files in a folder.

Collections

Objects can contain collections of other objects. For example, a Recordset object can contain a collection of field objects. A one-to-many relationship exists between the parent object and the child objects. You can specify an object in a collection by using the collection name with the name of the object of interest in the collection. For example, the following code prints the names of all the fields in a recordset that was retrieved from the OLS1 MEMBERS table:

```
Sub MemberFields()
Dim rst1 As ADODB.Recordset
Dim fld1 As ADODB.Field
```

```
'Open table and print field names
Set rst1 = New ADODB.Recordset
rst1.Open "MEMBERS", CurrentProject.Connection
For Each fld1 In rst1.Fields
     Debug.Print fld1.Name
Next fld1

'Clean up before exiting
rst1.Close
Set rst1 = Nothing

End Sub
```

The For Each...Next structure loops through all the fields in the MEMBERS table, printing the name of each field as it goes. After processing the last field, execution continues beyond the loop, cleaning things up and then terminating. The 'cleaning up' consists of closing and resetting things to return the system to the state it was in before the procedure executed.

Creating Database Objects with the ADOX Object Model

As you have seen in the previous section, the ADODB library gives you the tools to manipulate the data in an existing database. This assumes that the database structure already exists. The ADOX library gives you the tools to create that structure. ADOX stands for ADO Extensions for DDL and Security; DDL stands for Data Definition Language. The DDL is that part of SQL that you use to define a database and the objects that are in it.

As with the ADODB library, the ADOX library includes objects that can contain collections, which, in turn, can contain other objects. VBE's Object Browser lists all the objects that are contained in all the active libraries, including the ADOX library.

Figure 15-3 shows the structure of the ADOX object model.

The Catalog object

The Catalog object is at the top of the ADOX library's hierarchy. The members of the Catalog object define the schema of the database model and its security provisions.

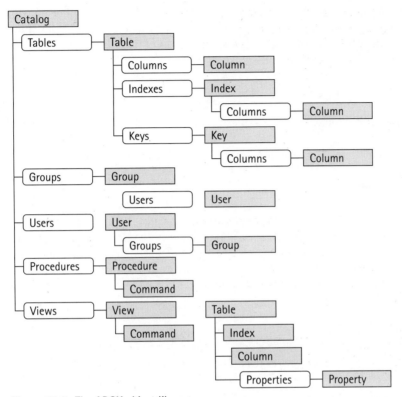

Figure 15-3: The ADOX object library.

The `Catalog` object contains the following collections:

- Tables
- Groups
- Users
- Procedures
- Views

TIP Because only one catalog is associated with each database, catalogs need not have names.

The `Catalog` object contains the `ActiveConnection` property. With this property, you can assign a `Connection` object to a catalog. This gives your application access to the database that's referenced by the catalog. Use a catalog's `Create` method to open a new database and access its catalog.

The Table object

The `Table` object is a member of the Tables collection, which in turn is a member of the `Catalog` object.

The `Table` object includes a number of different kinds of tables, such as

- System tables
- Linked tables
- Views
- Normal Access tables

The `Table` object includes the following collections:

- Columns
- Indexes
- Keys

The Column object

The `Column` object is a member of the Columns collection, which can be a member of the `Table` object but alternatively could be a member of the `Index` object or the `Key` object. This means that both the Index object and the Key object can contain a Columns collection.

Tables clearly need to have columns (or they would not be very useful). Likewise, indexes and keys must contain at least one column to be meaningful.

The following properties are required for all `Column` objects:

- `Name`: Allows them to be identified.
- `Type`: Indicates what type of data the column may hold.

The following properties are optional for all `Column` objects:

- `Attributes`: Indicates whether the column may contain null values.
- `DefinedSize`: Gives the maximum number of characters that the column may hold.
- `SortOrder`: Defines the order in which records will be sorted.

◆ Numeric columns may have the following properties:

  ■ NumericScale: Indicates the scale of a numeric value in a column.

  ■ Precision: Indicates the maximum precision of data values in a column.

 Check VBE's Object Browser for additional properties that may be relevant to your development effort.

The Index object

The Index object is a member of the Index collection, which in turn is a member of the Table object. The Index object sets indexes for the table.

The Index object includes five properties and two collections. The collections are as follows:

◆ Columns

◆ Properties

The properties are as follows:

◆ Name

◆ PrimaryKey: Tells whether this index applies to the table's primary key (Boolean value)

◆ Unique: Tells whether every entry in the index must be unique (Boolean value)

◆ IndexNulls: Tells what to do if a null value appears in the index

◆ Clustered: Tells whether the order of the indexes matches the physical order of the rows in the table (Boolean value)

The Key object

The Key object specifies the characteristics of keys. It has the following properties:

◆ Name

◆ Type: This key distinguishes among the following:

  ■ Primary keys

  ■ Foreign keys

  ■ Unique keys that are not primary keys

◆ RelatedTable: Applies to foreign keys; specifies the table that is linked to the foreign key.

◆ UpdateRule: Specifies the action after a primary key is updated.

◆ DeleteRule: Specifies the action after a primary key is deleted.

The Key object also contains a Columns collection.

The Group object

The Group object, a member of a Catalog's Groups collection, contains the Users collection for a particular group of users, as follows:

◆ SetPermissions **method:** Assigns different access rights to the members of different groups

◆ GetPermissions **method:** Retrieves the current permissions that are in effect for the group

◆ ParentCatalog **property:** Connects a group to its parent catalog

◆ Name **property:** Identifies the Group object

The User object

The User object is a member of the Users collection, which is a member of the Group object. The properties and methods of the User object identify the user and determine each user's access rights.

The Procedure object

The Procedure object is a member of the Procedures collection. The Procedures collection contains Access queries of various types, including the following:

◆ Parameter queries

◆ Action queries

◆ Union queries

◆ Cross-tab queries

 ADOX procedures are not the same as VBA procedures; they are Jet SQL statements, rather than VBA routines.

The View object

View objects, like Procedure objects, are stored Jet SQL statements. The View objects are simpler because the statements are simpler. The statements do not involve parameters or multiple SELECT statements, such as a union query would.

Creating a database

You can create a new database by first instantiating a catalog and then creating a database to go with it. The following procedure code shows how this is done:

```
Sub CreateAccessDB()
Dim str1 As String

'Specify the name of the new database
str1 = "C:\LunarSociety\NewDB.mdb"

'Check for duplicate database name and handle error
On Error GoTo CreateAccessDBErrorTrap
Dim cat1 As New ADOX.Catalog

'Instantiate the new catalog
Set cat1 = New ADOX.Catalog

'Create the new database
cat1.Create "Provider=Microsoft.Jet.OLEDB.4.0;" _
    & "Data Source=" & str1

CreateAccessDBExit:
'Clean up before exiting
Set cat1 = Nothing
Exit Sub

CreateAccessDBErrorTrap:
If Err.Number = -2147217897 Then
'If a prior version of this DB exists, kill it
    Debug.Print str1
    Kill (str1)
    Resume
Else
'If a different error has occurred display its description
    Debug.Print Err.Number, Err.Description
    MsgBox "Check Immediate window for error information.", _
        vbInformation
```

```
End If

End Sub
```

This code creates a new database named `NewDB.mdb` unless an error occurs.

 TIP   If you try to create a database with the same name as an already existing database, Access deletes the old version and replaces it with the new, empty database that you are creating. In some cases, you may want this behavior; in other cases, you may want to give your new database a different name. Think about under what circumstances a duplicate name may arise, and handle the situation accordingly.

Creating tables

After you have created a database, the next step is usually to create some tables. Using the `Table` object and the `Column` object from the ADOX library, you can add tables to any database, including one that you have just created, as we did in the previous section.

The following code shows you one way to create a table:

```
Sub AddTableToNewDB()
Dim cat1 As ADOX.Catalog
Dim str1 As String
Dim tbl1 As ADOX.Table
Dim cnxn As ADODB.Connection

'Specify the database that tables will be added to, and the
'columns that the table will contain
str1 = "C:\LunarSociety\NewDB.mdb"
Set cnxn = New ADODB.Connection
cnxn.Open "Provider=Microsoft.Jet.OLEDB.4.0;" _
      & "Data Source=" & str1
Set cat1 = New ADOX.Catalog
Set cat1.ActiveConnection = cnxn

'Create and name the table
Set tbl1 = New ADOX.Table
With tbl1
      .Name = "Donors"
      Set .ParentCatalog = cat1
      With .Columns
```

```
                .Append "DonorID", adInteger
                .Item("DonorID").Properties("AutoIncrement") = True
                .Append "FirstName", adVarWChar, 20
                .Append "LastName", adVarWChar, 25
                .Append "FirstDonationDate", adDate
        End With
End With


'Append new table to Tables collection of NewDB
cat1.Tables.Append tbl1

'Clean up before exiting
Set tbl1 = Nothing
Set cat1 = Nothing
cnxn.Close
Set cnxn = Nothing

End Sub
```

The `Set .ParentCatalog` statement is needed if the table contains an `AutoIncrement` field, which this one does (`DonorID`).

TIP   Even if your table has no `AutoIncrement` field, it's a good habit to include the `Set .ParentCatalog` statement.

After the preceding code is executed, the new table is a part of the database. It is still not complete, however, because no primary key has been named.

XREF   Keys are added to tables in the Adding a Primary Key section of this chapter.

Deleting tables

As time goes on, requirements sometimes change, particularly in the initial stages of a development effort or even after delivery to the customer. These changes may call for the deletion of existing tables and the creation of new ones. The ADOX library provides the tools for table deletion as well as table creation.

Suppose, in addition to the Donors table, that you had previously created a preliminary version of the table named OldDonors. Now you want to get rid of that redundant and distracting OldDonors table. You can do that with the following code:

```
Sub DeleteOldDonors()
Dim cat1 As ADOX.Catalog

'Instantiate a catalog for the table to be deleted
Set cat1 = New ADOX.Catalog
cat1.ActiveConnection = "Provider=Microsoft.Jet.OLEDB.4.0;" _
    & "Data Source=" & "C:\LunarSociety\NewDB.mdb"

'Use the table's Delete method
cat1.Tables.Delete "OldDonors"

'Clean up before exiting
Set cat1 = Nothing

End Sub
```

Creating indexes

Indexes can dramatically speed the process of retrieving records from a database table. With an index, a query can reach directly into a large table and extract the desired records, instead of scanning the records sequentially to find them.

If you know which fields in a table are likely to be used as the basis for a retrieval, you can create indexes for them using the following sample code:

```
Sub CreateIndex()
Dim cat1 As New ADOX.Catalog
Dim tbl1 As ADOX.Table
Dim index1 As New ADOX.Index

'Specify database engine, data source, and table to index
cat1.ActiveConnection = "Provider=Microsoft.Jet.OLEDB.4.0;" _
    & "Data Source = C:\LunarSociety\NewDB.mdb"
Set tbl1 = cat1.Tables("Donors")

'Set index properties
With index1
    .Name = "PKindex"
    .Unique = True
    .IndexNulls = adIndexNullsDisallow
End With
```

```
'Append column to index, and specify sort order
index1.Columns.Append "DonorID"
index1.Columns(0).SortOrder = adSortAscending

'Append index to table
tbl1.Indexes.Append index1

'Clean up before exiting
Set cat1 = Nothing
Set tbl1 = Nothing
Set index1 = Nothing

End Sub
```

In creating the index, the preceding code performs the following tasks:

◆ Names the index (PKindex)

◆ Specifies that every entry in the index must be unique

◆ Declares that null values are not allowed

These values are appropriate for DonorID, which is the primary key of the Donors table.

The preceding code also specifies that the records in the index are sorted in ascending order.

 Ascending order is the default and need not be specified. An index can also be sorted in descending order.

Types of keys

There are two types of keys:

◆ **Primary keys:** Uniquely identify individual records within a database table

◆ **Foreign keys:** Link one table to another

You can add keys to tables by either of the following methods:

◆ Using Access's Table Design view

◆ Adding keys programmatically through VBA and the ADOX library

ADDING A PRIMARY KEY

A *primary key* is an index into a table. Because primary keys must be unique, they are among the best indexes for retrieval speed. When you retrieve a table record by its primary key, the index that is associated with the primary key points directly to the desired record. This is the fastest retrieval that Access can make.

To add a primary key to an existing table that does not yet have a primary key, use code similar to the following:

```
Sub AddPrimaryKey()
On Error GoTo PKErrorTrap
Dim cat1 As ADOX.Catalog
Dim tbl1 As ADOX.Table
Dim index1 As ADOX.Index
Dim loopvar As Integer

Set cat1 = New ADOX.Catalog
Set tbl1 = New ADOX.Table
Set index1 = New ADOX.Index

'Specify database engine, data source, and table to index
cat1.ActiveConnection = "Provider=Microsoft.Jet.OLEDB.4.0;" _
     & "Data Source=C:\LunarSociety\NewDB.mdb"
Set tbl1 = cat1.Tables("Donors")

'Set index properties for primary key
'Label SetIndexVariable provides an entry point after error recovery
SetIndexVariable:
With index1
     .Name = "PKindex"
     .PrimaryKey = True
     .Unique = True
     .IndexNulls = adIndexNullsDisallow
End With

'Append column to index, and specify sort order
index1.Columns.Append "DonorID"
index1.Columns(0).SortOrder = adSortAscending

'Append index to table
tbl1.Indexes.Append index1

'Clean up before exiting
RoutineExit:
Set cat1 = Nothing
Set tbl1 = Nothing
```

```
Set index1 = Nothing
Exit Sub


PKErrorTrap:
Select Case Err.Number
'Key addition will fail if table is open
    Case -2147217856
            MsgBox "Table Donors in use. Close and retry."
            Resume RoutineExit
'Key addition will fail if a primary key already exists.
'Delete existing primary key
    Case -2147467259
            For Each index1 In tbl1.Indexes
                If index1.PrimaryKey = True Then
                        tbl1.Indexes.Delete (loopvar)
                        Resume SetIndexVariable
                End If
                loopvar = loopvar + 1
            Next index1
'Key addition will fail if an index already exists for the
'column or columns you are attempting to declare as a
'primary key. Delete existing index, then resume.
    Case -2147217868
            For Each index1 In tbl1.Indexes
                If index1.Name = "PKindex" Then
                        tbl1.Indexes.Delete (loopvar)
                        Resume SetIndexVariable
                End If
                loopvar = loopvar + 1
            Next index1
'Something else bad has happened
    Case Else
            MsgBox "Open Immediate window for error message"
            Debug.Print Err.Number; Err.Description
End Select

End Sub
```

The preceding code handles the following problems that may arise in an attempt to add a primary key to a table:

◆ Because a primary key is such a fundamental part of a table, when you are adding a primary key, other users should not be accessing the table. Thus, if the table is open, the primary key add operation fails. The preceding code traps this failure and displays a helpful message.

◆ If a primary key has already been created for the table in question, a new primary key cannot be created that would conflict with it. A table can have only one primary key. If this error occurs, the preceding code does the following:

- Deletes the old primary key

- Retries to create the new primary key

◆ If the field or fields that the code designates as the table's primary key are already indexed, a failure occurs. This problem is also handled by deleting the old index then retrying. Any other error conditions are handled by the catch-all Else clause, which merely prints the error number and a brief description of the error in VBE's Immediate window.

ADDING A FOREIGN KEY

Foreign keys are more complicated to create and maintain than primary keys. In addition to all the things that pertain to primary keys, foreign keys must do the following:

◆ Deal with two tables, instead of only one

◆ Determine how changes or deletions from one table affect the other

A primary key in one table could be a foreign key in a related table. The database designer must decide whether to cascade or restrict updates and deletions from the first to the second table. This decision is embedded in the foreign key that resides in the second table.

As with primary keys, if a particular foreign key for a table pair already exists, you must delete it before you create a new instance of that foreign key.

 Why recreate a foreign key to join two tables, if such a key already exists? The only reason is to change the definition of the key, such as how to treat the table containing the foreign key if a record in the other table is changed or deleted.

Because you cannot create a foreign key to relate two tables if a foreign key joining them already exists, you must first test to see if such a key exists and then delete the old foreign key if it does. Only then can you create a new instance of that foreign key.

The following code first checks whether a foreign key already exists that has the same name as the one that you propose to add. If such a key exists, information about its characteristics is displayed in the Immediate window, and then the key is deleted.

After the old key is gone, the new version of the key is easily created. This sub-procedure uses a couple of functions to provide the data that is displayed whenever a preexisting key is deleted. This information could be valuable if you ever wanted to restore the database to its original key structure.

```
Sub AddForeignKey()
Dim cat1 As ADOX.Catalog
Dim key1 As ADOX.Key
Dim col1 As ADOX.Column

'Specify database engine, data source, and table to index
Set cat1 = New ADOX.Catalog
cat1.ActiveConnection = "Provider=Microsoft.Jet.OLEDB.4.0;" _
    & "Data Source=C:\LunarSociety\OLS1.mdb"

'Check for preexisting foreign key.
'If it exists, document it, then delete it.
For Each key1 In cat1.Tables("MEM-RES").Keys
    With key1
        If .Name = "MemberIDFK" Then
            Debug.Print .Name
            Debug.Print String(4, " ") & "Key Type = " & _
                KeyType(.Type)
            Debug.Print String(4, " ") & "Related Table = " & _
                .RelatedTable
            For Each col1 In _
                cat1.Tables("MEM-RES").Keys(.Name).Columns
                Debug.Print String(4, " ") & "Key column name = " _
                    & col1.Name
            Next col1
            Debug.Print String(4, " ") & "Update Type = " & _
                RuleType(.UpdateRule)
            Debug.Print String(4, " ") & "Delete Type = " & _
                RuleType(.DeleteRule)
            cat1.Tables("MEM-RES").Keys.Delete .Name
        End If
    End With
Next key1

'Create new foreign key. Permit cascading updates.
Set key1 = New ADOX.Key
With key1
    .Name = "MemberIDFK"
    .Type = adKeyForeign
    .RelatedTable = "MEMBERS"
```

```
        .Columns.Append "MemberID"
        .Columns("MemberID").RelatedColumn = "MemberID"
        .UpdateRule = adRICascade
    End With
    cat1.Tables("MEM-RES").Keys.Append key1

    'Clean up before exiting
    Set key1 = Nothing
    Set cat1 = Nothing

    End Sub

    Function KeyType(intType As Integer) As String
        Select Case intType
            Case adKeyPrimary
                KeyType = "adKeyPrimary"
            Case adKeyForeign
                KeyType = "adKeyForeign"
            Case adKeyUnique
                KeyType = "adKeyUnique"
            Case Else
                KeyType = CStr(intType)
        End Select
    End Function

    Function RuleType(intType As Integer) As String
        Select Case intType
            Case adRINone
                RuleType = "adRINone"
            Case adRICascade
                RuleType = "adRICascade"
            Case adRISetNull
                RuleType = "adRISetNull"
            Case adRISetDefault
                RuleType = "adRISetDefault"
            Case Else
                RuleType = CStr(intType)
        End Select
    End Function
```

Checking what keys you have

You can lose track of what keys are assigned to the various tables of a database, particularly if the database includes many tables that are interconnected with foreign key links. The following code demonstrates how to get a listing for a database's keys. The listing shows the following:

- ◆ Key names

- ◆ The tables that the key names are associated with

- ◆ Key types

 TIP   This listing can be particularly valuable for a maintenance programmer who did not develop the database but now must keep it functional.

```
Sub ShowKeys()
Dim cat1 As ADOX.Catalog
Dim tbl1 As ADOX.Table
Dim key1 As ADOX.Key
Dim maxlen As Integer

'Specify database engine and data source
Set cat1 = New ADOX.Catalog
cat1.ActiveConnection = "Provider=Microsoft.Jet.OLEDB.4.0;" _
    & "Data Source=C:\LunarSociety\OLS1.mdb"

'Find longest key name
maxlen = 8
For Each tbl1 In cat1.Tables
    For Each key1 In cat1.Tables(tbl1.Name).Keys
        If maxlen < Len(key1.Name) Then maxlen = Len(key1.Name)
    Next key1
Next tbl1
maxlen = maxlen + 1

'Display key report heading
Debug.Print "Key Names and Types for OLS1.mdb"
Debug.Print "Table Name"
Debug.Print String(5, " ") & "Key Name" & _
    String(maxlen - 8, " ") & "Key Type"

'Examine all tables and display key information
For Each tbl1 In cat1.Tables
    If tbl1.Type = "table" And _
        Left(tbl1.Name, 4) <> "~TMP" Then
        Debug.Print tbl1.Name
```

```
        For Each key1 In tbl1.Keys
            Debug.Print String(5, " ") & key1.Name & _
                String(maxlen - Len(key1.Name), " ") & _
                KeyType(key1.Type)
        Next key1
    End If
Next tbl1

'Clean up before exiting
Set cat1 = Nothing

End Sub
```

When you run the code in the preceding listing against the Lunar Society's OLS1.mdb database, it produces the following result:

```
Key Names and Types for OLS1.mdb
Table Name
     Key Name              Key Type
AUTHORS
     PrimaryKey            adKeyPrimary
AUTH-PAP
     AUTHORSAUTH-PAP       adKeyForeign
     PAPERSAUTH-PAP        adKeyForeign
     PrimaryKey            adKeyPrimary
AUTH-RES
     AUTHORSAUTH-RES       adKeyForeign
     PrimaryKey            adKeyPrimary
     RESEARCHTEAMSAUTH-RES adKeyForeign
MEMBERS
     AUTHORSMEMBERS        adKeyForeign
     PrimaryKey            adKeyPrimary
MEM-RES
     MemberIDFK            adKeyForeign
     MEMBERSMEM-RES        adKeyForeign
     PrimaryKey            adKeyPrimary
     RESEARCHTEAMSMEM-RES  adKeyForeign
PAPERS
     PrimaryKey            adKeyPrimary
     RESEARCHTEAMSPAPERS   adKeyForeign
RESEARCHTEAMS
     PrimaryKey            adKeyPrimary
```

All the tables are listed with their keys and key types, as follows:

- Primary keys are identified by `PrimaryKey`, not by a field name.

  Because primary keys could be composite keys made up by combining multiple fields, the primary keys do not have unique names.

- Foreign keys can be uniquely identified, as follows:

  - If you create foreign keys using Access, not VBA, you have no opportunity to give them names, so Access assigns names. For example, the foreign key in the AUTH-PAP table that connects AUTH-PAP to the AUTHORS table is named `AUTHORSAUTH-PAP`.

  - If you create a foreign key using VBA, as shown in the preceding section, where the `MemberIDFK` foreign key was created in the MEM-RES table to connect it to the MEMBERS table, the name that you assign to the foreign key appears in the key listing.

Summary

For an Access application to use a database, it must first connect to that database. For the current Access product, that connecting is done primarily through ActiveX Data Objects, using either the ADODB library or the ADOX library. In this chapter, we discussed the ADO object model and the ADOX object model. Each has a different emphasis and a different set of objects that can perform the functions that you need.

Chapter 16

Access Events

ALL MAJOR OPERATING SYSTEMS today, such as Microsoft Windows, Linux, and OS X are *event-driven* operating systems. This means that they respond to events that occur at a specific point in time. Examples of user-initiated events are the clicking of a mouse button, the pressing of a keyboard key, or even the mere movement of the mouse from one location to another. The user interacts with the application that she is using by way of events. Errors that occur are also events, as are timeouts and other things. As a VBA programmer, you can control what happens whenever an event occurs. Access responds to events; when an event occurs, if an event-handling procedure (an *event handler*) has been written, Access transfers control to it. By writing these procedures, you can control how the system responds to any event. In this chapter, we discuss the major event types and what you can do in response to them.

Event Types That Access Can Monitor

Access can respond to the following major categories of events:

◆ **Form events:** Things that happen on screen forms, such as the clicking of a button or the entering of text into a text box. The occurrence of such an event can invoke a procedure that you write, called an *event handler*. Because you write the event handlers, you can control the way that the application interacts with the user.

◆ **Report events:** Stages in the preparation of a report for viewing, such as before Access formats a section, before it re-enters a previous section, or before it prints a section. You can write event handlers to change settings at any of these points in the printing process.

◆ **ADO events:** Apply to connection to a database and the creation of recordsets based on data that is extracted from the database.

◆ **Pivot events:** Apply only to PivotTable or PivotChart view.

◆ **Section events:** Occur within a section of a form.

◆ **Control events:** Occur in response to user actions.

All these event types give you, the programmer, control over the flow of execution, as follows:

◆ Control interactions with the user through the following:

  ▪ Form events

  ▪ Pivot events

  ▪ Section events

  ▪ Control events

◆ Control interactions with the data source that your application is communicating through ADO events

Form Events

As the name implies, form events occur when a user is interacting with a form on the screen. Form events are considered to be high-level or low-level, as follows:

◆ High-level events handle major form operations, such as inserting, updating, or deleting data from the form.

◆ Low-level events give you fine-grained control over what happens in response to a user action, such as Click and KeyPress.

You can write an event procedure for any of the standard events. Whenever that event occurs, your procedure runs.

High-level form events

Access's high-level form events, and the occasions when they occur, are as follows:

◆ Current: Occurs under the following conditions:

  ▪ When a form containing data is first opened.

  ▪ When you move to a new record.

♦ BeforeInsert: Occurs when data is first entered into a new record.

This makes the record *dirty*.

♦ AfterInsert: Occurs after the new record is saved.

Saving cleans up the *dirty* condition.

♦ Undo: Occurs before the undo operation is executed. This occurs when the user reverses changes on a form by either of the following:

   ▪ Pressing Esc, Ctrl+Z.

   ▪ Choosing Edit→Undo from the main menu.

♦ BeforeUpdate: Occurs immediately before edits to the current record are saved.

♦ AfterUpdate: Occurs immediately after edits to the current record are saved.

♦ Delete: Occurs immediately before a record is deleted.

♦ BeforeDelConfirm: Occurs after all specified records are deleted but before displaying the confirmation dialog box.

♦ AfterDelConfirm: Occurs in either of the following cases:

   ▪ After a record is deleted.

   ▪ After canceling the deletion of a record.

♦ Open: Occurs immediately after the form is loaded but before controls or data is loaded.

♦ Load: Occurs after a form is loaded and its record source is opened.

This happens after the Open event and before the Current event.

♦ Resize: Occurs whenever the form is resized (including when the form is opened).

♦ Activate: Occurs when the form receives focus.

♦ Deactivate: Occurs when the form loses focus.

♦ GotFocus: Occurs after the form gets focus.

This occurs only when the form contains no controls that can receive the focus.

♦ LostFocus: Occurs before the form loses focus.

This occurs only when the form contains no controls that can receive the focus.

◆ Unload: Occurs when the form close operation has begun but before the form is actually closed.

◆ Close: Occurs when the form is closed.

Some events (such as those in the preceding list) apply to an entire form; others apply to controls within a form. Some events (such as GotFocus and LostFocus) could apply to either an entire form or to a control within a form.

The high-level events give programmers control over the interaction with the user that is often sufficient for your purposes.

When fine-grained control is needed, you can make use of the lower-level events, such as the keyboard and mouse events.

Mouse form events

Several of the most common form events, for which you may want to write event procedures, are mouse events.

Other mouse events, discussed elsewhere in this chapter, are associated with controls on a form. Additional mouse events can occur outside the context of forms.

The following events are associated with the form as a whole. They are triggered either by button clicks or mouse movement.

◆ Click: Occurs when you click the left mouse button in either of the following cases:

■ On the record selector for a record being displayed

■ In the dead space on a form

◆ DblClick: Occurs when you double-click the left mouse button in either of the following cases:

■ In the record selector for a record being displayed

■ In the dead space on a form

◆ MouseDown: Occurs before the click event fires when you depress the left mouse button in either of the following cases:

■ On the record selector for a record being displayed

■ In the dead space on a form

- ◆ MouseMove: Occurs when you move the mouse over either of the following:
  - The record selector
  - The dead space on a form
- ◆ MouseUp: Occurs before the click event fires when you release the left mouse button in either of the following cases:
  - On the record selector for a record being displayed
  - In the dead space on a form
- ◆ MouseWheel: Occurs when you turn the wheel on a Microsoft Intellimouse or compatible device

Keyboard form events

Keyboard form events depend on the form's KeyPreview property. These events allow you to preempt the action of control events on the form.

When the KeyPreview property is set to True, keyboard form events fire before keyboard events for any controls on the form, as follows:

- ◆ KeyDown: Depends on the KeyPreview state, as follows:
  - **True:** Depressing a key anywhere on the form fires the KeyDown form event.
  - **False:** The KeyDown event fires only if the record selector is selected when a key is depressed.
- ◆ KeyUp: Depends on the KeyPreview state, as follows:
  - **True:** Releasing a key anywhere on the form fires the KeyUp form event.
  - **False:** The KeyUp event fires only if the record selector is selected when a key is released.
- ◆ KeyPress: Depends on the KeyPreview state, as follows:
  - **True:** Depressing and releasing a key anywhere on the form fires the KeyPress form event.
  - **False:** The KeyPress event fires only if the record selector is selected when a key is depressed and then released.

Error events

Run-time data errors are events. Access handles them with relatively generic messages to the user. You may want to make a more specific response. You can do so with an error event procedure. We now present an example.

Our OLS1 example database has a MEMBERS table and an AUTHORS table. For a person to be an author of a scientific paper that was issued by the Oregon Lunar Society (OLS), the person must first be a member of the OLS. We enforce this rule by placing a referential integrity constraint on the AUTHORS table. To add a person to the AUTHORS table, that person must first exist in the MEMBERS table. Figure 16-1 shows what happens when a user tries to add a person to the AUTHORS table when that person does not exist in the MEMBERS table.

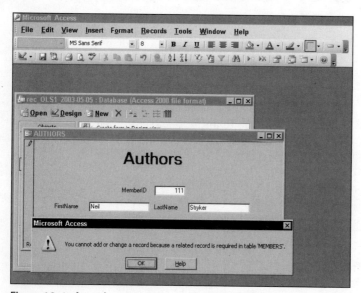

Figure 16-1: Access's response to a referential integrity error.

Access displays a message box that tells the user that a record cannot be added to the AUTHORS table unless a corresponding record already exists in the MEM-BERS table. This is quite helpful, but it could be even more helpful. The absence of an author from the MEMBERS table is probably an oversight. No one would be allowed to be an author of an OLS paper unless the person is a member. Therefore, it would be good to display the entry form for the MEMBERS table when this error occurs so that the user can add the author to the MEMBERS table before adding him to the AUTHORS table. This different response to the error can be placed into a form error event procedure, as shown in the following code:

```
Private Sub Form_Error(DataErr As Integer, HideStdMsg As Integer)
    Dim intResponse As Integer
    If DataErr = 3201 Then          'A referential integrity error
                                    'has been detected
        intResponse = MsgBox("An author must be a member of _
```

```
                OLS. Would you like to add a record to _
                the MEMBERS table?", vbYesNo)
        If intResponse = vbYes Then
            DoCmd.OpenForm "MEMBERS", , , , acFormAdd, acDialog
        End If
    Else
        intResponse = MsgBox("Non-referential integrity error _
                    has occurred.")
    End If
    HideStdMsg = acDataErrContinue
End Sub
```

After the preceding event procedure is added to the AUTHORS form, Access acts differently when a user attempts to add a new person to the AUTHORS table who is not already in the MEMBERS table. Figure 16-2 shows how the system responds now. The HideStdMsg = acDataErrContinue line suppresses the display of Access's standard error message for this error code (3201).

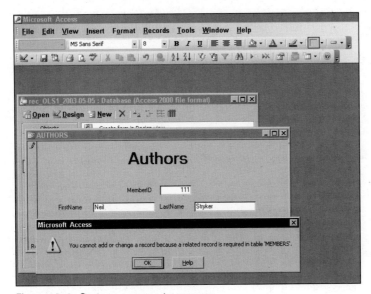

Figure 16-2: Custom response to an error.

If the user clicks the Yes button, the MEMBERS form, shown in Figure 16-3, appears.

The user can now enter a record for the author into the MEMBERS table using the MEMBERS form, and then into the AUTHORS table using the AUTHORS form. Referential integrity is preserved, and the error does not reappear.

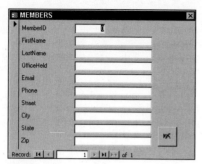

Figure 16-3: The MEMBERS form is displayed by
the event procedure.

Filter events

Filters are properties of forms and reports that allow you to extract a subset of a
recordset in much the way that an SQL WHERE clause does. You don't need VBA to
apply a filter, although you can certainly apply one using VBA. For example, if you
had queried the OLS1 database for rows in the MEMBERS table, you could restrict
the retrieval to people living in Oregon with a command similar to the following:

```
DoCmd.ApplyFilter WhereCondition:="State = OR"
```

Access considers filtering an event, and you can write an event procedure that is
executed before any filtering takes place. You could use this opportunity to do the
following:

♦ Change what Access displayed on the form

♦ Take some other action

♦ Cancel the filtering operation

Suppose that you wanted to trap the filter event to see if the user had activated
a filter. You could do so with the following code:

```
Private Sub Form_ApplyFilter(Cancel As Integer, ApplyType As
Integer)
    Dim strMsg As String
    If (ApplyType = acApplyFilter Or ApplyType = _
                acApplyServerFilter) _
                And Len(Me.Filter) > 0 Then
        strMsg = "You have asked to filter the form " & _
            "given the following condition:"
        strMsg = strMsg & vbCrLf & vbCrLf & Me.Filter
        strMsg = strMsg & vbCrLf & vbCrLf & "Proceed?"
```

```
      If MsgBox(strMsg, vbYesNo Or vbQuestion, _
          "ApplyFilter") = vbNo Then
          Cancel = True
      End If
   ElseIf ApplyType = acShowAllRecords Or Len(Me.Filter) = 0 Then
      strMsg = "You have asked to show all the records."
      strMsg = strMsg & vbCrLf & vbCrLf & "Proceed?"
      If MsgBox(strMsg, vbYesNo Or vbQuestion, "ApplyFilter") _
          = vbNo Then
          Cancel = True
      End If
   End If
End Sub
```

If the user clicks the ApplyFilter icon to invoke the form's filter and an active filter exists, a message box tells the user what the filter is and asks if she wants to proceed. Figure 16-4 shows this message box.

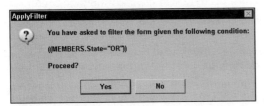

Figure 16–4: Response of a filter event procedure when the filter is active.

If the user clicks the ApplyFilter icon and an active filter does not exist, a message box tells the user that she has requested all records from the recordset and asks if she wants to proceed, as shown in Figure 16-5.

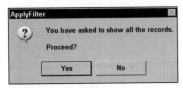

Figure 16–5: Response of a filter event procedure when he filter is not active.

 If the user chooses not to proceed, the event is canceled and a run-time error results. You must handle the error as described in the preceding section on error events, or your code halts.

Before you can apply a filter, the filter must exist. You can create a new filter or edit an existing one by either of the following methods:

◆ Select Records→Filter→Filter by Form from the main menu.

◆ Click the Filter by Form icon in the Form View toolbar.

Timer events

Every form has a `TimerInterval` property that you can set to some number of milliseconds. This number determines how often the `Timer` event fires, as follows:

◆ When the `TimerInterval` property is 0, the timer event is not triggered.

◆ When you set the `TimerInterval` property to a positive number, the `Timer` event is triggered on a regular basis. For example, if you set a form's TimerInterval property to 10,000, the Timer event fires every 10 seconds (10,000 milliseconds).

For example, you may write an event procedure that checked the lock condition of a database record. Whenever your routine found the record to be unlocked, it could update the record.

You may want to perform a variety of operations automatically after a specific interval of time has passed, or on a repeating basis. The `Timer` event is an ideal way to perform time-related operations.

Pivot events

Pivot events take place while a user is operating on a form in either PivotTable view or PivotChart view. PivotTables are features of both Access and Excel.

◆ Pivot events enable you to rearrange the presentation of a form's data in a way that emphasizes the relationships between fields.

◆ Pivot events give you summarization functions.

Figure 16-6 shows the Datasheet view of a form that displays the sales results of a company's sales associates for the first quarter of a year.

This is informative, but it could be more so. Selecting View→PivotTable from the main menu displays an empty PivotTable and the Field List for the Q1Sales table. An alternative, and possibly better, way to create a PivotTable is to create a form using the Form Wizard. One of the wizard's options is to create a PivotTable form. Dragging fields from the Field List onto the PivotTable results in the display that is shown in Figure 16-7.

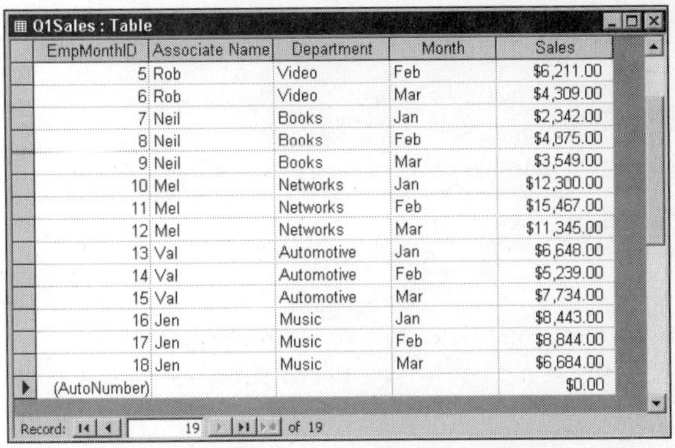

Figure 16-6: Datasheet view of Q1 sales results.

Figure 16-7: PivotTable view of Q1 sales results.

The Associate Name field was dragged to the area marked Drop Row Fields Here, and Month was dragged to the area marked Drop Column Fields Here. The Sales field was dropped into the large area marked Drop Totals or Detail Fields Here. With the resulting PivotTable view, it is easier to quickly see how each sales associate performed in each month of the quarter, compared to finding this information in Datasheet view. You can make the form even more informative by selecting the cell in the upper-left corner of the detail area (Jen's January sales) and then clicking on the AutoCalc icon, which looks like the capital Greek letter sigma (Σ). A menu drops down, listing various summarization functions. Clicking the Sum function alters the PivotTable, as shown in Figure 16-8.

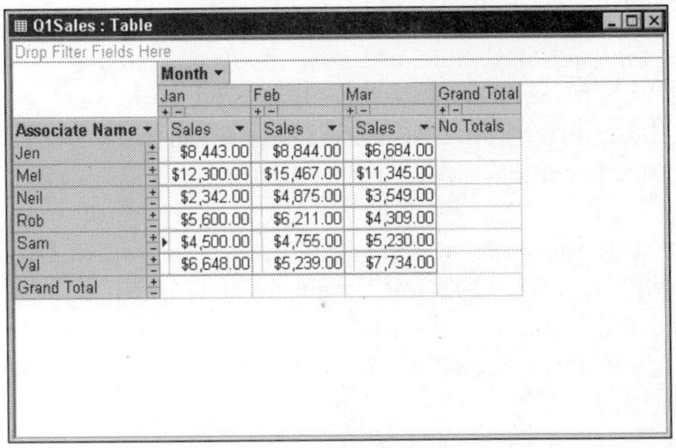

Q1Sales : Table				
Drop Filter Fields Here				
	Month ▼			
	Jan	Feb	Mar	Grand Total
	+ −	+ −	+ −	+ −
Associate Name ▼	Sales ▼	Sales ▼	Sales ▼	Sum of Sales
Jen	$8,443.00	$8,844.00	$6,684.00	$23,971.00
	$8,443.00	$8,844.00	$6,684.00	
Mel	$12,300.00	$15,467.00	$11,345.00	$39,112.00
	$12,300.00	$15,467.00	$11,345.00	
Neil	$2,342.00	$4,875.00	$3,549.00	$10,766.00
	$2,342.00	$4,875.00	$3,549.00	
Rob	$5,600.00	$6,211.00	$4,309.00	$16,120.00
	$5,600.00	$6,211.00	$4,309.00	
Sam	$4,500.00	$4,755.00	$5,230.00	$14,485.00
	$4,500.00	$4,755.00	$5,230.00	
Val	$6,648.00	$5,239.00	$7,734.00	$19,621.00
	$6,648.00	$5,239.00	$7,734.00	
Grand Total	$39,833.00	$45,391.00	$38,851.00	$124,075.00

Figure 16-8: PivotTable view of Q1 sales results, with subtotals and grand total.

The full quarter's sales totals for each associate are now displayed at the right edge of the table, and monthly totals for all associates are displayed at the bottom. The grand total of all sales for the quarter appears in the lower-right corner. This view of the data is helpful indeed – much easier to comprehend than in the Datasheet view.

Figure 16-9 shows the PivotChart view of the PivotTable in Figure 16-8. It is generated by selecting View→PivotChart View. To put the PivotChart in final form, you should put appropriate axis titles in place of the placeholders that are currently displayed. But even in this unfinished form, the chart shows who sells the most and the trends that are developing.

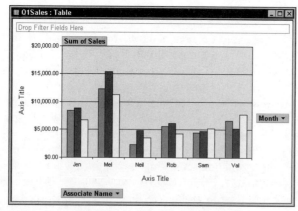

Figure 16-9: PivotChart view of Q1 sales results.

Many events apply to PivotTables and PivotCharts. The following events are implemented by components in the Microsoft Office XP Web Components library:

- ◆ BeforeScreenTip: Occurs before the component displays a screen tip

- ◆ CommandEnabled: Occurs when the component checks to see whether a particular command is enabled

- ◆ CommandChecked: Occurs when the component checks to see if a particular command is checked

- ◆ CommandBeforeExecute: Occurs before a particular command is executed

- ◆ CommandExecute: Occurs after a particular command is executed

- ◆ DataChange: Occurs when the data displayed in the PivotTable is changed

- ◆ DataSetChange: Occurs when the PivotTable's underlying data is changed

- ◆ PivotTableChange: Occurs when a field, field set, or category is added to or deleted from a PivotTable

- ◆ SelectionChange: Occurs when the selection is changed

- ◆ ViewChange: Occurs when the view of the data is changed without changing the data

- ◆ OnConnect: Occurs after a PivotTable connects to its data source

- ◆ OnDisconnect: Occurs after a PivotTable disconnects from its data source

- ◆ BeforeQuery: Occurs before a PivotTable sends a query to its data source

- ◆ Query: Occurs after a PivotTable sends a query to its data source

- ◆ AfterLayout: Occurs after the rendering engine determines the layout of a PivotChart but before any chart elements are plotted

- ◆ BeforeRender: Occurs before each element of a PivotChart is drawn

- ◆ AfterRender: Occurs after each element of a PivotChart is drawn

- ◆ AfterFinalRender: Occurs after an entire PivotChart has been drawn.

You can write a procedure that is triggered by any of the preceding events. This enables you to intervene anywhere you want in the process of generating or operating on either a PivotTable or PivotChart.

To add an event procedure to a PivotTable or PivotChart, the form's HasModule property must be set to Yes. You can do this from the Design view. To display the list of PivotTable events, switch to Form view and click somewhere on the form that is not a control. When the Form dialog box is displayed, click the Event tab and then select the event that you want to target for an event procedure.

Section events

Because forms can be divided into sections, some events apply to just a section of a form. You don't find many such events, and they aren't often useful, but they are available if you need them. The following list describes the section events and the actions that invoke them:

◆ Event: Indicates when the event occurs.

◆ Click: Occurs when you click the background of a section.

◆ DblClick: Occurs when you double-click the background of a section.

◆ MouseDown: Occurs when you press either mouse button when the cursor is located over the background of a section. This happens before the Click event.

◆ MouseUp: Occurs when you release either mouse button when the cursor is located over the background of a section. This happens before the Click event.

◆ MouseMove: Occurs when you move the mouse over the background of a section.

Control events

Controls are those things on a form that the user can interact with. Common examples are as follows:

◆ Command buttons

◆ Labels

◆ Text boxes

◆ Option buttons

Because these controls differ from each other, the events that apply to them may differ from one control to another. Some events apply to most controls; some apply to only a few.

The following list describes the control events and indicates when they occur:

◆ Before Update: Occurs before changes to a control are committed with either of the following commands:

■ Moving to another control

■ Saving

◆ After Update: Occurs after changes to a control are saved.

◆ Dirty: Occurs before a change is made by the user.

◆ Undo: Occurs before the undo operation is executed but after a user performs a command to reverse changes that are made to a control with any of the following commands:

- Pressing Ctrl+Z

- Pressing Esc

- Selecting Edit→Undo from the standard menu

◆ Updated: Occurs when the user inserts or updates a source OLE object.

This event applies only to the Object Frame control.

◆ Change: Occurs whenever data in a control changes.

◆ NotInList: Occurs when you enter a new value into a combo box.

This event fires only when the combo box's LimitToList property is set to Yes.

◆ Enter: Occurs when you move to a control but before the control gets focus.

◆ Exit: Occurs when the user moves away from a control but before the control loses focus.

◆ Got Focus: Occurs after a control gets focus.

◆ Lost Focus: Occurs before a control loses focus.

◆ Click: Occurs when the user clicks a control with either the left or the right mouse button.

◆ DblClick: Occurs when you double-click a control with the left mouse button.

◆ Mouse Down: Occurs when the user depresses either mouse button on a control before the Click event fires.

◆ Mouse Move: Occurs when the user moves the mouse pointer over a control.

◆ Mouse Up: Occurs when the user releases either the left or right mouse button on a control before the Click event fires.

◆ Key Down: Occurs when the user presses a key while a control has focus.

◆ Key Up: Occurs when the user releases a key while a control has focus.

◆ Key Press: Occurs when the user presses and releases a key while a control has focus.

Table 16-1 lists the form controls and shows which events apply to each.

TABLE 16-1 CONTROLS AND CORRESPONDING EVENTS

Control Name	Before Update	After Update	Dirty	Undo	Change	Enter	Exit	Got Focus	Lost Focus	Click	DblClick	Mouse Down	Mouse Move	Mouse Up	Key Down	Key Up	Key Press	Updated	NotInList
Label										Click	DblClick	Mouse Down	Mouse Move	Mouse Up					
Image										Click	DblClick	Mouse Down	Mouse Move	Mouse Up					
Rectangle										Click	DblClick	Mouse Down	Mouse Move	Mouse Up					
Text Box	Before Update	After Update	Dirty	Undo	Change	Enter	Exit	Got Focus	Lost Focus	Click	DblClick	Mouse Down	Mouse Move	Mouse Up	Key Down	Key Up	Key Press		
Combo Box	Before Update	After Update	Dirty	Undo	Change	Enter	Exit	Got Focus	Lost Focus	Click	DblClick	Mouse Down	Mouse Move	Mouse Up	Key Down	Key Up	Key Press		NotInList
List Box	Before Update	After Update				Enter	Exit	Got Focus	Lost Focus	Click	DblClick	Mouse Down	Mouse Move	Mouse Up	Key Down	Key Up	Key Press		
Toggle Button[1]	Before Update	After Update				Enter	Exit	Got Focus	Lost Focus	Click	DblClick	Mouse Down	Mouse Move	Mouse Up	Key Down	Key Up	Key Press		
Option Button[2]	Before Update	After Update				Enter	Exit	Got Focus	Lost Focus	Click	DblClick	Mouse Down	Mouse Move	Mouse Up	Key Down	Key Up	Key Press		
Check Box[3]	Before Update	After Update				Enter	Exit	Got Focus	Lost Focus	Click	DblClick	Mouse Down	Mouse Move	Mouse Up	Key Down	Key Up	Key Press		
Option Group	Before Update	After Update				Enter	Exit			Click	DblClick	Mouse Down	Mouse Move	Mouse Up					

Control Name	Before Update	After Update	Dirty	Undo	Change	Enter	Exit	Got Focus	Lost Focus	Click	DblClick	Mouse Down	Mouse Move	Mouse Up	Key Down	Key Up	Key Press	Updated	NotInList
Command Button						Enter	Exit	Got Focus	Lost Focus	Click	DblClick	Mouse Down	Mouse Move	Mouse Up	Key Down	Key Up	Key Press		
Tab					Change					Click	DblClick	Mouse Down	Mouse Move	Mouse Up	Key Down	Key Up	Key Press		
Object Frame	Before Update	After Update				Enter	Exit	Got Focus	Lost Focus	Click	DblClick	Mouse Down	Mouse Move	Mouse Up	Key Down	Key Up	Key Press	Updated	
Subform						Enter	Exit												

[1] *When toggle button is part of an option group, option group events apply.*
[2] *When option button is part of an option group, option group events apply.*
[3] *When check box is part of an option group, option group events apply.*

The following example demonstrates a typical control event by adding a procedure to the Vol DAR Details form in the Senior Vols database. Figure 16-10 shows the Vol DAR Details form.

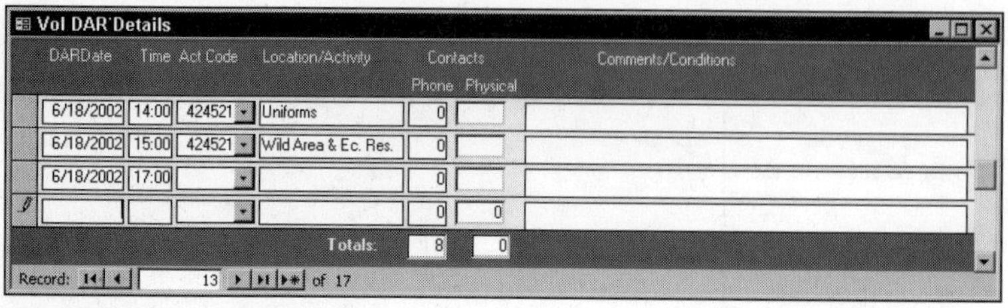

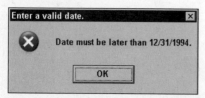

Figure 16-10: Vol DAR Details form.

The DAR Date field records the date that the subject senior volunteer performed a service. As a validity check, if a date earlier than January 1, 1995, is entered, an error message is displayed and the cursor is returned to the DAR Date field so that a valid date can be entered. The code is as follows:

```
Private Sub DARDate_Exit(Cancel As Integer)
'Do not accept any date before 01/01/1995.
If Me.DARDate < #1/1/1995# Then
    MsgBox "Date must be later than 12/31/1994.", vbCritical, _
        "Enter a valid date."

    Cancel = True
End If

End Sub
```

If the user enters a date earlier than January 1, 1995, a message box is displayed and the user is given another opportunity to enter a valid date. Figure 16-11 shows the message box that results from the entry of an invalid date.

Figure 16-11: Invalid date message box.

ADO Events

ADO events apply to the following major kinds of objects:

- ◆ Connection objects
- ◆ Recordset objects

ADO events occur in one of the following cases:

- ◆ Before an operation starts
- ◆ After an operation completes

 An ADO event is actually a notification that an operation is about to start or has just completed.

You can write event handlers to take action whenever an ADO event occurs. The events that occur after an operation completes are particularly important, because ADO supports asynchronous operation. This means that an application can initiate an action, such as opening a recordset, and then move on to other tasks, as follows:

1. In parallel to what the application is doing, ADO is opening the recordset.

2. When ADO finishes the job, it fires an ExecuteComplete event.

3. An event handler that you write can then redirect execution so that you can start making use of the recordset that is now open.

Connection object events

Nine connection object events are available. The following list describes when they occur:

- ◆ BeginTransComplete: Occurs after the current transaction on the connection has started

- ◆ CommitTransComplete: Occurs after the current transaction on the connection has committed

- ◆ RollbackTransComplete: Occurs after the current transaction on the connection has rolled back

- ◆ WillConnect: Occurs before the current connection has started

◆ ConnectComplete: Occurs after the current connection has started

◆ Disconnect: Occurs after the current connection has ended

◆ WillExecute: Occurs before the execution of the current command on the connection has started

◆ ExecuteComplete: Occurs after the execution of the current command on the connection has ended

◆ InfoMessage: Occurs during the current operation, notifying you of additional information about the operation

Recordset object events

Eleven recordset object events are available. The following list describes when they occur:

◆ FetchProgress: Occurs during a data retrieval operation

◆ FetchComplete: Occurs after a data retrieval operation has completed

◆ WillChangeField: Occurs before the value of the current field has changed

◆ FieldChangeComplete: Occurs after the value of the current field has changed

◆ WillMove: Occurs before the current position of the cursor in the recordset changes

◆ MoveComplete: Occurs after the current position of the cursor in the recordset changes

◆ EndOfRecordset: Occurs after the current position of the cursor in the recordset has reached the end of the recordset

◆ WillChangeRecord: Occurs before the current record is changed

◆ RecordChangeComplete: Occurs after the current record has changed

◆ WillChangeRecordset: Occurs before something in the current recordset has changed

◆ RecordsetChangeComplete: Occurs after something in the current recordset has changed

Visual Basic's Help facility has detailed descriptions of both connection events and recordset events, which we don't duplicate here. Instead, we create a form and use it to demonstrate the use of several ADO events. Figure 16-12 shows a form that was created to demonstrate ADO event programming.

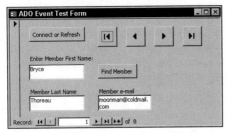

Figure 16-12: Form to demonstrate ADO event programming.

To test the functionality of the form in Figure 16-12, perform the following steps:

1. Click on the Connect or Refresh button to connect to the record source.

2. Click any of the following buttons to move around in the recordset:

   ■ Move Next

   ■ Move Last

   ■ Move Previous

   ■ Move First

   Verify that the values in the text boxes change appropriately.

3. Enter a valid first name into the FirstName text box, and then click the Find button.

   Verify that the appropriate record shows up in the text boxes.

The following listing is the code that creates the form:

```
Option Compare Database
Option Explicit
Const str1 = "Provider=Microsoft.Jet.OLEDB.4.0; Data _
Source=C:\LunarSociety\OLS1.mdb;"
Const strDefaultSQL = "SELECT * FROM MEMBERS"


'Enable events
Dim WithEvents cnxn As ADODB.Connection
Dim WithEvents rst1 As ADODB.Recordset


'Connect to record source
Private Sub Form_Load()
'Connect to source specified by str1
    Set cnxn = New ADODB.Connection
    cnxn.Open str1

End Sub
```

```vba
'Retrieve a recordset
Private Sub ConnectOrRefresh_Click()
On Error GoTo Err_ConnectOrRefresh_Click
Dim strSQL As String
strSQL = strDefaultSQL

'Instantiate a recordset object
Set rst1 = New ADODB.Recordset

'Fetch the recordset and report on progress
With rst1
    .CursorLocation = adUseClient
    .Properties("Initial Fetch Size") = 2
    .Properties("Background Fetch Size") = 2
    .Open strSQL, cnxn, , , adAsyncFetch
End With

Exit_ConnectOrRefresh_Click:
    Exit Sub

Err_ConnectOrRefresh_Click:
    MsgBox Err.Description
    Resume Exit_ConnectOrRefresh_Click

End Sub

' Move cursor to first record and display contents
Private Sub GoToFirst_Click()
On Error GoTo Err_GoToFirst_Click

    rst1.MoveFirst

'Display First Record
DisplayCurrent

Exit_GoToFirst_Click:
    Exit Sub

Err_GoToFirst_Click:
    MsgBox Err.Description
    Resume Exit_GoToFirst_Click

End Sub
```

```
'Move cursor to previous record and display contents
Private Sub GoToPrevious_Click()
On Error GoTo Err_GoToPrevious_Click

    rst1.MovePrevious

'Display Previous Record
DisplayCurrent

Exit_GoToPrevious_Click:
    Exit Sub

Err_GoToPrevious_Click:
    MsgBox Err.Description
    Resume Exit_GoToPrevious_Click

End Sub

'Move cursor to next record and display contents
Private Sub GoToNext_Click()
On Error GoTo Err_GoToNext_Click

    rst1.MoveNext

'Display Next Record
DisplayCurrent

Exit_GoToNext_Click:
    Exit Sub

Err_GoToNext_Click:
    MsgBox Err.Description
    Resume Exit_GoToNext_Click

End Sub

'Move cursor to last record and display contents
Private Sub GoToLast_Click()
On Error GoTo Err_GoToLast_Click

    rst1.MoveLast

'Display Last Record
DisplayCurrent
```

```
Exit_GoToLast_Click:
    Exit Sub

Err_GoToLast_Click:
    MsgBox Err.Description
    Resume Exit_GoToLast_Click

End Sub

'Move cursor to selected record and display contents
Private Sub FindMember_Click()
On Error GoTo Err_FindMember_Click

'Get specified record and display info from it
rst1.Find "" & "FirstName = " & "'" & _
    txtFirstName & "'" & "", , adSearchForward, adBookmarkFirst

'Display Found Record
DisplayCurrent

Exit_FindMember_Click:
    Exit Sub

Err_FindMember_Click:
    MsgBox Err.Description
    Resume Exit_FindMember_Click

End Sub

Private Sub DisplayCurrent()
'Fix possible out of range condition
If rst1.BOF Then
    rst1.MoveFirst
ElseIf rst1.EOF Then
    rst1.MoveLast
End If
Me.txtFirstName = rst1("FirstName")
Me.txtLastName = rst1("LastName")
Me.txtEmail = rst1("Email")

End Sub
```

If you decide to try this code on your own system, put the correct address to your record source in the str1 string. You may also want to set Initial Fetch Size and Background Fetch Size to larger numbers. We set them to 2 in this example, because we are operating on a small recordset of fictitious data[ES1].

Summary

Events give Access the ability to act according to the current operation of the program. Events can be user actions or program operations.

Chapter 17

Interacting with Other Applications

IN THIS CHAPTER

- Using data that originated outside of Access

- Controlling other applications with Automation

- Acting as an Automation server

- Acting as a data source for Word documents

- Using Automation objects and ActiveX controls

- Dealing with compatibility problems

ACCESS IS A PART OF Microsoft Office, a suite of applications, each of which performs a unique function. The function of Access is to build and maintain databases and database applications. Other Office members, such as Word, Excel, and Outlook, have other functions. Because each Office application has its own strengths and weaknesses, none of them is the best tool for tasks that cross disciplinary boundaries. For example, you may have data stored in a spreadsheet that would benefit from the kind of analysis that Access can do. Alternatively, you may have data stored in an Access database that you want to include in a Word document, a FrontPage Web site, or a PowerPoint presentation. VBA is a tool that you can use to transfer data from one application to another, greatly increasing the value of Office.

Data that may be valuable to you comes in many forms and can be found in all kinds of places. In addition to the other members of Microsoft Office, data sources such as dBASE files, Paradox files, Lotus 1-2-3 files, or even ASCII text files may hold information that you would like to import into your Access application. VBA can give you a means of connecting to all these different data sources. We first explore the three primary methods of using data from external sources: importing, linking to, and opening.

Importing, Linking to, and Opening External Data Sources

To import data into an Access database is to copy it into Access tables from the external source that it resides in. Linking to external data means leaving it in its original source file and operating on it there. Opening an external data source also leaves the data in its original form. We now examine each of these three methods in more depth.

Importing external data

Access supports the importation of the following commonly used file types:

- dBASE III, dBASE IV, dBASE 5
- Microsoft Access
- Microsoft Excel
- Microsoft Exchange
- HTML
- Lotus 1-2-3
- Microsoft Outlook
- Paradox
- Sharepoint Team Services
- ASCII text files
- XML
- ODBC-compliant databases

If the data that you want to process with Access is in any of these formats, you can import it into new tables in an Access database. You can do this either from the Access user interface or with VBA code.

Importing data into an Access database makes sense if you are migrating it to Access and you don't want to use it again with its original application. Once you start modifying it with Access, those modifications will not be present in the original file that you imported from. If you do not intend to modify the data with Access but only need to read it to produce reports, importing may also be the best way to proceed.

To import data programmatically, the `DoCmd` object has three methods. Each method is tailored to handle one particular kind of data, as follows:

◆ `TransferDatabase` performs Access, dBASE, Paradox, and ODBC importations.

◆ `TransferSpreadsheet` performs Lotus and Excel importations.

◆ `TransferText` performs ASCII importations.

An example using `TransferDatabase` is as follows:

```
Sub ImportMembers()
DoCmd.TransferDatabase _
     acImport, _
     "Microsoft Access", _
     "C:\LunarSociety\OLS1.mdb", _
     acTable, _
     "MEMBERS", _
     "tblOLSmembers"


End Sub
```

The preceding code imports the MEMBERS table from the `OLS1.mdb` Access database into the currently open database. You can use the same type of procedure to import tables from other personal database sources, such as Paradox or dBASE. Just substitute the appropriate database type and fully qualified path and filename.

You can import a text file into a database table in a similar manner. The following syntax does the job:

```
Sub ImportPlanetarySystems()
DoCmd.TransferText _
     acImportDelim, , _
     "tblPlanetarySystems", _
     "C:\LunarSociety\PlanetarySystems.txt", _
     True


End Sub
```

The preceding code imports the contents of the text file `PlanetarySystems.txt` into the table named tblPlanetarySystems in the currently open database, provided that the table has columns defined that correspond to the comma-delimited fields in the text file. The True keyword signifies that the first line of the text file contains the column titles for the data that follows. The following text file produces the table shown in Figure 17-1:

```
"Host Star","Planet","Distance from Earth","Magnitude","Planet Mass"
"16 Cygni","16 Cygni b",70,6.2,1.5
"47 Ursae Majoris","47 Ursae Majoris b",43,5.1,2.41
"47 Ursae Majoris","47 Ursae Majoris c",43,5.1,0.76
"51 Pegasi","51 Pegasi b",48,5.5,0.47
"55 Cancri","55 Cancri b",44,5.95,0.84
"55 Cancri","55 Cancri c",44,5.95,0.21
"55 Cancri","55 Cancri d",44,5.95,4
"70 Virginis","70 Virginis b",72,5,6.6
"Epsilon Eridani","Epsilon Eridani b",10.4,3.73,0.86
"Epsilon Eridani","Epsilon Eridani c",10.4,3.73,0.1
```

Figure 17-1: Table produced by importing the text file.

Linking to a table in another Access database

In the preceding section, we showed how to import a table from another Access database. You may want to do that in some situations, but potential problems also exist. As soon as you make one change to the table in your current database, the table differs from the source table in the other database. This lack of synchronicity can lead to data corruption or misleading conclusions, if the contents of both databases are ever considered together later. One way to avoid that problem is to link to the table in the other database rather than import it. This way, the table stays in the other database, and any changes that you make are visible to applications that use either database. When you are finished with any operations that you want to perform, you can break the link, reestablishing it whenever you need to. The following example code links to an external Access database:

```
Sub LinkToPapers()
DoCmd.TransferDatabase _
     acLink, _
     "Microsoft Access", _
```

```
        "C:\LunarSociety\OLS1.mdb", _
        acTable, _
        "PAPERS", _
        "tblOLSpapers"
End Sub
```

This code links the PAPERS table in the `OLS1.mdb` database to the current database, giving it the name tblOLSpapers. The table remains in `OLS1.mdb`, but it *seems* to be in the currently open database. You can operate on it as if it were a part of the currently open database.

Linking to an external database

With ODBC, you can link to any database that is ODBC-compliant. This includes Microsoft's SQL Server, IBM's DB2, Oracle 9i, and many others. The syntax for linking to an ODBC data source is similar to what you have seen already. An example for linking to an SQL Server database is as follows:

```
Sub LinkToODBCStores()

DoCmd.TransferDatabase _
    acLink, _
    "ODBC Database", _
    "ODBC;DSN=Publications; UID=Allen; PWD=; DATABASE=pubs", _
    acTable, "dbo.stores", "dbo_stores"
End Sub
```

A link is established to a table named stores in the pubs database and is given a moniker of dbo_stores in the currently open database. The code presupposes that a data source named Publications exists and that it points to the database named pubs. You can build such a data source from Windows by selecting Start→Control Panel→Administrative Tools→Data Sources (ODBC) and specifying at that time the database that you want to connect to.

You can now operate on the linked table as if it were local. Changes that you make in Access are reflected in the original SQL Server database.

Opening an Excel spreadsheet

One of the most common applications of the ability of Office applications to share data occurs when sharing data between Access and Excel. For years, people have been storing data of many types in Excel spreadsheets. Excel is capable of significant manipulation of data that is stored in its spreadsheets, and is thus of great value to its users. However, when more sophisticated analysis is called for, Access is a far more powerful tool. In addition to operating on its own `.mdb` and `.adp` files, Access can also deal with data in other formats, including Excel `.xls` files.

Access connects to data sources through small programs called *drivers*. Each different kind of data source has its own driver. To make Excel data available to Access, you can use an ISAM (Indexed Sequential Access Method) driver. To show you how to make the connection to an Excel spreadsheet, the following VBA sub procedure connects to a spreadsheet named `BookSalesRank.xls`. In the first column, the spreadsheet contains a date, and in the second and following columns, it contains sales rankings on the `Amazon.com` and `BN.com` Web sites for several books.

```
Sub Connect2SpreadsheetThenPrint()
' Connect to Sales Rank Spreadsheet and Print Data
Dim cnxn As New ADODB.Connection
Dim rst1 As ADODB.Recordset

' Connect to Excel data source
cnxn.Open "Provider=Microsoft.Jet.OLEDB.4.0;" & _
    "Data Source=C:\APP Example Files\BookSalesRank.xls;" & _
    "Extended Properties=Excel 8.0;"
' Open a read-only recordset based on the Excel source file
Set rst1 = New ADODB.Recordset
rst1.CursorType = adOpenForwardOnly
rst1.LockType = adLockReadOnly
rst1.Open "ranks", cnxn, , , adCmdTable

'Print Fields from the first record
Debug.Print rst1.Fields(0).Value, rst1.Fields(1).Value, _
    rst1.Fields(2).Value, rst1.Fields(3).Value _
    rst1.Fields(4).Value, rst1.Fields(5).Value

'Clean up before exiting
rst1.Close
Set rst1 = Nothing
cnxn.Close
Set cnxn = Nothing

End Sub
```

This routine connects to a spreadsheet data source, creates a recordset based on a named range of cells in the spreadsheet (ranks), and then prints in the Immediate window the contents of the first several fields in the first row of the recordset. This verifies that a connection has indeed been made to the spreadsheet and that data can be imported into Access from it. When we ran the routine, we got the following result:

1/2/2003   5174   7959   81191   63691

On January 2, 2003, Amazon gave the first book a rank of 5,174, and Barnes & Noble gave it a rank of 7,959. These companies ranked the second book 81,191 and 63,691, respectively.

Getting data from an Excel spreadsheet is useful, but even more important is the ability to operate on that data with VBA. This is just as easy as operating on data from a normal Access database file. In the next example, we again take data from the range of cells named ranks in the BookSalesRank.xls spreadsheet. This time, in the following code, we loop through all the rows, looking for Amazon's lowest value of sales rank for the first book. This corresponds to the book's best sales performance for that time interval.

```
Sub BestRankPrint()
' Connect to Sales Rank Spreadsheet, find best rank and print it
Dim cnxn As New ADODB.Connection
Dim rst1 As ADODB.Recordset
Dim bestRank As Double
Dim currentRank As Double

' Connect to Excel data source
cnxn.Open "Provider=Microsoft.Jet.OLEDB.4.0;" & _
     "Data Source=C:\APP Example Files\BookSalesRank.xls;" & _
     "Extended Properties=Excel 8.0;"
' Open a read-only recordset based on the Excel source file
Set rst1 = New ADODB.Recordset
rst1.CursorType = adOpenForwardOnly
rst1.LockType = adLockReadOnly
rst1.Open "ranks", cnxn, , , adCmdTable

'Find best sales rank
bestRank = 3000000
Do Until rst1.EOF
     currentRank = rst1.Fields(1)
     If currentRank < bestRank Then
          bestRank = currentRank
     End If
rst1.MoveNext
Loop

Debug.Print bestRank

End Sub
```

In the preceding code, the connection is made to the BookSalesRank.xls spreadsheet in the same way that it was done in the previous example. A recordset is created, based on the range of cells named ranks in the spreadsheet. A Do . . . Until loop goes through each record in the recordset, comparing Amazon's rank for the current record to the lowest rank previously found. If the current rank is lower, it replaces the previous lowest rank. After the recordset has been completely processed, the lowest rank is printed in the Immediate window.

Operating on Outlook contacts and e-mail messages

You can use an ISAM driver to read information in Outlook folders in much the same way that you can use an ISAM driver to read spreadsheet records in an Excel spreadsheet. In both cases, an ISAM driver gives you read-only access to the files that were created by Excel or Outlook. The following code, using an ISAM driver, reads the records in Outlook's Contacts folder. It retrieves a recordset from Outlook and then prints in the Immediate window the first name, last name, and e-mail address of all the people in the Contacts folder.

```
Sub ReadOutlookRecord()
Dim rst1 As ADODB.Recordset

'Instantiate a recordset
Set rst1 = New ADODB.Recordset

'Open rst1 on the Outlook Contacts folder
rst1.Open "SELECT First, Last, [Email Address] " & _
     "FROM Contacts IN 'C:\Windows\Temp\;'" & _
     "[Outlook 9.0;MAPILEVEL=Personal Folders|;];", _
     CurrentProject.Connection

'Print fields from records in the Contacts folder
Do Until rst1.EOF
     Debug.Print rst1(0), rst1(1), rst1(2)
     rst1.MoveNext
Loop

'Clean up before exiting
rst1.Close
Set rst1 = Nothing

End Sub
```

You can do more using the Outlook ISAM driver that is shown in the preceding example. For example, you could search through all the e-mail messages in your Inbox and display only those that contain a specified word or phrase. After opening a new database named Outlook Mining, we used Design View to create the form that is shown in Figure 17-2.

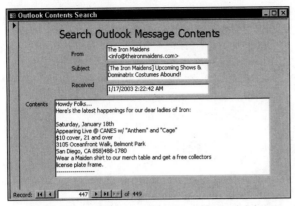

Figure 17-2: Form for data mining in an Outlook Inbox.

The Control Source settings for the text boxes specify which field from the recordset (From, Subject, Received, Contents) is to be displayed in each box. I wrote a procedure that executes when the form loads, opening a recordset that consists of messages in my Outlook Inbox that contain the word *Book* in the Contents field. The recordset contains 449 records that include that word. The code is as follows:

```
Option Compare Database
Option Explicit
Private rst1 As ADODB.Recordset

Private Sub Form_Load()
'Dim rst1 As ADODB.Recordset

'Instantiate a recordset and open it on a subset of the
'columns and rows in the Outlook Inbox
Set rst1 = New ADODB.Recordset
rst1.CursorLocation = adUseClient
rst1.Open "SELECT [From], Subject, Received, Contents " & _
    "FROM Inbox IN 'C:\Windows\Temp\;'" & _
    "[Outlook 9.0;MAPILEVEL=Personal Folders|;]" & _
    "WHERE InStr(Contents, 'Book') > 0;", _
    CurrentProject.Connection, , , adCmdText

'Open Outlook Contents Search and assign rst1 to it
DoCmd.OpenForm "Outlook Contents Search"
Set Application.Forms("Outlook Contents Search").Recordset = rst1

'Clean up before exiting
rst1.Close
```

```
Set rst1 = Nothing

End Sub
```

Wow, 449 e-mail messages that contain the word *Book!* I really ought to clean out my Inbox more often.

Controlling Other Applications with Automation

Automation is a Microsoft technology for interoperating between Office products such as Word, Excel, Outlook, and PowerPoint. Two applications are involved, an application server and an application client. The *application server* is the application that is being controlled. It is doing the bidding of the *application client.* This book is about Access, so we will give you a couple of examples of Access acting as a client and controlling the operation of Excel and Outlook. Then, we flip the coin and show Access acting as the server, dishing off information to Word as the client.

For Automation to work, the client application must be cognizant of the objects, properties, methods, and events of the server application. This knowledge resides in a type library for each application. Make sure that the server application's type library is loaded before trying to perform an Automation operation. The next section describes how to load a type library.

Controlling Excel with Automation

The preceding examples showed you how to connect to an Excel spreadsheet from Access and make use of the spreadsheet's data. There is another way to access Excel data. Rather than connecting to the data from Access, by using Automation you can cause Access to take control of Excel and have Excel manipulate its own spreadsheet data. To use Automation, you must be familiar not only with Access's object model but also with the object model of the application that you will control from Access, Excel in this case.

You need to break your application into two procedures, one involving only the Access object model that calls a second, which makes use of the Excel object model.

As an example, we write a procedure that takes control of Excel and loads a spreadsheet. We then have the procedure execute a second procedure that causes Excel to perform a simple operation on the spreadsheet.

The first thing you must verify is that your copy of Access includes the Excel type library. If it does not, you receive an error message when you try to refer to an Excel object. To add the library that you need, select Tools→References from the VBE menu, and in the References dialog box, make sure that Microsoft Excel 11.0 Object Library is checked. While you are at it, you may want to check the boxes next to Microsoft Outlook 11.0 Object Library and Microsoft Word 11.0 Object Library as well. If your system doesn't have version 11.0, check the version that you have.

You must next verify that your Excel security setting is not High. A High setting does not allow an unsigned macro or procedure to execute, and the procedure below (AverageRank()) is not signed. You can change Excel's security level by choosing Tools→Macro→Security from Excel's main menu.

The following are two procedures that, from Access, cause Excel to compute the average sales rank of the first book during the period of time covered by the ranks range of dates. The first procedure is in an Access module, and the second is in an Excel procedure that's located in ThisWorkbook. Create the Access procedure with an instance of Access's VBE, and create the Excel procedure with an instance of Excel's VBE.

```
Sub LaunchExcel()
Dim excelWorkbook As Excel.Workbook

'Connect to the Excel workbook and display it
Set excelWorkbook = GetObject("C:\APP Example _
Files\BookSalesRank.xls")
excelWorkbook.Application.Visible = True
excelWorkbook.Application.Windows("BookSalesRank.xls").Visible = _
True

'Launch the Excel procedure
excelWorkbook.Application.Run "ThisWorkBook.AverageRank"

'Save the modified spreadsheet and close the Automation object
excelWorkbook.Application.ActiveWorkbook.Save
excelWorkbook.Application.Quit
Set excelWorkbook = Nothing

End Sub
```

The LaunchExcel procedure does several simple things:

1. It connects to an Excel workbook named BookSalesRank.xls.

2. It runs the following application (AverageRank), which resides in that workbook.

3. It saves changes to the workbook and breaks the connection.

Remember that AverageRank is an Excel procedure. It performs three operations, enumerated right after the code below.

```
Sub AverageRank()
Dim mainSheet As Worksheet
Dim iRow As Integer
Dim lastRow As Integer

'Set reference to the worksheet
Set mainSheet = Worksheets(1)
With mainSheet
      lastRow = Range("ranks").Rows.Count

'Compute average Amazon sales rank for book 1 within date range
      Cells(Range("ranks").Rows.Count + 620, 1).Select
      ActiveCell.Formula = "Average"
      ActiveCell.Offset(0, 1).Activate
      ActiveCell.Formula = "=Average(b618:b" & lastRow & ")" & ""
End With

End Sub
```

The `AverageRank` procedure, running under Excel, uses the Excel object model. `AverageRank` deals with spreadsheet objects such as cells, formulas, and offsets. It does a few simple things:

◆ It computes how many rows are in the range named ranks.

◆ It computes the average sales rank for the first book (Column b), for the dates in that range. The range starts at row 618, so that is where the formula for the average starts.

◆ It prints the word *Average* in the first column of the spreadsheet and then the average that it has computed in the second column, two rows beyond the last row in the range.

The Excel object model is rich, so you could perform much more complex operations than this. This example demonstrates how to make the connection and perform a simple task. Doing a more complicated processing task is a simple extrapolation of what we show here. Because this book is about Access and not Excel, we leave the more ambitious spreadsheet processing to the reader.

Operating on Outlook objects with Automation

Rather than having Access deal directly with Outlook files, as it does through ISAM drivers, with Automation, Access tells Outlook what to do and Outlook does the work. Now would be a good time to use Automation to delete unneeded files from my Inbox. It is really tedious to delete them manually one by one. In the following example, I use Automation to delete multiple obsolete e-mail messages in one operation. The first step in that direction is to write a procedure that deletes all the e-mail messages from a specified sender. This will be an Outlook module written in VBA. You can write it by selecting Tools→Macro→Visual Basic Editor from the Outlook menu. As was the case when using Automation to control Excel, make sure that Access has a copy of the Outlook 11.0 Object Library, and make sure that your security setting is not High before trying to write a procedure like the one below. The following code is one way to delete all e-mail messages that were received from a specified From address:

```
Option Explicit
Sub DeleteObsolete(strEmail)
On Error GoTo notFoundTrap
Dim myOlApp As Outlook.Application
Dim myNameSpace As NameSpace
Dim myFolder As Items
Dim myItem As MailItem
Dim strFilter As String

'Launch an instance of Outlook
'Reference its MAPI Namespace
'Reference MAPI's Inbox folder
Set myOlApp = CreateObject("Outlook.Application")
Set myNameSpace = myOlApp.GetNamespace("MAPI")
Set myFolder = _
    myNameSpace.GetDefaultFolder(olFolderInbox).Items

'Find obsolete messages and delete them
loopTop:
strFilter = "[From] = """ & strEmail & """"
Set myItem = myFolder.Find(strFilter)

    myItem.Delete
    GoTo loopTop

deleteSpamExit:
'Clean up before exiting
Set myOlApp = Nothing
Exit Sub

notFoundTrap:

    If Err.Number = 91 Or Err.Number = 13 Then
        GoTo deleteSpamExit
```

```
      Else
          MsgBox Err.Number & ": " & vbCrLf & _
              Err.Description, vbCritical, _
              "Application Power Programming with VBA"
      End If

'Clean up before exiting
Set myOlApp = Nothing

End Sub
```

The parameter `strEmail` that `DeleteObsolete` uses as input specifies the From address of the messages that you want to delete. All messages that were received from that sender are deleted.

 These messages are *really* deleted. They are not transferred to the Deleted Items folder.

The procedure traps for the following specific errors:

◆ Error 91 occurs when no messages in the Inbox have a sender that matches the value of `strEmail`. You always get error 91 after the last message from the specified sender has been deleted. In this case, you do not want to stop execution with a message box that the user must acknowledge.

◆ Error 13, which is a type mismatch error, can sometimes occur after the last message from the target sender has been deleted. You don't want to stop after this message either.

In the case of both error 91 and error 13, `DeleteObsolete` exits immediately rather than displaying an error message.

To delete all the messages from a list of senders, you need an additional procedure. This procedure calls `DeleteObsolete` once for each sender in the list. The following code is for such a program:

```
Sub ZapObsoleteMessages()
Dim rst1 As New Recordset

'Open the table with the target e-mail senders
With rst1
    .ActiveConnection = CurrentProject.Connection
```

```
      .Open "EmailDelete"
End With

'Process all table records to delete obsolete messages
Do Until rst1.EOF
      DeleteObsolete (rst1.Fields(0))
      rst1.MoveNext
Loop

'Clean up before exiting
rst1.Close
Set rst1 = Nothing

End Sub
```

This procedure opens the table, named EmailDelete, which contains the names of
the e-mail senders that you want to delete. It puts those names into recordset `rst1`.
It then loops through the table records, calling `DeleteObsolete` every time through
the loop. `DeleteObsolete` deletes the messages from the Inbox that correspond to
the current value of `rst1.Fields(0)`, which is the name of an e-mail sender.

Acting as an Automation Server

When you write VBA code to control an application such as Excel or Outlook, that
application is the source of the data being handled. It is the Automation server.
Access can also take the role of an Automation server by providing database data
to another application. Users frequently want to incorporate data that is stored in an
Access database into a document that was generated by Word. Perhaps the earliest
and most useful example of cooperation between a database and a word processor
was the printing of form letters that pulled specific information, such as an
addressee's name and address, from a database file.

The ability to easily generate form letters is so universally recognized as valuable
that Word is already capable of doing it, without any need for programming or even
launching Access. However, at other times, it is valuable to include database data in
a document. For example, many documents include tables of items. This book is an
example of such a document. Others may be financial reports, scientific reports, or
articles that contain sports statistics. If the needed information is stored in an
Access table, a procedure for transferring data from an Access table to a table in a
Word document would come in handy.

As an example of taking data from an Access database and putting it into a table
in a Word document, we now take the list of papers stored in the PAPERS table of
the OLS1 database and put the list into a table in a Word document. This would be
a typical thing for the Oregon Lunar Society to do as part of its annual report of its

activities to its members and other interested parties. The following code demonstrates one way to take data from an Access table and insert it into a Word table:

```
Option Compare Database
Option Explicit

Sub PopulateWordTable()
Dim aWordApp As Word.Application
Dim aRange As Word.Range, aTable As Word.Table
Dim aCell As Word.Cell, iCol As Integer
Dim rst1 As New Recordset, iRow As Integer

'Open the PAPERS table
With rst1
    .ActiveConnection = CurrentProject.Connection
    .Open "PAPERS", , adOpenKeyset, adLockOptimistic, adCmdTable
End With

'Create an instance of a Word application
Set aWordApp = CreateObject("Word.Application")

'Add a document to the application and a table to the document
'Specify # of rows to be one more than # of rows in PAPERS table
aWordApp.Documents.Add
Set aRange = aWordApp.ActiveDocument.Range(0, 0)
aWordApp.ActiveDocument.Tables.Add Range:=aRange, _
    NumRows:=rst1.RecordCount + 1, NumColumns:=3

'Transfer table column headings
With aWordApp.ActiveDocument.Tables(1).Rows(1)
    .Cells(1).Range.Text = rst1.Fields(0).Name
    .Cells(2).Range.Text = rst1.Fields(2).Name
    .Cells(3).Range.Text = rst1.Fields(3).Name
End With

'Insert paper number, title, and author from PAPERS table
For iRow = 2 To aWordApp.ActiveDocument.Tables(1).Rows.Count
    iCol = 0
    For Each aCell In _
        aWordApp.ActiveDocument.Tables(1).Rows(iRow).Cells
        aCell.Range.Text = IIf(IsNull(rst1.Fields(iCol)), _
            "", rst1.Fields(iCol))
        If iCol = 0 Then
            iCol = iCol + 2
        Else
```

```
                    iCol = iCol + 1
            End If
        Next aCell
        rst1.MoveNext
Next iRow

'Reformat column widths
aWordApp.ActiveDocument.Tables(1).AutoFitBehavior wdAutoFitContent

'Make Word visible
aWordApp.Visible = True

End Sub
```

This code produces the Word document that is shown in Figure 17-3.

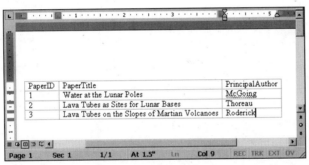

Figure 17-3: The Word table that is produced from data in the OLS1 PAPERS table.

Summary

In this chapter we looked at how you can use VBA to share data between Access and other Microsoft Office applications. Importing data into Access from external data sources, linking to external data sources, and opening external data sources and pulling data from them were covered. In addition, we discussed Automation as it relates to Access, where Access plays both the client and the server roles.

Chapter 18

XML Support

IN THIS CHAPTER

◆ What is XML?

◆ Importing XML data

◆ Exporting Access data as XML

XML HAS BECOME A BUZZWORD that is bandied about in just about any conversation about computer software. People judge software packages based on whether they have XML capability, often without even knowing what that means. In this chapter we explore what XML is, how it relates to Access, and how you can use it.

What is XML?

XML (eXtensible Markup Language), like HTML (HyperText Markup Language), is a child of SGML (Standard Generalized Markup Language). XML differs from HTML because HTML is strictly a formatting language that controls the formatting of a document. XML is a metalanguage that enables users to create markup languages that are designed to deal with specific domains. For example, markup languages designed for mathematics and chemistry have been created and standardized using XML. You can use XML to identify the specific content that your own documents deal with.

XML is ideal for transporting data that is typically held in databases from one place to another. The source and destination need not be compatible with each other in any way other than that they both have the ability to handle XML. XML has become outrageously popular and is well on its way to universal acceptance as the file format of choice for transporting data between dissimilar computers. It is also the preferred way of making database data available on the World Wide Web.

As an example of an XML file, the following code is a truncated version of the result of exporting the MEMBERS table from the Access 2003 database OLS1:

```
<?xml version="1.0" encoding="UTF-8" ?>
<dataroot xmlns:od="urn:schemas-microsoft-com:officedata"
xmlns:xsi="http://www.w3.org/2001/XMLSchema-instance"
xsi:noNamespaceSchemaLocation="MEMBERS.xsd">
    <MEMBERS>
```

```
        <MemberID>101</MemberID>
        <FirstName>Bryce</FirstName>
        <LastName>Thoreau</LastName>
        <OfficeHeld>Treasurer</OfficeHeld>
        <Email>moonman@coldmail.com</Email>
        <Phone>(503) 555-8004</Phone>
        <Street>154 Polk St.</Street>
        <City>Carver</City>
        <State>OR</State>
        <Zip>97003</Zip>
    </MEMBERS>
    <MEMBERS>
        <MemberID>102</MemberID>
        <FirstName>Cheryl</FirstName>
        <LastName>Lancaster</LastName>
        <OfficeHeld>Secretary</OfficeHeld>
        <Email>starlass@cosmos.net</Email>
        <Phone>(503) 555-8080</Phone>
        <Street>213 Adams Ave.</Street>
        <City>Redland</City>
        <State>OR</State>
        <Zip>97047</Zip>
    </MEMBERS>
    <MEMBERS>
        <MemberID>103</MemberID>
        <FirstName>Tom</FirstName>
        <LastName>Charges</LastName>
        <Email>waldo@magic.com</Email>
        <Phone>(503) 555-3211</Phone>
        <Street>132 22nd St.</Street>
        <City>Portland</City>
        <State>OR</State>
        <Zip>97245</Zip>
    </MEMBERS>
</dataroot>
```

The components of XML

An XML document is made up of a number of components. Each component tells you something about the document. The primary components of an XML document are as follows:

- The XML declaration

- Tags

- Elements

- The dataroot element and the namespace declaration

- Attributes

- Literal data

- Comments

- Processing instructions

THE XML DECLARATION

The first line of a well-written XML document is the XML declaration. In the preceding XML example, the XML declaration is as follows:

```
<?xml version="1.0" encoding="UTF-8" ?>
```

Although it is possible to have a valid XML file without an XML declaration, it is good practice to include one. Access includes an XML declaration in any file that it exports in XML format. Access can import XML files, regardless of whether they have an XML declaration.

XML TAGS AND ELEMENTS

Most XML files are primarily made up of tags and elements.

TAGS Tags come in pairs: a *start tag* and an *end tag*. These are defined as follows:

- The start tag is enclosed in angle brackets, like this:

  ```
  <Tag>
  ```

- The corresponding end tag is enclosed in angle brackets but is also preceded by a forward slash, like this:

  ```
  </Tag>
  ```

XML tags look like HTML tags, but that is where the similarity ends. XML is much more flexible. You can make up your own tags and give them any name you like. HTML tags, such as `<H1>Heading</H1>`, have a fixed meaning that is defined by the HTML specification.

ELEMENTS Between the start tag and the end tag is the *element* that is named by the tags. An element name must follow these rules:

- It can contain any *alphanumeric* character, *underscores, hyphens,* and *periods.*

- It must start with either a *letter* or an *underscore* character.

- It may not contain any *white space* (that is, blank spaces).

In the following example of a single element, City is the name of the element and Carver is the value of the element:

```
<City>
    Carver
</City>
```

You can nest one or more elements within an outer, enclosing element. If you do, close the inner elements with their appropriate end tags before starting another inner element or closing the outer element. For example, the following is legal XML:

```
<MEMBERS>
    <MemberID>
        103
    </MemberID>
    <FirstName>
        Tom
    </FirstName>
    <LastName>
        Charges
    </LastName>
    <Email>
        waldo@magic.com
    </Email>
    <Phone>
        (503) 555-3211
    </Phone>
    <Street>
        132 22nd St.
    </Street>
    <City>
        Portland
    </City>
    <State>
        OR
    </State>
    <Zip>
        97245
    </Zip>
</MEMBERS>
```

Every tag that is started must end before another tag on the same level begins. No lower-level tag ends after a higher-level tag ends. The following is not legal XML:

```
<MEMBERS>
    <MemberID>
        103
    </MemberID>
    <FirstName>
    <LastName>
        Tom
        Charges
    </FirstName>
    </LastName>
    <Email>
        waldo@magic.com
    </Email>
    <Phone>
        (503) 555-3211
    </Phone>
    <Street>
        132 22nd St.
    </Street>
    <City>
        Portland
    </City>
    <State>
        OR
    </State>
    <Zip>
        97245
    </MEMBERS>
    </Zip>
```

In the preceding code, two problems exist. Either one of the following errors is enough to make the XML file invalid:

◆ The FirstName and LastName tags overlap.

◆ The outer /MEMBERS tag comes before the inner /Zip tag.

DATAROOT AND THE XML TREE

Every XML document has a single root element named *dataroot*. All other elements are nested within the dataroot element, giving the entire document a tree structure. Within the dataroot start tag is a *namespace declaration*. The purpose of the namespace declaration is to make sure that any tags in the document refer to one and only one thing. The tags in the document are identified with a namespace.

Attributes or Elements

XML supports an alternate way of expressing data besides nesting inner elements within outer elements. This alternate method assigns attributes to elements instead of nesting subsidiary elements inside them.

The following is an example that shows an element with attributes:

```
<?xml version="1.0" encoding="UTF-8" ?>
<dataroot xmlns:od="urn:schemas-microsoft-com:officedata"
    xmlns:xsi="http://www.w3.org/2001/XMLSchema-instance"
    xsi:noNamespaceSchemaLocation="MEMBERS.xsd">
      <MEMBERS MemberID="101" FirstName="Bryce"
LastName="Thoreau"
          OfficeHeld="Treasurer" Email="moonman@coldmail.com"
          Phone="(503) 555-8004" Street="154 Polk St."
          City="Carver" State="OR" Zip="97003"/>

</dataroot>
```

Access always exports XML using the element/nested element format, not the element and attributes format. If you try to import an XML file that contains attributes, Access can't parse it.

The following is an example of a namespace declaration:

```
<dataroot xmlns:od="urn:schemas-microsoft-com:officedata"
    xmlns:xsi="http://www.w3.org/2001/XMLSchema-instance"
    xsi:noNamespaceSchemaLocation="MEMBERS.xsd">
```

The namespace declaration contains the following parts:

- ◆ xmlns: Indicates to the XML parser that a namespace declaration follows.

- ◆ **Prefix of the namespace:** In the preceding example, the prefix is od.

- ◆ **Uniform Resource Indicator (URI) for this namespace:** In the preceding example, the URI is urn:schemas-microsoft-com:officedata.

In the example above, a second namespace, xsi, follows with some additional information about the file.

REPRESENTING LITERAL DATA

Elements that contain regular alphanumeric characters are no problem for XML parsers, but special characters, such as apostrophes, ampersands, and quotation marks, present a challenge. You can solve this problem with either of the following solutions:

◆ Replace each special character with an *entity reference* that the parser recognizes.

The following are example entity references:

- " replaces " (quotation mark)

- ' replaces ' (apostrophe)

- & replaces & (ampersand)

- < replaces < (left angle bracket)

- > replaces > (right angle bracket)

If you have an element named `College` with a value of Lewis & Clark, it could be represented like this:

```
<College>
    Lewis &amp; Clark
</College>
```

The entity reference form is necessary to import data that contains special characters. It can also be used for data export.

◆ Include literal data that contains special characters in a *CDATA section*. A CDATA section can represent any amount of literal data. The following is an example:

```
<College>
    <![CDATA[Lewis & Clark]]>
</College>
```

Access uses CDATA to export data that contains special characters.

COMMENTS

You can include comments in an XML document. The parser recognizes a comment and ignores it, because comments are meant to be read by humans. Comments are

Parsers: Validating and Nonvalidating

Before XML can do anything with an XML document, it must verify that the document is well formed. A *well-formed document* is one without syntax errors. Nonvalidating parsers check to make sure that all opening tags have corresponding closing tags and that nesting is done properly. Nonvalidating parsers do not check that the proper tags are being used, because they do not know what tags are proper and what tags are not.

Validating parsers go one step beyond nonvalidating parsers. Validating parsers verify that the document conforms to a specific Document Type Definition (DTD) or schema. The DTD documents the structure of a document. (Gee, isn't *document* a versatile word? We can use it as both a verb and a noun in the same sentence.) The DTD ensures that other organizations can use the document. If a validating parser finds code in your document that does not conform to the DTD, it flags that line of code as an error.

not a functional part of the document and are identified by an opening and a closing character string. The opening string is `<!--` and the closing string is `-->`. The following is an example:

```
<!-- This is a comment. -->
```

You may place comments anywhere within a document, except for the following restrictions:

- ◆ You may not place comments within a tag pair.
- ◆ One comment may not be nested within another.

PROCESSING INSTRUCTIONS

Processing instructions that are embedded in an XML document are meant to be read by programs that process XML documents. These instructions tell the processing program additional facts about the document so that the program can process the document properly.

The following is an example of a processing instruction:

```
<?xml version="1.0" encoding="UTF-8" ?>
```

Exporting Access Data as XML

One of the nice things about Access's support of XML is that you do not have to be an XML expert to create XML documents. Access creates the documents for you. In fact, you don't even have to be a programmer to create XML documents. You can

Creating XML Documents

Creating XML documents is a major subject in itself, and numerous big, thick books are available on the subject. We don't try to cover that material here in a single chapter. To create such documents, refer to one or more of those big, thick books. To ease yourself into the subject, you can try *XML For Dummies*, by Ed Tittel (Wiley Publishing, Inc.).

export an Access record source, such as a table or query result set, to an XML file directly from the user interface.

Data export formats

You can export the following three aspects of database objects. Each of these is exported to a different file with the corresponding extension.

- ◆ **Data:** Exported as an `.xml` file.

- ◆ **Schema:** Exported as an `.xsd` file.

- ◆ **Presentation:** Exported as an `.xsl` file. (This is also known as *formatting information.*)

Exporting without programming

To export a database object to an XML file, follow these steps:

1. **Select the object that you want to export, and then choose File→Export.**

   This displays the Export Object dialog box, as shown in Figure 18-1.

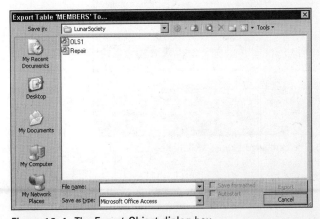

Figure 18-1: The Export Object dialog box.

2. Select the directory where you want Access to write the file, and then name the file.

3. In the Save as type text box, select XML.

4. Click the Export button.

The Export XML dialog box appears, as shown in Figure 18-2.

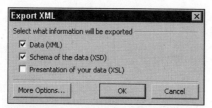

Figure 18-2: The Export XML dialog box.

5. Select the dialog box options that are appropriate for the application of this XML data.

There are three options in the dialog box and three checkboxes for you to select: *data, schema,* and *presentation*. In the case of this example, exporting the Planetary Systems table, let's export the data and the schema, but not worry about the presentation. For a table, presentation is not an issue. It would be an issue if you were exporting a report.

If you click on the More Options button, the dialog box expands as shown in Figure 18-3.

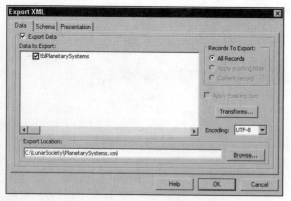

Figure 18-3: The expanded Export XML dialog box.

There are tabs for data, schema, and presentation, with various options available for each. For this example, we will just accept the default options. Clicking OK causes the XML data file and the XSD schema file to be written. That's all there is to it. Exporting database objects to XML files from the Access user interface is pretty straightforward.

Exporting data by program

You may want to export database objects to XML files automatically, without human intervention. In such cases, Access gives you a couple of tools that you can use to do this.

EXPORTXML

You can invoke the ExportXML method of the `Application` object in your VBA code.

TIP

To import an XML database into another copy of Access, use the ExportXML method. ExportXML exports data in the *element/nested element* format. This is the format that Access uses to import XML data.

The general form of the ExportXML method is as follows. Optional arguments are shown in square brackets ([ ]).

```
Application.ExportXML(ObjectType As AcExportXMLObjectType, _
    DataSource As String, [DataTarget As String], _
    [SchemaTarget As String], [PresentationTarget As String], _
    [ImageTarget As String], _
    [Encoding as AcExportXMLEncoding = acUTF8], _
    [OtherFlags As Long])
```

NOTE

Although `DataTarget`, `SchemaTarget`, and `PresentationTarget` are optional, you must specify at least *one* of them. These variables name the files that are created.

The arguments have the following meanings:

- *ObjectType:* Any type of Access object that contains data. These include `acExportForm`, `acExportFunction`, `acExportQuery`, `acExportReport`, `acExportServerView`, `acExportStoredProcedure`, or `acExportTable`.

- *DataSource:* The name of the object that you want to export.

- *DataTarget:* The name of the XML file that you are creating.

◆ *SchemaTarget:* The name of the XSD schema file that you are creating.

◆ *PresentationTarget:* The name of the XSLT file that you are creating.

◆ *ImageTarget:* The path for exported images when you are exporting a report.

◆ *Encoding:* Either UTF-16 or UTF-8.

◆ *OtherFlags:* A collection of flags that can control the export.

The following code exports the OLS1 MEMBERS table to XML as an .xml file, an .xsd file, and an .xsl file:

```
Sub ExportMEMBERS()
    Application.ExportXML acExportTable, "MEMBERS", _
        "C:\LunarSociety\MEMBERS.xml", _
        "C:\LunarSociety\MEMBERS.xsd", _
        "C:\LunarSociety\MEMBERS.xsl"

End Sub
```

Figure 18-4 shows what the first part of the .xml file looks like.

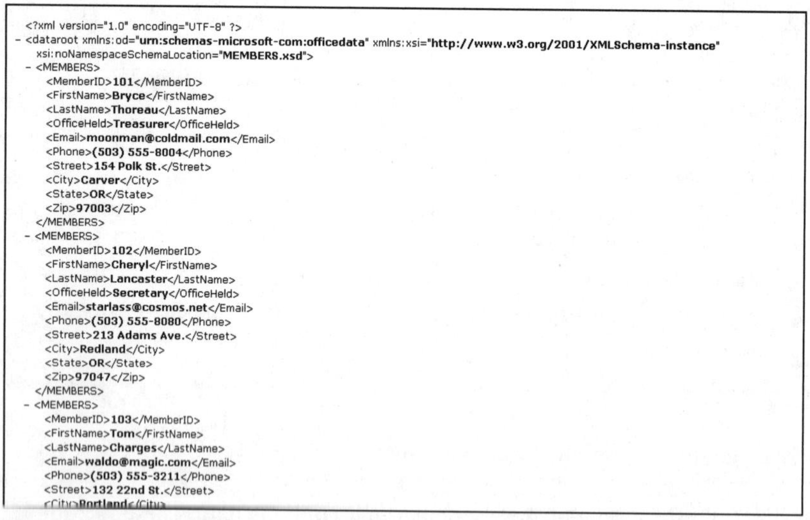

```
<?xml version="1.0" encoding="UTF-8" ?>
- <dataroot xmlns:od="urn:schemas-microsoft-com:officedata" xmlns:xsi="http://www.w3.org/2001/XMLSchema-instance"
    xsi:noNamespaceSchemaLocation="MEMBERS.xsd">
  - <MEMBERS>
      <MemberID>101</MemberID>
      <FirstName>Bryce</FirstName>
      <LastName>Thoreau</LastName>
      <OfficeHeld>Treasurer</OfficeHeld>
      <Email>moonman@coldmail.com</Email>
      <Phone>(503) 555-8004</Phone>
      <Street>154 Polk St.</Street>
      <City>Carver</City>
      <State>OR</State>
      <Zip>97003</Zip>
    </MEMBERS>
  - <MEMBERS>
      <MemberID>102</MemberID>
      <FirstName>Cheryl</FirstName>
      <LastName>Lancaster</LastName>
      <OfficeHeld>Secretary</OfficeHeld>
      <Email>starlass@cosmos.net</Email>
      <Phone>(503) 555-8080</Phone>
      <Street>213 Adams Ave.</Street>
      <City>Redland</City>
      <State>OR</State>
      <Zip>97047</Zip>
    </MEMBERS>
  - <MEMBERS>
      <MemberID>103</MemberID>
      <FirstName>Tom</FirstName>
      <LastName>Charges</LastName>
      <Email>waldo@magic.com</Email>
      <Phone>(503) 555-3211</Phone>
      <Street>132 22nd St.</Street>
      <City>Portland</City>
```

Figure 18-4: The first part of MEMBERS.xml.

Figure 18-5 shows part of the .xsd schema file, as displayed by Visual Studio.

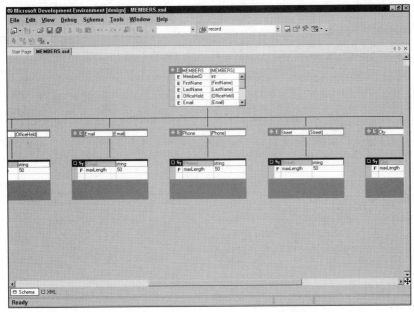

Figure 18-5: The center part of `MEMBERS.xsd`, as displayed by Visual Studio.

Figure 18-6 shows the first lines of the `.xsl` presentation file.

```
<?xml version="1.0" encoding="UTF-8" ?>
- <xsl:stylesheet version="1.0" xmlns:xsl="http://www.w3.org/1999/XSL/Transform" xmlns:msxsl="urn:schemas-microsoft-com:xslt"
    xmlns:xd="urn:schemas-microsoft-com:office:xdocs" xmlns:aj="urn:office-microsoft-com:xdocs-designer-xhtml" xmlns:fx="#fx-
    functions" exclude-result-prefixes="msxsl fx">
    <xsl:output method="html" version="4.0" indent="yes" xmlns:xsl="http://www.w3.org/1999/XSL/Transform" />
- <xsl:template match="//dataroot" xmlns:xsl="http://www.w3.org/1999/XSL/Transform">
  - <html xmlns:xd="urn:schemas-microsoft-com:office:xdocs">
    - <head>
        <title>MEMBERS</title>
        <style type="text/css" />
        <style tableEditor="TableStyleRulesID">TABLE.xdLayout TD { BORDER-RIGHT: medium none; BORDER-TOP: medium
        none; BORDER-LEFT: medium none; BORDER-BOTTOM: medium none } TABLE.msoUcTable TD { BORDER-RIGHT:
        1pt solid; BORDER-TOP: 1pt solid; BORDER-LEFT: 1pt solid; BORDER-BOTTOM: 1pt solid } TABLE { BEHAVIOR: url
        (#default#urn::tables/NDTable) }</style>
        <style id="controlStyle">.xdControl { DISPLAY: inline-block } .xdTextBox { BORDER-RIGHT: #dcdcdc 1px solid;
        PADDING-RIGHT: 1px; BORDER-TOP: #dcdcdc 1px solid; PADDING-LEFT: 1px; PADDING-BOTTOM: 1px; MARGIN-
        LEFT: 1px; BORDER-LEFT: #dcdcdc 1px solid; MARGIN-RIGHT: 1px; PADDING-TOP: 1px; BORDER-BOTTOM: #dcdcdc
        1px solid } .xdRichTextBox { BORDER-RIGHT: #dcdcdc 1px solid; PADDING-RIGHT: 1px; BORDER-TOP: #dcdcdc 1px
        solid; PADDING-LEFT: 1px; PADDING-BOTTOM: 1px; MARGIN-LEFT: 1px; BORDER-LEFT: #dcdcdc 1px solid; MARGIN-
        RIGHT: 1px; PADDING-TOP: 1px; BORDER-BOTTOM: #dcdcdc 1px solid } .xdTextList { PADDING-LEFT: 30pt;
        MARGIN: 0ptS } .xdListBox { MARGIN: 1px } .xdComboBox { MARGIN: 1px } .xdCollection { PADDING-RIGHT: 2pt;
        PADDING-LEFT: 5px; PADDING-BOTTOM: 2pt; MARGIN: 2pt; PADDING-TOP: 2pt } .xdGroup { BORDER-RIGHT:
        #dcdcdc 1pt solid; PADDING-RIGHT: 2pt; BORDER-TOP: #dcdcdc 1pt solid; PADDING-LEFT: 2pt; PADDING-BOTTOM:
        2pt; MARGIN: 2pt; BORDER-LEFT: #dcdcdc 1pt solid; PADDING-TOP: 2pt; BORDER-BOTTOM: #dcdcdc 1pt
        solid } .xdPicture { MARGIN-LEFT: 1px } .xdTextList .xdTextBox { BORDER-RIGHT: 0px; BORDER-TOP: 0px;
        VERTICAL-ALIGN: text-top; BORDER-LEFT: 0px; WIDTH: 100%; BORDER-BOTTOM:
        0px } .xdTextList .xdRichTextBox { BORDER-RIGHT: 0px; BORDER-TOP: 0px; VERTICAL-ALIGN: text-top; BORDER-
        LEFT: 0px; WIDTH: 100%; BORDER-BOTTOM: 0px } LABEL { DISPLAY: inline-block } BODY {layout-
        grid:none;} .xdListItem {width:100%;vertical-align:text-top;} .xdListBox,.xdComboBox{margin:1px;} .xdPicture
        {margin:1px;} BEHAVIOR: url(#default#urn::xdPicture) url(#default#urn::controls/Binder) } TABLE.xdFormLayout
        TD{BEHAVIOR: url(#default#LayoutText);} .xdBehavior_Formatting,.xdBehavior_FormattingNoBUI{BEHAVIOR:
        url(#default#urn::controls/Binder) url(#default#Formatting);} .xdStaticText{margin: 1px;padding:
        1px;} .xdCollection{border:1px solid #FFFFFF;padding:7px;} .xdGroup{border:1px solid
        #FFFFFF;padding:7px;} .xdBehavior_GhostedText,.xdBehavior_GhostedTextNoBUI{BEHAVIOR: url
        (#default#urn::controls/Binder) url(#default#TextField) url
```

Figure 18-6: The first part of `MEMBERS.xsl`.

By including the presentation information with the schema and the data, the data from the MEMBERS table can now be displayed by a browser, such as Internet Explorer, in an easily readable format (see Figure 18-7).

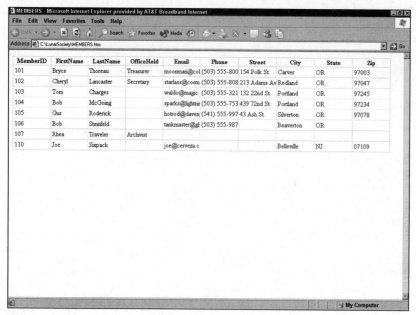

Figure 18-7: Browser view of the data from the MEMBERS table.

ADO export

You can use ADO to save a database object as XML for use by many XML-fluent programs.

 Access is not able to directly import XML that is saved using the ADO method. To import XML back into Access, use the ExportXML method. ExportXML exports data in the *element/nested element* format; ADO exports data in the *element and attribute* format.

To illustrate the exporting of an Access object using the ADO method, the following code includes these two procedures:

♦ A general procedure for exporting an object to XML using ADO

♦ A short wrapper program that calls the first procedure, feeding it parameters that specify what database object to export and what file to export it to

```
Sub ExporttblPlanetarySystems()
    Dim str1 As String
```

```
    Dim str2 As String

    str1 = "tblPlanetarySystems"
    str2 = "PlanetarySystems"
    Call ExportADOXML(str1, str2)

End Sub
```

The preceding code specifies the object to be exported (tblPlanetarySystems) and the name of the file to export it to (PlanetarySystems.xml). The following procedure, ExportADOXML(str1, str2), actually does the export operation.

```
Public Sub ExportADOXML(strTableName As String, strXMLFileName As String)
    'Export Access table as ADO-format XML file
    Dim rst1 As ADODB.Recordset

    On Error GoTo ErrorHandler

    'Instantiate recordset, open source table, save to XML file
    Set rst1 = New ADODB.Recordset
    rst1.Open strTableName, CurrentProject.Connection
    rst1.Save strXMLFileName, adPersistXML

    rst1.Close
    Set rst1 = Nothing

ExitRoutine:
    Exit Sub

ErrorHandler:
    MsgBox Err.Number & ": " & Err.Description, vbCritical, "ExportADOXML"
    Resume ExitRoutine

End Sub
```

The preceding code uses the Open and Save methods of a recordset object. These are in the Microsoft ADO Ext. 2.7 for DDL and Security library, which must be loaded for this procedure to work. If you do not have this library loaded, you can load the library by choosing Tools→References and selecting Microsoft ADO Ext. 2.7 for DDL and Security.

Importing XML Data

Regardless of whether you create XML documents yourself, you may need to import XML data into an Access database from an external source. You can do this manually, from the Access user interface, without programming. Or, you can perform the import from a VBA program.

Importing data without programming

Importing an XML file into an Access database is easy, although not particularly flexible.

Follow these steps to import the XML file:

1. **Choose File→Get External Data→Import.**

   This displays a dialog box of the contents of a folder. If necessary, switch to the folder that contains the XML file that you want to import.

2. **From the Files of Type drop-down menu, select XML.**

   This should display the desired file in the dialog box's main pane.

3. **Click the Import button.**

   This displays the Import XML dialog box, as shown in Figure 18-8.

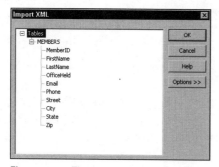

Figure 18-8: The Import XML dialog box.

4. **In the Import XML dialog box, click the Options button.**

   The dialog box expands to display three options and their associated option buttons.

5. **Select the appropriate import option:**

- Structure Only

- Structure and Data (the default)

- Append Data to Existing Table(s)

6. **Click OK.**

Importing an XML file this way works smoothly as long as the XML file is compatible with Access's XML import tool. The import should work flawlessly if the XML file being imported was originally exported from another Access database.

One possible source of problems is the form of the XML file. If the file is syntactically correct and in the element/nested element format, the import should go smoothly. If syntax errors exist or if the file is in the element and attributes format, Access can't import it correctly. Because XML that was created by ADO from a recordset is always in the elements and attributes format, you can't use this simple method to bring that kind of XML file into Access.

Importing data by program

If you have XML files in the element/nested element format, you can use the ImportXML method of the `Application` object to import the file's structure, data, or both into an Access database. For files in the element and attributes format, you must take a different approach.

IMPORTING FILES IN THE ELEMENT/NESTED ELEMENT FORMAT

Access can import XML in the element/nested element format with the greatest of ease. A VBA example of how to do that is as follows:

```
Sub ImportXMLFileIntoAccessTable()

'Import the MEMBERS XML file that came from the OLS1 database
Application.ImportXML _
    "E:\Access Power Programming\MEMBERS.xml", acStructureAndData

End Sub
```

It doesn't get much easier than that. Just apply the ImportXML method of the `Application` object, with the following two parameters:

◆ The first parameter is the location of the XML file.

◆ The second parameter specifies whether you want to import:

- Just the table structure

- Both the structure and data

- Just the data (to be added to an existing table)

IMPORTING FILES IN THE ELEMENT AND ATTRIBUTES FORMAT

Importing a file in the element and attributes format is not nearly as easy as the preceding example, which imports a file in element/nested element format, but it's possible.

An XML file in the element and attributes format is as follows:

```
<xml xmlns:s='uuid:BDC6E3F0-6DA3-11d1-A2A3-00AA00C14882'
    xmlns:dt='uuid:C2F41010-65B3-11d1-A29F-00AA00C14882'
    xmlns:rs='urn:schemas-microsoft-com:rowset'
    xmlns:z='#RowsetSchema'>
<s:Schema id='RowsetSchema'>
    <s:ElementType name='row' content='eltOnly'>
        <s:AttributeType name='c0' rs:name='Host Star' rs:number='1'
rs:nullable='true' rs:maydefer='true' rs:writeunknown='true'>
            <s:datatype dt:type='string' dt:maxLength='50'/>
        </s:AttributeType>
        <s:AttributeType name='Planet' rs:number='2'
rs:nullable='true' rs:maydefer='true' rs:writeunknown='true'>
            <s:datatype dt:type='string' dt:maxLength='50'/>
        </s:AttributeType>
        <s:AttributeType name='c2' rs:name='Distance from Earth'
rs:number='3' rs:nullable='true' rs:maydefer='true'
            rs:writeunknown='true'>
            <s:datatype dt:type='r4' dt:maxLength='4'
rs:precision='7' rs:fixedlength='true'/>
        </s:AttributeType>
        <s:AttributeType name='Magnitude' rs:number='4'
rs:nullable='true' rs:maydefer='true' rs:writeunknown='true'>
            <s:datatype dt:type='r4' dt:maxLength='4'
rs:precision='7' rs:fixedlength='true'/>
        </s:AttributeType>
```

```
        <s:AttributeType name='c4' rs:name='Planet Mass'
rs:number='5' rs:nullable='true' rs:maydefer='true'
rs:writeunknown='true'>
            <s:datatype dt:type='r4' dt:maxLength='4'
rs:precision='7' rs:fixedlength='true'/>
        </s:AttributeType>
        <s:extends type='rs:rowbase'/>
    </s:ElementType>
</s:Schema>
<rs:data>
    <z:row c0='16 Cygni' Planet='16 Cygni b' c2='70'
Magnitude='6.1999998' c4='1.5'/>
    <z:row c0='47 Ursae Majoris' Planet='47 Ursae Majoris b' c2='43'
Magnitude='5.0999999' c4='2.4100001'/>
    <z:row c0='47 Ursae Majoris' Planet='47 Ursae Majoris c' c2='43'
Magnitude='5.0999999' c4='0.75999999'/>
    <z:row c0='51 Pegasi' Planet='51 Pegasi b' c2='48'
Magnitude='5.5' c4='0.47'/>
    <z:row c0='55 Cancri' Planet='55 Cancri b' c2='44'
Magnitude='5.9499998' c4='0.83999997'/>
    <z:row c0='55 Cancri' Planet='55 Cancri c' c2='44'
Magnitude='5.9499998' c4='0.20999999'/>
    <z:row c0='55 Cancri' Planet='55 Cancri d' c2='44'
Magnitude='5.9499998' c4='4'/>
    <z:row c0='70 Virginis' Planet='70 Virginis b' c2='72'
Magnitude='5' c4='6.5999999'/>
    <z:row c0='Epsilon Eridani' Planet='Epsilon Eridani b' c2='10.4'
Magnitude='3.73' c4='0.86000001'/>
    <z:row c0='Epsilon Eridani' Planet='Epsilon Eridani c' c2='10.4'
Magnitude='3.73' c4='0.1'/>
</rs:data>
</xml>
```

This is different from files in the element/nested element format. It contains both data and schema information, and Access cannot handle it directly. You can, however, write a procedure that brings the data and schema into Access.

Let's do it. Let's Import the planetary systems file that we used ADO to export to XML in the previous section, but give the resulting table a different name. We use the procedure/subprocedure form that we used in the ADO export example. A wrapper routine that specifies the XML source file and the destination table calls a generic import subprocedure that does the actual importing. First, the wrapper is as follows:

```
Sub ImportPlanetarySystemsFile()
    Dim str1 As String
    Dim str2 As String

    str1 = "C:\LunarSociety\PlanetarySystems.xml"
    str2 = "ADOPlanetarySystems"
    Call ImportADOXML(str1, str2)

End Sub
```

The preceding code holds all the specific information about this particular operation and calls the general import routine, ImportADOXML, as follows:

```
Public Sub ImportADOXML(strXMLFileName As String, strTableName As String)
    'Import an ADO-formatted XML file into a table with a specified name
    Dim rst1 As ADODB.Recordset
    Dim rst2 As ADODB.Recordset
    Dim cat1 As ADOX.Catalog
    Dim tbl1 As ADOX.Table
    Dim col1 As ADOX.Column
    Dim fld1 As ADODB.Field

    On Error GoTo ErrorHandler

    Set cat1 = New ADOX.Catalog
    Set cat1.ActiveConnection = CurrentProject.Connection

    'Create ADO recordset from XML file
    Set rst1 = New ADODB.Recordset
    rst1.Open strXMLFileName, , , , adCmdFile

    'Create new table
    Set tbl1 = New ADOX.Table
    tbl1.Name = strTableName

    'Create table's columns
    For Each fld1 In rst1.Fields
        Set col1 = New ADOX.Column
        col1.Name = fld1.Name
        col1.Type = fld1.Type
        col1.DefinedSize = fld1.DefinedSize
        tbl1.Columns.Append col1
    Next fld1
```

```
'Save the new table
cat1.Tables.Append tbl1

'Open a recordset on the new table
Set rst2 = New ADODB.Recordset
rst2.Open strTableName, CurrentProject.Connection, _
        adOpenKeyset, adLockOptimistic

'Transfer records from recordset to new table
Do Until rst1.EOF
    rst2.AddNew
        For Each fld1 In rst1.Fields
            rst2(fld1.Name) = rst1(fld1.Name)
        Next fld1
    rst2.Update
    rst1.MoveNext
Loop

'Clean up after yourself
rst1.Close
Set rst1 = Nothing
rst2.Close
Set rst2 = Nothing
Set col1 = Nothing
Set tbl1 = Nothing
Set cat1 = Nothing

'Display the new table
Application.RefreshDatabaseWindow

ExitRoutine:
    Exit Sub

ErrorHandler:
    MsgBox Err.Number & ": " & Err.Description, vbCritical, _
        "ImportADOXML"
    Resume ExitRoutine

End Sub
```

After running the preceding code, a new table named ADOPlanetarySystems resides in the currently active database.

It is possible to use ADO to export to XML and import from XML, but considering how easy it is to accomplish the same thing with the Application object's `ExportXML` and `ImportXML` methods, you have little reason to do so, unless you are working with another program that must use the elements and attributes format of the XML file instead of the element/nested element format.

Summary

XML provides a great mechanism for transporting data from one software environment to another. Because so many different environments support the importing and exporting of data in XML format, you have tremendous freedom in taking data from anywhere and using it in Access, or vice versa. You will never have to go through the drudgery of writing format conversion routines again.

This chapter describes what XML is, and how to import and export data in XML format with Access.

Chapter 19

Add-Ins

IN THIS CHAPTER

◆ Creating add-ins

◆ Registering add-ins

◆ Installing add-ins

ACCESS HAS TWO DIFFERENT INTERFACES, designed to be used by two different kinds of people. First, Access features the familiar graphical user interface, with its windows, wizards, and menus. It is aimed at people who may have no knowledge of programming. Nevertheless, they can gain tremendous value from using Access. Such people are Access's main target audience. The second interface is VBA. It is aimed at application developers who use VBA to develop custom applications for the first group of users, the nonprogrammers.

Adding to Access's Capabilities

Add-ins provide a bridge between the two user communities. Programmers can write VBA functions that add new features to Access's graphical user interface. Features that are not a part of Access's graphical user interface, but would nonetheless be valuable to the nonprogramming users in your organization – or even the programming users – can be added to the basic capabilities of Access. Once you create, register, and install these new functions, they become a permanent part of Access and are available for all future projects. With this capability, you can customize the copies of Access that are owned by your organization to address the organization's specific needs.

Due to the presence or absence of such add-ins, one copy of Access may be able to do things that a second copy cannot. If you decide to enhance the functionality of Access with an add-in to support an application that you are building, be sure that the add-in is present on all the machines that will be running your application.

Several different kinds of add-ins exist, including builders, wizards, menu add-ins, and COM add-ins. Each type is briefly discussed in the following sections.

Builders

A *builder* is an add-in that breaks down the task of building a mathematical expression into a series of visual steps. Using a builder, even algebraically challenged users are able to build complex expressions. Builders are usually in the form of a dialog box, with controls that guide the user through the construction of an expression or another data element.

ACCESS'S EXPRESSION BUILDER – AN EXAMPLE OF A BUILDER ADD-IN

Even a "stock" copy of Access contains add-ins. One is the Expression Builder, which is used to help users construct expressions. When you create a table in Design view, you can specify a number of things about each field in the table. Figure 19-1 shows the Design view of the MEMBERS table in the OLS1 database.

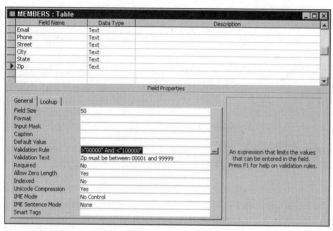

Figure 19-1: The MEMBERS table in Design view.

The selected field in the Field Properties section, Validation Rule, has a Build button that contains an ellipsis (...) to the right of the text-entry area. When you click the Build button, the Expression Builder, shown in Figure 19-2, is displayed.

The Expression Builder helps users build complex expressions, such as the range specification in the text box at the top, by allowing them to click the operator buttons below the text box or to select operators from the pane on the bottom right. Constants and functions can also be selected. This is a user-friendly alternative to just typing the validation rule directly into the Validation Rule field in Design view. When the user finishes the expression and clicks the OK button, the new validation rule appears in the Design view window, as shown in Figure 19-1.

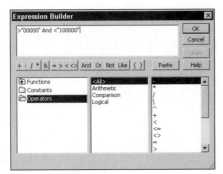

Figure 19-2: The Expression Builder.

Wizards

Wizards are similar to builders but are more flexible. The purpose of a wizard is to guide the user through a procedure that may not be particularly obvious. Thus, you find considerable diversity in the clan of wizards. This is especially true because you can create custom wizards to add to the ones that are provided by Microsoft. Granting the value of diversity and freedom of expression, it is good to give your wizards an appearance that is consistent with that of Microsoft's wizards so that users will already be somewhat familiar with them the first time they use them.

ACCESS'S TABLE CREATION WIZARD

One example of an Access wizard is the Table Creation Wizard, which you can use to create database tables. When you first start to create a database, you are faced with the following three options for creating a table:

- ◆ Create a table in Design view
- ◆ Create a table by using a wizard
- ◆ Create a table by entering data

Creating a table in Design view is the most flexible and will probably be the choice of advanced users. Creating a table by entering data is the least flexible and the least efficient, because Access makes numerous default assumptions about what the user wants. This option is also the easiest for the user to deal with, because it only requires data to be entered into a grid of rows and columns and then saved.

Creating a table by using a wizard is a compromise between the two extremes of maximum flexibility and maximum ease of use. A wizard can offer options from which the user can make selections. This is easier than Design view's requirement that the user know enough to create the table from scratch. And, it is more flexible than the method of creating a table by entering data. The wizard offers the most common personal and business table candidates and likely field names for them.

You can change the name of a field, and you can change the name of the table. You can even specify your own primary key or accept the one that Access automatically creates.

Figure 19-3 shows the opening screen of the Table Wizard.

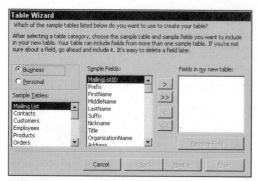

Figure 19-3: The Table Wizard.

After the user selects a table from the Sample Tables list box and then chooses fields from the Sample Fields list box, she places them in the Fields in my new table list box. From there, a series of dialog boxes walks the user through the creation of a table. It is a painless way to create a table. Other wizards make it equally easy to accomplish other functions.

CREATING A CUSTOM WIZARD

Wizards are clearly cool supplements to Access. Even cooler is the fact that you can create your own wizards, customized to the needs of your organization, and have them integrated into Access so tightly that they appear to be an integral part of it. To show how you do this integration, we create a custom wizard that enables users to change the text that is displayed on a form's command buttons.

Suppose that you are working for a firm that has two distinct user communities, one that is accustomed to very formal use of the English language and another that prefers an informal approach to language. For either audience, several of the forms in your applications have command buttons indicating that the user accepts the information being offered. For the informal crowd, that button would carry the legend OK. The formal folk, however, would not be comfortable with that, so you want those same buttons on their copies of the application to say Yes instead of OK.

You can create a wizard that enables a person to switch all the command buttons in a database from OK to Yes, or vice versa. If a person of the opposite persuasion later takes possession of that computer, the text on the button can be switched back.

You may never be confronted with the problem of supporting different user communities with different text on command buttons, but by studying the following example, you can see the general steps that are needed to create a custom wizard.

BUILDING THE FORMALITY CHANGER WIZARD   To change the formality of command button legends on all a database's forms in a single operation, you need to loop through its forms, changing formality as you go. To do that, you first have to create a table that stores the name of each form, the controls on each form that are affected, the informal legend, and the formal legend in each case. The first step in the process is to create a new database file to hold your add-in wizard. This makes the wizard independent of a particular application and accessible to all who want to use it. Add-in databases are generally given an .mda extension rather than .mdb. Follow these steps to construct the Formality Changer Wizard:

1. **Launch a new database by choosing File→New.**

2. **Save the database with the name** Formality.mda.

   Be sure that the Save as type menu choice is set to All Files. If you accept the default, the file is saved as Formality.mda.mdb, which is not what you want.

3. **Create a new table with the following fields:**

Field Name	Data Type	Field Length
FormName	Text	20
ControlName	Text	20
ControlType	Text	20
LatestUpdate	Date/Time	
Informal	Text	20
Formal	Text	20

4. **Set a composite primary key on both** FormName **and** ControlName.

   You can do this by highlighting both rows and clicking the Primary Key icon. Once the primary key is set, key icons appear on the left edge of the FormName and ControlName rows, as shown in Figure 19-4.

5. **Save the table as tblFormality and close it.**

6. **Using VBE, create a new module and select Tools→References.**

   Clear the check box next to Microsoft ActiveX Data Objects 2.1 Library, and then select the check box next to Microsoft DAO 3.6 Object Library.

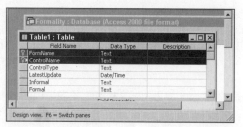

Figure 19-4: Table definition with the composite primary key.

7. Click the OK button to close the References dialog box.

8. In the empty module, enter the following code:

```
Private Const Formality_Table As String = "tblFormality"
```

9. Add a procedure to loop through all the forms in the database, as follows:

```
Public Sub EnumerateForms(bolExtract As Boolean, strFormality
As String)

    Dim db As Database
    Dim recFormal As Recordset
    Dim objAO As AccessObject
    Dim objCP As Object

    ' Open the database and font style recordset
    Set db = CurrentDb()
    Set recFormal = db.OpenRecordset(Formality_Table)
    recFormal.Index = "PrimaryKey"

    'Enumerate the forms
    Set objCP = Application.CurrentProject
    If bolExtract Then
        For Each objAO In objCP.AllForms
            ExtractCaptions recFormal, strFormality, objAO.Name
        Next objAO
    Else
      For Each objAO In objCP.AllForms
            SetCaptions recFormal, strFormality, objAO.Name
        Next objAO
    End If

    ' Clean up after yourself
    recFormal.Close

End Sub
```

10. **Using the following code, extract the existing command button captions from the forms and add them to the tblFormality table:**

```
Private Sub ExtractCaptions(recFormal As Recordset,
strFormality As String, strFormName As String)
    Dim frmF As Form
    Dim ctlC As Control
    Dim strControlName As String
    Dim datNow As Date
    Dim intControlType As Integer

    'Open the form, hidden, in Design View
    DoCmd.OpenForm strFormName, acDesign, , , , acHidden
    datNow = Now()

    'Add the form caption
    Set frmF = Forms(strFormName)
    With recFormal
        .Seek "=", strFormName, strFormName

        'Add a record to or update a record in the Formality
Changer table
        If .NoMatch Then
            .AddNew
        Else
            .Edit
        End If

        'Specify field contents
        !FormName = strFormName
        !ControlName = strFormName
        !ControlType = "Form"
        !DateUpdated = datNow
        .Fields(strFontStyle) = frmF.Caption
        .Update

        'Loop through the controls
        For Each ctlC In frmF.Controls

            intControlType = ctlC.ControlType
            If intControlType = acCommandButton Then
                'Find the control in the tblFormality table
                strControlName = ctlC.Name
                .Seek "=", strFormName, strControlName

                'Add a record for or update the existing record
```

```
                         'for the control in the Formality Changer table
                         If .NoMatch Then
                             .AddNew
                         Else
                             .Edit
                         End If

                         'Specify field contents
                         !FormName = strFormName
                         !ControlName = strControlName
                         !ControlType = "Command button"
                         !DateUpdated = datNow
                         .Fields(strFontStyle) = ctlC.Caption
                         .Update
                     End If
                 Next
             End With

             'Close and save the form
             DoCmd.Close acForm, strFormName, acSaveYes

         End Sub
```

11. **Use a second procedure to reverse the effect of the** ExtractCaptions **procedure.**

    This second procedure takes the captions that are in the tblFormality table and applies them to the corresponding command buttons on the database's forms, as follows:

```
    Private Sub SetCaptions(recFormal As Recordset, strFormality
    As String, strFormName As String)

        Dim frmF As Form
        Dim ctlC As Control
        Dim strControlName As String
        Dim intControlType As Integer

        'Open the form, hidden, in Design View
        DoCmd.OpenForm strFormName, acDesign, , , , acHidden

        'Add the form caption
        Set frmF = Forms(strFormName)
        With recFormal
            .Seek "=", strFormName, strFormName

            'Add or update the form in the font weight table
```

```
        If .NoMatch Or IsNull(.Fields(strFormality)) Then
            frmF.Caption = ""
        Else
            frmF.Caption = .Fields(strFormality)
        End If


        'Loop through the controls
        For Each ctlC In frmF.Controls

            'We are only interested in the command buttons
            intControlType = ctlC.ControlType
            If intControlType = acCommandButton Then
                'Find the control in the tblFormality table
                strControlName = ctlC.Name
                .Seek "=", strFormName, strControlName

                'Add or update the control in the tblFormality
table
                If .NoMatch Or IsNull(.Fields(strFormality)) Then
                    ctlC.Caption = ""
                Else
                    ctlC.Caption = .Fields(strFormality)
                End If
            End If
        Next
    End With


    'Close the form and save it
    DoCmd.Close acForm, strFormName, acSaveYes

End Sub
```

12. **Compile the wizard, and save it as the Formality Changer Wizard.**

    At this point, the wizard is functionally complete.

13. **Test the new wizard on a form before you apply it to production forms.**

    Create a new form in a new database, and place a command button on the form. Assign the command button a caption of OK.

14. **Save the form as Form1.**

15. **Type the following code into the VBE Immediate window:**

    ```
    EnumerateForms True, "Informal"
    ```

    If you have not made any errors, the code will run, populating tblFormality with Informal data.

16. **View the tblFormality table in Access.**

    The table should look like that shown in Figure 19-5.

tblFormality : Table

FormName	ControlName	ControlType	LatestUpdate	Informal	Formal
Form1	Command0	Command button	03 6:36:40 PM	OK	
Form1	Form1	Form	03 6:36:40 PM		

Record: 3 of 3

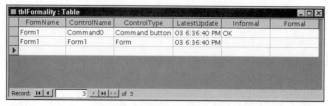

Figure 19-5: The tblFormality table, populated with Informal data.

You see two rows in the table, one for the form itself (`Form1`), and the other for the command button that you placed on the form (`Command0`). Because you set the caption of the button to OK, that is what now appears in the cell at the intersection of the `Informal` column and the `Command0` row in the tblFormality table.

17. **Add a more formal equivalent of OK to the `Formal` column in the cell that's next to the OK in the `Informal` column.**

    Type Yes into that cell. This gives you the table that is shown in Figure 19-6.

tblFormality : Table

FormName	ControlName	ControlType	LatestUpdate	Informal	Formal
Form1	Command0	Command button	03 6:36:40 PM	OK	Yes
Form1	Form1	Form	03 6:36:40 PM		

Record: 3 of 3

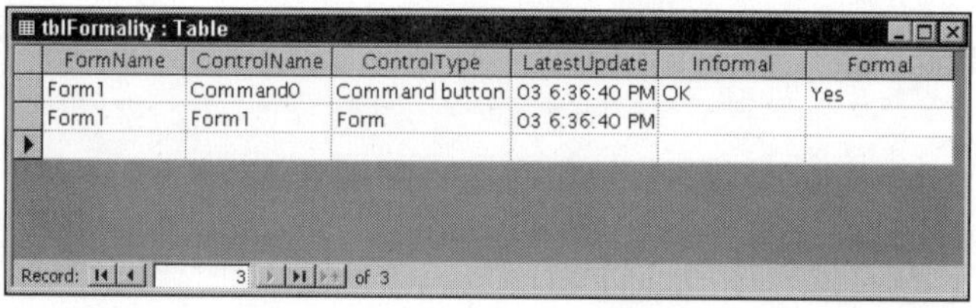

Figure 19-6: The tblFormality table, populated with both Informal and Formal data.

18. **Close the tblFormality table, and return to VBE Immediate window.**

    To switch the caption on your test command button, enter the following command:

```
EnumerateForms False, "Formal"
```

19. **After the code has run, switch back to Access and view your form.**

    The form should look like that shown in Figure 19-7.

    You can switch back to Informal by executing the following code:

```
EnumerateForms False, "Informal"
```

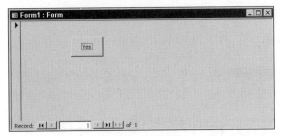

Figure 19-7: Form1, showing that the button caption
has changed from OK to Yes.

The major work on this wizard is now done. However, you need to complete a
few important details.

CREATING THE WIZARD'S FORM   Because the whole purpose of wizards is to make
things easy for the user, it is unacceptable to require users to first know about VBE,
to second open the Immediate window, and to third type in a cryptic command. The
solution is for the users to express their preference for either formality or informal-
ity with a custom form. The next step in the wizard-creation process is to create
that form.

The user should be able to do the following three things:

◆ Extract the captions from all the command buttons on all the database's
forms and store them in the appropriate column of the tblFormality table.

◆ Set the captions on all the command buttons on all the database's forms,
based on the values in the appropriate column of the tblFormality table.

◆ Exit the wizard.

The form must make it easy for the user to select a formality level (formal or informal) and to choose whether to extract, set, or exit. Figure 19-8 shows an example of
what such a form may look like.

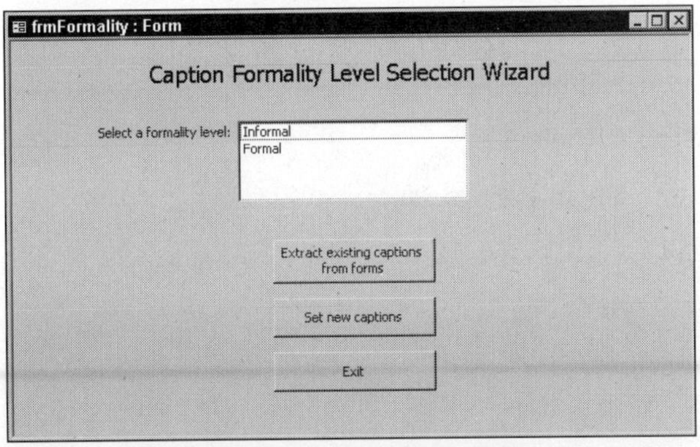

Figure 19-8: The formality form, frmFormality.

The list box at the top of Figure 19-8 should have the properties that are shown in Figure 19-9.

Figure 19-9: The Property sheet for the list box in the Formality form, frmFormality.

The first five properties on the Property sheet, described as follows, are the only ones that you need to consider:

♦ Select a name for the list box, in this case lstFormalityLevels.

♦ Leave the Control Source field blank.

♦ Select a Row Source Type of Value List.

♦ Add Row Source options of Informal and Formal.

♦ Set Column Count to 1.

Next, give each of the command buttons a name and an event procedure. The event procedure specifies what action is to be performed when the button is clicked.

Name the top button cmdExtractCaption, and enter the following code for its On Click event procedure:

```
If lstFormalityLevels.ListIndex = -1 Then
    MsgBox "Please select a formality level."
Else
    EnumerateForms True, lstFormalityLevels
End If
```

This procedure first checks to see whether a selection has been made. If none has been made, the code displays Please select a formality level. If a selection *has* been made, the selected formality level determines which column in tblFormality receives the extracted captions.

Now name the middle command button cmdSetCaption, and enter the following code for its On Click event procedure:

```
 If lstFormalityLevels.ListIndex = -1 Then
    MsgBox "Please select a formality level."
Else
    EnumerateForms False, lstFormalityLevels
End If
```

This procedure also checks to see whether a selection has been made. If a selection has been made, the captions of the selected formality level are set on all the command buttons on all the database's forms.

Finally, name the bottom button cmdExit, and enter the following event procedure for its On Click event:

```
DoCmd.Close
```

ACCESSING THE WIZARD'S FORM   Now that you have created the wizard's form, you need to provide a mechanism for users to access it. You can do that with a public function. Follow these steps:

1. **Create a new module.**

2. **Add the following code to the new module:**

   ```
   Public Function formalityLevel()
      DoCmd.OpenForm "frmFormality"
   End Function
   ```

3. **Save this module as** Formality Level Entry Point.

PREPARING THE DATABASE FOR THE NEW WIZARD   Users invoke custom wizards with the Add-In Manager, which is available from Access's Tools menu. To give the users a more meaningful name than Formality to select, you should set the properties for the Formality database. Select File→Database Properties. This displays a dialog box that you can populate in a manner similar to that shown in Figure 19-10.

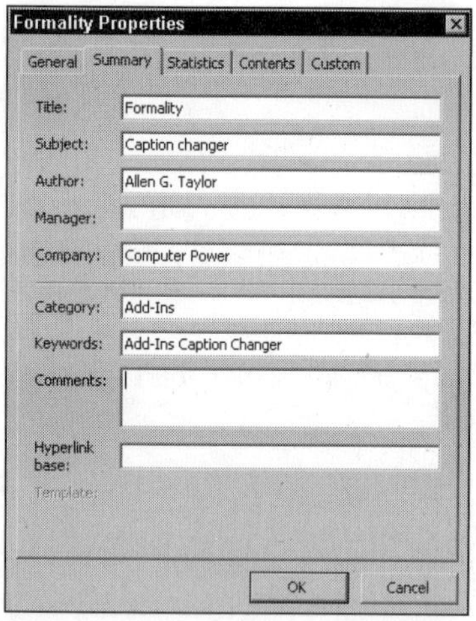

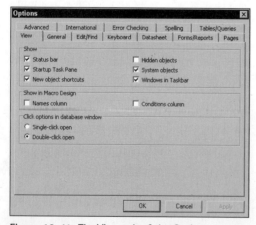

Figure 19-10: Database properties for the Formality database.

Now, all that remains is to register the wizard add-in so that it is available to all users on every machine that it is installed on.

REGISTERING THE WIZARD AS AN ACCESS ADD-IN   Before you can register the new wizard, you must make sure that your system has a USysRegInfo table. This is a special table that is normally hidden. To see whether it is present in the Formality database, select Tools→Options. From the View tab, make sure that the System objects option is checked. Figure 19-11 shows this option.

Figure 19-11: The View tab of the Options menu.

Figure 19-12 shows the result. A number of previously invisible system tables are now visible, but no USysRegInfo table exists. You can either build one from scratch or import one from a database that already has one, and then modify it to fit your needs.

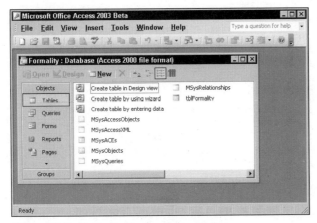

Figure 19-12: Tables in the Formality database.

To create a new USysRegInfo table, use the field definitions and properties that are shown in Table 19-1.

TABLE **19-1 FIELD DEFINITIONS AND PROPERTIES**

Field Name	Data Type	Field Length	Allow Zero Length	Unicode Compression
Subkey	Text	255	No	No
Type	Number			
ValName	Text	255	No	No
Value	Text	255	No	No

Save the table with the name USysRegInfo. You don't need to specify a primary key for this table.

Once you have created the USysRegInfo table, you must fill it with the data that allows both Access and the user to locate the new wizard. Figure 19-13 shows the USysRegInfo table after the appropriate data has been added to it.

USysRegInfo : Table						
Subkey			Type	ValName	Value	
▶	HKEY_CURRENT_ACCESS_PROFILE\Menu Add-Ins\Caption changer		0			
	HKEY_CURRENT_ACCESS_PROFILE\Menu Add-Ins\Caption changer		1	Expression	=formalityLevel()	
	HKEY_CURRENT_ACCESS_PROFILE\Menu Add-Ins\Caption changer		1	Library	|ACCDIR\Formality.mda	
*			0			

Record: ◄◄ ◄ 1 ► ►► ►* of 3

Figure 19-13: The populated USysRegInfo table.

INSTALLING THE NEW WIZARD Now that you have built a custom add-in, you must install it in any databases that will be using it. Following is a step-by-step procedure on how to do it:

1. **Close the** `Formality.mda` **add-in database, and open another database.**

   You can open any other database, as long as it has at least one form. Rather than using a production database, you should use a database that isn't important to you, in case things don't go as planned.

2. **Select Tools→Add-Ins→Add-In Manager.**

   The Add-In Manager may already list some add-ins, or it may be empty. Figure 19-14 shows what ours looks like. It already has an add-in for the Crystal Reports 9 Wizard.

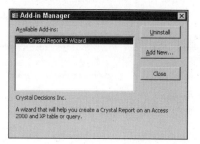

Figure 19-14: The Add-In Manager.

3. **Click the Add New button.**

   From the list of add-ins that appears, select `Formality.mda` and then click the Open button. This installs the add-in. The installation is confirmed by an X that appears to the left of Formality in the Add-In Manager, as shown in Figure 19-15.

4. **Close the Add-In Manager.**

   Before you can use the Formality add-in wizard in the current database, you must import the tblFormality table from the `Formality.mda` database.

5. **Choose File→Get External Data→Import.**

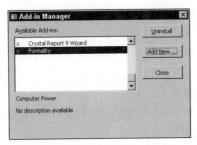

Figure 19-15: Formality.mda is now
installed in the Add-In Manager.

6. In the File dialog box, select the Formality.mda database and then click
   the Open button.

   The Import Objects dialog box appears.

7. Select tblFormality from the Import Objects dialog box, and click OK.

   This copies the Formality table into the current database.

8. Choose Tools→Add-Ins→Caption changer.

   The Formality form appears, waiting for the user to select a formality
   level, as shown in Figure 19-16.

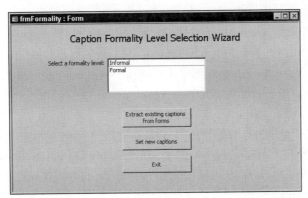

Figure 19-16: Selecting the Caption changer add-in displays
the formality form.

9. Select Informal from the list box, and then click the Extract existing
   captions from forms command button.

10. Open the tblFormality table.

    You now see an OK in the Informal column. The wizard has extracted the
    caption on your test button and placed it in the table.

11. In the `Formal` column of tblFormality, in the same row as the OK entry, enter Yes.

    This determines the formal caption for the button that is informally known as OK.

12. Close the table, and save the database.

13. From the Caption Formality Level Selection Wizard form (frmFormality), select Set new captions.

    The procedure runs quickly, and your test button's caption has now changed from OK to Yes.

You have just created a functional custom add-in wizard, and it works! However, your wizard is not yet ready for prime time. Note the following rough edges:

◆ You have to manually import the formality table into any database that is to use the wizard. A production-quality custom add-in would do that automatically the first time that someone tried to use the wizard.

◆ Adding new levels of formality, such as Very Formal, Casual, or Street Lingo, requires you to edit the formality table. A production-quality custom add-in would allow adding or deleting formality levels with a form or dialog box that is reachable from the add-in's main form.

From the foregoing examples, you can see that creating a custom wizard add-in is a fairly complex undertaking. You have many opportunities to go astray, leading to barely comprehensible error messages along the way. However, once you have negotiated the steep learning curve, you will have a valuable skill. You will be able to customize Microsoft Access.

Summary

Access's extensive capabilities can be expanded even further with add-ins. Some add-ins come from Microsoft and are built into Access. It hardly seems right to call such things add-ins when they are an integral part of the product. However, they have the same structure as custom add-ins that are not a part of Access. You can create custom add-ins to help users perform tasks that may be specific to your organization or your industry. Add ins come in the form of builders and wizards. This chapter describes how to create, register, and install both builders and wizards, enabling you to upgrade Access in ways that specifically meet the needs of your users.

Part V

Developing Applications with VBA

CHAPTER 20
Developing User-Oriented Applications

CHAPTER 21
Developing Multi-User Applications

Chapter 20

Developing User-Oriented Applications

IN THIS CHAPTER

- ◆ Defining a user-oriented application
- ◆ Understanding application development concepts

SO FAR IN THIS BOOK, we have provided you with a wide variety of techniques that you can use to make your Access applications better. We have told you about the various elements of VBA and how to use them. We have covered how to write and debug VBA code. We have given examples of how to create Access objects and how to handle events. We have demonstrated how to interact with other applications. One thing we have not yet talked much about is how the application you write interacts with the user who runs it.

What Is a User-Oriented Application?

The best, most powerful, most functional, fastest-delivered, and least expensive application in the world is of little value if its intended users don't use it. If the users find your application unfamiliar, unresponsive, clunky, or cryptic, they will not use it. If they do not use it, the investment that their organization has made in it is wasted. This will not be a feather in your cap. Thus, it is important to factor in the needs, desires, and past experience of the user community when you are designing an application.

Delivering the desired functionality

Although usability is an important factor, your first priority is to deliver an application that does what it is supposed to do. This seems to be a straightforward requirement, but it is usually more complex than it seems on the surface.

Chapter 2 emphasizes the importance of the Statement of Requirements in any development effort. The purpose of this document is to assure that both the developer and all the relevant people in the client organization agree on exactly what the proposed system will do. In an ideal world, this is enough to prevent problems from miscommunication. Unfortunately, the world we live in is far from ideal.

Because your domain of expertise as an application developer probably has little in common with the domains of expertise of the various people you are developing for, each of you probably has a somewhat different interpretation of what the Statement of Requirements means. Of course, you will try your best to minimize these differences, but some will occur nonetheless. To resolve these differences to the mutual satisfaction of all involved requires you to add negotiation and diplomacy to your tool kit of skills, right alongside your technical skills in designing robust databases and applications, and in writing VBA code.

The best time to arrive at an understanding of what is going on in your client's mind, and what her expectations are, is at the beginning of the project. Take extra care to understand the following:

◆ What the client wants

◆ Why the client wants it

◆ What the client expects it to do for her

Making the application easy to use

Once you know what the application should do, and what you need to do to deliver that functionality, you need to design the user interface with your specific target audience in mind. An interface that is intuitive and logical to one user may be incomprehensible to another. This is why it is so important to know everyone who is likely to use your application and to know his or her experiences, preferences, and expectations.

LOGICAL, UNCLUTTERED USER INTERFACE

A user interface should make sense to the people who are called upon to work with it. It should be logical from *their* point of view, which may not coincide with your point of view. Pick out a typical user from the group that will use your application. Imagine that you are that person. If you were that person, what would make the most sense to you? Ask yourself this question, and then design the relevant aspects of the user interface according to how you answer that question.

Most likely, you will find several classes of users of your application: Some interact with the screen and use some subset of the controls that you place there.

Others interact with a different subset. Some users never see any of your screens but instead read your printed reports. You probably need to adjust various parts of your application's user interface to match the types of people who use those parts.

SCREENS AND CONTROLS

Each screen should be designed specifically for the audience that views it and should have the following features:

- It should contain only the displays and controls that enable the user to perform a single function or a tightly connected group of related functions.

- No extraneous material should distract the user from the primary task.

- Even closely related items should be distributed across multiple screens if there are more than five or six items.

TIP Don't present a user with more than five or six different things to respond to on a single screen. It is better to use multiple screens, providing access to these things with tabs or navigation buttons.

Controls should be consistent throughout an application. One of the important drivers of the success of the Microsoft Office applications is that the controls are consistent in their appearance, function, and screen location across all the applications in the Office suite. If you can work the menus in Microsoft Word, you can quickly get up to speed in Excel, PowerPoint, or any other Office application. The applications that you write should have that same self-consistency.

TIP If the target audience for your application is already using other applications, such as Microsoft Office programs, you can considerably shorten the time they need to become proficient in your application by making your displays and controls similar to the application displays and controls that they already use. Microsoft does not discourage this kind of design reuse and even provides tools to make it easy.

REPORTS

Printed reports, if your application has them, are as much a part of the user interface of the application that you are creating as are the windows and dialog boxes on the screen. Typically, the reports are aimed at a different audience than are the screens and dialog boxes, and that difference must be taken into account. The general rule is the same: Format your reports so that their intended users can easily understand and use them.

 Often, an organization has a standard format for both internal documents and for documents that have a wider distribution. Make sure that you are aware of such conventions and adhere to them as much as possible.

If you must make innovations in the way that information is presented, be sure to relate the presentation to something that is already familiar to the people who are likely to be reading your report.

Application Development Concepts

Beyond the strictly technical details of designing a system so that all its functions are easy to understand and use by their varied intended audiences, the developer must keep in mind a larger, more strategic set of considerations. The following two questions must be asked:

- What is the immediate impact of this application on the organization for which it is designed?

- What are the long-term consequences to the organization of adopting this application?

Solving the immediate problem

Generally, no application development project is initiated unless the following perceptions exist:

- A problem exists.

- A new application can solve that problem (or at least reduce it).

Usually, the perception that a problem exists is correct, but sometimes the root cause of the problem is not properly identified. This could lead to the development of an application that masks the symptoms of the problem instead of solving the problem itself. Such an outcome is not beneficial to anyone involved. An important part of the developer's task is to determine that the solution requested by the client is indeed a solution to the real problem. If it is not, further discussions with the client are called for to assure a satisfactory result. These discussions should be documented so that in the event that the application delivered does not result in the hoped-for improvement in operations, the developer's early reservations are on the record. The developer should not be obliged to provide any additional work beyond what was originally agreed in the project's Statement of Requirements.

Taking the long view

A major database application can have an impact on an organization's operation that goes far beyond the solution of the particular problem that it was designed to solve. A major application can affect an organization's structure and even its culture. It would not be unreasonable to consider such possible impacts before embarking on a project. This is not to say that major projects should be abandoned if a risk of affecting corporate culture exists. It just means that if you are aware of the possible organizational changes that such a project may bring about, you can plan proactively to handle such situations as they arise. These concerns are more the province of the client than they are of the developer, but often clients are not aware of such impacts; the developer has seen similar situations in the past. The professional thing to do is to discuss possible scenarios early on with the client to make sure that development, phase-in, and use of the new system are a net positive for the client organization and are not disruptive.

Summary

It's not enough to create applications that are efficient and reliable, and that perform all the functions laid out in the Statement of Requirements. It is also important to understand the users in all their diversity, and to specifically target your application to them. Beyond the impact of the application on the users, you must also consider both its short term and long term impact on the users' organization. Will the application change the way people work and interact with each other? If so, will that change be detrimental? Sometimes the effect of a new way of doing things on an organization's culture does not become evident until after the cultural change has taken place. At that point, it may not be possible to return to the amicable state of affairs that prevailed before the application was installed. Think about potential cultural changes in the planning stages, when things are still fluid enough to divert into a favorable direction.

Chapter 21

Developing Multi-User Applications

IN THIS CHAPTER

◆ Using locking to prevent data errors

◆ Facing security issues

◆ Compiling for performance

◆ Encrypting a database to thwart snoopers

APPLICATIONS THAT ARE simultaneously accessed by multiple users present challenges that are nonexistent or of little concern when an application never deals with more than one user at a time. Security and reliability are much more important when applications are designed for many users.

The following two categories of problems are more serious in a multiuser system:

◆ Unauthorized people may be able to see, change, or destroy information that they should not be allowed to see, change, or destroy.

◆ Legitimate users, doing what they are authorized to do, may interfere with each other and corrupt their database in the process.

You need to protect the database against both of these very different kinds of threats. Specific remedies are available for both classes of problems. First, let's look at the more common case where legitimate users might corrupt data by interfering with each other.

Memory Access Conflicts and Locking

Often, two users make changes to the same database table at the same time. A salesperson may be adding notes to a memo field in the CUSTOMER table based on a just-completed phone contact. Simultaneously, a clerical worker may be updating the customer's memo field with information from a payment that was received yesterday. Both workers obtain a working copy of the customer's record, and each makes her own changes. What happens when they attempt to save their changes to the database? Without *concurrency control*, the first change saved is lost, and the person making that change has no way of knowing. The second saved change overwrites and obliterates the first change.

Access avoids this kind of data loss with a *locking system*. When one user locks a database object (such as a record, a page, a table, or an entire database), no other user can make changes to the locked object.

 This strategy protects database integrity, but at a cost. While an object is locked by one user, other users are denied access to it.

Granularity

Locking a database object to prevent an access conflict raises another conflict: *granularity.* To minimize the interference of one user upon another, set fine-grained locks. Locking the smallest possible object reduces the likelihood that another user will try to edit the same object at the same time.

♦ The *finest* grain lock is an individual record (record lock), also called a row lock.

♦ The *coarsest* grain lock is a *database* lock. It denies access to the entire database to everyone except the person who set the lock.

Only a database administrator (DBA) should apply a lock at the database level.

The primary types of locking that Access does support are page locking and record locking.

You know what a record is, but what is a page?

Database data is stored on a hard disk. Hard disk access times are measured in milliseconds, that is, thousandths of a second. Data that is stored in semiconductor chips is accessible with access times measured in nanoseconds, that is, billionths of a second. Clearly, if you are operating on data, performance is much better if that data is in semiconductor memory than if the data is out on a hard disk. For that reason, Access partitions data into pages of 4K bytes each. These pages are swapped into semiconductor memory from disk memory when you start working on them. Thus, on the first operation on any record on the page, access time is slow, but after that it is very fast.

Several locking schemes are employed by other database management systems. The Microsoft Access scheme is rudimentary compared to those used by more robust systems, such as Oracle or DB2. However, the Access scheme is still complicated enough to require some explaining.

Access supports the following two primary database locking types:

◆ **Single records:** Other users can edit other records on the same 4K data page. Record locks may *increase* overall database performance if multiple users will probably want to access other records on the same data page at the same time. Applying many record locks in quick succession may *reduce* performance by increasing overhead.

◆ **Pages of records:** Other users can't edit records on the same 4K page, even though the user setting the lock is not affecting the records that they want to edit. Page locking minimizes overhead because only one lock per page exists. Page locking may be preferable if multiple users will seldom want to edit records in the same page at the same time.

For any database that you maintain, you can select whether you want page locking or record locking. To do so, follow these steps:

1. **Choose Tools→Options.**

2. **In the Options dialog box, choose the Advanced tab.**

   This shows a dialog box that is similar to the one in Figure 21-1.

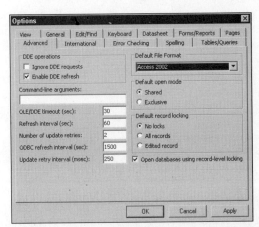

Figure 21-1: The Advanced tab of the Options dialog box.

3. **Select the locking method by either checking or clearing the Open databases using record-level locking option. Each method is described as follows:**

- For record-level locking, place a check mark in the box for this option. When a database is created, this box is checked by default.
- For page-level locking, clear the check box.

 For safety's sake, in a multiuser environment, only change records within a transaction. Begin a transaction with the `BeginTrans` method and end it with either the `CommitTrans` method (if your update was successful) or the `Rollback` method (if your update was not successful). This enhances performance and eliminates some of the dangers of user conflicts.

Optimistic locking or pessimistic locking?

I (AGT) try to be an optimist about everything. I think it is just a better way to live. It is certainly a more enjoyable way to live. However, when it comes to locking, sometimes it is better to be a pessimist. To understand the difference between optimistic locking and pessimistic locking, you need to think about how changes are made to a database.

Suppose that you want to edit a record in a table. You can edit it directly in datasheet view, using a form, or directly with an SQL UPDATE statement. The optimistic view of the situation is to assume that everything will be fine, that is, that no other user will edit that same record at the same time. In such situations, you would specify optimistic locking. When optimistic locking is in effect, the record (or page) that you are editing is not locked until you save it. After the save is completed, the lock comes off. Thus, the lock is in place for the minimum amount of time, and your interference with other users is minimized. This is clearly a desirable state of affairs. However, what if your assumption is wrong?

What if someone else is editing the same record at the same time as you are? The first one of you to save the record (perhaps it's you) succeeds, but the second user receives a run-time error when she attempts to save her work. A dialog box appears asking the second user whether she wants to save her changes, copy the changes to the clipboard, or abandon her changes. If she chooses to save her changes, they overwrite yours, and you aren't informed of this destruction of your work! Not good at all! If this kind of situation could happen in your organization, you should probably not use optimistic locking.

So what is pessimistic locking? In this case, as soon as a user starts to operate on a record, a lock is applied. The locked record or page remains locked and thus unavailable to all other users until either you save your record or abandon the edit. This guarantees that the dangerous situation that was described in the previous paragraph cannot happen, but at a cost. The record (or page) in question is locked for a much longer time. Heaven forbid that the user who has the record or page locked should take his afternoon break before completing the operation. Work in the office could come to a screeching halt for 15 or 20 minutes.

As you can see, there are benefits and dangers to both optimistic and pessimistic locking. Before specifying one or the other, carefully consider how the database in question will be used and what the chances are of two users trying to edit the same record or page at the same time. This decision is entangled with deciding whether to use record locking or page locking. If you use page locking, pessimistic locking is more likely to affect the unlucky users who do not apply the lock first.

On the Advanced tab of the Options dialog box in Figure 21-1, note the Default record locking panel. The three options are No locks, All records, and Edited record. The No locks option corresponds to optimistic locking. A record is locked only during the interval of time that it is being saved. The Edited record option corresponds to pessimistic locking. In this mode, a record is locked from the instant that it is first edited until it is saved or the edit is abandoned. The All records option locks the entire table, which could be thousands or even millions of records. Only the database administrator (DBA) should use this option and only when changing the structure of the table. When this lock is in place, no one can change anything in the table.

Exclusive versus shared locks

Another area on the Advanced tab of the Options dialog box shown in Figure 21-1 is the Default open mode panel, with Shared and Exclusive options. Shared is the default choice for this option, and with good reason. If you have a database open and select the Exclusive option here, you are commandeering exclusive access to that database. No one else can access the database until you either close your connection to the database or change the option back to Shared. An exclusive lock is the most restrictive lock available on an Access database.

A shared lock allows multiple people to access the database at the same time, but restrictions may still exist on what they can do, depending on whether optimistic, pessimistic, or All records locking is in effect.

How should you configure your locks?

The major negative aspect of pessimistic locking is that it degrades concurrency, because the locked object is unavailable to other users while the first person to acquire it is working on it. This can be significant if page locking is in effect, but it is much less important when record locking is being employed. The chance that two users would want to edit the same record at the same time is much less than the chance that two users would want to edit two records that happen to be on the same page at the same time. In general, because pessimistic locking is safer, it is a good choice on systems where record locking is in effect.

Because locking strategy affects an entire database, it should not be something that ordinary users modify. Leave locking decisions to the DBA, based on input from users and performance benchmarks.

Locking records using a form

In addition to setting locking strategy from a dialog box, you can also control locks from an application that's written with VBA. One way to do this is to set the locking options for all records that are edited using a form. Table 21-1 shows the relationships between the locking options that are available on the Advanced tab of the Options dialog box and the equivalent VBA code.

TABLE 21-1 LOCK OPTIONS AND VBA EQUIVALENTS

Option	Lock Type	VBA	Effect
No locks	Optimistic	.RecordLocks = 0	Locks only when saving
All records	Database	.RecordLocks = 1	Locks entire database
Edited record	Pessimistic	.RecordLocks = 2	Locks when an edit is started

The following is an example of applying pessimistic locking to a form in the OutlookMining database:

```
Private Sub PessimisticLocks()
    Dim frm1 As Form

    DoCmd.OpenForm "AddinTestForm"
    Set frm1 = Forms!AddinTestForm
    frm1.RecordLocks = 2
End Sub
```

This changes the default optimistic locking for the tables that are affected by the form named AddinTestForm to pessimistic locking.

Locking records in recordsets

Setting the locking behavior for a recordset is a little more involved than it is for a form. The following code creates a recordset that is based on the OLS1 MEMBERS table. The code then opens the recordset with optimistic locking. This is in contrast to the ADO default, which is read-only. As an example of a possible edit, the OfficeHeld field of the first record in the recordset is changed to Vice President, giving Bryce Thoreau an instant upgrade from Treasurer. The update is performed, and the lock is in effect only during the update operation. Finally, the recordset and the connection are closed, and the routine is ended.

```
Sub SetADORecordsetLockOptimistic()

    Dim cnxn As ADODB.Connection
    Dim rstOpt As ADODB.Recordset

    Set cnxn = CurrentProject.Connection
    Set rstOpt = New ADODB.Recordset

    ' Open a recordset with optimistic locking
    ' Default is read-only

    rstOpt.Open "MEMBERS", cnxn, adOpenKeyset, _
        adLockOptimistic, adCmdTable

    rstOpt!OfficeHeld = "Vice President"
    ' Optimistic locking locks the record only during save
    rstOpt.Update
    rstOpt.Close

    Set rstOpt = Nothing
    cnxn.Close
    Set cnxn = Nothing

End Sub
```

You can set a pessimistic lock with the `adLockPessimistic` constant in Access 2003. Earlier versions of Access do not support this when you set the connection to `CurrentProject.Connection`. You must open a new connection to set a pessimistic lock in Access 2002 and earlier versions.

Dealing with record-locking errors

When optimistic locking is in effect, the second person to attempt to save an edited database object (either a page or a record) receives a run-time error. A dialog box appears, asking the user to do one of the following three things:

- ◆ Save her changes, overwriting the changes that were made by the first user to save.

This option is very dangerous and should be used with extreme care.

◆ Save her changes to the clipboard and handle them after seeing what changes the first user has made.

This is a viable option, but only for a fairly sophisticated user.

◆ Drop her changes, refresh the record (which now includes the first user's changes), and reenter her edits.

Dropping changes can be frustrating, particularly if the changes were extensive. However, in many cases, this is the best option.

Run-time errors are also possible with pessimistic locking but are much less likely, because the "window of vulnerability" is much shorter. The chance that two people would save the same record or page at the same instant is pretty slim.

The dreaded deadlock and how to avoid it

No, deadlocks are not trendy hairstyles originating in Jamaica and other Caribbean islands. They are far more insidious. Deadlock is also known in some circles as deadly embrace. In a *deadlock* situation, two users are locked together such that neither one can make any progress. Both are frozen in place, waiting perpetually to acquire a resource that will never become available.

Here's an example of how deadlock can happen. Suppose that Susan wants to perform an operation that involves two tables, AUTHORS and PAPERS. She locks AUTHORS and then attempts to lock PAPERS. Meanwhile, Brenna, in another department, wants to perform a different operation on those two tables. Brenna locks PAPERS and attempts to lock AUTHORS. Susan cannot acquire PAPERS because Brenna has locked it. Brenna cannot acquire AUTHORS because Susan has locked it. This is a classic deadlock, and it could easily happen.

You can virtually eliminate the possibility of deadlock in Access by wrapping all your database maintenance operations in *transactions*. If the transaction does not complete successfully, you can instruct it to *roll back*. A rollback returns all the tables in the database to the state that they were in before you started and releases all the locks that you have placed. You can now retry the transaction. Chances are that the person whose operation conflicted with yours will not retry at exactly the same time that you do.

More-sophisticated database management systems than Access have *deadlock detection* and *deadlock breaking logic.* Access has neither.

Facing Security Issues

Should you be concerned about the security of your Access database? The answer is a definite maybe. Access offers an elaborate security structure that enables you to protect databases and applications in a variety of ways. These facilities add overhead to the system and add hassle to the legitimate users who must contend with them. You must ask yourself whether the increased security is worth the overhead and hassle.

Access is so common and easy to use that it is employed in applications where the data is not particularly sensitive or important. In such cases, adding security overhead may be unnecessary and may discourage use of the system. On the other hand, many applications handle sensitive data or procedures. You may want (or be required by law) to restrict access to these data and procedures. Access provides the means to do this.

Password protection

The simplest and most indiscriminate form of protection is to put a password on your database that enables only those who possess the password to open and use the database. This is great for keeping out people who have no business nosing around your database, but it does not differentiate between people who should have limited access to some of the database and people who should have complete access to all of it.

PROTECTING DATABASES

To set a password on a database, you must first have exclusive access to the database. This means that you must open the database in *exclusive mode.* Follow these steps to open the database in exclusive mode and set the password:

1. Select File→Open.

2. In the Open dialog box, select the desired database file and click the drop-down menu to the right of the Open button.

3. From the drop-down menu, select Open Exclusive, as shown in Figure 21-2.

   This gives you exclusive access to the database, which ensures that no other user can be active in the database while you are changing the password.

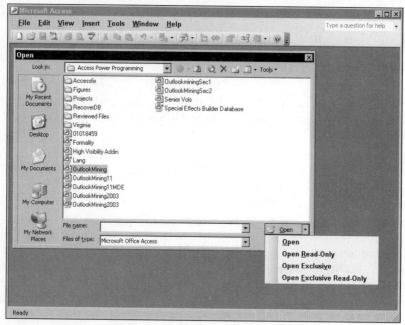

Figure 21-2: Open the database in Exclusive mode.

4. **Select Tools→Security→Set Database Password from the main menu.**

   This displays the Set Database Password dialog box, which is shown in Figure 21-3.

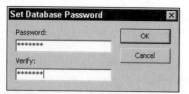

Figure 21-3: The Set Database Password dialog box.

5. **Enter the same new password in the following fields:**

   ■ Password

   ■ Verify

   The entries that you type are represented by asterisks so that anyone who is looking over your shoulder can't see what you have typed.

6. **When you are sure that you have entered the password you want in both fields, click the OK button.**

   The password changes from the default (no password) to the new password that you entered.

Remember the password. Without it, you can't access your database.

PROTECTING VBA CODE

In some cases, you may not see the need to protect your database with a password, but you may still want to keep your application code confidential. VBE provides a password protection mechanism for the code that you write with it. Follow these steps:

1. **In VBE, select Tools→<project name> Properties.**

   This displays the dialog box that is shown in Figure 21-4.

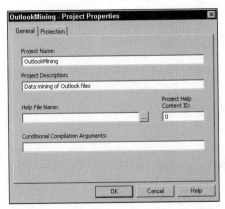

Figure 21-4: The Project Properties dialog box.

2. **Click the Protection tab, as shown in Figure 21-5.**

3. **To password-protect your code, select the Lock project for viewing check box.**

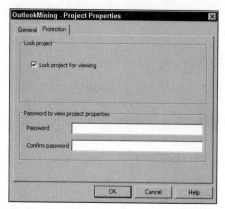

Figure 21-5: The Protection tab of the Project Properties dialog box.

 If you do not select the Lock project for viewing check box, subsequent users can read your source code but they can't open the Properties dialog box for your project.

4. Enter the same new password in the following fields:

   ■ Password

   ■ Verify

   The entries that you type are represented by asterisks so that anyone who is looking over your shoulder can't see what you have typed.

5. When you are sure that you have entered the password you want in both fields, click the OK button.

   The password changes from the default (no password) to the new password that you have entered.

   Any users who follow you must enter the password to see your VBA code.

USER-LEVEL SECURITY

A variety of people in an organization perform a variety of functions. Therefore, they require varying levels of access to database objects. You can set a group of permissions for the following:

   ◆ Individual users

   ◆ Groups of users

Maintaining permissions for a group is much easier than maintaining permissions for each member of the group separately. You can set up a workgroup for each class of user, for example, salesperson or payroll clerk. The permissions for workgroups are kept in a Workgroup Information File (WIF). You can do the following:

◆ Use the User-Level Security Wizard to create a WIF

◆ Use VBA to modify the WIF

Setting up a Workgroup Information File (WIF)

Access provides an easy step-by-step process for creating a WIF. Because this is a one-time operation for each workgroup, you don't need to use VBA.

Follow these steps to create a WIF from the Access user interface:

1. Choose Tools→Security→User-Level Security Wizard, as shown in Figure 21-6.

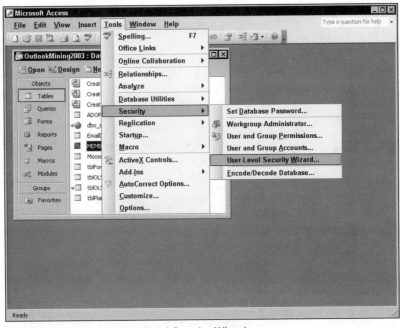

Figure 21-6: Select the User-Level Security Wizard.

2. As shown in Figure 21-7, choose to do one of the following:

■ Create a new WIF

■ Modify an existing WIF

If there is no existing WIF, the second option is unavailable.

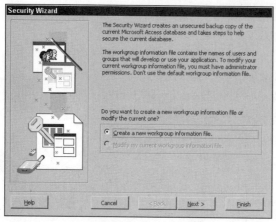

Figure 21-7: Choose to create a new WIF.

3. **Give your WIF a name, and specify whether you want it to apply to either of the following:**

   ■ All databases

   ■ The current database

   Figure 21-8 shows these choices. If you select 'I want to make this my default workgroup information file,' it will apply to all databases. If you select 'I want to create a shortcut to open my security-enhanced database,' the WIF file applies only to the current database.

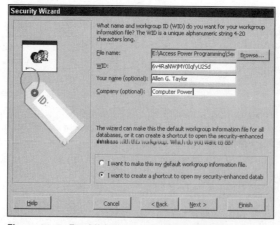

Figure 21-8: Establish the scope of the WIF.

4. Specify the database objects that you want to secure, as shown in Figure 21-9.

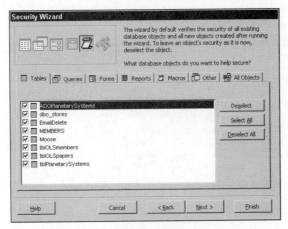

Figure 21-9: Specify the objects to secure.

5. Specify the groups that you want to include in the WIF. Check the following boxes, as appropriate:

- **Full Permissions:** A group that you are a member of can have full access to the database.

- **Lesser permission levels:** You can add users with various needs to appropriate groups.

Figure 21-10 shows that no groups are included by default.

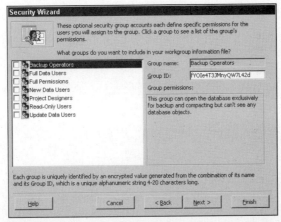

Figure 21-10: Specify the groups that are to be included in the WIF.

If you do not check any boxes here, the WIF is created without permissions and no one can access the database. If this happens, you are not totally hosed. A nonsecured backup file is created as part of the WIF creation process. You can delete the useless secure file and convert the backup file to an active database. Then you can re-create the WIF file, with appropriate permissions.

6. **In the Security Wizard, choose whether you would like to grant some permissions to the Users group, as shown in Figure 21-11.**

   Any permissions that you grant to members of the Users group are also granted to anyone who has a copy of Access and a copy of your database.

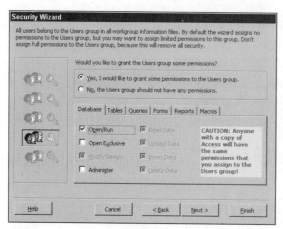

Figure 21-11: Granting permissions to members of the Users group.

The default selection is No, which is not much use. If you keep this default selection, users can't open the database.

7. **After creating groups, add users to the WIF.**

   Figure 21-12 shows the screen to add users.

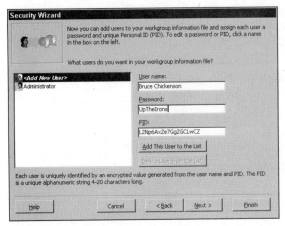

Figure 21-12: Adding a user to a WIF.

8. When the WIF contains both groups and users, assign specific users to the appropriate groups.

   Figure 21-13 shows the screen to assign users.

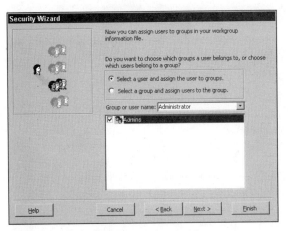

Figure 21-13: Assigning users to groups.

9. Name your backup file, as shown in Figure 21-14.

   Thankfully, Access creates an unsecured backup database before applying security to your database. If you have made a mistake in applying security, you can delete your secure database and start from scratch on the backup. You can keep doing this until you have a database with the exact level of security that you want for every potential user of the system.

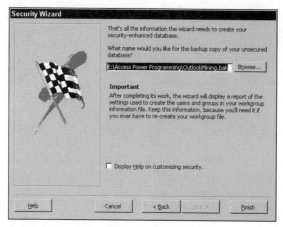

Figure 21-14: Name the backup database.

Upon finishing, the Security Wizard creates a report that provides a record of what you have done (see Figure 21-15). This may prove valuable later, if you want to change your security settings.

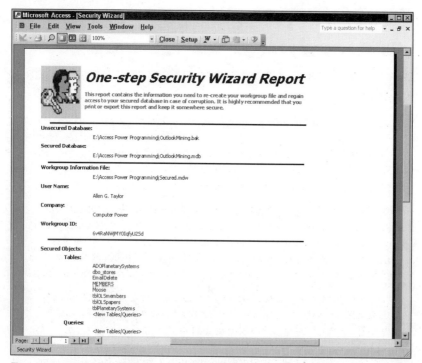

Figure 21-15: The One-step Security Wizard Report.

Compiling Code Affects Performance and Security

Basic was originally an interpreted language. What that means is that as a program was run, each instruction was translated from human-readable source code to computer-readable machine code, and then the machine code was executed. Compared to compiled languages, such as Fortran or C, this limited performance, because the translation from source code to machine code had to be done every time the program was run. Compilation, on the other hand, translates the source code to machine code once and stores it. After that, the machine code can be executed immediately. Early versions of Access were interpreted, but recent versions, using VBA, make use of compilation. You don't have to compile your applications before running them, but you can.

 TIP   In most cases, it is best not to compile an application while it is being developed and debugged. You are not in a production environment, so on-the-fly compilation is less onerous than the hassle of compiling every time you make a change to your code or to one of your forms or reports. However, you should compile before releasing the project to your users.

Why Compile VBA Code?

VBA code must be compiled to run. The question is not whether to compile; it is when to compile. When you compile an Access application, your VBA code is converted to a tokenized form called *p-code*. If you don't compile a project before executing it, Access compiles your source to p-code on the fly just before it executes it. The performance issue here is that this compilation takes time while you are running the program.

When you compile a project in advance of executing it, the source is converted into p-code, and both source code and p-code are stored on disk. Later, when you execute the program, only the p-code is loaded into memory and executed. Compiling only happens once, not every time you execute the application, and it happens at a time when performance is typically not critical (at compile time instead of at execute time).

Compiled code saves more than time. When you execute a compiled application, only the p-code code gets loaded into memory. To execute an uncompiled application requires both the source code and the p-code to be loaded into memory. This not only increases load time, but it also takes up more memory. The extra memory that is consumed may degrade overall performance because of a memory squeeze that forces virtual memory swaps to disk.

How to compile a project with VBE

Compiling a VBA project is easy. From the VBE main menu, select Debug→Compile <project name>, as shown in Figure 21-16.

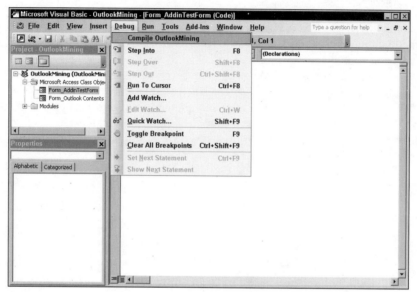

Figure 21-16: Compile a project from the Debug menu.

That's all there is to it. This sure beats the series of steps that we used to have to go through to compile a program in the old days. If you have no recollection of turning in decks of Hollerith cards at the vestibule of the "glass house," thank your lucky stars. Be glad that you live in the modern age.

Should you use the Compile On Demand option?

The answer is maybe. A typical application has multiple modules, forms, and reports. After an application is substantially finished, you may have occasion to go back into several of these modules, forms, or reports and make minor changes. If you inadvertently neglect to test all the changed objects, a compilation error may lurk in one of them.

Compile On Demand, which is the default setting in Access 2003, means that only objects that are about to be used are compiled. If you don't initially use the faulty module, form, or report, the error doesn't appear. The benefit of Compile On Demand is that it shortens compile time, because only the objects that you actually use are compiled. This benefit is offset by the fact that you cannot be sure that your application is free of compile errors.

It may be best to turn off the Compile On Demand option. To do so, select Tools→Options→General from the main menu. This displays the dialog box that is shown in Figure 21-17.

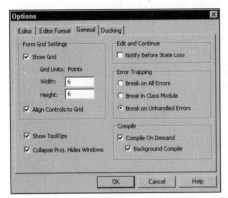

Figure 21-17: The General tab of the Options dialog box.

Uncheck the Compile On Demand option in the Compile panel. Compilations may take a little longer, but if compile errors exist in your code, you know right away and can fix them while you remember what you did to cause them.

Now that we have made a case for turning off Compile On Demand, we make a case for leaving it on, thanks to the Background Compile option.

Using the Background Compile option

In the Compile panel, Background Compile is also checked by default (see Figure 21-17). If you elect to leave Compile On Demand in effect, when the Background Compile option is active, Access takes advantage of idle time by compiling your application in the background. Background Compile is not available if Compile On Demand is not in effect. By compiling all the objects that you are using when you use them, and compiling all the rest during idle time, when your computer is doing little processing, Access attempts to optimize overall performance. Depending on the application, it may be best to leave both Compile On Demand and Background Compile checked. Application size is probably the biggest determinant here. You may want to run tests of both options and choose the one that gives the best overall performance.

Decompiling and recompiling

Decompiling is the reverse of compiling. It is the translation of machine code into human-readable source code. Access does not actually decompile machine code into source code, but it seems like it does. When you compile a VBA application, both the uncompiled source code and the compiled p-code are stored on disk. When you run the compiled application, the p-code is interpreted into machine code, which is executed. At some later time, if you edit module code or a form or report, that object is flagged as being "dirty," meaning that it has been modified and the compiled version is no longer valid. Only the uncompiled version is left. The next time that you execute the application, any dirty objects are compiled on the fly before being executed.

After modifying any object in a compiled application, you should recompile the changed object by recompiling the project.

MDE files

Users have an amazing ability to use applications in a manner that you never anticipated. In so doing, they get themselves into trouble, and of course, the developer is blamed for the problem. Try as you might to make the application as foolproof as possible, someone will find a way to use it incorrectly.

Users can *really* cause serious problems if they change the VBA code in your modules or modify your forms or reports. In an ordinary .mdb file, you can't prevent users from making such modifications. If you cannot completely protect your users from themselves, at least you can prevent the major disasters that may follow from ill-conceived modifications to VBA source code, forms, or reports. You can do this by creating and distributing an .mde file, instead of an .mdb file.

A compiled .mdb file contains both the VBA source code and the compiled p-code, while an .mde file contains only the p-code. Users who are running your application are not able to modify or even look at your source code, because they don't have it. This not only protects your application from damaging modification, but it also prevents users from seeing how you have implemented the functions that they are using. This can prevent users from reverse-engineering your application.

Saving an Access application to an .mde file is easy once you meet all the conditions. Unfortunately, quite a few conditions must be met. These are described as follows:

◆ The .mdb file that you want to convert must be in the same format as the copy of Access that you are using.

For example, Access 2003 doesn't convert an .mdb file that is in Access 2000 format. You must convert the .mdb file to Access 2003 format first and then create the .mde file. This has the disadvantage that the file isn't readable on Access 2000 and Access 97 machines.

◆ You must have password access to the VBA code.

◆ If your database is replicated, you must remove all the replication system tables before you can create an .mde file.

◆ If your database references another database or an add-in, the referenced database or add-in must be created as `.mde` files before you can create the referencing database as an `.mde` file.

◆ You must have exclusive access to the database before you can create an `.mde` file from it.

After you meet all of these conditions, you can create an `.mde` file by selecting Tools→Database Utilities→Make MDE File from the Access main menu, as shown in Figure 21-18.

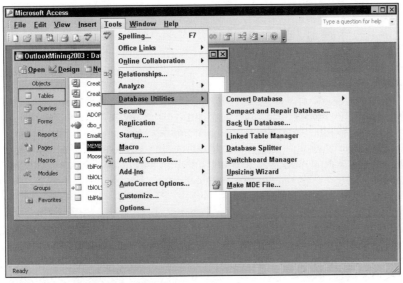

Figure 21-18: Making an `.mde` file.

If you have met all the preceding conditions, that is all there is to it. Access asks you for a name and location for the new file, and when you supply this information, it creates the new file. The old `.mdb` file is retained undisturbed.

TIP   Hang onto your `.mdb` file, even if you are sure that the `.mde` file is perfect. You may have to change something later. The `.mde` file cannot be changed, but you can change your original `.mdb` file and then create a new `.mde` file from it.

After you create an .mde file, if you attempt to open a code module with VBE, you see the brief dialog box that is shown in Figure 21-19.

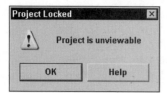

Figure 21-19: What you see when you try to look into an .mde code module.

Encrypting a Database

Although putting your application into an .mde file protects your code from prying eyes and dancing fingers, and password-protecting your data restricts access to people who possess the password, your data is still vulnerable to a very unsophisticated attack. All a person has to do is open your database in a simple text editor, such as Notepad, to see the data that is in it. The reader will see a lot of unreadable garbage, but nestled within the garbage is the data that you have saved, which may be confidential. Figure 21-20 shows an example.

Figure 21-20: The text editor view of part of the OutlookMining database.

Figure 21-20 shows the contact information for an officer of the Oregon Lunar Society, which is perhaps something that should be kept confidential. To maintain confidentiality, you can encrypt your database so that it *all* looks like garbage when viewed with a text editor. To encrypt a database, choose Tools→Security › Encode/Decode Database from the Access main menu, as shown in Figure 21-21. Access asks you for a name and location for the encoded database and then saves it in encoded form. Keep the unencoded version in a safe place where unauthorized people never have physical access to it.

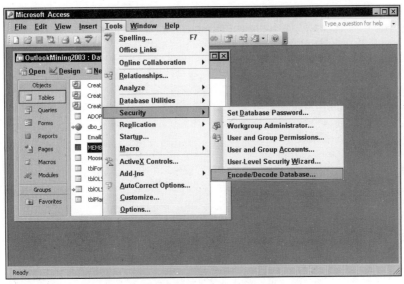

Figure 21-21: Create an encoded version of your database.

Backing Up an Access Database

It's always a good idea to retain backup copies of any computer code or data that is important to you. Stuff happens. Files get corrupted. You don't want anything bad to happen to your only copy of important work.

Make multiple copies of things and remove them from your computer. In fact, send the copies *off-site,* as follows:

◆ If you are part of a large organization, many vendors can offer secure storage for your database copy (and other essential corporate documents).

◆ A small business can store copies of essential records, such as databases, in a safe-deposit box where you bank.

If you have backup copies, it is a minor inconvenience if your working copies are damaged or destroyed, not a major disaster.

Enough said.

Summary

When a database application can be simultaneously accessed by multiple users, a number of database integrity and security concerns arise which are not issues when only one user at a time is active. To address these concerns, Access provides several tools. The problem of database corruption due to simultaneous access of the same data by different users is addressed by a locking scheme. The locking scheme itself can cause problems, such as deadlock, if not used properly. Deciding how best to set up the locking of a system is complicated and best left to an expert such as an organization's database administrator.

Security is a major concern for organizations of all sizes and types. Access provides password protection of both Access database files and of VBA programs. In addition, you can encrypt both databases and VBA programs to keep unauthorized personnel from appropriating their secrets.

Performance of an application system depends on whether code is left in interpreted form at runtime or compiled. Compilation ahead of runtime provides additional security by preventing application modification in the field.

Multiuser operation raises serious concerns, but Access addresses them all in a satisfactory manner.

Part VI

Other Important Topics

CHAPTER 22
Compatibility Issues

Chapter 22

Compatibility Issues

IN THIS CHAPTER

♦ Defining compatibility

♦ Understanding compatibility problems

♦ Dealing with Access versions and compatibility

♦ Understanding how new features affect compatibility

IN THE WILLAMETTE VALLEY in western Oregon, a popular saying is, "If you don't like the weather, just wait 5 minutes. It'll change." That saying is an exaggeration, but there is a kernel of truth to it. If anything competes with Oregon weather for frequency of change, it is computer software. New releases of Microsoft Windows and Microsoft Office are practically annual affairs. If one hasn't changed recently, the other has.

By and large, these changes are all for the good. Usually, significant improvements in the latest release make the upgrade worthwhile. Along with the improvements, however, problems are also a part of the package. Because the new version is "improved," it may not work exactly as the older version did when applied to the same data. Your existing data is now considered *legacy data*, and it is looked upon somewhat askance by software vendors. Microsoft Access, like other members of the Microsoft Office Suite, is a full participant in the upgrade merry-go-round. There will never be an "ultimate" version of Access that does everything that everyone could possibly want it to do. Thus, issues will always exist about whether an application that worked fine before the latest upgrade will still work after it is installed. Another issue arises when different computers in an organization are running different versions of Access. Will they be able to share files? Maybe — and maybe not.

What is Compatibility?

According to Webster's New World Dictionary, two people are compatible if they are capable of living together harmoniously or if they get along well together. Two things are compatible if they can be mixed without adverse effects. When it comes to the relationship between a database management system (DBMS) and a database, compatibility means that the DBMS can use the data without problems. In this context, incompatibilities can arise in several ways. We discuss these incompatibilities in the following sections.

Types of Compatibility Problems

Every DBMS has its own proprietary format for database files. This leads to the first kind of incompatibility. Oracle cannot operate on IBM DB2 files, and neither of those can operate on Access files. Access cannot handle Oracle or DB2 files either. Microsoft Access .mdb files are not usable by Microsoft SQL Server (although .adp files are usable). Often, translations are possible from one database format to another, but making such a translation is an extra operation and is not always error-free. One solution to this kind of compatibility problem is XML, which we discuss later in this chapter.

Although you may expect compatibility problems between two dissimilar database management systems, it probably seems reasonable to expect any Access file that you may have to be compatible with the copy of Access that you have installed on your computer. Such compatibility is not assured. Because multiple versions of Access, released over a decade, exist, databases and applications that were created with those various versions may not work with versions other than the one that created them.

It is probably unreasonable to expect any DBMS vendor to continue to support every version of its DBMS that has ever existed. Some vendors are more conscientious than others in supporting past versions. Microsoft is pretty good in this regard, continuing to support the Access 97 file format as well as the Access 2000 and Access 2002 formats after the introduction of Access 2003. However, that does not mean that no compatibility issues will crop up among the supported versions of Access.

Compatibility across Access Versions

Access has come a long way since Access 1.0. Microsoft no longer supports Access 1.0, Access 2.0, and Access 95. If you have database applications that were written with any of those products, you may have trouble using them with Access 2003. You may even have a problem mixing any version with any other version. We now look at the major dividing lines between versions and the types of problems that may arise.

Naturally, it is a goal of Microsoft to maintain backward compatibility between a new version of Access and all previous versions. Customers have major investments in databases and applications that were written with those earlier versions. However, the addition of new functionality sometimes comes at the expense of reduced backward compatibility. Other times, a bug in the new version breaks backward compatibility but isn't discovered until it is too late to fix. New applications may have already been written that rely on the buggy code remaining the way it is.

Versions prior to Access 97

In general, compatibility is not much of an issue among Access 1.0, Access 2.0, and Access 95. The DAO 3.0 Object Library that was released with Access 95 includes methods and properties that replace those in earlier versions. However, Access 95 still runs all code that was written to the earlier versions, providing that you reference the DAO 2.5/3.0 Compatibility Library. This happy situation is small comfort to most people, because the capabilities of Access 95 are so far surpassed by later versions that upgrading beyond Access 95 is virtually mandatory.

Access 97

Substantial differences exist between Access 97 and all previous versions of Access. Microsoft provides a migration path from those earlier versions to Access 97 that works for most people. However, problems can arise in certain situations.

CONVERTING A DATABASE TO ACCESS 97 FORMAT

The preferred solution is to *convert* databases and code that were created in earlier versions to Access 97 databases and code. This is an automatic procedure that you can select from the Access 97 main menu. The main problem with this approach is that once you convert a database to Access 97 format, you cannot open it in earlier versions of Access. This can be a problem if multiple users on a network want to access the database but they have not all upgraded to Access 97.

The conversion to Access 97 operation may not be perfect, depending on which functions the legacy database has used. A number of incompatibilities are not handled by the automatic conversion routine. In such cases, manual adjustments may need to be made to the converted database and accompanying code. The following are a few examples of potential problem areas:

- Intrinsic constants in Access 95 and 97 differ from those in Access 2.0. The older constants still work in Access 97, but their functionality in future versions is not assured, so they should probably be changed.

- Windows 95 OLE Automation code may need to be changed if it references an obsolete version of an Office product.

- Code that was created by wizards in Access 2.0 and Access 95 may need to be changed if it references functions that are replaced by newer versions.

- The `DoCmd` statement in Access 2.0 is replaced by the `DoCmd` object in Access 95 and later versions, with a corresponding difference in the syntax that is used with it.

- ◆ Changes to the menu structure in Access 97 may cause `SendKeys` statements to fail.

- ◆ New reserved words in Access 97 may conflict with module names in legacy applications.

- ◆ Error codes in Access 97 differ, in some cases, from the codes for the same errors in earlier versions. This causes error traps that refer to specific error codes to fail.

- ◆ Databases that include many forms, reports, or modules increase dramatically in size when converted to Access 97.

The preceding list is just a sampling of the many potential problems in converting a database that was created with Access 95 or an earlier version to Access 97 or a later version. In extreme cases, it may be easier to re-create the code modules of an application instead of trying to fix the converted modules. Usually, the adjustments that you must make to a converted database are minor.

 Before converting a database, or performing any structural modification to one, back it up. If the conversion does not succeed, you can restore your system from the backup and be no worse than you were before attempting the conversion.

ENABLING A LEGACY DATABASE TO RUN UNDER ACCESS 97

One alternative to converting a database that was created by an earlier version of Access is to enable it in Access 97. To *enable* a database that was created with an earlier version of Access is to run the database in Access 97 without converting it. An enabled database can be opened and used in Access 97, but you cannot change the design of the database or use any of the new features of Access 97 that were not available in the version of Access that originally created the database.

Enabling a legacy database, rather than converting, it makes sense on a network where multiple computers are accessing a single database. If only some of those computers are updated to Access 97, all users can continue to use the enabled database. This would not be the case if the database were converted to Access 97 format.

SPLITTING A LEGACY DATABASE TO RUN UNDER ACCESS 97

You have a second alternative to converting a database when different users are running different versions of Access. You can split an Access `.mdb` file into two files: one containing the tables and the other containing the queries, forms, reports, macros, modules, and shortcuts to data access pages. Leave the back-end database, containing the tables, at the lowest version that any of the users is running, but convert each front-end database, containing all the other database objects, to the version that is current for each user. In this way, users of newer versions can take advantage of the features of their newer versions, while users of older versions can still access the database as they were previously able to do. Using this technique, users could be updated to newer versions of Access at convenient times instead of requiring everyone to update at the same time.

To split an Access database, select Tools→Database Utilities→Database Splitter. The Database Splitter Wizard dialog box leads you step by step through the procedure of separating the data from the other objects that are in an application.

Access 2000

When considering the compatibility between Access 2000 and previous versions of Access, your options are much the same as we discussed in the previous section about Access 97. The difference between Access 2000 and Access 97 is not as major as the difference between Access 97 and Access 95, but compatibility is an issue nonetheless. You can convert an Access 97 database to Access 2000 format, and because of the relative closeness of the two versions, you can also convert an Access 2000 database to Access 97 format. This is helpful if you upgrade from Access 97 to Access 2000, convert your database, and then decide that the upgrade was a bad idea and that you should have stayed with Access 97.

 After you convert a database to Access 2000 format, you can't open it with an earlier version of Access.

 Before converting a database, or performing any structural modification to one, back it up. If the conversion does not succeed, you can restore your system from the backup and be no worse than you were before the conversion.

Access 2000 does not support the DAO 2.5/3.x Compatibility Library. If you try to convert an Access database that contains older versions of DAO objects, methods, or properties that depend on the DAO 2.5/3.x Compatibility Library, you receive compilation errors. To overcome this problem, before converting, remove all references to objects, methods, or properties that depend on the DAO 2.5/3.x Compatibility Library from your code. After a successful conversion, you can add back newer equivalents of the things that you removed.

If your database uses add-ins or library databases that were created with an earlier version of Access, you must convert them, too.

ENABLING A LEGACY DATABASE TO RUN UNDER ACCESS 2000

You can enable Access 2000 to operate on a database in Access 97, Access 95, or Access 2.0 format instead of converting it. You can add, delete, and modify the data in the database's tables, but you can't change the database's structure or its security settings. To maintain full security, you should convert the database instead of enabling it.

You cannot link or import an Access 2000 database into a database that was created with an earlier version of Access.

Whenever you enable a database, it increases in size because the Visual Basic project must store information in the format of each version. This can be a problem if you enable an Access 2.0 database into Access 95, enable it again into Access 97, and enable it again into Access 2000. Don't even think about enabling it another time into Access 2002 and then Access 2003!

Access 2000 does not support the DAO 2.5/3.x Compatibility Library. If you attempt to enable a database containing older versions of DAO objects, methods, or properties, the enable operation fails.

SPLITTING A LEGACY DATABASE TO RUN UNDER ACCESS 2000

With Access 2000 you can split a legacy Access database as we described in the preceding Access 97 section on splitting a legacy database, allowing users operating with different versions of Access to use the database. By converting only the front-end parts, where appropriate, everyone can continue working with the version that they have installed.

A BUG IN ACCESS 2000

Automation clients that were written in Access 97 may have problems when run under Access 2000, 2002, or 2003. In Access 2000, both the `Report` and `Form` objects have new properties or methods that were inserted in the middle of their interfaces. This causes the binary layout of each object's vtable (virtual function table) to be changed, while the interface identifiers were unchanged. The vtable is a table of pointers to the interface identifiers. Thus, some interface identifiers in Access 2000 do not match those in previous versions. Clients written in earlier versions that use early binding can expect calls to these objects to fail, because the methods that they intended to call are not the ones that they will retrieve. The recommended workaround for this problem is to use late binding instead of early binding.

Access 2002

If you add code to one of the new events in Access 2002 and then try to compile the database in Access 2000, the compile fails. The only solution to this problem is to refrain from compiling such code in Access 2000. You can add or edit such code in Access 2000 as long as you don't compile it there. Compile code that contains events that are new in Access 2002 or a later version.

Access 2003

The comments that we made earlier about converting, enabling, and splitting apply equally well to Access 2003. Just remember to back up your database before attempting to convert or split it.

Should You Avoid Using New Features?

Because compatibility problems are usually caused by new features that are introduced in a version of Access, one may wonder if it is best to avoid using such new features to reduce the possibility of having compatibility problems. The answer to that question depends on several factors.

The first factor is whether, when you upgrade to a new version of Access, you will still have some systems in your organization that are running an older version of Access. If you don't have any such systems, you have no reason not to use the new features that are offered by the latest version. Compatibility is not an issue because you have nothing to remain compatible with. However, if you have a mixed facility, with several versions of Access in use, you must decide whether the applications that you are creating on the latest version will ever need to run on one of the older versions. If the answer to that question is yes, you should consider foregoing the new features.

A second, and perhaps more important, factor is whether you really need the new features of the newer version of Access. If a new capability makes your job significantly easier or if it delivers functionality that is required but that is unavailable without the new feature, you may decide to use the new feature and handle any compatibility problems that may arise later. This is a judgment call.

XML

Probably the most significant new feature of Office 2003 is its support of XML. XML can transfer data from any member of the Office 2003 Suite to any other. From Access 2003, you can export any database object, such as a table, form, or report in XML format. It can then be imported into other suite members, such as Excel and Word. This new level of interoperability among Office Suite members greatly eases the task of moving data from one application to another.

XML relates to Access 2003 in that Access can export database objects in XML format as well as a number of other formats that are supported by previous versions of Access. Access 2003 can also import XML files, as long as they are in the element/nested element format. (See Chapter 18 for details.) Because the XML code is always external to the database itself, you have no reason not to use XML if it is to your advantage to do so. You can't import the XML files into earlier versions of Access that do not support XML. If people in your organization are still using such earlier versions, you can export, just for them, in a format that they can handle, such as the normal Access format.

Smart Tags

Smart Tags, introduced in Office XP in applications other than Access, provide a quick and easy link from an Office application such as Word or Excel to information that is external to the application, on the Web, for example. With Office 2003, an enhanced version of Smart Tags is available in Access. Users of Access applications that you create can quickly and easily display information from a variety of sources. You can use existing Smart Tags that were created by Microsoft and numerous third-party sources, or you can build your own Smart Tags to provide access to the exact information that you want, from forms or data access pages in your application. To demonstrate Smart Tags, we add one to a text box in a form in one of our databases. Figure 22-1 shows the form.

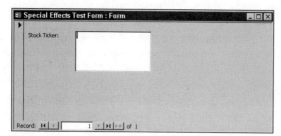

Figure 22-1: The form with a text box.

We have labeled the field Stock Ticker because we are going to use one of the Smart Tags that comes with Access 2003. The tag displays financial information about any exchange-listed stock in a browser window after you enter a ticker symbol. Follow these steps to add the Stock Ticker Smart Tag to the text box:

1. **Right-click in the text box, and select Properties from the pop-up menu that appears.**

   The Properties dialog box that is shown in Figure 22-2 appears.

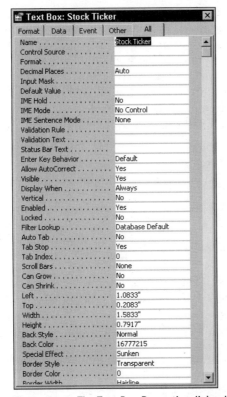

Figure 22-2: The Text Box Properties dialog box.

2. **Select the Smart Tags property from the Data tab.**

   A Build button (...) appears at the right of the data-entry field.

3. **Click the Build button.**

   This displays the Smart Tags dialog box that is shown in Figure 22-3.

4. **Select Financial Symbol, and click the OK button.**

   This fills in the Smart Tags field of the text box's Properties dialog box with the Uniform Resource Name (URN) of the data source that the Smart Tag links to.

   Now, when you type in a stock ticker symbol, such as MSFT, into the text box, a Smart Tag icon appears to the lower right of the text box, as shown in Figure 22-4.

Figure 22-3: The Smart Tags dialog box.

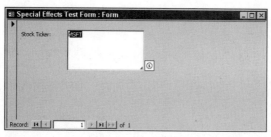

Figure 22-4: The Smart Tag icon appears to the right of the text box.

5. Click the Smart Tag icon to display the menu that is shown in Figure 22-5.

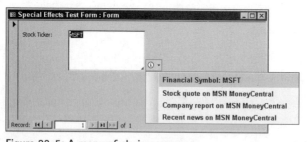

Figure 22-5: A menu of choices appears.

6. Select one of the options on the menu, for example, Stock quote on MSN MoneyCentral.

   Figure 22-6 shows an example of what appears.

7. Type in a different stock ticker symbol to display another quote.

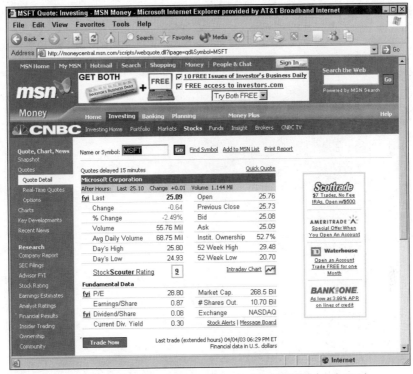

Figure 22-6: The Browser view of the stock quote from MSN MoneyCentral.

In addition to the several Smart Tags that are preinstalled with Access 2003, you can install more. Many are available. To see them, click the More Smart Tags button in the lower-left corner of the Smart Tags dialog box. The Smart Tags feature in Access 2003 is significantly enhanced compared to the one in Access 2002. The enhancements are primarily aimed at increasing flexibility for the developer. In any case, Access 2002 does not support Smart Tags.

So, should you use this cool new feature of Access 2003? If you are creating a database for systems that have Access 2002 or earlier, Smart Tags don't work on those systems. If all your users have at least Access 2003, you can deliver some fancy functionality to them with Smart Tags.

Summary

Considering the frequency with which Access is updated, backward compatibility concerns everyone. If you develop an application with one version of Access, then upgrade to a newer version, your existing application may not run in the new environment. Be sure to consider such compatibility problems *before* you upgrade to a new version. Microsoft will try to encourage you, or even, through discontinuing support for older versions, coerce you to upgrade. Be sure you know what effect upgrading will have on your existing applications before you make a massive switchover. These caveats are especially important if multiple versions of Access are running in your organization.

Part VII

Appendixes

Appendix A

Helpful Web Links

THE FOLLOWING ARE WEB links to sources of information about Microsoft Access and VBA. A wealth of information is available on the official Microsoft sites. You can also find considerable resources at non-Microsoft sites.

- ◆ Microsoft Office Tools on the Web: `http://office.microsoft.com/default.aspx`

  This is Microsoft's main support page for Microsoft Office. It is loaded with links to sites for Access and the other Office applications.

- ◆ Microsoft Developer Network (MSDN) Access page: `http://msdn.microsoft.com/library/default.asp?url=/nhp/default.asp?contentid=28000550`

  This is Microsoft's Office page on the MSDN site. The Microsoft Developers Network is the primary source of technical information about Microsoft products.

- ◆ Microsoft Access Home Page: `www.microsoft.com/office/access/default.asp`

  This is the main Access page on Microsoft's Web site. It's a good starting point for information and links.

- ◆ Tony's Main Microsoft Access Page: `www.granite.ab.ca/accsmstr.htm`

  This independent Web site, maintained by Tony Toews, contains a wealth of tips, downloads, links, and other useful information.

- ◆ The Access Web: `www.mvps.org/access/`

  The Access Web is a popular site, with many frequently asked questions and answers.

- ◆ A basic Access tutorial: `http://cisnet.baruch.cuny.edu/holowczak/classes/2200/access/accessall.html`

  This is Professor Holowczak's tutorial on using Access without programming.

- ◆ The Microsoft Access Compendium: `www.cyber-matrix.com/access.htm`

  This site has links to a variety of sites that are resources for Access knowledge.

◆ Another basic Access tutorial:
`www.fgcu.edu/support/office2000/access/`

A university-based tutorial on Access without VBA.

◆ Access VBA coding forum: `www.tek-tips.com/threadminder.`
`cfm?spid=705&newpid=705`

This is a forum that you can join, where you can get your questions
answered by experts who have already "been there and done that." After
a while, you could become one of the experts yourself!

Appendix B

VBA Statements and Functions

THIS APPENDIX CONTAINS A complete listing of all VBA statements and built-in functions. For details, consult Access's online help.

TABLE B-1 SUMMARY OF VBA STATEMENTS

Statement	Action
AppActivate	Activates an application window
Beep	Sounds a tone using the computer's speaker
Call	Transfers control to another procedure
ChDir	Changes the default directory
ChDrive	Changes the current drive
Close	Closes all open files or the selected file
Const	Declares a value as a constant
Date	Sets the current system date
Declare	Declares a reference to an external procedure in a DLL
DefBool	Sets the default data type to Boolean for variables that begin with specified letters
DefByte	Sets the default data type to byte for variables that begin with a specified letter
DefDate	Sets the default data type to date for variables that begin with a specified letter
DefDec	Sets the default data type to decimal for variables that begin with a specified letter

Continued

TABLE B-1 SUMMARY OF VBA STATEMENTS *(Continued)*

Statement	Action
DefDouble	Sets the default data type to double for variables that begin with a specified letter
DefInt	Sets the default data type to integer for variables that begin with a specified letter
DefLng	Sets the default data type to long for variables that begin with a specified letter
DefObj	Sets the default data type to object for variables that begin with a specified letter
DefSng	Sets the default data type to single for variables that begin with a specified letter
DefStr	Sets the default data type to string for variables that begin with a specified letter
DefVar	Sets the default data type to variant for variables that begin with a specified letter
DeleteSetting	Deletes a section or key setting from an application's entry in the Windows registry
Dim	Declares a variable
Do-Loop	Cycles through a loop until a specified condition is met
End	Used by itself, exits the program. End is also used to end a block of statements that begin with If, With, Sub, Function, Property, Type, and Select.
Erase	Clears current contents of an array
Error	Simulates a specific error condition
Event	Creates a user-defined event
Exit Do	Exits a block of Do-Loop code
Exit For	Exits a block of Do-For code
Exit Function	Exits a function procedure
Exit Property	Exits a property procedure
Exit Sub	Exits a subroutine procedure

Statement	Action
FileCopy	Copies a file
For Each-Next	Cycles through a collection of objects or items in an array
For-Next	Loops until the necessary value is reached
Function	Declares the name and arguments for a function procedure
Get	Retrieves information from an open file and places it in a variable
GetAllSettings	Returns a list of key settings and their respective values
Get Attributes	Returns an Integer representing the attributes of a file, directory, or folder
Get Object	Returns a reference to an object provided by an ActiveX component
GetSetting	Returns a key setting value from an application's entry in the Windows registry
GoSub...Return	Branches to a piece of code within a subroutine or function
GoTo	Branches to out-of-sequence set of code
If-Then-Else	Processes statements conditionally
Implements*	Specifies an interface or class that will be implemented in a class module
Input #	Reads data from a sequential input or binary file
Kill	Deletes a file from a disk
Let	Assigns the value of an expression to a variable or property
Line Input #	Reads a line of data from a sequential text file
Load	Loads an object but doesn't show it
Lock...Unlock	Controls access to parts of the current file or other process
LSet	Left-aligns a string within a string variable
Mid	Replaces characters in a string with other characters
MkDir	Creates a new directory or folder
Name	Renames a file, directory, or folder

Continued

TABLE B-1 SUMMARY OF VBA STATEMENTS *(Continued)*

Statement	Action
On Error	Branches on an error
On...GoSub	Jumps to subroutine based on value of numeric index
On...GoTo	Branches execution to a subroutine
Open	Opens a file for reading or writing
Option Base	Sets default lower limits for arrays
Option Compare	Sets the default comparison mode when comparing strings
Option Explicit	Forces declaration of all variables in a module
Option Private	Indicates that an entire module is private
Print #	Writes data to a sequential file
Private	Declares a local array or variable private to form module or routine
Property Get	Declares the name and arguments of a property retrieval routine
Property Let	Declares the name and arguments of a property definition routine
Property Set	Declares a property reference routine
Public	Declares a public array or variable
Put	Writes a variable to a current file
RaiseEvent	Fires a user-defined event
Randomize	Initializes the random number generator
ReDim	Changes the dimensions of an array
Rem	Specifies a line of comments (same as an apostrophe ['])
Reset	Closes all disk files opened with the open statement
Resume	Resumes execution when an error-handling routine finishes
RmDir	Removes an existing directory or folder
RSet	Right-aligns a string within a string variable
SaveSetting	Saves or creates an application entry in the Windows registry
Seek	Returns the current read/write position of an open file

Statement	Action
Select Case	Processes statements conditionally
SendKeys	Sends one or more keystrokes to the active window
Set	Assigns an object reference to a variable or property
SetAttr	Sets attribute information for a file
Static	Makes a variable persistent after procedure ends
Stop	Pauses the program
Sub	Declares the name and arguments of a sub procedure
Time	Sets the system time
Type	Defines a custom variable type
Unload	Removes an object from memory
While...Wend	Cycles through a loop
Width #	Sets the output line width of a text file
With	Sets a series of properties for an object
Write #	Writes data to a specified open file

TABLE B-2 SUMMARY OF VBA FUNCTIONS

Function	Action
Abs	Returns the absolute value of a number
Asc	Returns the first character of a string to its ASCII value
Atn	Returns the arctangent of an angle
CallByName	Executes a method, or sets or returns a property of an object
Cbool	Converts an expression to a Boolean data type
Cbyte	Converts an expression to a byte data type
Ccur	Converts an expression to a currency data type
Cdate	Converts an expression to a date data type

Continued

TABLE B-2 SUMMARY OF VBA FUNCTIONS *(Continued)*

Function	Action
CDbl	Converts an expression to a double data type
CDec	Converts an expression to a decimal data type
Choose	Selects and returns a value from a list of arguments
Chr	Converts a character code to a string
CInt	Converts an expression to an integer data type
CLng	Converts an expression to a long data type
Command	Returns the argument portion of the command line
Cos	Returns the cosine of an angle
CreateObject	Creates and returns a reference to an ActiveX object
CSng	Converts an expression to a single data type
CStr	Converts an expression to a string data type
CurDir	Returns the current path
Cvar	Converts an expression to a variant data type
CVDate	Converts an expression to a date data type (for compatibility, not recommended)
CVErr	Returns a user-defined error value that corresponds to an error number
Date	Returns the current system date
DateAdd	Adds a time interval to a date
DateDiff	Returns the time interval between two dates
DatePart	Returns a specified part of a date
DateSerial	Returns the date for a specified year, month, and day
DateValue	Converts a string date to a date value
Day	Returns the numeric day of the month of a date
DDB	Returns the depreciation of an asset
Dir	Returns the name of a file, directory, or folder that matches a pattern

Function	Action
DoEvents	Yields execution so the operating system can process other events
Environ	Returns an operating environment string
EOF	Returns True if the end of a text file has been reached
Err	Returns the error message that corresponds to an error number
Error	Returns the error message that corresponds to an error number
Exp	Returns the base of the natural logarithms (e) raised to a power
FileAttr	Returns the file mode used to open a file
FileDateTime	Returns the date and time when a file was last created or modified
FileLen	Returns the number of bytes in a file that is not open
Filter	Returns a subset of a string array, filtered
Fix	Returns the integer portion of a number
Format	Displays an expression in a particular format
FormatCurrency	Returns an expression formatted with the system currency symbol
FormatDateTime	Returns an expression formatted as a date or time
FormatNumber	Returns an expression formatted as a number
FormatPercent	Returns an expression formatted as a percentage
FreeFile	Returns the next available file number when working with text files
FV	Returns the future value of an annuity
GetAllSettings	Returns a list of settings and values from the Windows registry
GetAttr	Returns a code representing a file's attributes
GetObject	Returns a reference to an object provided by an ActiveX environment
GetSetting	Returns a specific setting from the application's entry in the Windows registry
Hex	Returns a string equivalent to the hexadecimal value of a number
Hour	Returns the hour of the day
IIf	Evaluates an expression and returns one of two parts

Continued

TABLE B-2 SUMMARY OF VBA FUNCTIONS *(Continued)*

Function	Action
InputBox	Displays a dialog box to prompt a user for input
InStr	Returns the position of a string within another string
InStrRev	Returns the position of a string within another string, from the end of the string
Int	Returns the integer portion of a number
Ipmt	Returns the interest payment for a given period of an annuity
IRR	Returns the internal rate of return for a series of cash flows
IsArray	Returns True if a variable is an array
IsDate	Returns True if a variable is a date
IsEmpty	Returns True if a variable has not been initialized
IsError	Returns True if an expression is an error value
IsMissing	Returns True if an optional argument was not passed to a procedure
IsNull	Returns True if an expression contains a null value
IsNumeric	Returns True if an expression can be evaluated as a number
IsObject	Returns True if an expression references an object
Join*	Combines strings contained in an array
LBound	Returns the smallest subscript for a dimension of an array
LCase	Returns a string converted to lowercase
Left	Returns a specified number of characters from the left of a string
Len	Returns the number of characters in a string
Loc	Returns the current read or write position of an open file
LOF	Returns the number of bytes in an open file
Log	Returns the natural logarithm of a number
LTrim	Returns a copy of a string with no leading spaces
Mid	Returns a specified number of characters from a string
Minute	Returns the minute of the hour

Function	Action
MIRR	Returns the modified internal rate of return for a series of periodic cash flows
Month	Returns the numeric month of a date
MonthName	Returns the month, as a string
MsgBox	Displays a modal message box
Now	Returns the current system date and time
NPer	Returns the number of periods for an annuity
NPV	Returns the net present value of an investment
Oct	Returns a string representing the octal value of a number
Partition	Returns a string representing a range in which a value falls
Pmt	Returns a payment amount for an annuity
Ppmt	Returns the principal payment amount for an annuity
PV	Returns the present value of an annuity
QBColor	Returns an RGB color code
Rate	Returns the interest rate per period for an annuity
Replace*	Returns a string in which a substring is replaced with another string
RGB	Returns a number representing an RGB color value
Right	Returns a specified number of characters from the right of a string
Rnd	Returns a random number between 0 and 1
Round	Returns a number rounded to a specified number of decimal places
RTrim	Returns a copy of a string with no trailing spaces
Second	Returns the seconds portion of a specified time
Seek	Returns the current position in a file
Sgn	Returns an integer that indicates the sign of a number
Shell	Runs an executable program
Sin	Returns the sine of an angle
SLN	Returns the straight-line depreciation for an asset for a period

Continued

TABLE B-2 SUMMARY OF VBA FUNCTIONS *(Continued)*

Function	Action
Space	Returns a string with a specified number of spaces
Split	Returns a one-dimensional array containing a number of substrings
Sqr	Returns the square root of a number
Str	Returns a string representation of a number
StrComp	Returns a value indicating the result of a string comparison
StrConv	Returns a converted string
String	Returns a repeating character or string
StrReverse	Returns a string, reversed
Switch	Evaluates a list of expressions and returns a variant value or expression associated with the first True expression
SYD	Returns the sum-of-years' digits depreciation of an asset for a period
Tan	Returns the tangent of an angle
Time	Returns the current system time
Timer	Returns the number of seconds since midnight
TimeSerial	Returns the time for a specified hour, minute, and second
TimeValue	Converts a string to a time serial number
Trim	Returns a string without leading spaces and/or trailing spaces
TypeName	Returns a string that describes the data type of a variable
UBound	Returns the largest available subscript for a dimension of an array
UCase	Converts a string to uppercase
Val	Returns the number formed from any initial numeric characters of a string
VarType	Returns a value indicating the subtype of a variable
Weekday	Returns a number indicating a day of the week
WeekdayName	Returns a string indicating a day of the week
Weekday	Returns a number representing a day of the week
Year	Returns the numerical year of a date

Appendix C

VBA Constants

THIS APPENDIX CONTAINS A complete listing of the VBA constants that can simplify your programming. They can be used anywhere in your VBA code in place of actual values. The constants are listed by usage, for example, Calendar Constants, MsgBox Constants, and KeyCode Constants.

For complete details, consult Access's online help.

Constant Type	Constant	Value	Description
Calendar	vbCalGreg	0	Indicates Gregorian calendar is used
	vbHijri	1	Indicates Hijri calendar is used
CallType	vbMethod	1	Indicates that a method has been invoked
	vbGet	2	Indicates a Property Get procedure
	vbLet	4	Indicates a Property Let procedure
	vbSet	8	Indicates a Property Set procedure
Color	vbBlack	0x0	Black
	vbRed	0xFF	Red
	vbGreen	0xFF00	Green
	vbYellow	0xFFFF	Yellow
	vbBlue	0xFF0000	Blue
	vbMagenta	0xFF00FF	Magenta
	vbCyan	0xFFFF00	Cyan
	vbWhite	0xFFFFFF	White

Continued

Constant Type	Constant	Value	Description
Comparison	vbUseCompareOption	−1	Performs a comparison using the setting of the Option Compare statement
	vbBinaryCompare	0	Performs a binary comparison
	vbTextCompare	1	Performs a textual comparison
	vbDatabaseCompare	2	For Microsoft Access (Windows only), performs a comparison based on information contained in your database
Date – First DayOfTheWeek	vbUseSystem	0	Use NLS API setting
& Return Values	vbSunday	1	Sunday (default)
	vbMonday	2	Monday
	vbTuesday	3	Tuesday
	vbWednesday	4	Wednesday
	vbThursday	5	Thursday
	vbFriday	6	Friday
	vbSaturday	7	Saturday
Date – First Day of theYear	vbUseSystem	0	Use NLS API setting
	VbUseSystemDayOfWeek		Use the day of the week specified in your system settings for the first day of the week
	VbFirstJan1	1	Start with the week in which January 1 occurs (default)

Constant Type	Constant	Value	Description
	vbFirstFourDays	2	Start with the first week that has at least four days in the new year
	vbFirstFullWeek	3	Start with the first full week of the year
Date Format	vbGeneralDate	0	
	vbLongDate	1	
	vbLongTime	3	
	vbShortDate	2	
	vbShortTime	4	
File Attribute	vbNormal	0	Normal (default for Dir and SetAttr)
	vbReadOnly	1	Read-only
	vbHidden	2	Hidden
	vbSystem	4	System file
	vbVolume	8	Volume label
	vbDirectory	16	Directory or folder
	vbArchive	32	File has changed since last backup
	vbAlias	64	On the Macintosh, identifier is an alias
First Week of the Year	vbFirstFourDays	2	
	vbFirstFullWeek	3	
	vbFirstJan1	1	
	vbUseSystem	0	
Form	vbModeless	0	
	vbModal	1	

Continued

Constant Type	Constant	Value	Description
IMEStatus	vbIMEModeAlpha	8	Half-width alphanumeric mode
	vbIMEModeAlphaFull	7	Full-width alphanumeric mode
	vbIMEModeDisable	3	IME disabled
	vbIMEModeHiragana	4	Full-width Hiragana mode (Japanese)
	vbIMEModeKatakana	5	Full-width Katakana mode (Japanese)
	vbIMEMode-KatakanaHalf	6	Half-width Katakana mode (Janapese)
	vbIMEModeHangul	10	Half-width Hangul mode (Korean)
	vbIMEModeHangulFull	9	Full-width Hangul mode (Korean)
	vbIMEModeOff	2	IME off
	vbIMEModeOn	1	IME on
KeyCode	vbKeyLButton	0x1	Left mouse button
	vbKeyRButton	0x2	Right mouse button
	vbKeyCancel	0x3	CANCEL key
	vbKeyMButton	0x4	Middle mouse button
	vbKeyBack	0x8	BACKSPACE key
	vbKeyTab	0x9	TAB key
	vbKeyClear	0xC	CLEAR key
	vbKeyReturn	0xD	ENTER key
	vbKeyShift	0x10	SHIFT key
	vbKeyControl	0x11	CTRL key
	vbKeyMenu	0x12	MENU key
	vbKeyPause	0x13	PAUSE key
	vbKeyCapital	0x14	CAPS LOCK key

Constant Type	Constant	Value	Description
	vbKeyEscape	0x1B	ESC key
	vbKeySpace	0x20	SPACEBAR key
	vbKeyPageUp	0x21	PAGE UP key
	vbKeyPageDown	0x22	PAGE DOWN key
	vbKeyEnd	0x23	END key
	vbKeyHome	0x24	HOME key
	vbKeyLeft	0x25	LEFT ARROW key
	vbKeyLButton	0x1	Left mouse button
	vbKeyRButton	0x2	Right mouse button
	vbKeyCancel	0x3	CANCEL key
	vbKeyMButton	0x4	Middle mouse button
	vbKeyBack	0x8	BACKSPACE key
	vbKeyTab	0x9	TAB key
	vbKeyClear	0xC	CLEAR key
	vbKeyReturn	0xD	ENTER key
	vbKeyShift	0x10	SHIFT key
	vbKeyControl	0x11	CTRL key
	vbKeyMenu	0x12	MENU key
	vbKeyPause	0x13	PAUSE key
	vbKeyCapital	0x14	CAPS LOCK key
	vbKeyEscape	0x1B	ESC key
	vbKeySpace	0x20	SPACEBAR key
	vbKeyPageUp	0x21	PAGE UP key
	vbKeyPageDown	0x22	PAGE DOWN key
	vbKeyEnd	0x23	END key
	vbKeyHome	0x24	HOME key
	vbKeyLeft	0x25	LEFT ARROW key

Continued

Constant Type	Constant	Value	Description
	vbKeyUp	0x26	UP ARROW key
	vbKeyRight	0x27	RIGHT ARROW key
	vbKeyDown	0x28	DOWN ARROW key
	vbKeySelect	0x29	SELECT key
	vbKeyPrint	0x2A	PRINT SCREEN key
	vbKeyExecute	0x2B	EXECUTE key
	vbKeySnapshot	0x2C	SNAPSHOT key
	vbKeyInsert	0x2D	INSERT key
	vbKeyDelete	0x2E	DELETE key
	vbKeyHelp	0x2F	HELP key
	vbKeyNumlock	0x90	NUM LOCK key
	vbKeyA	65	A key
	vbKeyB	66	B key
	vbKeyC	67	C key
	vbKeyD	68	D key
	vbKeyE	69	E key
	vbKeyF	70	F key
	vbKeyG	71	G key
	vbKeyH	72	H key
	vbKeyI	73	I key
	vbKeyJ	74	J key
	vbKeyK	75	K key
	vbKeyL	76	L key
	vbKeyM	77	M key
	vbKeyN	78	N key
	vbKeyO	79	O key
	vbKeyP	80	P key

Constant Type	Constant	Value	Description
	vbKeyQ	81	Q key
	vbKeyR	82	R key
	vbKeyS	83	S key
	vbKeyT	84	T key
	vbKeyU	85	U key
	vbKeyV	86	V key
	vbKeyW	87	W key
	vbKeyX	88	X key
	vbKeyY	89	Y key
	vbKeyZ	90	Z key
Keyboard Numbers	vbKey0	48	0 key
	vbKey1	49	1 key
	vbKey2	50	2 key
	vbKey3	51	3 key
	vbKey4	52	4 key
	vbKey5	53	5 key
	vbKey6	54	6 key
	vbKey7	55	7 key
	vbKey8	56	8 key
	vbKey9	57	9 key
Numeric Keypad	vbKeyNumpad0	0x60	0 key
	vbKeyNumpad1	0x61	1 key
	vbKeyNumpad2	0x62	2 key
	vbKeyNumpad3	0x63	3 key
	vbKeyNumpad4	0x64	4 key
	vbKeyNumpad5	0x65	5 key
	vbKeyNumpad6	0x66	6 key

Continued

Constant Type	Constant	Value	Description
	vbKeyNumpad7	0x67	7 key
	vbKeyNumpad8	0x68	8 key
	vbKeyNumpad9	0x69	9 key
	vbKeyMultiply	0x6A	MULTIPLICATION SIGN (*) key
	vbKeyAdd	0x6B	PLUS SIGN (+) key
	vbKeySeparator	0x6C	ENTER key
	vbKeySubtract	0x6D	MINUS SIGN (–) key
	vbKeyDecimal	0x6E	DECIMAL POINT (.) key
	vbKeyDivide	0x6F	DIVISION SIGN (/) key
Function Keys	vbKeyF1	0x70	F1 key
	vbKeyF2	0x71	F2 key
	vbKeyF3	0x72	F3 key
	vbKeyF4	0x73	F4 key
	vbKeyF5	0x74	F5 key
	vbKeyF6	0x75	F6 key
	vbKeyF7	0x76	F7 key
	vbKeyF8	0x77	F8 key
	vbKeyF9	0x78	F9 key
	vbKeyF10	0x79	F10 key
	vbKeyF11	0x7A	F11 key
	vbKeyF12	0x7B	F12 key
	vbKeyF13	0x7C	F13 key
	vbKeyF14	0x7D	F14 key
	vbKeyF15	0x7E	F15 key
Miscellaneous	vbCrLf	Chr(13) + Chr(10)	Carriage return/ linefeed combination
	vbCr	Chr(13)	Carriage return character

Constant Type	Constant	Value	Description
	vbLf	Chr(10)	Linefeed character
	vbNewLine	Chr(13) + Chr(10) or, on the Macintosh, Chr(13)	Platform-specific new line character; whichever is appropriate for current platform
	vbNullChar	Chr(0)	Character having value 0
	vbNullString	String having value 0	Not the same as a zero-length string (""); used for calling external procedures
	vbObjectError	–2147221504	User-defined error numbers should be greater than this value. For example: `Err.Raise Number = vbObjectError + 1000`
	vbTab	Chr(9)	Tab character
	vbBack	Chr(8)	Backspace character
	vbFormFeed	Chr(12)	Not useful in Microsoft Windows or on the Macintosh
	vbVerticalTab	Chr(11)	Not useful in Microsoft Windows or on the Macintosh
MsgBox Results	vbOK	1	OK button pressed
	vbCancel	2	Cancel button pressed
	vbAbort	3	Abort button pressed
	vbRetry	4	Retry button pressed
	vbOgnire	5	Ignore button pressed
	vbYes	6	Yes button pressed

Continued

Constant Type	Constant	Value	Description
	vbNo	7	No button pressed
MsgBox Style	vbOKOnly	0	OK button only (default)
	vbOKCancel	1	OK and Cancel buttons
	vbAbortRetryIgnore	2	Abort, Retry, and Ignore buttons
	vbYesNoCancel	3	Yes, No, and Cancel buttons
	vbYesNo	4	Yes and No buttons
	vbRetryCancel	5	Retry and Cancel buttons
	vbCritical	16	Critical message
	vbQuestion	32	Warning query
	vbExclamation	48	Warning message
	vbInformation	64	Information message
	vbDefaultButton1	0	First button is default (default)
	vbDefaultButton2	256	Second button is default
	vbDefaultButton3	512	Third button is default
	vbDefaultButton4	768	Fourth button is default
	vbApplicationModal	0	Application modal message box (default)
	vbSystemModal	4096	System modal message box
	vbMsgBoxHelpButton	16384	Adds Help button to the message box
	VbMsgBoxSetForeground	65536	Specifies the message box window as the foreground window

Constant Type	Constant	Value	Description
	vbMsgBoxRight	524288	Text is right aligned
	vbMsgBoxRtlReading	1048576	Specifies text should appear as right-to-left reading on Hebrew and Arabic systems
QueryClose	vbAppTaskManager	3	
	vbAppWindows	2	
	vbFormCode	1	
	vbFormControlMenu	0	
	vbFormMDIForm	4	
Shell	vbHide	0	Window is hidden and focus is passed to the hidden window
	vbMaximizedFocus	3	Window is maximized with focus
	vbMinimizedFocus	2	Window is displayed as an icon with focus
	vbMinimizedNoFocus	6	Window is displayed as an icon. Curently active window remains active.
	vbNormalFocus	1	Window has focus and is restored to its original size and position
	vbNormalNoFocus	4	Window is restored to its most recent size and position. Currently active window remains active.
StrConv	vbFromUnicode	128	
	vbHircegana	32	
	vbKatakama	16	
	vbLowerCase	2	

Continued

Constant Type	Constant	Value	Description
	vbNarrow	8	
	vbProperCase	3	
	vbUnicode	64	
	vbUpperCase	1	
	vbWide	4	
SystemColor	vbScrollBars	0x80000000	Scroll bar color
	vbDesktop	0x80000001	Desktop color
	vbActiveTitleBar	0x80000002	Color of the title bar for the active window
	vbInactiveTitleBar	0x80000003	Color of the title bar for the inactive window
	vbMenuBar	0x80000004	Menu background color
	vbWindowBackground	0x80000005	Window background color
	vbWindowFrame	0x80000006	Window frame color
	vbMenuText	0x80000007	Color of text on menus
	vbWindowText	0x80000008	Color of text in windows
	vbTitleBarText	0x80000009	Color of text in caption, size box, and scroll arrow
	vbActiveBorder	0x8000000A	Border color of active window
	vbInactiveBorder	0x8000000B	Border color of inactive window
	vbApplication-Workspace	0x8000000C	Background color of multiple-document interface (MDI) applications
	vbHighlight	0x8000000D	Background color of items selected in a control

Constant Type	Constant	Value	Description
	vbHighlightText	0x8000000E	Text color of items selected in a control
	vbButtonFace	0x8000000F	Color of shading on the face of command buttons
	vbButtonShadow	0x80000010	Color of shading on the edge of command buttons
	vbGrayText	0x80000011	Grayed (disabled) text
	vbButtonText	0x80000012	Text color on push buttons
	vbInactive-CaptionText	0x80000013	Color of text in an inactive caption
	vb3DHighlight	0x80000014	Highlight color for 3-D display elements
	vb3DDKShadow	0x80000015	Darkest shadow color for 3-D display elements
	vb3DLight	0x80000016	Second-lightest 3-D color after vb3DHighlight
	vbInfoText	0x80000017	Color of text in ToolTips
	vbInfoBackground	0x80000018	Background color of ToolTips
Tristate	vbFalse	0	
	vbTrue	−1	
	vbUseDefault	−2	
VarType	vbEmpty	0	Uninitialized (default)
	vbNull	1	Contains no valid data
	vbInteger	2	Integer
	vbLong	3	Long integer

Continued

Constant Type	Constant	Value	Description
	vbSingle	4	Single-precision floating-point number
	vbDouble	5	Double-precision floating-point number
	vbCurrency	6	Currency
	vbDate	7	Date
	vbString	8	String
	vbObject	9	Object
	vbError	10	Error
	vbBoolean	11	Boolean
	vbVariant	12	Variant (used only for arrays of variants)
	vbDataObject	13	Data access object
	vbDecimal	14	Decimal
	vbByte	17	Byte
	vbUserDefinedType	36	Variants that contain user-defined types
	vbArray	8192	Array
	vbEmpty	0	Uninitialized (default)
	vbNull	1	Contains no valid data

Appendix D

VBA Error Codes

THIS APPENDIX CONTAINS A COMPLETE LISTING OF the error codes for trappable errors. This information is useful for error trapping at run time. For complete details, consult Access's online help.

Error code	Message
3	Return without GoSub.
5	Invalid procedure call or argument.
6	Overflow (for example, value too large for an integer).
7	Out of memory. This error rarely refers to the amount of physical memory installed in your system. Rather, it usually refers to a fixed-size area of memory used by Access or Windows (for example, the area used for graphics or custom formats).
9	Subscript out of range. You also get this error message if a named item is not found in a collection of objects.
10	This array is fixed or temporarily locked.
11	Division by zero.
13	Type mismatch.
14	Out of string space.
16	Expression too complex.
17	Can't perform requested operation.
18	User interrupt occurred. This error occurs if the user interrupts a macro by pressing the Cancel key.
20	Resume without error. This error probably indicates that you forgot the Exit Sub statement before your error handler code.
28	Out of stack space.
35	Sub or function or property not defined.

Continued

Error code	Message
47	Too many code resource or DLL application clients.
48	Error in loading code resource or DLL.
49	Bad code resource or DLL calling convention.
51	Internal error.
52	Bad file name or number.
53	File not found.
54	Bad file mode.
55	File already open.
57	Device I/O error.
58	File already exists.
59	Bad record length.
61	Disk full.
62	Input past end of file.
63	Bad record number.
67	Too many files.
68	Device unavailable.
70	Permission denied.
71	Disk not ready.
74	Can't rename with different drive.
75	Path/file access error.
76	Path not found.
91	Object variable or With block variable not set.
92	For loop not initialized.
93	Invalid pattern string.
94	Invalid use of Null.
97	Cannot call Friend procedure on object which is not an instance of the defining class.

Error code	Message
98	A property or method call cannot include a reference to a private object, either as an argument or as a return value.
298	System resource or DLL could not be loaded.
320	Can't use character device names in specified file names.
321	Invalid file format.
322	Can't create necessary temporary file.
325	Invalid format in resource file.
327	Data value named not found
328	Illegal parameter; can't write arrays.
335	Could not access system registry.
336	Component not correctly registered.
337	Component not found.
338	Component did not run correctly.
360	Object already loaded.
361	Can't load or unload this object.
363	Control specified not found.
364	Object was unloaded.
365	Unable to unload within this context.
368	The specified file is out of date. This program requires a later version.
371	The specified object can't be used as an owner form for show.
380	Invalid property value.
381	Invalid property-array index.
382	Set not supported at run time.
383	Property Set can't be used with a read-only property.
385	Need property array index.
387	Property Set not permitted.
393	Property Get can't be executed at run time.

Continued

Error code	Message
394	Property Get cannot be executed on write-only property.
400	Form already displayed; can't show modally.
402	Code must close topmost modal form first.
419	Permission to use object denied.
422	Property not found.
423	Property or method not found.
424	Object required. This error occurs if text following a dot is not recognized as an object.
425	Invalid object use.
429	Component can't create object or return reference to this object.
430	Class does not support Automation or does not support expected interface.
432	Filename or class name not found during Automation operation.
438	Object doesn't support this property or method.
440	Automation error.
442	Connection to type library or object library for remote process has been lost.
443	Automation object does not have a default value.
445	Object doesn't support this action.
446	Object doesn't support named arguments.
447	Object doesn't support current locale setting.
448	Named argument not found.
449	Argument not optional or invalid property assignment.
450	Wrong number of arguments or invalid property assignment.
451	Object not a collection.
452	Invalid ordinal
453	Specified code resource not found.
454	Code resource not found.
455	Code resource lock error.

Error code	Message
457	This key is already associated with an element of this collection.
458	Variable uses an Automation type not supported in Visual Basic.
459	This component does not support the set of events.
460	Invalid clipboard format.
461	Method or data member not found.
462	The remote server machine does not exist or is unavailable.
480	Can't create AutoRedraw image.
481	Invalid picture.
482	Printer error.
483	Printer driver does not support specified property.
484	Problem getting printer information from the system. Make sure the printer is set up correctly.
485	Invalid picture type.
486	Can't print form image to this type of printer.
520	Can't empty clipboard.
521	Can't open clipboard.
735	Can't save file to TEMP directory.
744	Search text not found.
746	Replacements too long.
31001	Out of memory.
31004	No object.
31018	Class is not set.
31027	Unable to activate object.
31032	Unable to create embedded object.
31036	Error saving to file.
31037	Error loading from file.

Appendix E

ANSI Codes

THIS APPENDIX CONTAINS THE ANSI decimal codes, the default characters (if any) that the codes produce, the hex value of the codes, the binary value of the codes, and the keystrokes (if any) that generate the codes. Some of the codes do not result in displaying characters but are used as control characters. These entries show a title rather than the equivalent keystroke. Values in the character set above 127 are determined by the code page that is specific to your operating system.

 The actual character that is displayed may depend on the font in use.

ANSI code	Character	Hex Code	Binary Code	Title or Keystroke*
1	<None>	&H01	0000 0001	Start of heading
2	<None>	&H02	0000 0010	Start of text
3	<None>	&H03	0000 0011	End of text
4	<None>	&H04	0000 0100	End of transmission
5	<None>	&H05	0000 0101	Enquiry
6	<None>	&H06	0000 0110	Acknowledge
7	<None>	&H07	0000 0111	Bell
8	<Backspace>	&H08	0000 1000	Backspace
9	<Tab>	&H09	0000 1001	Tab
10	<Line feed>	&H0A	0000 1010	Line feed
11	<None>	&H0B	0000 1011	Line tabulation

Continued

ANSI code	Character	Hex Code	Binary Code	Title or Keystroke*
12	<None>	&H0C	0000 1100	Form feed
13	<Carriage return>	&H0D	0000 1101	Carriage return
14	<None>	&H0E	0000 1110	Shift out
15	<None>	&H0F	0000 1111	Shift in
16	<None>	&H10	0001 0000	Datalink escape
17	<None>	&H11	0001 0001	Device control 1
18	<None>	&H12	0001 0010	Device control 2
19	<None>	&H13	0001 0011	Device control 3
20	<None>	&H14	0001 0100	Device control 4
21	<None>	&H15	0001 0101	Negative acknowledge
22	<None>	&H16	0001 0110	Synchronous idle
23	<None>	&H17	0001 0111	End of transmission block
24	<None>	&H18	0001 1000	Cancel
25	<None>	&H19	0001 1001	End of medium
26	<None>	&H1A	0001 1010	Substitute
27	<None>	&H1B	0001 1011	Escape
28	<None>	&H1C	0001 1100	File separator
29	<None>	&H1D	0001 1101	Group separator
30	<None>	&H1E	0001 1110	Record separator
31	<None>	&H1F	0001 1111	Unit separator
32	<Space>	&H20	0010 0000	Space
33	!	&H21	0010 0001	!
34	"	&H22	0010 0010	"
35	#	&H23	0010 0011	#
36	$	&H24	0010 0100	$
37	%	&H25	0010 0101	%

ANSI code	Character	Hex Code	Binary Code	Title or Keystroke*
38	&	&H26	0010 0110	&
39	'	&H27	0010 0111	'
40	(	&H28	0010 1000	(
41	)	&H29	0010 1001	)
42	*	&H2A	0010 1010	*
43	+	&H2B	0010 1011	+
44	,	&H2C	0010 1100	,
45	-	&H2D	0010 1101	-
46	.	&H2E	0010 1110	.
47	/	&H2F	0010 1111	/
48	0	&H30	0011 0000	0
49	1	&H31	0011 0001	1
50	2	&H32	0011 0010	2
51	3	&H33	0011 0011	3
52	4	&H34	0011 0100	4
53	5	&H35	0011 0101	5
54	6	&H36	0011 0110	6
55	7	&H37	0011 0111	7
56	8	&H38	0011 1000	8
57	9	&H39	0011 1001	9
58	:	&H3A	0011 1010	:
59	;	&H3B	0011 1011	;
60	<	&H3C	0011 1100	<
61	=	&H3D	0011 1101	=
62	>	&H3E	0011 1110	>
63	?	&H3F	0011 1111	?

Continued

ANSI code	Character	Hex Code	Binary Code	Title or Keystroke*
64	@	&H40	0100 0000	@
65	A	&H41	0100 0001	A
66	B	&H42	0100 0010	B
67	C	&H43	0100 0011	C
68	D	&H44	0100 0100	D
69	E	&H45	0100 0101	E
70	F	&H46	0100 0110	F
71	G	&H47	0100 0111	G
72	H	&H48	0100 1000	H
73	I	&H49	0100 1001	I
74	J	&H4A	0100 1010	J
75	K	&H4B	0100 1011	K
76	L	&H4C	0100 1100	L
77	M	&H4D	0100 1101	M
78	N	&H4E	0100 1110	N
79	O	&H4F	0100 1111	O
80	P	&H50	0101 0000	P
81	Q	&H51	0101 0001	Q
82	R	&H52	0101 0010	R
83	S	&H53	0101 0011	S
84	T	&H54	0101 0100	T
85	U	&H55	0101 0101	U
86	V	&H56	0101 0110	V
87	W	&H57	0101 0111	W
88	X	&H58	0101 1000	X
89	Y	&H59	0101 1001	Y
90	Z	&H5A	0101 1010	Z

ANSI code	Character	Hex Code	Binary Code	Title or Keystroke*
91	[	&H5B	0101 1011	[
92	\	&H5C	0101 1100	\
93	]	&H5D	0101 1101	]
94	^	&H5E	0101 1110	^
95	_	&H5F	0101 1111	_
96	`	&H60	0110 0000	`
97	a	&H61	0110 0001	a
98	b	&H62	0110 0010	b
99	c	&H63	0110 0011	c
100	d	&H64	0110 0100	d
101	e	&H65	0110 0101	e
102	f	&H66	0110 0110	f
103	g	&H67	0110 0111	g
104	h	&H68	0110 1000	h
105	i	&H69	0110 1001	i
106	j	&H6A	0110 1010	j
107	k	&H6B	0110 1011	k
108	l	&H6C	0110 1100	l
109	m	&H6D	0110 1101	m
110	n	&H6E	0110 1110	n
111	o	&H6F	0110 1111	o
112	p	&H70	0111 0000	p
113	q	&H71	0111 0001	q
114	r	&H72	0111 0010	r
115	s	&H73	0111 0011	s
116	t	&H74	0111 0100	t

Continued

ANSI code	Character	Hex Code	Binary Code	Title or Keystroke*
117	u	&H75	0111 0101	u
118	v	&H76	0111 0110	v
119	w	&H77	0111 0111	w
120	x	&H78	0111 1000	x
121	y	&H79	0111 1001	y
122	z	&H7A	0111 1010	z
123	{	&H7B	0111 1011	{
124	|	&H7C	0111 1100	|
125	}	&H7D	0111 1101	}
126	~	&H7E	0111 1110	~
127	<None>	&H7F	0111 1111	Delete
128		&H80	1000 0000	Alt+0128
129	<None>	&H81	1000 0001	Alt+0129
130	,	&H82	1000 0010	Alt+0130
131	ƒ	&H83	1000 0011	Alt+0131
132	„	&H84	1000 0100	Alt+0132
133	…	&H85	1000 0101	Alt+0133
134	†	&H86	1000 0110	Alt+0134
135	‡	&H87	1000 0111	Alt+0135
136	ˆ	&H88	1000 1000	Alt+0136
137	‰	&H89	1000 1001	Alt+0137
138	_	&H8A	1000 1010	Alt+0138
139	‹	&H8B	1000 1011	Alt+0139
140	Œ	&H8C	1000 1100	Alt+0140
141		&H8D	1000 1101	Alt+0141
142	_	&H8E	1000 1110	Alt+0142
143		&H8F	1000 1111	Alt+0143

ANSI code	Character	Hex Code	Binary Code	Title or Keystroke*
144		&H90	1001 0000	Alt+0144
145	'	&H91	1001 0001	Alt+0145
146	'	&H92	1001 0010	Alt+0146
147	"	&H93	1001 0011	Alt+0147
148	"	&H94	1001 0100	Alt+0148
149	•	&H95	1001 0101	Alt+0149
150	–	&H96	1001 0110	Alt+0150
151	—	&H97	1001 0111	Alt+0151
152	˜	&H98	1001 1000	Alt+0152
153	(tm)	&H99	1001 1001	Alt+0153
154	_	&H9A	1001 1010	Alt+0154
155	›	&H9B	1001 1011	Alt+0155
156	œ	&H9C	1001 1100	Alt+0156
157	_	&H9D	1001 1101	Alt+0157
158	_	&H9E	1001 1110	Alt+0158
159	Ÿ	&H9F	1001 1111	Alt+0159
160	<None>	&HA0	1010 0000	Alt+0160
161	¡	&HA1	1010 0001	Alt+0161
162	¢	&HA2	1010 0010	Alt+0162
163	£	&HA3	1010 0011	Alt+0163
164		&HA4	1010 0100	Alt+0164
165	¥	&HA5	1010 0101	Alt+0165
166	_	&HA6	1010 0110	Alt+0166
167	§	&HA7	1010 0111	Alt+0167
168	¨	&HA8	1010 1000	Alt+0168
169	(c)	&HA9	1010 1001	Alt+0169

Continued

ANSI code	Character	Hex Code	Binary Code	Title or Keystroke*
170	ª	&HAA	1010 1010	Alt+0170
171	«	&HAB	1010 1011	Alt+0171
172	¬	&HAC	1010 1100	Alt+0172
173		&HAD	1010 1101	Alt+0173
174	(r)	&HAE	1010 1110	Alt+0174
175	¯	&HAF	1010 1111	Alt+0175
176	°	&HB0	1011 0000	Alt+0176
177	±	&HB1	1011 0001	Alt+0177
178	²	&HB2	1011 0010	Alt+0178
179	³	&HB3	1011 0011	Alt+0179
180	´	&HB4	1011 0100	Alt+0180
181	>	&HB5	1011 0101	Alt+0181
182	¶	&HB6	1011 0110	Alt+0182
183	·	&HB7	1011 0111	Alt+0183
184	¸	&HB8	1011 1000	Alt+0184
185	¹	&HB9	1011 1001	Alt+0185
186	º	&HBA	1011 1010	Alt+0186
187	»	&HBB	1011 1011	Alt+0187
188	1/4	&HBC	1011 1100	Alt+0188
189	1/2	&HBD	1011 1101	Alt+0189
190	3/4	&HBE	1011 1110	Alt+0190
191	¿	&HBF	1011 1111	Alt+0191
192	À	&HC0	1100 0000	Alt+0192
193	Á	&HC1	1100 0001	Alt+0193
194	Â	&HC2	1100 0010	Alt+0194
195	Ã	&HC3	1100 0011	Alt+0195
196	Ä	&HC4	1100 0100	Alt+0196

ANSI code	Character	Hex Code	Binary Code	Title or Keystroke*
197	Å	&HC5	1100 0101	Alt+0197
198	Æ	&HC6	1100 0110	Alt+0198
199	Ç	&HC7	1100 0111	Alt+0199
200	È	&HC8	1100 1000	Alt+0200
201	É	&HC9	1100 1001	Alt+0201
202	Ê	&HCA	1100 1010	Alt+0202
203	Ë	&HCB	1100 1011	Alt+0203
204	Ì	&HCC	1100 1100	Alt+0204
205	Í	&HCD	1100 1101	Alt+0205
206	Î	&HCE	1100 1110	Alt+0206
207	Ï	&HCF	1100 1111	Alt+0207
208	–	&HD0	1101 0000	Alt+0208
209	Ñ	&HD1	1101 0001	Alt+0209
210	Ò	&HD2	1101 0010	Alt+0210
211	Ó	&HD3	1101 0011	Alt+0211
212	Ô	&HD4	1101 0100	Alt+0212
213	Õ	&HD5	1101 0101	Alt+0213
214	Ö	&HD6	1101 0110	Alt+0214
215	–	&HD7	1101 0111	Alt+0215
216	Ø	&HD8	1101 1000	Alt+0216
217	Ù	&HD9	1101 1001	Alt+0217
218	Ú	&HDA	1101 1010	Alt+0218
219	Û	&HDB	1101 1011	Alt+0219
220	Ü	&HDC	1101 1100	Alt+0220
221	–	&HDD	1101 1101	Alt+0221
222	–	&HDE	1101 1110	Alt+0222

Continued

ANSI code	Character	Hex Code	Binary Code	Title or Keystroke*
223	ß	&HDF	1101 1111	Alt+0223
224	à	&HE0	1110 0000	Alt+0224
225	á	&HE1	1110 0001	Alt+0225
226	â	&HE2	1110 0010	Alt+0226
227	ã	&HE3	1110 0011	Alt+0227
228	ä	&HE4	1110 0100	Alt+0228
229	å	&HE5	1110 0101	Alt+0229
230	æ	&HE6	1110 0110	Alt+0230
231	ç	&HE7	1110 0111	Alt+0231
232	è	&HE8	1110 1000	Alt+0232
233	é	&HE9	1110 1001	Alt+0233
234	ê	&HEA	1110 1010	Alt+0234
235	ë	&HEB	1110 1011	Alt+0235
236	ì	&HEC	1110 1100	Alt+0236
237	í	&HED	1110 1101	Alt+0237
238	î	&HEE	1110 1110	Alt+0238
239	ï	&HEF	1110 1111	Alt+0239
240	_	&HF0	1111 0000	Alt+0240
241	ñ	&HF1	1111 0001	Alt+0241
242	ò	&HF2	1111 0010	Alt+0242
243	ó	&HF3	1111 0011	Alt+0243
244	ô	&HF4	1111 0100	Alt+0244
245	õ	&HF5	1111 0101	Alt+0245
246	ö	&HF6	1111 0110	Alt+0246
247	÷	&HF7	1111 0111	Alt+0247
248	ø	&HF8	1111 1000	Alt+0248
249	ù	&HF9	1111 1001	Alt+0249

ANSI code	Character	Hex Code	Binary Code	Title or Keystroke*
250	ú	&HFA	1111 1010	Alt+0250
251	û	&HFB	1111 1011	Alt+0251
252	ü	&HFC	1111 1100	Alt+0252
253	_	&HFD	1111 1101	Alt+0253
254	_	&HFE	1111 1110	Alt+0254
255	ÿ	&HFF	1111 1111	Alt+0255

For keystrokes that require you to press Alt, use the numeric keypad with Num Lock on.

Index

Symbols

A

continued

continued

continued

continued